Nicholas M

Nicholas Murray was educated at Li
and is a writer and poet. He is
critical biography of Bruce Cha

A Life of
Matthew Arnold

NICHOLAS MURRAY

SCEPTRE

First published in 1996 by Hodder and Stoughton
First published in paperback in 1997 by Hodder and Stoughton
A division of Hodder Headline PLC
A Sceptre Paperback

British Library Cataloguing in Publication Data

Murray, Nicholas
    A Life of Matthew Arnold
    1. Arnold, Matthew, 1822–1888 – Biography
    2. Poets, English – 19th century – Biography
    I. Title
    821.8

    ISBN 0 340 62489 2

Printed and bound in Great Britain by
Cox & Wyman Ltd, Reading, Berkshire

Hodder and Stoughton
A division of Hodder Headline PLC
338 Euston Road
London NW1 3BH

To my parents

'Our actual obligations to Matthew Arnold are almost beyond expression.'

G. K. Chesterton

'They could not understand, and were greatly inclined to resent, the appearance of this bright, playful, unconventional spirit, happy and brilliant himself, and loving the happiness and brilliancy of the world; with not an ounce of pomposity in his own nature, and with the most irreverent demeanour towards pomposity in other people.'

G. W. E. Russell

'. . . the born lover of ideas, the born hater of commonplaces must feel in this country that the sky over his head is of brass and iron.'

Matthew Arnold, *Heinrich Heine*

Contents

List of Illustrations

The earliest photograph of Arnold at 33 years old.
A page from Arnold's *Pilgrim Love* which he wrote at the age of seven.
Portrait of Arnold's father, Dr Thomas Arnold, after Thomas Philips RA.
Sketch by Arnold's sister, Jane.
The school at Laleham-on-Thames where Arnold was born.
Cardinal John Henry Newman in 1889.
Mrs Mary Arnold, Matthew Arnold's mother.
Jane Martha Arnold.
Frances Arnold.
Frances Arnold with her elderly mother.
Arnold's younger brother, Tom, in 1848.
Arthur Hugh Clough, from the 1860 painting by Samuel Rowse.
Fragment of *Lines Written in Kensington Gardens*.
Ink drawing by Jane Arnold of Fox How, Ambleside.
Fox How today.
An early portrait of Arnold – 'the elegant Jeremiah'.
Fanny Lucy, Arnold's wife.

Scenes from the interior of the Athenaeum Club.
Two caricatures of Arnold: one from *Vanity Fair*, 1871 and one by Max Beerbohm.
The old chain ferry on the Thames by Henry Taunt.
Taunt's Berkshire shepherd.
Arnold's unmistakable central parting and bushy sidewhiskers which were seized upon by caricaturists.
Lady Louisa de Rothschild with her lapdog, Elfie.
Arnold's two daughters, Lucy and Eleanor.
Arnold in middle-age with his daughter Eleanor and his two dogs.
Managing a rare smile for the camera.
A cartoon of Arnold as a trapeze artist from *Once a Week* magazine, 1872.
Photographs of Bablock-hythe today.
The churchyard at Laleham where Arnold and his wife are buried.

PREFACE

'MATTHEW ARNOLD', WROTE E. M. Forster, 'is of all the Victorians most to my taste: a great poet, a civilised citizen, and a prophet who has managed to project himself into our present troubles, so that when we read him now he seems to be in the room.'[1]

As a poet, Arnold may have lacked the music of Tennyson, the abundant energy of Browning, but he deserves his traditional ranking as one of the finest three or four poets of the mid-Victorian era. His output was slender by the standards of his peers but his poetry has always guaranteed him a high place in the affections of readers of English poetry. His contemporaries never doubted that he would be remembered chiefly as a poet and the early departure of his poetic gift has always been regretted.

But Arnold was also a major critic – of literature, life, religion and politics. His criticism, unlike his poetry, may have passed through periods of relative neglect, but, nearly half a century on, Forster's declaration has lost none of its force: *when we read him now he seems to be in the room.*

Arnold was the son of the famous, severe and intensely moralistic Dr Arnold of Rugby. He inherited – though with a lighter, more playful touch, at odds with all those grave, bewhiskered portraits that seem to bespeak high Victorian earnestness – that sense of public mission that was enjoined, in the judgement of an Arnold, on every 'civilised citizen'. Arnold's struggle with that inheritance, which was partly acknowledged, partly resisted, is one of the themes of this book. In his youth his demeanour could seem an amalgam of Prince Hamlet (with his antic disposition adopted as a strategy to hide true feelings and inner uncertainty) and Prince Hal (with his youthful irresponsibility quickly put off in maturity). His emergence as a poet of deep seriousness and haunting melancholy surprised all who knew him. The bright gaiety of his social existence – coupled to his purposeful optimism in politics and the world of ideas – threw the sadness of his poetry into a curious relief.

Matthew Arnold worked all his adult life as an inspector of schools. The relentless burden of travelling, marking papers, testing pupil-teachers, quizzing little children, and being cordial to provincial school-managers, created strains that were sometimes intolerable for a writer and a poet. His friends on occasion despaired of the fate that had been assigned to him. But, if he sometimes complained about this 'incessant grind', his devotion to the cause of universal compulsory state education was total. By speaking out on educational matters and criticising the politicians who were his employers he put his career at risk but he believed so passionately in the cause of bringing education to the working class that he never counted the personal cost. His social criticism, therefore, was written out of practical personal experience of Victorian England in the grip of an epoch of massive, and visible, change. It was not written from the vantage point of a college study or a cloister. The author of *Culture and Anarchy* had snow on his boots.

In the sphere of public debate – which he entered by lectures, contributions to the periodical press and a ceaseless flow of books on literature, culture, religion and politics – Arnold was both ambitious (in seeking nothing less than to change the whole intellectual culture of his fellow countrymen) and controversial in the outspoken, elegant and witty way in which he conducted his polemics. So many of his prophecies have been fulfilled – that we would become more and more European, that art would increasingly fill what Salman Rushdie has called 'the God-shaped hole' in the secular mind of the twentieth century, that religion must update itself if it wished to survive, that the rise of the mass media would force us to confront the question of the value and legitimacy of literature and art in an age of mass democracy, that Parliament would slowly be marginalised by other forces in the modern world, that England's problems with Ireland would be solved by justice not by coercion, that the study of the classics would inevitably decline – the list could easily be extended.

Matthew Arnold was a happy man who could easily have been otherwise, as he watched his poetic gift evaporate. The word 'playful' occurs again and again in accounts of him by his friends. Zest, humour and spontaneous liveliness are among the defining characteristics of his personality. His private life, although marred by the death of three of his sons in childhood, was invariably happy and he loved his wife and children, his pets (to excess), and his Surrey garden which became a retreat from the demands of a London literary society that was always so keen to solicit his attendance.

Although those who knew him always observed a certain grand manner, an undeniable streak of vanity, in their friend, they equally often added that it was cancelled out by his delight in guying himself in ways that immediately brought him back down to earth. They also observed a simplicity in his personality. It is this characteristic of Arnold which has given an opening to his critics – notoriously T. S. Eliot who, in addition to being tone-deaf to Arnold's poetry, which he dismissed as 'academic', said of the man who in truth had helped to establish the tradition in which the later critic triumphed: 'He had no real serenity, only an impeccable demeanour.' Eliot disliked Arnold's liberal human-ism, his unwillingness to submit to orthodoxy in religion and politics. More recent critics – like the polymathic comparative critic George Steiner who feels that Arnold, by remaining, for all his aspiring Europeanism, too limited and English a figure,[2] could not equip the modern mind to cope with the evils of the twentieth century – have indicted Arnold for not being complicated enough.

But, increasingly, Arnold's calm and lucid temperament, his good faith, his Orwellian decency, his putting of the ideal of 'disinterested-ness' or 'the return upon oneself' above instant partisanship, his passion for directing ideas at the widest possible audience and seeking for them broad consent rather than sectarian self-satisfaction, are turning out to be not weaknesses but strengths. The old dichotomies of public debate are breaking down (both Left and Right having tended to hold Arnold at arm's length for most of the post-war period) and Matthew Arnold as 'a prophet who has managed to project himself into our present troubles' may just be about to come once more into his own.

At the present time – when so many literary critics and theorists in the academy speak to each other in a barbarous 'discourse' fashioned out of mannered obfuscation, tortured and grimly unfunny wordplay, and unctuous correctness – the elegance and clarity of Arnold's critical prose can seem as refreshing as a mountain rill.

PART ONE

The Making of the Poet

CHAPTER ONE:
THE MIGHTY OAK
[1822–1841]

Papa . . . while he held a thing, he held it very hard, and without the sense some people always have that there are two sides to the question.[1]

1

One crisp November morning in 1822, Mary Arnold, the thirty-year-old wife of a young schoolmaster four years her junior, Thomas Arnold – who took private pupils in a large, rambling house at the village of Laleham-on-Thames, some sixteen miles west of London – was out riding when her pony kicked suddenly and threw her to the ground. 'My confinement was so soon expected that I was considerably alarmed, but thank God! no mischief followed',[2] she wrote with relief in her diary. The birth of her first child, Jane, on 1 August the previous year, had been difficult enough, followed as it was by a violent fever which nearly killed her. Fortunately, the birth of Matthew a month after the fall, on Christmas Eve, was without incident.

Mary Arnold's eldest boy was to grow up in the shadow of his father: that powerful personality was to mark him for life. All young men struggle to break free from paternal influence but, in the case of Matthew Arnold, his father's overwhelming presence offered a peculiar challenge. At the time of Matthew's birth, Thomas Arnold was apparently an obscure schoolmaster but he was soon to become the most famous headmaster in the history of the English public school. Known to posterity by the imperial title of 'Arnold of Rugby', his reputation, in spite of the skilful mockery of this Victorian idol by Lytton Strachey in *Eminent Victorians* (1918), has never been at risk of under-estimation. His distinction as an educational reformer – his admirers would say his greatness – was less in any curricular innovations than in the peculiar moral atmosphere he engendered at Rugby. Although even his contemporaries would from time to time voice concern about his effect on impressionable young boys, the power of his personality and the earnestness of his Sunday sermons, preached in Rugby chapel to the 'Christian gentlemen' he saw as being the proper product of his school, created a formidable legend. He was also a serious religious thinker, strongly influenced by the Coleridge of *The Constitution of Church and State* (1829) and sharing Coleridge's belief in the necessity of a national church which would work as a counterweight to the materialism and frantic getting and spending that had begun to characterise early-nineteenth-century England. He was also a historian of some reputation.

Filial reaction, if not revolt, is a constant theme in later Victorian literature, as a younger generation, feeling its way deeper into an age of unbelief, came to resent (or suspect the true tenacity of) the certainties of its fathers. Matthew Arnold never entered into open rebellion against his father, although his laziness at Oxford and his early foppish manner – all part of a strategy to create some space for himself – would dismay the earnest Dr Arnold. Arnold grew up knowing that his father's fame was greater than his own. For most of his life he would assume that posterity would take the same view. Yet – without revolt, and while rarely missing a chance to record earnestly filial tributes to his father's memory (at any rate, in family letters) – Arnold's whole career can be seen, in some sense, as a subtle reaction against the dominant personality of his father. His lifelong crusade on behalf of moderation, temperate judgement, 'sweetness and light', or 'seeing the object as in itself it really is', was partly an example of what Rilke termed a poet's tendency to 'hate the approximate'. But it was also an implicit – and quietly powerful – rejection of the example of a parent whose fulminations, zealotry, and lack of delicacy or tact were everything that his son set himself against. No official rebellion, but perhaps a suppressed resentment: Arnold's narrative poem *Sohrab and Rustum*, written in his late twenties, is the story of a man who unconsciously slaughters his son.

To understand the life of Matthew Arnold, therefore, we must first take the measure of his famous parent. Thomas Arnold was born on 13 June 1795 at Cowes on the Isle of Wight where his father was a collector of customs. He was the seventh child of William Arnold and Martha Delafield. The Arnolds originally came from Lowestoft in Suffolk where they had been fishermen for generations, although Thomas Arnold's grandfather, William, had been the first Arnold to work for the customs and excise, firstly at Northwood in West Cowes and later at Slattwoods near Whippingham in East Cowes. Little is known of the Delafields except that they were of Puritan stock. Martha's brother John Delafield emigrated to New York, made a fortune, and was eventually made a freeman of New York City. There is nothing here to support an odd conjecture that gained currency after Matthew Arnold's death that there was some Jewishness in the Arnolds – Frank Harris declared, after looking at Matthew Arnold: 'there was surely Hebrew blood in his veins'.[3] Arnold, in one of his Oxford lectures on Celtic literature, was to muse on the fact that 'my very name expresses that peculiar Semitico-Saxon mixture which makes the typical Englishman'.[4] Although some have felt uneasy with Arnold's famous dichotomy between 'Hellenic' and 'Hebraic' culture, and seen in it grounds for imputing anti-Semitism,[5] it is probably fairer to see him as in truth a philosemite, warm towards Disraeli, who reciprocated the liking and joked with him about his more famous catchwords, and to Lady Louisa de Rothschild who was a lifelong friend and correspondent, enjoying an intimacy with Arnold which those who have been disappointed at the absence of scandal in his biography have often examined hopefully.

Thomas Arnold was educated at Winchester and Oxford after a childhood upbringing which resulted, in Strachey's portrait, in the formation of a rather absurd and pompous prig ('but, after all, what else could be expected from a child who, at the age of three, had been presented by his father, as a reward for proficiency in his studies, with the twenty-four volumes of Smollett's *History of England*'[6]). Strachey's essay – still a wicked pleasure to read – has been influential in creating a sort of counter-legend of Dr Arnold and, although there is more than a grain of truth in the picture of this particular eminent – and vexingly high-minded – Victorian, it must also be seen as an essay which was serving the interests of Bloomsbury as much as those of truth. In 1918, the expiry of glad, confident liberalism on the Somme, combined with the desire of alienated intellectuals like Strachey to dethrone what they saw as the frigid, moralistic heroes of an earlier generation, made the attack on Arnold inevitable. Thomas Arnold, however, had real distinction as a religious thinker, and as an author of works on Roman history which were taken seriously enough for him to be appointed as Regius Professor of Modern History at Oxford. He was also a reformer of the English public school – although, other than private tutoring, he knew only Winchester where he had been as a boy, and Rugby where he spent his entire public school career. He was an ardent Broad Churchman and advocate of church reform, and even Catholic emancipation (though he had little love for Catholicism). He drew the line, however, at the Tractarians and the Oxford Movement which he saw as a fatal weakening of the national church. He wanted, he said, to 'Christianise the nation', to establish a little of heaven on earth, and although he was aware of Continental critical theories about biblical inspiration – like his son he was an ardent European – he believed that the aim of religion was to inculcate goodness not to chop logic. The Thirty-nine Articles of the Church of England, to which its members were expected to subscribe, were not central to him; although like many of his contemporaries, he objected to some of them, yet even his biographer was in some difficulty in establishing what those objections were.[7] His principal quarrel with Newman and the Oxford Movement was that it placed such matters as the apostolic succession above the pursuit of practical Christian morality. He believed in an Established Church that would be broad enough to include even the Dissenters, and, with some marginal adjustments, even the Quakers and Unitarians. But he drew the line at Catholics and Jews. One of the few inheritances we can trace in Matthew Arnold back to his father is this powerful notion of centrality. The latter's belief in a unifying national culture – transcending what he saw as the unloveliness and isolation of, for example, the provincial Nonconformists – was in some sense a reprise of his father's passionate commitment to the idea of a national church. In a truculent essay on the treacherous 'Oxford Malignants' (the memorable title was in fact supplied by the editors of the periodical) in the *Edinburgh Review* in April 1836, he famously anathematised the Tractarians. He thoroughly disapproved of John Henry Newman, whose 'intellectual delicacy' by contrast worked a charm over his son. The dalliance of the Oxford Movement with 'priestcraft' instead of contending on behalf of the national church was something Thomas Arnold found hard to tolerate. Tolerance, indeed, was not one of his cardinal virtues. When provoked, he could easily succumb to terrible rage. His great grandson Arnold Whitridge describes this peculiar temper of Dr Arnold, giving no source but presumably writing with some inherited knowledge of family tradition: 'He was always boiling over with indignation about something . . . There was occasionally an almost Berserker rage about

Dr Arnold . . . He translated the most trivial events in everyday life as well as the most momentous political problems into adventures in righteousness.'[8]

As a school reformer (confined, in sharp contrast to his son, to the limited sphere of the public schools) Thomas Arnold's achievement was essentially to transform the disorder and moral anarchy of the early-nineteenth-century English boarding school into a more disciplined environment where a muscular Christian ethic became the dominant force in the life of the school. One of his contemporary critics, the Reverend Thomas Mozley, paints a picture of him at Rugby living 'in a world of his own, as despotic at his writing-desk as in his school, and wielding his pen as if it were a ferule . . . He seemed to live in a jungle, where every moving of the reeds was fearfully significant'.[9] There is more than a hint here of that paranoid tendency which often accompanies the fundamentalist sensibility. Because of the tempestuous energy and force of his character – and his love of engaging in controversy with everyone from school governors (who disliked his eagerness to expel undesirable pupils) to theological opponents – Thomas Arnold became famous in his day. In consequence, any of his children would be thought of primarily as the son or daughter of Dr Arnold.

To emphasise this image of vehement righteousness is to risk neglecting an equally important, and more amiable, side of Thomas Arnold. As the diarist Henry Crabb Robinson put it: 'He was physically strong, had excellent spirits, and was joyous and boyish in his intercourse with his children and his pupils.'[10] This romping, energetic, childlike side of his nature was in evidence in the long walks he took with his children – all of whom had individual nicknames but were collectively known as 'the dogs' or 'the fry' – on the Westmorland fells around the holiday home at Fox How, Ambleside, which he built when they were children, or in boisterous games in the garden at Laleham-on-Thames. This eager domesticity was one of a number of characteristics Matthew Arnold shared with his father. He also had his father's love of nature and outdoor pursuits – and his utter insensitivity to music and indifferent feel for the visual arts. His younger brother, Tom, writing to his fiancée Julia Sorell in 1850, tried to reassure her about an impending visit to the intimidatingly correct Arnolds at Fox How (now bereft of their Papa but still dedicated to his memory and continuing in their traditional ways): 'You need not be afraid, my dear Julia, of my family's being too good; they are much like other people, and when we are all at home, there is nothing but joking and fun from morning to night . . .'[11]

At first, people noticed only the superficial contrasts between father and son. The scholar and Oxford Regius Professor Goldwin Smith wrote in his *Reminiscences*: 'Matthew Arnold was outwardly a singular contrast to his almost terribly earnest sire . . . His outward levity was perhaps partly a mask, possibly in some measure a recoil from his father's sternness.'[12] But it was considered by Whitridge that underneath this superficial variance could be found 'the solid substratum of righteousness inherited from the militant headmaster'.[13] This may be so, but in spite of the frequent pious references to 'Papa' which are scattered through his correspondence, and the stiff tribute of the poem *Rugby Chapel* written in his thirties fifteen years after his father's death:

> We who till then in thy shade
> Rested as under the boughs
> Of a mighty oak . . .,

Arnold was certainly developing in a different direction, towards an appreciation of some of those qualities of 'intellectual delicacy' for which his father had no time. Phrases distributed through his essays – 'a combative, rigid, despotic nature of which the characteristic was energy',[14] 'more vehemence than truth and more heat than light',[15] or 'the acrid tone and temper of the fanatic'[16] – seem to call to mind Dr Arnold and his furious zeal. They cause his ghost to flit across the many passages where Arnold is advocating 'harmonious perfection' and 'sweetness and light'.

2

'Tradition says that I was born at Laleham in 1822 on the 24th of December', wrote Matthew Arnold in 1836,[17] already, at the age of thirteen, an accomplished ironist. When his wife fell from her horse, Thomas Arnold was already two weeks into his latest piece of historical hack-work, a history of Rome from Gracchi to Trajan, for the *Encyclopaedia Metropolitana* done for seven guineas a sheet. He had arrived by the Thames in Laleham in 1819 with his brother-in-law John Buckland to start a private school, and by 1822 they had six pupils. He had come to teaching after what had begun as a promising academic career, reading theology at Corpus Christi College, Oxford, followed by election as a Fellow of Oriel in 1815. His one ambition was to be a parson but he was assailed by doubts which made him uneasy about subscribing to the Thirty-nine Articles. Although he was ordained deacon on 20 December 1818 the doubts returned and he was forced to accept that the priesthood was not for him.

Thomas Arnold had now to ask himself what he would do with his life. His sister Frances was married to John Buckland who was running a successful small school for the sons of the local gentry in the old vicarage at Hampton. Buckland was ambitious and saw the scope for a larger private school which, as an alternative to private tuition, would prepare boys for the public schools and universities. When Buckland approached his brother-in-law to suggest a joint enterprise the idea seemed attractive. The two young men, only in their early twenties, spent the summer of 1819 scouring the Thames-side villages for suitable properties to rent and, after a long search, they eventually found what they were looking for at Laleham-on-Thames near Staines, about sixteen miles from London. Buckland chose a house that belonged to a local doctor and Arnold the property of an East India captain. Buckland's house still stands, with an oblique view of the river, but Arnold's was demolished in 1864 to make way for a new vicarage and school. At the age of twenty-four Arnold had for the first time a home of his own, and he invited his mother, Martha Arnold, his aunt, Susan Delafield and his disabled sister Susannah, who was carried from the ferry on the shoulders of the Thames boatman, to share it with him. When he eventually married on 11 August 1820 a house became available for rent next door to the Bucklands and into it he moved mother, sister, and aunt.

Thomas Arnold's wife was Mary Penrose, a Cornishwoman, four years older than her husband. Aubrey de Vere recorded a visit to the Lake District on 5 March 1845 where he met Wordsworth ('in great force and indignation about the railways') and, that evening, 'Was introduced to Mrs Arnold – a dark, eager, enthusiastic, vivid, interesting, and apparently strong-minded woman.'[18] Mary Arnold outlived her husband by more than thirty years and, from her retreat at Fox How, preserved his memory and a certain Arnoldian *hauteur*. Her eldest son was very aware that his notorious 'vivacity' and love of chaffing his opponents was viewed with some coolness at Fox How. When he sent his younger brother Tom a copy of *Essays in Criticism* in 1865 he revealed: 'At Fox How they didn't much like the Preface – there is a vein of strictness in our family which makes them a little averse to that sort of thing . . .'[19] Mrs Arnold remained, if it is possible to use the term in a neutral sense, a provincial, making very occasional trips to London to see her children but displaying no particular affection for metropolitan life. Her eldest child, Jane Arnold, who was always referred to by her childhood nickname 'K', and who married the Liberal politician William Forster, and was thus required to live in London, was very unhappy in her first years in the capital. Matthew was perhaps the most ardent metropolitan of the Arnolds but he would join in the teasing of his wife, Fanny Lucy, as 'a Cockney' because of her shrewd Belgravian knowledge of how to find her way around central London. Arnold loved, in particular, his central London club, the Athenaeum, and once found his old friend, the MP and editor John Morley, confessing to him in an 'unthinking dream' that if he could have chosen his lot in life he would have chosen Wordsworth's life 'among the lakes and fells'. Arnold was cheerfully dismissive of this bucolic idyll into which his normally robust friend had slipped: 'No, no,' he said, 'you would not; it was a peasant's life: you would soon have longed for us two to be dining together at the Athenaeum.'[20] Arnold loved good food, good conversation, the clubman's brandy and cigars and conviviality. The 'peasant's life' was certainly not for him. But in spite of the gulf of urbanity between him and Fox How he loved to visit there, to walk and to fish, and he wrote a letter to his mother every week of her life, filled with his doings and those of his adored wife and children.

The Cornish element in Arnold's make-up – which he acknowledged in private but which, oddly, he did not explicitly refer to in his lectures on Celtic literature – has been seen by some as a key to understanding the juxtaposition of gaiety and melancholy in his personality.[21] For obvious reasons we in the twentieth century are more cautious than the Victorians were about the consequences of glib racial theories, but the mercurial passage between glitter and gloom – whether or not we term it a 'Celtic temperament' – could just as easily be seen as another instance of the poet's internalised war against the Arnoldian inheritance, the struggle between aesthetic joy and moral rectitude. The dichotomy in Arnold is paralleled in the conflict between the poet and the writer of prose.[22] Urbane as he might seem to the world, Arnold was kept in check by an efficient internal policing system.

Mrs Arnold's father, the Reverend John Penrose, and his wife Jane – a Trevenen – left the parish of Carwythenick or Crannick in Cornwall in 1801 for a new living at Fledborough in Nottinghamshire. Better prospects tempted them but Jane Penrose found it hard to leave her native Cornwall. They set off one February morning in a Welsh car pulled by a sturdy old horse whose reputation was enhanced by the name of Mercury. When the carriage reached the border of Devon and Cornwall, Mrs Penrose ordered it to stop, 'got out, and stooped down and kissed the dust on the road saying that it was her tender farewell to the land she loved'.[23] Much later, when she had reluctantly settled in to the Fledborough Parsonage, Mrs Penrose mentioned, in a letter of 22 November 1817, her son Thomas Trevenen's undergraduate friend who occasionally stayed with them and who was 'rising in reputation and wins all the Oxford prizes he tries for'.[24] This paragon was Thomas Arnold who had begun to take notice of Thomas Trevenen's sister, Mary. They were eventually married on 11 August 1820 and their first child, Jane, was born in the summer of the following year at Laleham.

3

Although Laleham would be, for Thomas Arnold, a mere phase of preparation for the role of Arnold of Rugby, for his young family it would be a period of uncomplicated happiness, and would remain in affectionate, perhaps even sentimental, memory for the rest of their lives. 'Ambitious friends wrote to complain of his Boetian retirement', it has been claimed,[25] but he was happy, if not fully stretched, at Laleham. Matthew Arnold spent the first five years of his life here, on the banks of the Thames which, brimming and wide, flows past what is still an attractive spot today. His passion for rivers in general and for the Thames and its surrounding countryside in particular is one of the marked characteristics of his poetry, most explicitly in *The Scholar-Gipsy* who is apostrophised:

> O born in days when wits were fresh and clear,
>   And life ran gaily as the sparkling Thames;
>   Before this strange disease of modern life,
>   With its sick hurry, its divided aims,
>   Its heads o'ertaxed, its palsied hearts, was rife . . .

Arnold's childhood belongs to that imagined innocence and we are indebted to the family's fondness for writing and recording in sketches, poems, and family albums, their trivial doings, for the relatively full picture we have of their Thames-side idyll. The Arnolds seem to have been peculiarly susceptible to the spirit of place and the force of nostalgia – the spirit which animates much of *The Scholar-Gipsy* – and Laleham became, for all the Arnolds, a special region of the heart. Tom Arnold – the younger and hopelessly unworldly brother whom Arnold so often tried to help into official posts or get settled – described Laleham in his autobiography, *Passages in a Wandering Life*:

> At the southern end of the village were the house and gardens of Lord Lucan; on a short cross road running down to the river was the villa belonging to the Hartwell family, where Louis XVIII and other members of the French royal family found an asylum for many years . . . My father . . . rented an old red-brick mansion in the middle of the village, built in that semi-Dutch style, comfortable to inhabit and not unpleasing to behold, which prevailed in the home counties during the greater part of the last century. Behind it was a large lawn, flanked by some fine cedars; beyond the lawn was a greenhouse.[26]

Late one summer night at the end of July in 1852 Arthur Hugh Clough arrived at Laleham by ferry to see for the first time the place where his adolescent idol Dr Arnold had lived and worked: 'We found our way to the house he used to occupy, a solidish red brick place, with a narrow turn for a carriage in front and a tolerable garden alongside it'. By now the house was unoccupied so Clough and his companion went to look at the church, peering through the window where they made out 'the pulpit whence he used to fulminate'.[27] Matthew Arnold frequently mentions Laleham in his letters, and one Sunday in 1862 he took his eldest son Trevenen ('Budge') to see his Aunt Buckland – a revisiting which 'greatly touched' him. After lunch they walked from Chertsey to the Laleham ferry,

> which so long as I live will always rise to my mind when I hear or read the word ferry: and that view, which is the first I remember, of the beautiful turn of the river under Lord Lucan's towards Chertsey Bridge – opposite Aunt Susannah's house, the Hartwells' old place with its huge willows, and the short road running up to the Bucklands.[28]

Budge was to go to the Bucklands' school, which was still functioning. As Arnold observed to his mother: 'We who were brought up in the country, with fields and gardens, have no notion what the country can do, even for school, in the eyes of a London boy'. Tom, too, was nostalgic about Laleham: 'In my boyish memory and imagination the lawn, bathed in perpetual sunshine, stretched out for a quarter of a mile between the house and the greenhouse, and the whole scene was parklike and beautiful.' But when he actually returned some years later he had to admit that distance had lent enchantment: 'the spacious lawn was but some eighty yards across; everything was altered and shrunken in my eyes; disillusion could not be more complete'.

Arnold's attachment to Laleham was so great that he once told his mother: 'My desire is, if ever I get a great sale for my books to restore that poor neglected church at Laleham – and I think very much of this . . .'[29] That 'great sale' never came and Arnold's prediction that he would always be, comparatively speaking, 'an unpopular author' was fulfilled. At another reflective moment, in 1868, when the rest of the family had gone to Laleham to look at the fresh grave of his youngest child Basil he wrote from Harrow, where he was then living, to his mother: 'You will be well able to fancy the feelings and recollections which Laleham in the summer evening calls up to me. It was certainly a good place to be born in; it has something so abiding and peaceful.'[30] And Laleham was on the Thames, which flowed through his poems, sometimes, perhaps, in disguise as the Oxus or the 'lone Chorasmian stream',[31] sometimes more grandly as the River of Life, often as itself.[32] Arnold once wrote to Tom from Llysdinam in Breconshire, where he was staying at the house owned by George Venables of the *Saturday Review*: 'I have a passion for beautiful rivers in general, and for the Wye, that "wanderer of the woods", in particular.'[33]

Writing in her family journal in 1828, Mrs Arnold looked back at Laleham, where 'the first years of our married happiness had been past' and remembered 'the six little cribs' in the nursery. Addressing herself to the children she knew would later read the account she went on:

> Some of you will I hope remember that lovely garden – where there was so much shade and liberty – where your little steps first tottered along on the level turf till becoming stronger and stronger you ran through the walks with your hoops and whips – or gathered violets in the springtime, both blue and white in the ash plantation – or delighted in your little gardens at the bottom of the orchard. Or when the long summer days made the confinement of your nursery irksome – sat with your nurses in the shade and sometimes had your tea underneath the beautiful Cedar of Lebanon.[34]

Arnold was christened at the church of All Saints, Laleham, in whose churchyard he was eventually to be buried. The christening, on 23 January 1823, came three weeks after his first excursion, in the arms of his nurse, a Mrs Jerome from Thomas Arnold's native Isle of Wight, to see his grandmother at the other end of the village. Matthew was accompanied to the font by his two godfathers, the Reverend John Tucker and the Reverend John Keble. The latter would be one of the first of the 'Oxford Malignants' when he preached his famous sermon on 'National Apostasy' in 1833, generally seen as the firing of the starting pistol for the Tractarian Movement, but for now he was just Thomas Arnold's old college friend from Corpus.[35] Mrs Arnold wrote: 'I shall never forget the cheerful earnestness of Mr Keble's look as he shook me by the hand as we went to Church.'[36] There was no premonition of future rupture. The other clergyman, Reverend John Tucker, made an even more powerful impression, as they strode towards the church, by 'an account of his attendance at a mad-house to give religious instruction'. Later that year, on 14 September, Mrs Arnold recorded that Matthew 'first took notice of the moon'.[37]

In the summer of 1836 when Arnold was thirteen years old his elder sister by a year, 'K', wrote out a three-page manuscript which has survived, *The History of Jane's Life*.[38] She explains that when they lived at Laleham, where six of the nine children of Thomas Arnold were born, they had 'a nice large garden' with 'a digging place in it'. Digging was a favourite pursuit of the children and, when they were exhausted by it, their dog, Spot, obligingly carried on scratching out the earth for them. Spot also pulled a dog-cart around the garden with Matthew or one of the others as his passenger. 'Papa took pupils, I forget how many, but they were very kind to us', she goes on. Her little history has an addendum by Matthew who agreed about the kindness of the pupils although he was a little more acerbic in his estimate of them: 'One of the first things I remember is my asking one of Papa's pupils, who were very kind to us, one morning after breakfast to get me a bough and he greatly vexed me by making a bow.' The lively, boisterous, and rapidly growing family obviously struck a chord with the older children being taught by Thomas Arnold. John Buckland taught younger pupils and eventually the two men made this division of labour permanent by forming two separate schools. The children were all given nicknames by their father which Jane carefully enumerates: 'Papa gave us all new names when we were quite babies and we have kept them ever since. I was K and now I am called K much oftener than Jane [which was to be the case for the rest of her life]. Matt is Crab, Tom, Prawn, Mary, Bacco, Edward, Didu, Willy, Widu, Susy, Babbat Apbook, Fan, Bonze, and Walter, Quid.'

The nickname given to Matthew – 'Crab' or 'Crabby' – takes on a different aspect when he recalls – in addition to 'being obstinate' – going up to London 'about my crooked legs, and wearing irons'. Although the adolescent Arnold's tone here is deliberately breezy and bumptious ('I think my memory must be very good, for I remember such quantities of things which occurred . . . I have not however any string of facts in my head, but only abstruse ones') the experience must have been a very mortifying one for a sensitive young boy, for all his attempted insouciance. The most obvious explanation for the leg-irons was vitamin deficiency causing rickets, but we cannot be certain. The Arnolds seem to have been reluctant to agree to the irons (which in the nineteenth century were so heavy as to be at risk of being a cure worse than the disease). In the summer of 1824, however, after a brief trip to the Penroses' at Fledborough – where Thomas Arnold and the children went out on the Trent in a rowing boat called the *Frolic* and they were allowed to row ('or fancied they did so')[39] – the Arnolds realised they had to confront the issue. On Wednesday 18 August the local doctor, Mr Tothill, examined Matthew's leg again 'and recommended irons'. Accepting the doctor's judgement, Thomas Arnold took his son up to town the following morning to consult another doctor who sent him to a specialist brace-maker called Callum who pronounced that 'he should be measured immediately for irons to be made under his directions'.

On 7 September, his mother wrote in the family journal: 'Matt's irons came.' A week later his father again took Matthew up to London to have the irons properly fitted by Callum. Although the Arnolds again consulted their doctor in October 1825, he told them 'the Irons were doing what he intended and must be continued'. The young boy was to wear them for two years. His parents remained uneasy, however, and Mrs Arnold's journal records: 'The confinement was become so irksome and in every way so disadvantageous to our dear boy that from this time we gradually discontinued them – & without any bad effect. His clumsy manner of walking and heavy movement and inactive habits shew even now the mischief which attended the great good which he gained from them.' Yet she seemed willing to concede that 'the prompt use of these incumbering irons probably saved him from permanent lameness or deformity'[40] so he wore them on and off until the summer of 1826. By the end of that year Mrs Arnold was able to write with some relief in her journal in December: 'My Matt was made very happy on his birthday, Sunday 24th, by receiving his grandfather's very kind present of a rocking horse – which had long been promised when he left off his fetters.'[41]

Before this, however, Matthew was to meet with an accident, very probably connected with the wearing of the 'fetters'. On 5 December 1825, a couple of weeks before his third birthday, he clambered up on to the book-strewn sofa in his father's study where the materials for his latest work on Roman history for the *Encyclopaedia Metropolitana* were scattered and, rendered clumsy by the irons, tumbled off and broke open his head on the ugly claw foot of a table set just in front of the sofa. The wound took an unusually long time to heal and Tothill was brought in to examine it 'to make sure the mischief did not extend further than we had expected'. Mrs Arnold was so anxious about the slow healing of the wound that she delayed her Christmas visit to her relatives – and did not in fact feel confident enough to set off for Cornwall until 10 January 1826. In spite of these domestic anxieties, Mrs Arnold was able to finish her journal with the assertion that 1825 had been 'another happy year'.

At the beginning of 1827 she weighed Matthew in her Marriott scales and found the four-year-old to be a healthy 43 pounds. Arnold was always to be fond of outdoor pursuits, long walks and tennis, and showed no long-term consequences of his early period in leg-irons.

4

Life at Laleham came to an end in 1828 when the family moved to Rugby on Dr Arnold's appointment as headmaster. 'I was very sorry to leave dear Laleham I loved it so much',[42] wrote K. For Thomas Arnold, however, it was an enormous opportunity. He had the chance to make his name as a great reforming headmaster and to implement some of his ideas on realising a true Christian community (although he never had any illusions about the moral state of boyhood). The public schools of his day were in a sorry state. Drunkenness and disorder were rife and bullying was such that new boys returning home at the end of their first term at Rugby were often said to take lessons from local farmhands in boxing in order to defend themselves on their return next term. To this were added flogging and fagging, poor living conditions, and barbarous practices such as 'buffeting', 'chairing' and 'clodding'. Troops had been called in to suppress riots in some schools. Expulsions for homosexual rape were not unknown. It all seemed an entirely adequate field of wickedness on which Thomas Arnold could contend, with the aim of making 'Christian gentlemen' out of such very raw material. It has never been claimed that he was a significant innovator in the curriculum (although he did achieve some limited broadening of its scope by introducing mathematics and French) and the brass plate to his memory in Laleham Church probably sums up his order of priorities: 'Powerful to raise and train the intellect but desirous above all to impress religion and duty upon the hearts of his pupils.'

Arnold's popular fame as a headmaster rests in part on the novel by Thomas Hughes, *Tom Brown's Schooldays* (1857), which did much to create the Arnold legend.[43] Hughes was later to claim that he had introduced into the book details of practices which he knew had belonged to the time of Dr Arnold's predecessor.[44] But in general, in its curiously innocent way, it probably does give a true picture of a school where bird-nesting, fishing, poaching and fighting easily eclipsed any intellectual performance. The only glimpse we get of actual learning is of lessons where the classics are studied by means of cribs and 'vulgus books'. Perhaps the real function of this book for schoolboys (or for adult males who have not quite grown up) is to foster a myth of cheerful red-blooded Englishness. From this point of view the early part of the book – an excursion into Merrie England in the Vale of White Horse – very much sets the tone for what is to follow. 'Perhaps ours is the only little corner of the British Empire which is thoroughly, wisely, and strongly ruled just now', a master tells a boy. Tom Brown, too, offers a neat summation of the purpose of Rugby: 'I want to be A1 at cricket and football, and all the other games, and to make my hands keep my head against any fellow, lout or gentleman. I want to get into the sixth before I leave, and to please the Doctor; and I want to carry away just as much Latin and Greek as will take me through Oxford respectably.' Both these remarks indicate what a powerful personality was possessed by Dr Arnold and the eagerness with which he was obeyed. Whatever our final judgement on Rugby in the 1820s and 1830s, it is worth noting that Matthew Arnold did not send his children to Rugby nor did he make any substantial reference, in his own career as an educational reformer, to his father's example.

In contrast to the present day, Thomas Arnold was appointed to his post without interview and solely on the basis of written testimonials. From the Provost of Oriel, Dr Hawkins, he received perhaps one of the most famous character-references of the nineteenth century. If Arnold were chosen, wrote the Provost, he would 'change the face of education all through the public schools of England'. Egged on by his Oxford friends, the 32-year-old schoolmaster, who had never managed an establishment of more than eight pupils, was accepted by the twelve noblemen and gentlemen of Warwickshire who were trustees of the school, and triumphed over thirty other contenders. Like the rest of his family he was in two minds about leaving Laleham. Apart from a shrewd premonition of the 'perfect vileness which I must daily contemplate' at Rugby, he was apprehensive about 'the greater form and publicity of the life which we should there lead, when I could no more bathe in the clear Thames, nor wear old coats and Russia duck trousers, nor hang on a gallows, nor climb a pole, I grieve to think of the possibility of a change'.[45] But the prospect of a salary of £113 6s 8d per year, when the Arnolds had married 'with a considerable debt' and had already six children, proved decisive. On 18 January the Arnolds accepted the outgoing headmaster Dr Wooll's invitation to visit the school and on 1 June Thomas Arnold was ordained priest (partly to avoid being put at a disadvantage in the balance of power in the school *vis-à-vis* the chaplain). In November he took his degree of Doctor of Divinity. Although his wife found it 'ridiculous' to address him by his new title he was, at last, Dr Arnold of Rugby. On the day before he left Laleham he wrote to his friend the Reverend John Tucker: 'So ends the first act of my life since I arrived at manhood. For the last eight years it has been a period of as unruffled happiness as I think could ever be experienced by man.'[46]

On the morning of 5 August 1828 the Arnolds left Laleham. They filled the entire Oxford coach and in the confusion the loyal Spot was overlooked. 'Great were the lamentations when he was found not to make one of the travelling party',[47] wrote Mrs Arnold later. But by the time the coach had reached the crossroads the local bricklayer, Percy, was seen racing along to cut them off with Spot eagerly trotting along beside him. Percy's palm was crossed and Spot hauled on board. It was a beautiful morning but there was great gloom at parting from Laleham and Jane's face was swollen with tears. The party reached Oxford at 5 p.m. and spent the night at the Angel Inn. Next day they boarded the coach for Rugby – six children, two nurses and the governess, Miss Rutland, squeezed inside to escape the rain. On arrival at Rugby they were greeted by the housekeeper and servants and immediately began to unpack the heavy luggage that had preceded them. Dr Arnold wasted no time in settling in. He had to prepare for the pupils who would arrive by the end of the month. 'So here we are at Rugby', he wrote, 'in a house splendid beyond all my experience and expectations – with much to be thankful for in outward circumstances, if our inward mind corresponds with our situation.'[48] In the months and years that followed Dr Arnold would implement his plans for reform – which echoed the wider clamour for reform in English society at this time, in the difficult period of urban and rural unrest after the Napoleonic Wars. The most notable innovation was the institution of 'praepostors' or sixth-form prefects who would police the lower school on his behalf, like the compliant local élites in a colonial administration. His home, the School House, was always open to masters and senior boys. He was consciously trying to break down the aura of autocratic majesty gathered around him by his predecessor. On one occasion he told a group of praepostors what he saw as being the aim of the school – in a characteristic set of priorities: '1st, religious and moral principles; 2ndly, gentlemanly conduct' and, bringing up the rear, '3rd, intellectual ability'.[49]

Matthew, now aged five, was still giving his parents some anxiety. His legs continued to make him clumsy and awkward. Mrs Arnold thought of engaging a drill sergeant or a dancing master but when the former was eventually employed Matthew promptly developed, like his younger brother Tom, a stutter. A speech therapist, Mr Bull, was then engaged to treat the boys, but after an expensive fortnight at Rugby, he seemed to make little progress. The hesitation in speech continued for some time afterwards. Matthew's formal education had begun on 14 February 1828, shortly before leaving Lalcham, when he first opened the pages of a Latin grammar. At Rugby the children were at first instructed by a governness, Miss Rutland, but eventually the Arnolds decided that Matthew would make more progress by being sent back to Laleham to Buckland's school. A few months before he went, however, he produced what is the earliest piece of writing we have from the future poet and critic. Earlier in the year his godfather, John Keble, had presented him with a Bible 'with stories of animals for children'.[50] Written at the age of seven and inscribed 'from Matt to Papa, October 15th 1830', the tiny pencil-written booklet – fragile as the tissue paper which scholars today carefully unwrap when inspecting it in the library of Balliol College, Oxford – is entitled *Pilgrim Love* and is plainly influenced by Bunyan. It has a Preface addressed 'To His Highness, Lord Man' and begins with a dream of an encounter with Mr Knowledge, then of a castle in the wood owned by a Mr Freedom whose three sons are Self Love, Badthought, and Foolish. The narrative then introduces Pilgrim Love who, girding himself up with the (misspelt) shield of Faith despatches Self Love with the sword of the spirit and plunges into a cave in the middle of the wood out of which has been heard a great roaring. Love, by the agency of the same sword, finishes off the cave's two guardian giants called Hurt and Cruel. Thus ends the first of a promised four-volume allegory. The idea that writing and moral uplift are intertwined was plainly implanted very early in the education of an Arnold. About this time Mrs Arnold confided to her diary the children's pleasure in their magic lantern which they watched in the School House – 'greater experience of life and death', she added sententiously, 'will show them how we make our exits and our entrances like the figures on the curtain'.[51] But perhaps, too, young Matthew was well able to imagine for himself the giants of hurt and cruelty, transferring to them his anger at 'my crooked legs', and his speech impediments.

At the beginning of 1831 Dr and Mrs Arnold set off from Rugby with Matthew to Laleham to deliver him to Buckland's school, less than three years after leaving the Thames. The Arnolds were once again in two minds about their decision and a year later, on 14 February 1832, Mrs Arnold wrote as determinedly as she could: 'One dear child is absent from us – our dear eldest boy who has entered on his second year at his Uncle Buckland's school at Laleham & thank God: we feel satisfied that we judged right in sending him.'[52] His father wrote to his eight-year-old son at Laleham on 20 September 1831: 'I am sorry, my own Crabby, that you are in trouble about your Greek grammar: – it puts me very much in mind of my own trouble when I was first put into Phaedrus'.[53] It is a kind letter from the stern headmaster that admits to his own schoolboy shortcomings (his 'impositions' and 'knocks' received) and tells young Matt to keep his chin up and to 'expect trials in this life'. For 'you who wrote so nicely about Pilgrim Love will understand that we are all Pilgrims, and must expect to meet with enemies on our way, and must fight with them as with great and bloody Giants'. A month later, however, the tone was a little more stern: 'My dear Crabby, I am afraid that you are become a Tory . . . since you have got *Male* twice in one week . . . it makes me sadly afraid that my boy Matt is an idle boy, who thinks that God sent him into the world to play and eat and drink . . . I do not like writing to my Crabby when I am obliged to find fault with him.'[54] By 21 March 1832 the sunnier Dr Arnold was back with a playful remonstration about his son's tardy letters: 'O Crabby the great, who make your letters long to wait, that we get them about two weeks too late'.[55] And then it was summer time.

In December of the previous year the children had, according to Jane's history, first gone to the Lake District, to Rydal Mount, inaugurating a long Arnoldian love-affair with the Lakes – although the famous holiday home at Fox How would not be in use until 1834. In July 1832 Matthew was reunited with his brothers and sisters and writing home to Rugby from Kendal where they were all in the charge of a governess, Miss Ellen Robertson, who assured Mrs Arnold that Matthew had been 'a very good boy'. The opening words of Matthew's earliest surviving letter are: 'I have fished a good deal.'[56] He was to remain an ardent angler all his life, an obsession reflected even on his personal library bookplate which shows a large and scaly fish, wriggling above an improving Latin motto. On this occasion, however, in spite of being kept liberally supplied with fresh hooks by Miss Robertson, he had caught only 'a full-sized perch and a few minnows'.

The summer was over all too quickly and by September he was back at Uncle Buckland's, being written to this time by his younger brother Tom. His brother's letter shows that the children had brought their Laleham games and hoops to Rugby but 'poor old Spot' was now chained up outside the stables. 'The boys have begun football',[57] noted Tom. In his autobiography Tom later recalled the family games at Rugby: 'Little cricket, gymnastics, quoits, swinging, gardening'[58] and 'the chief amusement of all', digging. They dug out forts and assailed each other with clay missiles. And Dr Arnold 'delighted in our games and sometimes joined in them'. Although Tom believed his father to be neither witty nor humorous, he could appreciate humour in others and was strongly attracted by 'the comic and grotesque side of life' and 'there was a vein of drollery in him, a spirit of pure fun, which perhaps came from his Suffolk ancestry'. Although in one sense the children feared him, 'on the whole love cast out fear; for he never held us at a distance'.

In this same month, September 1832, Dr Arnold received a letter from William Wordsworth informing him that the owner of Fox How, at Rydal, a Mr Simpson, was willing to sell the estate for £800.[59] The Arnolds had first visited the Lakes – and begun their friendship with Wordsworth – in 1831. In 1833 they stayed in Grasmere and took out a rental for the whole year of a house at the head of the village called Allan Bank which had once been lived in by the Wordsworths. From this time onwards, wrote Crabb Robinson, the Arnolds and the Wordsworths would see a great deal of each other: 'They walked and talked and disputed and played whist together.' However, it was at the same time true that on these holiday visits, 'Wordsworth and Doctor Arnold did not see eye to eye either on political or religious questions.'[60]

Wordsworth was a potent early influence on Matthew Arnold who knew him as a poet but first as a man. When the poet came into their lives he had not published anything since *A Description of the Scenery of the Lakes* in 1822, the year of Matthew Arnold's birth and of Jeffrey's pronouncement in the *Edinburgh Review* that 'The Lake School of Poetry . . . is now pretty nearly extinct.'[61] It was to be the poet's most barren decade. Wordsworth was now in his early sixties, with his radical youthful energies put well behind him, but his affection for his new neighbours was sufficient to enable him to transcend his distaste for their liberal politics. He thought Dr Arnold a good man but, in a shrewd assessment in a letter to Henry Crabb Robinson, he judged that he was 'of too ardent a mind however to be always judicious on the great points of secular and ecclesiastical politics that occupied his mind and upon which he often wrote and acted under strong prejudices, and with hazardous confidence'.[62]

Matthew Arnold, who was an eight-year-old boy when he first met Wordsworth, was once encountered by the poet out walking on the fells. With Tom, he had been building a play fort on the side of Loughrigg, the mountain which towered over Fox How and, as his mother recorded for them, 'Mr Wordsworth came and found you in your Strong hold'.[63] The poetic influence – subtly inwrought with the influence of the Lake District scenery – would bear fruit later. Obvious Wordsworthian touches can be felt in many of Arnold's poems but the older poet's advocacy of natural language, of the poet's speech as needing to be that of 'a man speaking to men', and of the primacy of authentic experience and feeling, all find an echo in Arnold's poetic theory and practice – although his verse is more experimental and wide-ranging in its choice of subject than such a simple aesthetic would suggest.

One of Arnold's most famous critical essays is on Wordsworth, written in 1879, as the Preface to a popular selection of his poems for Macmillan. In the essay Arnold manages to suggest some of Wordsworth's limitations – he was one of the first to establish the critical commonplace that Wordsworth wrote too much and some of it of indifferent quality – while concluding that his great achievement, as one of 'the great glories of English poetry', was in 'the extraordinary power with which Wordsworth feels the joy offered to us in nature'. Arnold's tragedy was that he aspired to do the same but was born into another age, as he saw it, of doubt and confusion, in which it was no longer possible for a poet just to write of 'the simple primary affections'. He would later argue, in private letters, that Wordsworth's influence could be detrimental – in encouraging a habit of 'thinking aloud rather than making anything' – and he placed the poet beneath Goethe in intellectual power, including him in his general indictment of the Romantic English poets who 'did not know enough'. But he remained touched by Wordsworth's influence, as by Byron's – a poet whom he likewise simultaneously admired and criticised.

The physical presence of the poet – whether glimpsed striding the fells or comfortably settled in the drawing room at Fox How reading his own work – must have worked, with the surrounding presence of the countryside his poetry animated, an extraordinarily potent charm over the young boy who dreamed of being a poet. On a winter visit to Fox How, much later, at the age of twenty-five, Mrs Arnold recorded in a letter to Tom: 'Matt has been very much pleased I think by what he has seen of dear old Wordsworth since he has been at home, and certainly he manages to draw him out very well. The old man [Wordsworth was now 78] was here yesterday, and as he sat on the stool in the corner beside the fire which you knew so well, he talked of various subjects of interest, of Italian poetry, of Coleridge, etc etc; and he looked and spoke with more vigour than he has often done lately.'[64]

By December 1832 Dr Arnold had concluded that, in spite of Matthew's being, as he put it in a letter, 'a grand Crab . . . who can construe Virgil, and quote Ovid'[65] it was time to bring him home from Laleham and try to expose him to some 'home feelings'.[66] He accordingly hired an expensive tutor at a salary of £200 a year for both Matthew and Tom. Herbert Hill was a cousin of the poet Robert Southey and tutored the boys until they were sent to Winchester in 1836. In Tom's view: 'He was a good but rather a severe tutor; and we all made fair progress under him in Greek and Latin.' He also taught them Euclid, 'but here the bent of my brother's mind showed itself. Ratiocination did not at that time charm him; and the demonstration of what he did not care to know found him languid.'[67] Matthew at that time found war games a little more enticing than geometry. In a letter to his Uncle Trevenen Penrose written a few days before his eleventh birthday – after citing an impressive list of his achievements in Greek which showed that Mr Hill had already advanced the ten-year-old from mere Homer and Xenophon to Aeschylean choruses – Matthew explained that he would spear with Mr Hill, play battledore and shuttlecock in the afternoon, and drive his hoop around the Rugby schoolfield. But he also liked drawing 'armed men' and had instructed the obliging Mr Hill to bring back from Oxford after Christmas a model trooper so that he could adequately render the 'Spanish cap and feather' of a cavalier. 'I have got a wooden sword',[68] he added.

In January 1836 Matthew Arnold composed his first poem on the subject of Mary Queen of Scots' departure from France. It is no more than a talented thirteen-year-old's juvenilia which shows a certain taste for grandiloquent gesture which was to characterise many of his childhood verses. In March he wrote another poem, *The First Sight of Italy*, which is more interesting technically and shows the influence of reading in the English Romantic poets. It also contains a parenthetical salute to the Lakes, in whose valleys 'chiefly Nature rallies',[69] and where Matthew was beginning to visit regularly for holidays. His next effort was to be a piece of light-hearted doggerel written to his cousin Martha Buckland, the schoolmaster's daughter, on 14 May 1836. The manuscript, with its hasty scribble and crossings-out, indicates something done extempore and not as a considered poem. Its jogging rhyming couplets are not to be taken too seriously and are much in the spirit of the accompanying letter to Martha which explains that he has a terrible cold and has been 'barking continually'. He has none the less 'filled my sheet with nonsense, which was my special object'.[70] Adding sauce to facetiousness, he addresses her in the letter in a stray line of verse as 'Maid of the merry blue eye' with the implication that it is a snatch from one of his own poems ('by you know whom'). The letter ends with a sharply contrasting note of grave courtesy from Dr Arnold, conveying his good wishes to his niece.

A month or so later Matthew wrote another poem, sparked off by a declaration from his tutor Herbert Hill that he would never consider living by the sea. Arnold's 'Reply' to that declaration expresses, by contrast, his love of the sea ('I love to hear the bounding waves / In quick succession beating') and his sense (faintly prefiguring *Dover Beach*) that 'The ceaseless murmur of waves on the shore / Enlivens Fancy's power'.[71] In the summer of 1836, Matthew was in East Cowes on holiday with his parents, staying with his Arnold relatives. He wrote home to his younger brother Willy and sister Susy describing his itinerary through the Home Counties, including a visit to Windsor Great Park. He drew Willy's attention to Pope's poem *Windsor Forest* 'which Mr Pope wrote when he was only 13 years old', as was Arnold himself at this time.[72] There is an irony in the first recorded mention of an English poet by Arnold being of Pope, of whom he was later to be so disparaging. The journey continued to Winchester where he was to meet Dr Moberly, the headmaster of the public school. 'Dr Moberly's house is not near such a nice one as the School House at Rugby,' was all he had to say. They got some buns and set off for Eaglehurst to bathe. (Dr Arnold's sister, Lydia, was the second wife of Richard Lambart, seventh Earl of Cavan, whose country seat was at Eaglehurst.) On 12 July Mrs Arnold discovered after breakfast that 'Matt was missing'.[73] It turned out that he had gone down to the shore again 'but I do not think it would be guessed what he was doing there. I did not know till as we were driving along he put in at the carriage window a pencilled paper which proved that he had been poetizing.' His mother was struck by his 'facility in thought and composition' in the piece, *Lines Written on the Seashore at Eaglehurst*, another thalassic poem of naiads underneath 'the boundless ocean's swell'. By now, it seemed, his 'poetizing' was unstoppable.

On 31 August 1836 Matthew and Tom set off for Winchester. Arnold never spoke about Rugby with the same affection as he had spoken about Laleham and recollections of his relatively brief periods of continuous residence there are rare. Late in life, in a letter to Tom, written in one early December, he recalled: 'This is the season when you and I, Edward and Willy, used to play our little football behind the Close, with old Sam, his milk pails on his shoulders on the way to the farmyard, pausing to look on.'[74] Dr Arnold, oddly perhaps, was reluctant to put his two eldest sons through his own school and contemplated doing so 'with trembling'.[75] He was anxious, too, about Matthew who had given him innumerable problems and who, in spite of his emerging poetic talent, was considered less promising than Tom. One of the first things that Matthew did on arrival at Winchester was to write another poem, *Lines Written on First Leaving Home for a Public School*. It bears the mark of his enforced rote-learning of his godfather John Keble's *The Christian Year* (1827) and is a rather lugubrious production which shows that entry to his father's old school did not fill Matthew with any eager anticipation: 'One step in life is taken / And we must hurry on / And cheer our onward path as best we may.' The improving conclusion of the poem – that only God will prop 'our sinking hopes' – hardly disposes of the very real apprehension that Winchester is to be the first step on the ascent of 'life's toilsome hill'.[76] Tom explains in his autobiography that he and Matthew entered Winchester as Commoners. Because of some obscure objection of their father's to the Thirty-nine Articles, signing of which was necessary to become a Heathcote Scholar, Matthew declined Moberly's invitation to apply for the scholarship and remained a Commoner.

One day in the spring of 1837 the two brothers attended one of Dr Moberly's breakfasts for members of the upper forms. 'My brother always talked freely', says Tom pointedly, and on this occasion Matthew blithely announced that some part of his form work was 'light and easy' which prompted the headmaster to laugh: 'Indeed, we must see to that!'[77] Then, what Tom calls 'a stupid boy' from the senior part of the school came after Matthew when they got outside to let him know that a dim view was taken of such comments which risked harder work being imposed on the rest of the boys. The young poet's unpopularity in the school was thus established. Shortly afterwards, when the time came for a school ritual called 'Cloister peelings' which afforded the opportunity for the ritual humiliation of unpopular boys, Matthew 'was brought out, placed at the end of the great school, and, amid howls and jeers, pelted with a rain of "pontos" for some time'. A ponto, in Winchester *argot*, was a ball made of the soft inside of a fresh bread roll. Tom also records another, more triumphant, episode when Matthew won a verse-speaking contest against the whole school for his recitation of the speech in the penultimate scene of Byron's *Marino Faliero, Doge of Venice* (1820) when the Doge begins: 'I speak to Time and to Eternity, / Of which I grow a portion, not to man.' Byron remained a lifelong passion for Arnold – however much he was to adjust his critical estimate of the poet. The fact that it was 'the simplicity and distinctness of his delivery' that won Matthew the prize would indicate that all speech impediment was now behind him and he was growing more confident.

In the Easter of 1837 the boys went for a short London vacation during which they heard Grisi sing in *Don Pasquale* and saw Kemble and Macready in Shakespeare's *King John* at Covent Garden. In April Matthew met with a serious accident at school when he burnt his hand, apparently from a phosphorous flare from playing with a firearm, and his mother was anxious when it was slow to heal. When the summer vacation came the boys made their way home via the newly opened Grand Junction Railway and were 'whirled' from Birmingham to Manchester in five and a quarter hours. This was the great age of railway expansion and Arnold was frequently to use the railways as a symbol of the obsession with material progress (at the expense of spiritual transport) that gripped his contemporaries – a point whose subtlety amusingly evades the author of the *Oxford History of England* (1962) who points out: 'As an inspector of schools Matthew Arnold owed a great deal of his leisure and comfort to rapid travel, and yet he merely sneers at railways.'[78]

That summer Matthew made a trip to France with his parents. They left Rugby early on a bright August morning with both the postboy on the stage-coach and the horses decorated with the dark blue rosettes of the North Warwickshire Whigs. The 1837 general election, Matthew noted, 'caused a great ferment at the various inns in that part of the country'.[79] They arrived in London on 9 August to dine with some friends, the Halls, in Tavistock Square and make contact with the Bucklands, whose eldest son was to travel with them. They slept at Campbell's Family Hotel in Southampton Row, although the two boys were suspicious of the beds. With high adolescent facetiousness Matthew gave their verdict: 'The beds looked comfortable, but experience taught Buckland and myself that seeing was not feeling. Suffice it, however, without entering into particulars, to say that there were verminous little animals within them.' Next morning while Dr Arnold went off to see about passports in Poland Street, Matthew made notes from the latest issue of *The Times* about the election. He also found time to visit an optician in Great Russell Street, Harris's, with Mr Hall to buy an 'eye glass'. This is the first we hear about any eye problems and the next morning, on their way out of London, they called at another oculist, Mr Ware at 23 Bridge Street, Blackfriars, 'about my eyes and he told me not to wear a glass, and said plenty more which I need not report'.

As the stage-coach (on the first seventeen-mile stretch to Dartford) passed the London docks, the sight was a revelation to Matthew, whose notion of the Thames had hitherto been a gentle and pastoral one: 'The views of the Thames with its vessels, sail, and steamer, of Tilbury Port and Gravesend, through part of which we passed, were most beautiful, for I had never seen anything in that line before.' That night they slept at the George Inn, Sittingbourne, only to rise – 'Horresco referens!!!' – at 4 a.m. on Friday 11 August, for a breakfast of milk and water 'which was the only thing procurable'. This stage was a sixteen-mile one and, because the sun was not due to rise for another hour or so and the dew being copious, 'I was frizzled in a style no tonseur could have surpassed.' It was now the turn of Matthew's feet to play up and he had to buy some foot plaster at a chemist in Dover just before boarding the packet, the *Water Witch*. Sea-sickness was now added to the other ailments, although it was exciting to arrive at Boulogne and see 'quantities of white bathing machines and people thronging the piers'. The incipient Oxford dandy was fascinated by 'the blue short-tailed jackets with a broad red border covered with metal buttons' worn by the French postillions. As they bowled through

Northern France he was intrigued by the 'very picturesque and foreign' scenes, including, at Montreuil, a lamp-post 'such as men were in the habit of getting hanged upon in the French Revolution'. Tumblers of *vin ordinaire de Bourgogne* proved 'very refreshing' and, undeterred by his father's horror of the European Catholic clergy, he noted with interest 'a young priest in a long, black robe very like an English lady's riding habit'. At Abbeville they entered the cathedral church at dusk, 'and many people kneeling at their devotions up the aisle, and the solemn stillness of everything around, together with the indistinctly seen altar at the upper end had a very inspiring effect'. The following day, however, the brighter light inside the church of Blanquis revealed 'gewgaw ornament and worthless pictures' which abated a little his admiration for Catholic churches.

And on 16 August Matthew entered Paris for the first time, 'in fashion, elegance, public buildings' superior to almost any city in Europe. Soon they were off again and at Chartres he shrewdly noted that the congregation, in spite of their pious attitudes and missals, seemed no more attentive 'on closer inspection' than an English one. They went to Rambouillet and Versailles then back to Paris to the Louvre where he dutifully toured the galleries, preferring the paintings to the sculpture. There was also a glimpse of a giraffe at the Jardin du Roi. Now beginning to guy his own dandyish inclination he describes how 'I went with Mamma to a great draper's warehouse and assisted her with my exquisite taste in forming a selection of pelerines, lace, cambric, silks etc: a tasteful assortment of which it would have been impossible to have procured without my assistance.' By 21 August the trip was over and the family was back at Boulogne. 'No ten days tour ever gave more gratification,' concluded Matthew. His notes on this tour show the emergence of an observant, witty, playful personality that was to be the one so frequently described by his friends in later years and which was so remote from the picture of him held by his detractors.

After the summer holiday, fourteen-year-old Matthew returned to Rugby as a pupil at last, the Winchester experiment having failed. It had perhaps been the expense, or the boy's unhappiness, or anxiety about his accidents, or a desire to have him at home again, that made Dr Arnold take the decision to enrol him, in August 1837, as a member of the Upper Fifth. Arthur Hugh Clough was just about to leave for Balliol and noted in a letter to a friend on 26 August: 'Mat. Arnold is in the School and the Upper 5th. His Compos. Tutor is Lee, his Mathematical, Price – a balance of favour I suppose.'[80] The tutor, the Reverend James Prince Lee (later Bishop of Manchester) was probably responsible for setting Matthew an early Latin 'vulgus' composition exercise on a theme from Virgil's *Georgics* III beginning 'iuvat ire jugis . . .' (joyous it is to roam over heights where no forerunner's track turns . . .). It is recorded in a notebook dated 21 October 1837[81] and suggests already a familiarity with Lucretius. It is a characteristic exercise in disappointed expectation – the poet ascends a wintry summit (many of his later poems were to involve such ascents and high perspectives) only to be swept away by a divinely ordered avalanche just at the point where his senses have been deceived into joy ('sensus in gaudia fallunt') by the prospect of seeking out the secrets of matter ('rerum arcana'). It was partly the young boy's understanding of poetic convention that created the disparity between such melancholy poetic perceptions and the jaunty spirit of his ordinary self, and partly, no doubt, the readiness of all adolescents to be seduced by gloom. But the paradox – central to any understanding of Arnold – did not lessen with time.

5

The Arnolds spent the Christmas holiday of 1837 at Fox How: 'Most beautiful morning. At Chapel twice. Wordsworth walked back with us,' wrote Dr Arnold in his diary on New Year's Eve.[82] When Dr Arnold originally decided to build a house in the area he took Wordsworth's advice on a site, eventually buying one of twenty acres, as Matthew Arnold's niece Mrs Humphry Ward puts it in her autobiography, *A Writer's Recollections* (1918): 'on a "how" or rising ground in the beautiful Westmorland valley leading from Ambleside to Rydal'. Wordsworth came and sat on a little three-legged stool by the fire to discuss building design details. He offered to be unofficial clerk of works when the family returned to Rugby at the end of each holiday period. Fox How was completed in the summer of 1834 and Wordsworth had willingly supervised the building of the house which was described by Mrs Humphry Ward as 'a modest building, with ten bedrooms and three sitting-rooms. Its windows look straight into the heart of Fairfield, the beautiful semi-circular mountain which rears its hollowed front and buttressing scaurs against the north, far above the green floor of the valley'.[83] The Arnolds seemed unconcerned that the grey stone house was north facing and loved the garden with 'its mimic bridges, its encircling river, its rocky knolls, its wild strawberries and wild raspberries, its queen of birch-trees rearing a stately head against the distant mountain, its rhododendrons growing like weeds on its mossy banks, its velvet turf, and long silky grass in the parts left wild'.

Once the house was finished the Arnolds threw themselves into the life of walking, bathing, fishing and boating. One of Matthew's favourite pastimes was shooting snipe. Inside the house there were plenty of pursuits for evenings and rainy days, for, as Matthew Arnold's wife, Fanny Lucy, confided after her husband's death following a visit to Fox How in 1894: 'after more than 40 years acquaintance with the climate of Westmorland one does not expect a steady continuance of fine weather'.[84] Days indoors were filled with charades, plays, drawing, and, of course, reading. Sketches in family albums which have survived give a vivid picture of the various activities of the family in the Fox How drawing room. The most famous of these childhood exercises was the *Fox How Magazine*, produced by the children from 1838 twice a year until January 1842. Its pages are full of light poems occasioned by holiday events and mishaps, facetious mock-editorialising, Jane's sketches of the house and the surrounding fells, playful digs at 'great Matt', and numerous other high-spirited efforts to be expected from a lively and literate group of children. On 10 July 1838, fifteen-year-old Matthew poetised on a theme from the vivacious popular novelist Julia Pardoe whose *The City of the Sultan* (1836) gave him a story of a young Greek girl at Constantinople who nursed her dying lover in a plague hospital then retired to the mountains to die alone. When the family returned to Fox How for the second time that year to spend Christmas there, two more poems were added to the Magazine, signed as usual with Matthew's 'C.C.C': *Land of the East!* and a translation of some lines from the *Aeneid*,[85] possibly set as a holiday task. The following summer an elegiac poem on *Constantinople* fallen to the Turks, in its mood anticipating *Alaric at Rome*, appeared in the July issue of the Magazine.

Members of the Arnold family kept coming to Fox How throughout their lives, with their husbands and wives, and the house was not emptied of Arnolds until the death of 'Fan', Matthew's youngest unmarried sister, in 1923. Mrs Humphry Ward remembers Matthew Arnold's visits which were eagerly looked forward to 'because of the constant fun which his presence heralded. He had a genius for keeping up and remembering family jokes, a delight in family reminiscences, which he would keep going with his brothers and sisters'. And he loved his walks in the surrounding countryside: 'I can see him throw back his head and sniff up the air as though it did him good all through. And there were the hours when we children, playing in the garden, saw him through the study window and knew that he was busy with his Annual Report and must not be disturbed.'[86] Throughout his life, Fox How, remained a pleasant oasis for Arnold even if, from time to time, he rubbed up against its customary sobriety, with his irrepressible vivacity. And as well as play, there would be work to do: the annual chore of his school inspector's report or marking papers he had brought with him from London. Holidays, both for inspectors and headmasters, were lavish by today's standards. After Christmas 1837, Thomas Arnold returned to Rugby on 31 January 1838, noting in his diary: 'Thank God through Christ Jesus for his great goodness to me in giving me nearly seven weeks of rest and happiness at this beloved home'.[87] By 21 June, the day after term ended, he was back at Fox How, arriving at 9 p.m. and dining with the Wordsworths the following evening. He stayed until 7 August when, expressing proper thanks to his God for such copious leisure, he wrote: 'Left dearest Fox How after a most happy residence of 46 days – may God be thanked and make me thankful.' Dr Arnold enjoyed nearly a hundred days' holiday a year at Fox How.

'The Fox How portion of our life was a time of unspeakable pleasure to us all', wrote Tom.[88] There were also adventures. In the summer of 1838, when Jane was in charge of 'the fry' at Fox How while her parents were briefly away, Matthew went out in a boat, the *Black Dwarf*, on Windermere, and, not for the first time, failed to return for evening players. Jane raised the alarm and a search was made but not until noon the following day did Matthew reappear, explaining that he and his companions were 'knocked up' with rowing after apparently having become becalmed and had put in at the ferry for the night.

Making and racing model boats was another passion of the boys, and Tom writes of a tarn they discovered a mile from the house: 'Here for several years we used to race our boats – cutters, schooners, yawls, luggers, as the case may be – and never grew tired of the pastime.' As well as Wordsworth, the Arnolds met many of the other literary figures of the Lakes. One day in 1834, Dr Arnold took Matthew and Tom to see the poet Southey who lived at Greta Bank, Keswick. 'As we shyly advanced', writes Tom, 'Southey rose up and came to meet us, shook hands with us both, and said with a smile, "So, now you've seen a live poet!" '[89] Although by this time Coleridge had moved south, his son Hartley Coleridge was in the area and, as Tom puts it, 'a melancholy ruin' who one evening, when offered a jug of water by Dr Arnold after evening prayers, said to his host: 'Might I ask for a glass of *beer*?'[90]

On 20 August, back in School House, we get a glimpse of family life on a typical day for Matthew and his brothers and sisters, as preparations were made for the new term – one in which Matthew would start to be a Rugby schoolboy for the first time. After reading Homer and Tacitus and writing a few letters, Dr Arnold took 'the dogs' to bathe in the river. After splashing in the August sunshine for the afternoon, something more improving was required to finish the day. 'Read Gibbon to fry in the evening', is the terse entry in Dr Arnold's diary. This mixture of earnest instruction, discipline and animal high spirits which was Dr Arnold's regime for his children's upbringing is perfectly expressed in a set of mock-rules which their father devised for the summer of the following year, 1839: 'That the Dogs do travel to Rugby in the following order . . . That all Dogs, unless there is some positive engagement, do stay within doors and read for their canine edification from 10 o'clock to 12 . . . That all Dogs bear themselves reverently and discreetly towards Dog K, not barking, biting nor otherwise molesting her, under pain of a heavy judicium with many smites . . .'[91]

6

Although Matthew's Rugby life was punctuated by prizes for Latin verse, his parents recorded a general sense of disappointment. He was sometimes tardy in preparing lessons and late for class. He was, in other words, a normal schoolboy. And although he made friends at this time, such as Theodore Walrond and Thomas Hughes, it was the view of his father that he was 'not likely to form intimate friendships, being too gregarious an animal: he does not like being alone . . . Matt likes general society, and flitters about from flower to flower, but is not apt to fix.' As a result of this apparent butterfly disposition, 'I do not see how the sources of deep thought are to be reached in him.'[92] Dr Arnold was not the only person to be deceived by Arnold's exterior pose – the form of his later emergence as a poet was to take his family by surprise. They had read too much into his antic disposition.

In May 1840, however, Matthew entered a poem for the Rugby English prize which he won and read to the school on 12 June. *Alaric at Rome* was to be his first published poem – printed anonymously at Rugby in 1840 and only properly acknowledged by Arnold two months before he died in a letter to Edmund Gosse where he declared: 'Yes! *Alaric at Rome* is my Rugby prize-poem, and I think it is better than my Oxford one, *Cromwell*; only you will see that I had been very much reading *Childe Harold*.'[93] Certainly the Byronic influence is plain in a poem that seems in part written to facilitate the manner of its delivery, full of poetic sententiousness and conventional rhetorical properties. A contemporary, E. H. Bradby, who recalled being part of the original Rugby audience, described its launch: 'with a roll and vigour . . . unlike the timid utterance of the ordinary school poet'.[94] Mrs Arnold briefly reported: 'Matt has gained the English verse. It was I believe a unanimous vote.'[95] The poem is an attempt to envisage the thoughts of Alaric, leader of the Goths, who sacked Rome in the fifth century AD. It shows, however, that Arnold lacked skill in dramatising a scene vividly and this was to be a shortcoming to which future critics of his narrative poems would often return. Arnold's explanatory notes suggest that his father's readings of Gibbon to 'the fry' were not wasted since *Decline and Fall* is clearly a source. Alaric is represented as a 'lonely conqueror', pensive and apart like some proto-gipsy-scholar, meditating, even at the point of his triumph, on human mortality and transience ('The change of life, the nothingness of power').

In spite of their wish that he were a little more diligent as a scholar, Matthew's parents decided to put him up for the Balliol Scholarship and hired a tutor for the summer, William Charles Lake, a young Balliol graduate and former pupil of Dr Arnold's. Lake had won the Balliol Scholarship in 1834 and had been part of a triumvirate of friends in the Sixth, with Arthur Stanley and Charles Vaughan, who would continue their friendship at Oxford. But first a little fishing. On the last Thursday of the half-year Matthew and his cousin John Penrose went off to Derbyshire to fish. 'I had never seen Dovedale before so I was very glad to have the opportunity of fishing all through it,' he told his Laleham aunts.[96] He then pressed on to Bakewell, soon shedding his companions, and enjoyed a fortnight's blissful fishing which was finally interrupted by a summons from Lake to present himself at Chester for some more serious work. Lake already had another pupil with him, a young Irish boy called Carden, and the three spent the next fortnight touring North Wales. A letter from Tom reached them at Bangor to say he would be joining them from Ireland although he did not manage to do so until the end of their stay. The reading group then took lodgings at Beddgelert. Unfortunately, rain is as common in Snowdonia as it is in Westmorland, and it poured constantly for the whole two weeks. This quite put Arnold off Wales which was grumpily characterised as 'only a bad second edition of the Lakes'. He was 'heartily tired' by the time they came to transfer their lodgings to Abergele – which at least was by the sea. After another two weeks at Abergele the scholars took a boat to Liverpool and from thence travelled to Rugby.

On 17 August Dr Arnold wrote to Lake, pouring out all his concern about his eldest son:

> Matt does not know what it is to work because he so little knows what to think. But I am hopeful about him more than I was: his amiableness of temper seems very great, and some of his faults appear to me less; and he is so loving to me that it ought to make me not only hopeful, but very patient and long-suffering towards him. Besides, I think that he is not so idle as he was, and that there is a better prospect of his beginning to read in earnest. Alas! that we should talk of prospect only, and of no performance as yet which deserves the name of 'earnest reading'.[97]

This very frank letter, referring also to Tom's progress, reveals an anxiety on the part of the Doctor that his role as a parent and his role as Headmaster might be in conflict. 'I think that Rugby is good for them', he writes hopefully. 'I am sure that it does not weaken their affection for me, which might perhaps have been feared.'

Another of Dr Arnold's former pupils, Arthur Hugh Clough, wrote from Oxford a couple of months later, with rather more faith in the outcome of the scholarship: 'There are 2 candidates from Rugby, one of them Dr Arnold's son and he of the two has the best chance.'[98] Later that same month Matthew surprised and delighted – in equal measure – his parents by winning the Balliol Scholarship, against competition from thirty-three candidates from the public schools. The first winner to be announced was James Riddell of Shrewsbury and the remaining four semi-finalists were then examined orally until it was almost dark and Arnold's name was finally released.[99] 'I had not the least expectation of his being successful, and the news actually filled me with astonishment,' his father admitted. 'I have great hopes that success will act wholesomely on him.'[100]

The family, as usual, spent Christmas 1840 at Fox How where

Matthew celebrated his eighteenth birthday on Christmas Eve with a poem: *The Birthday, or Eighteen Years Ago.*[101] This was signed in the January 1841 issue of the Magazine with the initials CFLRFH which probably stood for 'Crab, floruit Laleham, Rugby, Fox How'. It is an amusing squib, playing on the fact that the eldest brother is now part of a family of nine children. He looks back with mock sadness to the time of his youth when 'Blind to my future woes', he had plenty of room to breathe ('No crowding then, no turns were in my way'). There is a sly dig at Dr Arnold's views on discipline ("Tis true that many a whipping was my lot; / Yet – seeing what I am – I murmur not') and complaints at the bruising of his ribs caused by mealtime crushes with brothers and sisters jostling each other at a table where a family of eleven sat down to dine. Tom riposted with a squib of his own making fun of 'Old fellow Matt.'s' alleged ineptitude at shooting wildfowl ('He shoots a Duck / But O bad luck, / It drops in the lake . . .').

Matthew was not to go up to Oxford until the autumn of 1841. That year – which was momentous for Dr Arnold in that it saw his election on 19 August as Regius Professor of History at Oxford – saw another trip to France for Matthew with his father, Tom and K. Dr Arnold set off on a walking tour along the banks of the Loire, Matthew in a straw hat in tow. In a baker's shop in Beauvais, while Dr Arnold spent three sous on some bread rolls, his son 'got some light cakes and disdained my bread'.[102] Matthew Arnold, who would later grow impatient with the insularity of his fellow countrymen, and rebuke them for their lack of interest in Europe, had acquired early the tendency to decline the plain fare of the honest-to-goodness Englishman in favour of more interesting Continental confections.

Arnold was now eighteen and clearly more self-confident – and with more to be self-confident about – after his academic triumph. At Oxford he would no longer be a schoolboy away from home but a young man moving slowly out of his father's shadow into his own adult world. His father would follow him, in a literal as well as a metaphorical sense, when he came to give his inaugural lecture at Oxford only weeks after his son had taken up residence at Balliol, but Dr Arnold had only another year to live. His son's increasingly recognised distinction, his bright personality, his now noticeable manners and airs, would draw him to everyone's attention. But they still did not know him. Arnold was in no sense precocious: the poet had still to emerge from his bright chrysalis and the future critic and moralist was yet more remote. At Oxford he would perform for just a little longer.

Chapter Two:
Oxford Scholars
[1841–1848]

And long the way appears, which seemed so short
To the less practised eye of sanguine youth.[1]

1

Oxford in the 1840s was still feeling the force of the Tractarian Movement which had blazed since the middle of the previous decade, filling the University with excited argument and the bitter divisiveness of *odium theologicum*. The eighteen-year-old undergraduate who started to unpack in his rooms at Balliol on 15 October 1841 to spend 'three of the happiest years of my life'[2] had arrived at a time of exceptional intellectual ferment. But the first report we have of Arnold, a few weeks after his arrival, indicates that such matters were far from his mind. 'Mat. Arnold has come up to reside as scholar of Balliol', wrote Arthur Hugh Clough to a friend on 10 November, 'and as a report whispered to me . . . has been going out with the Harriers.'[3] Arnold clearly preferred the hounds to theological controversy. From the start he took no interest in the Tracts. On matriculation day he told another freshman, Edward Walford, as they sat in the Vice-Chancellor's anteroom waiting for formal admission, of his 'great aversion to sundry statements in the Thirty-nine Articles, to which at that time we were forced to subscribe, especially that Article which expresses an approval of the Athanasian Creed, and that which denounces the Pope of Rome'.[4] Walford also remembered their first days at Oxford together, at table: 'I shall never forget how, in opposition to the

Tractarianism of the day, he used to say that the strict imposition of creeds had done more to break than to unite churches, and nations, and families, and how even then, in our small and highly privileged circle, he was the apostle of religious toleration in every direction.'

Arnold's own father had been one of the principal adversaries of the Tractarians of the Oxford Movement, as J. A. Froude, in his book *The Nemesis of Faith* (1849) was to acknowledge when he wrote that the magnetism of the great figure on the other side of the argument, John Henry Newman, 'took us all his own way; all, that is, who were not Arnoldised'. Matthew Arnold seems not to have been Arnoldised, either, and his admiration for Newman was unstinted, although not perhaps quite of the kind that Newman would have wished. In this he also differed sharply from his brother Tom, who came up to Oxford the following year, to University College. Tom had rooms directly opposite St Mary's, where Newman preached, but crossed the street to hear him only once. According to Arnold's niece, Mrs Humphry Ward, Tom on this occasion was 'repelled by the mannerism of the preacher'[5] – the very thing that attracted his elder brother's attention.

It was Newman's prose style, his urbanity in the conduct of an intellectual argument rather than his thought, that seduced Arnold. Beguiled by what Tom, in Mrs Humphry Ward's report, was to call 'that strange Newmanic power of words' (his later poem *The Voice*, probably written about 1844, records the impact on him of Newman's preaching, which 'Blew such a thrilling summons to my will, / Yet could not shake it'), Arnold was none the less 'never touched in the smallest degree by Newman's opinions'. Instinctively aware of this, Newman was always courteous but reserved. Arnold seems to have been less sensible of 'the great differences of opinion which separate us' as Newman expressed it in a letter to Arnold from the Oratory at Birmingham in 1872[6] and always insisted on his intellectual debt to Newman.

Newman has frequently been represented as being on the 'reactionary' side of this great Victorian theological debate – not least by contemporaries such as the Christian socialist F. D. Maurice. In rejecting liberalism and the Protestant conscience in favour of strict dogma, ceremonial and divine mystery, Newman appeared to be blaspheming against the Victorian deity – Progress. His belief that liberal theology and the Protestant emphasis on private judgement (as opposed to ecclesiastical authority or dogma) were the first steps on the slippery slope to atheism seemed to confirm the charge. His willingness to take seriously many theological beliefs and church practices which

Protestantism thought it had wholly interred and his willingness, even before his conversion, to see some good in Catholicism, was too much for men like Dr Arnold who embodied the venerable English prejudice against 'popery' and who, on his travels abroad, found Catholic Europe an awful provocation, as his travel diaries attest.

On the key issue that divided them, Newman rejected the notion of a State church. Dr Arnold, in turn, saw Newman as a defender of 'priestcraft' and a hieratic and obscurantist mode of church governance. Matthew Arnold, in addition to having no desire to fight his father's battles, was simply not interested in these dry arguments. His respect for Newman's methods of argument and his style, may, however, have been accompanied by a respect for a man who was prepared to go against the grain, to refuse to join in the euphoria of material progress, in order to probe a little deeper into the spiritual shortcomings of the age. Arnold was to risk something similar in his social and cultural criticism and would attract some of the same opprobrium for telling his contemporaries some things which they did not wish to hear.

Years later, when delivering a lecture on Emerson on his first trip to America in 1883, Arnold recalled, in a famous passage, the Newman of his undergraduate years (by 1883 Newman was in his eighties and living at the Oratory in Birmingham): 'Forty years ago he was in the very prime of life . . . he was preaching in St Mary's pulpit every Sunday; he seemed about to renew what was for us the most national and natural institution in the world, the Church of England.' Then Arnold slips into an eloquent, cadenced prose worthy of Newman himself: 'Who could resist the charm of that spiritual apparition, gliding in the dim afternoon light through the aisles of St Mary's, rising into the pulpit, and then, in the most entrancing of voices, breaking the silence with words and thoughts which were a religious music – subtle, sweet, mournful?'[7]

In February 1841, several months before Arnold arrived at Balliol, Newman had published Tract 90 which seemed to argue that certain passages in the Thirty-nine Articles could be interpreted in support of Catholic doctrine. Oxford had erupted, and Newman was eventually forced to resign his Oriel Fellowship and retire to Littlemore on the outskirts of Oxford, settling there in September 1843. The Tractarian Movement had reached its peak and was now to start to peter out, but the wider unsettlement of religious belief that was to characterise the Victorian period – the attacks from German scholarship and 'the higher criticism' on the literal inspiration of the Bible, and the challenge of scientific and evolutionary thought – continued to deepen.

One of Arnold's Oxford contemporaries was Frederick Temple, a future Headmaster of Rugby and Archbishop of Canterbury, who had come up to Balliol a year earlier, and who was the only Tory member of a debating society called 'The Decade', to which Arnold also belonged. In a memoir of Temple's early years, the Reverend J. M. Wilson described the mood of Oxford as it was when he took up residence:

> From Oxford the movement which had begun in 1833 was now vibrating through the whole country; and it was profoundly affecting the intellectual and spiritual life of Oxford society . . . It permeated more or less the whole mass . . . It was omnipresent; it was endlessly discussed; it was feared; but it could not be ignored . . . it resulted in a moral quickening, a stimulating warmth, a heightened pulse of spiritual life . . . it gave a certain shade of seriousness even to the boisterous.[8]

That last phrase might seem designed to embrace Arnold but he has left no record of any real involvement with the anguished theological questions which so racked his friend Clough. There was a coolness, a certain languor – some have seen it even as an intellectual laziness – about Arnold's mind which, as we shall see, also affected his political opinions during the European upheavals of 1848 – again in contrast to Clough. But he could not have avoided being drawn into the topics and the temper of the discussions held by the Decade. This society of undergraduates took its name from the fact that when founded it had, at any one time, only ten members. An indication that it did not take itself too seriously comes from a reference by John Duke Coleridge – a nephew of the poet and a lifelong friend of Arnold – to a Balliol scout who 'long since gone to his rest persisted in embodying the external world's judgement on it by always calling it the Decayed'.[9] Coleridge described its attraction for those young men who had come straight to Oxford from the public schools 'where we were taught to construe, to say by heart, to write verses, and Greek and Latin prose, but where our minds were allowed to lie fallow and to grow on, unclouded by thought, in an atmosphere of severe and unhealthy intelligence'.[10] Arriving at Balliol two years before Arnold, John Duke Coleridge remembered the day of his arrival as 'a day of fear and hope and of change'.

In addition to himself and Arnold, the Decade in 1841 included Clough (soon to progress to a Fellowship at Oriel), Lake (Arnold's summer tutor of 1840 and later Dean of Durham who had founded the Decade that year with Benjamin Brodie, later Professor of Chemistry at

Oxford), Arthur Stanley (the biographer of Dr Arnold and later Dean of Westminster), Temple, Walrond (Arnold's Rugby friend), Richard Church (later Dean of St Paul's and historian of the Oxford Movement) and Benjamin Jowett, later the legendary Master of Balliol and Greek scholar. Members at other times included Francis Turner Palgrave, the anthologist, Archibald Campbell Tait, another future headmaster of Rugby and Archbishop of Canterbury, and John Conington, classical scholar and fellow of University College.

This *dramatis personae* of early Victorian Oxford shows how intimate was the milieu from which the English ecclesiastical, academic and administrative class then drew its recruits. These men would move gently out into the world to occupy the commanding heights of the church, universities, and public schools, meeting each other on the steps of the Athenaeum or at Oxford and church ceremonials. But as undergraduates, John Duke Coleridge continues:

> We met in one another's rooms. We discussed all things, human and divine. We thought we stripped things to the very bone, we believed we dragged recondite truths into the light of common day and subjected them to the scrutiny of what we were pleased to call our minds. We fought to the very stumps of our intellects, and I believe that many of us, I can speak for one, would gladly admit that many a fruitful seed of knowledge, of taste, of cultivation, was sown on those pleasant, if somewhat pugnacious evenings.

Clough was a star performer in these discussions. As Tom Arnold describes it:

> no member of the society spoke in so rich, penetrating, original, and convincing a strain as Clough. He was not rapid, yet neither was he slow or hesitating; he seemed just to take time enough to find the right word or phrase . . . I remember one debate when he spoke to a resolution that I had proposed in favour of Lord Ashley's Ten Hours Bill. In supporting the resolution he combated the doctrines of *laissez-faire* and the omnipotence and sufficiency of the action of Supply and Demand, then hardly disputed in England, with an insight marvellous in one who had so little experience of the industrial life.[11]

Arnold, too, clearly enjoyed his participation in these evening meetings of the Decade, but as regards the wider theological debating-chamber his friend George Russell was probably right: 'The formal side of religion – the side of dogma and doctrine and rule and definition – had no attraction for him, and no terrors.'[12] His real interest was poetry but it was not well advertised. The German-born philologist and first Professor of Comparative Philology at Oxford, Friedrich Max-Müller, wrote in his autobiography: 'It strikes one that while he was at Oxford, few people only detected in Arnold the poet or the man of genius.'[13]

At Oxford, Arnold moved, too, in a yet smaller circle than the Decade, consisting of Tom, Clough and Theodore Walrond, and self-described as 'a little interior company'[14] or the 'Clougho-Matthean set'. These four friends shared walks in the landscape that would be re-imagined in *The Scholar-Gipsy* and *Thyrsis*, and they shared intellectual passions quite different from those of the Tractarians. 'They discovered George Sand, Emerson and Carlyle', wrote Mrs Humphry Ward, 'and orthodox Christianity no longer seemed to them the sure refuge that it had always been to the strong teacher who trained them as boys'. George Sand – although her novels, and in particular products of her maturity such as *Les Maîtres Sonneurs* (1852), strike us now as deeply moral works – offered a sense of risk for these progressively minded undergraduates which derived in part from reports of her private life. Their interest, however, was a genuine one. '*Consuelo* [1842] in particular, was a revelation to the two young men [Arnold and Tom] brought up under the "earnest" influence of Rugby', wrote Mrs Humphry Ward. 'It seemed to open to them a world of artistic beauty and joy of which they had never dreamed; and to loosen the bands of an austere conception of life, which began to appear to them too narrow for the facts of life.' Arnold and Clough discussed an early novel, *Indiana* (1831), passages of which Arnold was able to quote from memory. One in particular, is from a reproachful letter the heroine, Indiana Delmare, writes to her lover Raymon de Manière, criticising his hypocritical and formal religion and advocating a liberating theology which would see God as a bringer of equality and justice who would 'break the strong and raise up the weak'.[15] Arnold found in George Sand a spirit of freedom and Romantic idealism ideally suited to a liberal-minded undergraduate, and in responding in this way he was typical of many of his contemporaries.[16] His notebooks are peppered with quotations from George Sand, whom he was to call 'a friend and a power'. Although Arnold was to an extent disconcerted by her sexual freedom, he responded to her intelligence, her enormous energy and productivity, and her religious ideas. In his essay on George Sand (which is the only essay, apart from that on Tolstoy, that he ever wrote on a novelist) published in *Mixed Essays* (1879), Arnold distinguishes three phases in her life and writing: 'the cry of agony and revolt, the trust in nature and beauty, the aspiration toward a purged and renewed human society'.[17] These sound like the phases through which Arnold himself was to pass. In particular, Arnold singles out what he saw as her ruling idea – '*le sentiment de la vie idéale*' – the feeling for the ideal life and, more significantly, the belief that it might one day be realised. He also valued her love of nature and wild flowers – a particular passion of Arnold's – and her Wordsworthian celebration of the life of ordinary country people in her native region of the Berry.

Arnold's passion for George Sand's writing would endure into his maturity, his passion for her writing changing as it changed, and as he changed. He believed that she would be valued more highly in time than Balzac and that 'the immense vibration of George Sand's voice upon the ear of Europe will not soon die away'. But it was as a passionate young man attracted to her early phase of idealism and revolt that he went in the summer of 1846 to visit her at Nohant. That visit is recalled in his essay on the writer in *Mixed Essays* where he describes himself as one of those 'who, amid the agitations, more or less stormy, of their youth, betook themselves to the early works of George Sand'[18] Such ardent youthful readers, wrote Arnold, 'may in later life cease to read them, indeed, but they can no more forget them than they can forget *Werther*'. And then, recalling his passionate youth, Arnold turns suddenly rhapsodic: 'days of *Valentine*, days of *Lélia*, days never to return! They are gone, we shall read them no more, and yet how ineffaceable is their impression! How the sentences from George Sand's works of that period still linger in our memory and haunt the ear with their cadences! Grandiose and moving, they come, those cadences, like the sighing of the wind through the forest, like the breaking of the waves on the seashore.' Arnold wrote to his mother in 1869, on the death of Sainte-Beuve, the critic he admired above all others: 'When George Sand and Newman go, there will be no writers left living from whom I have received a strong influence: they will all have departed.'[19]

Strong as his passion for George Sand's writing was, however, what Mrs Humphry Ward calls her 'social enthusiasms' – the passion for equality as an ideal which Arnold shared – did not generate in him the same utopian plan for building a better world which seized his brother Tom. Arnold was always the more sceptical and disengaged of the 'little interior company' when it came to politics. This prefigured his later critical stance in *Culture and Anarchy* where he would advocate refusing to 'lend a hand' to immediate practical schemes for tackling definite social evils until thought and reflection had been given a chance to do their work.

While still at Oxford, probably in his final year, 1844, when the essays had just appeared, Arnold wrote a sonnet *Written in Emerson's Essays*, which complains of the world's indifference to the great thinker and his 'voice oracular'. Years later, when he visited America Arnold delivered a lecture on Emerson which recalled the mood of the 1840s: 'Forty years ago, when I was an undergraduate at Oxford, voices were in the air . . . a voice also from this side of the Atlantic, – a clear and pure voice . . . as new, and moving, and unforgettable, as the strain of Newman, or Carlyle, or Goethe'.[20]

Emerson's influence on the young Arnold, though less intense than that of George Sand or Goethe or even Newman, was considerable and the name of Concord where the sage lived was as resonant to him as that of Newman's Oxford or Goethe's Weimar. Words and phrases of Emerson 'fixed themselves in my mind as imperishably as any of the eloquent words' of those two other thinkers, he told his audience. He recalled such sentences and declared: 'These lofty sentences of Emerson, and a hundred others of like strain, I never have lost out of my memory; I never *can* lose them.' Yet Emerson's failure to produce memorable lines diminished him as a poet, Arnold felt, notwithstanding the fact that he was a 'beautiful and rare spirit'. He was not 'plain and concrete enough', Arnold argued 'in other words not poet enough' to achieve greatness in poetry. The same could be said of his philosophy: 'He cannot build; his arrangement of philosophical ideas has no progress in it, no evolution; he does not construct a philosophy.' Although Emerson's transcendentalist philosophy did not work for Arnold, the writer's appeal to the young poet at Balliol lay in a general sense that he was 'the friend and aider of those who would live in the spirit', he had 'a hopeful, serene, beautiful temper' and he was a force for optimism. In his later lecture on Emerson, Arnold makes reference to Carlyle, another early intellectual influence, but, like Emerson, a lesser one. He began by admiring Carlyle's vigorous style but in the end came to feel that he was not doing what Arnold always wanted a writer to do: showing the way forward. He grew weary of his rant and eventually described him in a letter to Clough as one of the 'moral desperadoes' in public life.[21]

The remaining major early influence on Arnold was Goethe, the poet and thinker for whom he retained throughout his life the highest possible regard.[22] He identified Goethe, in a letter to Newman, as one of the few men from whom he had learned 'habits, methods, ruling ideas, which are constantly with me'.[23] At Oxford, Tom claimed, Goethe displaced Byron in his brother's allegiance, and it was Carlyle who was responsible – through his translation of *Wilhelm Meister* (1795–6) in 1824 – for drawing the German poet to the attention of the Arnold circle at Balliol. Arnold's relationship with Goethe developed over time – in 1847, for example, he bought the sixty-volume edition of his works, and collected subsequent material – but the undergraduate influence was primarily in loosening his hold over orthodox Christianity by exposing him to Goethe's 'profound, imperturbable naturalism . . . absolutely fatal to all routine thinking' which he described in his essay on *Heinrich Heine* (1863). 'Nothing could be more really subversive of the foundations on which the old European order rested; and it may be remarked that no persons are so radically detached from this order, no persons so thoroughly modern, as those who have felt Goethe's influence most deeply.'[24] The common thread in all these intellectual influences was that they were in varying degrees liberating, challenging, or to use a word of Arnold's, 'loosening', as early intellectual influences generally tend to be. In the years ahead he would start to sift these inheritances, discarding some, entering more deeply into others, refining or altering preliminary estimates. All of them contributed to the growth of a mind of great seriousness that was still masked by outward levity and still kept largely hidden from most of those who knew him.

The comradeship of the four friends, however, was not solely in things of the mind. 'We used to go skiffing up the Cherwell', recalled Tom, 'or else in the network of river channels that meander through the broad meadows facing Iffley and Sandford.' And every Sunday morning in the years from 1842 to 1847 the four breakfasted in Clough's rooms at Oriel, falling eagerly on *The Spectator* to dissect its leading articles on politics, arguing about Sir Robert Peel's reforming ministry, or the intractable question of Ireland. 'Those were times of great enjoyment', concluded Tom.

One event, however, was to darken the life of the Arnolds in the early 1840s. On Thursday 2 December 1841 Dr Arnold delivered his inaugural lecture as Regius Professor of Modern History at Oxford in which, characteristically, he argued that the end of all societies 'should be good rather than truth'.[25] The lecture theatre was filled to capacity. The whole Arnold family had travelled up to Oxford to witness the triumph and they were graciously received by Matthew Arnold at his rooms in Balliol at the top of the second staircase in the corner of the second quad. K was meant to be impressed by her brother who, arrayed, as Tom describes it, 'in all the glory of a scholar's gown and three months' experience as a "University man" welcomed his rustic *geschwister* with an amused and superior graciousness'. In the Christmas issue of the *Fox How Magazine* Arnold wrote a witty 'dramatic fragment', *The Incursion*, to mark the visit of the Arnolds and their appearance at lodgings in Beaumont Street. He playfully describes his Papa: 'this ruthless chief / Who hath led hither his barbarian hordes / To brawl and riot in the heart of Oxford' and introduces a 'Spirit of Propriety' who wails like a Greek chorus at 'this strange, unmannered family'.[26]

The lecture itself was everything that the disciples of Dr Arnold could have wished for. Tom remembered for the rest of his life how 'my heart seemed to stand still' when his father described the French army before the invasion of Russia thus: 'Earthly state has never reached a prouder pinnacle than when Napoleon in June 1812 gathered his army at Dresden . . . and there received the homage of subject kings.'[27] Arthur Penrhyn Stanley, Dr Arnold's biographer, reflecting the pleasure his pupils always took in allowing themselves to yield to his mastery, takes up the story, in notes made a day or two later on Stanley's return to Rugby: 'I think I never shall forget the moment when the Inaugural Lecture began, when in that great building, once more in the relation of a pupil to a teacher, I heard that well known voice addressing a larger audience than had probably ever listened to a professor's lecture in Oxford since the middle ages. Throughout the hour during which it lasted the attention never flagged and it ended as it had begun in general applause.' Stanley was quite overcome by the 'most striking and touching scene'[28] which was shared with many of the Doctor's former pupils. After this, during the long half-year of 1842 there were more trips to Oxford to lecture. On 2 February Dr Arnold's diary records: 'Breakfasted with Crab . . . Dined in Hall at Oriel & met Newman.'[29] 'Crab', according to a mocking ballad written by K for the *Fox How Magazine* at Christmas, was every inch the 'fine young Oxford gentleman' with 'an eye-glass round his neck hung by a silken string' whose foppishness was more noticeable than any sort of scholarly inclination: 'Eau de Mille Fleurs, Eau de Cologne and twenty eaux besides / Rowland's Odonto, scented soaps, jostle his books aside . . .'[30]

During the middle part of the half-year at Rugby Dr Arnold fell ill with 'an eruption' on his right cheek but recovered. The recovery was short-lived, however, and on 12 June he died suddenly, at the age of forty-six, of an attack of the *angina pectoris* which had brought down his own father, William Arnold, at the age of fifty-six and which would be bequeathed to his son. Matthew Arnold was warned by 'an eminent surgeon' at the age of twenty-four that 'the action of his heart was not regular' and that he was 'in a certain sense doomed',[31] yet he contrived to put the knowledge aside and live an energetic and often highly stressful life. 'He knew for years that though he was strong and looked very young for his age', wrote Max-Müller of Matthew Arnold, 'the thread of his life might snap at any moment'. There was in all he said 'a kind of understood though seldom expressed sadness, as if to say, "It will soon be all over, don't let us get angry".'[32]

When Dr Arnold collapsed, the children had already set off for Fox How for the summer holidays and Lake was sent to break the news. The public grief at the death of Dr Arnold was universal, with even his enemies paying tribute to a man seen to have been struck down in his prime. According to Tom: 'This was a momentous moment for Matthew Arnold, who had lived till then, as he himself has told so well in the lines on "Rugby Chapel", under the shadow and shelter of a great and overpowering personality, which being withdrawn, his genius was freer to develop itself in its own way. The natural bent of his mind was very different from that of his father.'[33] Dr Arnold's widow now retreated permanently to Fox How where she would live for the rest of her life with her unmarried daughter Frances 'Fan' Arnold. The headmastership of Rugby would pass to Archibald Tait and in August Arnold wrote to him from Fox How an uncharacteristically stiff and pompous letter of congratulation, stressing repeatedly the importance of 'firm and consistent management' as a prerequisite of any intellectual proficiency.[34]

2

Arnold, as Tom hinted, was now to move a little more freely in Oxford circles and to develop what Max-Müller called his 'Olympian manners'.[35] It was no longer a case of struggling to emerge from his father's shadow but of trying to achieve the far more important aim of nurturing a poetic talent that was oddly reticent, camouflaged by his outward demeanour, still not confident enough to emerge in its own colours. 'He was cultivating his poetic gift carefully', Tom writes of the years after 1842, 'but his exuberant versatile nature claimed other satisfactions; his keen bantering talk made him something of a social lion among Oxford men; he even began to dress fashionably. Goethe displaced Byron in his poetical allegiance; the transcendental spells of Emerson wove themselves around him; the charm of an exquisite style made him, and long kept him, a votary of George Sand.' John Campbell Shairp, in a poem published in 1888, captures this under-graduate face of Arnold in the 1840s:

> The one wide-welcomed for his father's fame,
> Entered with free bold step that seemed to claim
> Fame for himself, nor on another lean.
>
> So full of power, yet blithe and debonair,
> Rallying his friends with pleasant banter gay,
> Or half a-dream chaunting with jaunty air
> Great words of Goethe, catch of Béranger,
> We see the banter sparkle in his prose,
> But knew not then the undertone that flows
> So calmly sad, through all his stately lay.[36]

The 'social lion' was rather less distinguished academically. During Arnold's Balliol residence, the Master, Richard Jenkyns, kept a 'Master's Examination Register' which allows us to see both what Arnold was expected to study and how his scholarly performance was judged. He was expected to study Divinity, Greek, Latin, Mathematics and Logic, and Morals. The Old Testament was read in translation but the New in Greek and he read the Greek poets and dramatists. At Winchester and at the hands of private tutors, Arnold had already developed skill at Latin composition but the Master's Register indicates that his skill at English prose composition was, as we might expect, considerable. His English essays, which were written 'with much ability', evinced 'considerable power & skill', but in those areas where hard work rather than natural gifts were in question the reports are less glowing. By 1842 his performance in Morals was 'respectable but desultory in habits of reading'. More than this, he was 'not sufficiently attentive to the rules of the College' and, a year later, he was conceded to be 'improved in diligence & attention but still deficient in both' and to be 'irregular'.[37] In March of that year a friend, J. Manley Hawker, wrote to John Duke Coleridge that 'Matt wastes his time consider-ably'.[38] In fairness to Arnold the Oxford classical curriculum at this time was hardly such as to inspire a gifted mind. Even the great classicist Jowett was later to admit that 'There was very little true interpretation of any book in those days.'[39]

Perhaps in an attempt at rehabilitation Arnold tried in March 1842 for the Hertford Scholarship but narrowly missed it with a *proxime accessit*. He was more successful with the Newdigate Prize which he won with *Cromwell* and which he was to have recited in the Sheldonian Theatre on 28 June 1843. But on that day there was uproar at Commemoration over the award of a degree to an American minister, Edward Everett, formerly a Unitarian preacher. But even the cries of '*Non placet!*' at this were drowned out by undergraduate howls against an unpopular proctor called Jelf of Christ Church. The proceedings continued, as *The Times* put it 'in dumbshow'. By the time Arnold's prize-winning poem was due to be read the proceedings had been abandoned. The occasion seems to have been considerably more exciting than the poem which is a rather lifeless exercise. The setting of the subject of Cromwell was timely in that Carlyle had only just mounted a defence of the Protector in his *Heroes and Hero-Worship* (1841) and celebration of him would be a rebuke to those parts of Tractarian Oxford which inclined more to the memory of Charles the martyred king. For his 240 lines in heroic couplets the undergraduate poet is said to have received ten pounds when it was published later in the year in an edition of 750 copies.[40] It concentrates on a series of Cromwell's reflections that never quite manage to break out of their rhetorical straitjacket and come to life.

The sense that Arnold's heart was not in this exercise is confirmed by a letter written to Coleridge on 11 March 1843 from Fox How – where snow prevented him from fly-fishing – in which he confesses 'the melancholy truth' that he has been 'slow in writing' the poem. He tells Coleridge that: 'As a boy, I used to write very quickly, and I declare that at first it was with an effort that I compelled myself to write more slowly and carefully, though I am ready to confess that now I could not write quicker if I would.'[41] Arnold was to remain a slow writer, a fact confirmed by John Morley: 'Nor did writing come very easily to him.'[42] In this instance, Arnold recognised that writing not done with great despatch needed to be done steadily if it was not to ossify: 'if people are to be allowed to write very slow, they ought, I confess, to write very constantly, or there is a great stiffness about their productions when they are complete'. This was precisely what had happened with *Cromwell* and was 'a great fault in my Poem', a flaw which combined 'ludicrously enough' with 'the fault of over-rapidity in the last part, which I had to finish in two or three days'.

This was to be the last of Arnold's dutiful prize poems and boyish exercises. His next poem, written probably in August 1843, *To a Gipsy Child by the Sea-shore*, was to mark the emergence of the poet who has a real claim on our attention. The uncertainty about the date is due to Tom Arnold who in his recollections was often vague about such matters and who thought the visit to the Isle of Man that was the occasion of the poem took place 'in 1843 or 1844'[43] – but we have firm evidence from Arnold's diary that he was in the Isle of Man in August 1845, which would render feasible an even later date for this poem. The Arnolds spent part of the long vacation at Douglas on the Isle of Man and one afternoon Arnold and Tom were at the pier, watching the arrival of the Liverpool steamer. Just in front of them in the crowd was a poor woman, who could have been a gipsy, looking down, like them, at the steamer. The child in her arms was looking backwards over her shoulder. 'Its pitiful wan face' recalled Tom, 'and sad dark eyes rested on Matthew for some time without change of expression.' Arnold loved children and was always sensitive to their sufferings. Years later, in *Culture and Anarchy*, in a tirade against fashionable economists, he would refer to the desperate state of the urban poor whom he glimpsed at first hand on his professional visits to the East End: 'children eaten up with disease, half-sized, half-fed, half-clothed, neglected by their parents, without health, without home, without hope'.[44]

The poem, at last, is one of real feeling as the young poet tries to apprehend the meaning of the poor child's 'soul-searching vision' and realises that the blithe Oxford undergraduate has never witnessed such pleading sadness: 'Glooms that go deep as thine I have not known.' He reflects, stoically, on the ability to endure: 'Thou hast foreknown the vanity of hope, / Foreseen thy harvest – yet proceed'st to live.' This would certainly be one of those poems that would contribute to the astonishment of Arnold's family and friends when his first volume was eventually published in 1849. His demeanour had not led them to expect such seriousness, such a tragic sense of what life had to offer.

As an undergraduate Arnold was high-spirited – he was said on more than one occasion to have leapt over the railings at Wadham – and he enjoyed playing the fool. He was not entirely studious, for there was plenty of bathing in the Cherwell and walks and talks with his friends. An entry in Clough's diary for May Day 1843 reads: 'bathed, break-fasted, rowed, and tead with Walrond and Mat.'[45] Coleridge's correspondent Hawker records a visit to Devon where they arrived, in July 1843, 'after sundry displays of the most consummate coolness on the part of our friend Matt, who pleasantly induced a belief into the passengers of the coach that I was a poor mad gentleman, and that he was my keeper'.[46] Hawker elsewhere records that 'Our friend Matt utters as many absurdities as ever, with as grave a face'. His brother Tom agreed that: 'Things which said by anyone else would have produced a deadly quarrel were said by him with such a bright playfulness, such a humorous masterfulness, that the victim laughed before he had time to feel hurt.'[47] But Lake accused him in a letter of being 'frivolous' and in spite of Tom's claim it is clear that his playful mockery was not always taken in the right spirit by his friends. In the summer of 1844 he was obliged to write to Coleridge to explain that his manner with his friends did not signal 'a want of interest' in them as they were increasingly ('it is an old subject') alleging. 'I laugh too much and they make one's laughter mean too much',[48] he complained to Coleridge. 'However, the result is that when one wishes to be serious one cannot but fear a half suspicion on one's friends' parts that one is laughing, and, so, the difficulty gets worse and worse . . .' It was Coleridge's marriage plans – and Arnold's apparent failure to make the right noises on that subject – that had prompted this declaration.

This was to be a problem for Arnold all his life, for although the Victorians were far less stuffy than they are generally supposed to have been, they were not always sure how to deal with Arnold's 'vivacities', as they were dubbed, and he frequently collided with their expectations of *gravitas* on public occasions. An acute observer of Arnold at Oxford was Max-Müller who wrote:

> He was beautiful as a young man, strong and manly, yet full of dreams and schemes. His Olympian manners began even at Oxford; there was no harm in them, they were natural, not put on. The very sound of his voice and the wave of his arm were Jovelike.[49]

Max-Müller, whilst he appreciated the Jovelike Balliol scholar, saw clearly enough the dangers of Arnold's compulsive levity when performed on a wider stage. 'A laugh from his hearers or readers seemed to be more valued by him than their serious opposition, or their convinced assent', he wrote. 'He trusted, like others, to *persiflage*, and the result was that when he tried to be serious, people could not forget that he might at any time turn round and smile, and decline to be taken *au grand sérieux*. People do not know what a dangerous game this French *persiflage* is, particularly in England, and how difficult it becomes to exchange it afterwards for real seriousness.'[50] Unease at this Arnoldian manner has persisted to the present day.[51] Perhaps, like many skilled polemical writers who are pleased to discover that they possess a talent to deride, Arnold began to enjoy the exercise of it too much. Today we take pleasure in his vivacities because we think that these darts are not aimed at us, but Arnold's original audience shifted uncomfortably in its seats and on occasion spluttered an objection.

By 1844, Arnold's last undergraduate year, his poor academic performance was beginning to cause concern. 'As an undergraduate', wrote Tom, 'he seemed bent on accumulating various experiences, he read a little with the reading men, hunted a little with the fast men, and dressed a little with the dressy men.'[52] He was, in short, becoming a dilettante. To the laughter of his friends, he mimicked the Master of Balliol, Dr Jenkyns, saying that he 'considered his proceedings *desultory*'. Others, however, were not so amused and in the summer of 1844 Arnold was taken in hand to avoid a disaster at his Classics Finals. His assigned saviour was to be Clough.

3

The relationship of Arnold and Clough, which culminated in *Thyrsis*, Arnold's elegy for his friend written three or four years after Clough's death in Florence in 1861, was the most complex and intense of his male friendships. Our knowledge of it largely derives from the letters Arnold wrote to Clough and which were unknown until they were published in 1932, his collected letters published in 1895 having contained nothing earlier than 1848 when Arnold was already twenty-five and living in London. Born in Liverpool on New Year's Day 1819, the son of a local merchant who took his family to Charleston, South Carolina to take advantage of the cotton export market, Clough entered Rugby in the summer of 1829. He was given the nickname 'Tom Yankee'. His separation from his family, coupled with a lonely and sensitive temperament, made him an object of concern for the headmaster's wife. As a boarder in the School House, Clough was mothered by Mrs Arnold and was frequently to be found in the private parts of the house. Tom recalled that 'my mother, who marked his somewhat delicate health, conceived a great liking for him; and his gentleness, and that unwonted *humanity* of nature which made him unlike the ordinary schoolboy, caused him to be a welcome guest in her drawing room'.[53] More significant, however, was the collision with Dr Arnold in the sixth form. Arthur Stanley wrote later of how Clough 'received into an unusually susceptible and eager mind the whole force of that electric shock which Arnold communicated to all his better pupils'.[54] It seems to have been an unfortunate conjunction of a highly scrupulous and sensitive youth and an overpowering personality in Dr Arnold. The latter told Clough's uncle that he regarded his nephew 'with an Affection and Interest hardly less than I should feel for my own son'.[55] Clough became more and more anxious to do his duty and be beyond reproach in the eyes of Dr Arnold. Oxford enlarged him to a certain extent but as his tutor William Ward later recalled, Clough's immersion in the Tractarian controversies was equally baneful: 'His intellectual perplexity preyed heavily on his spirits, and grievously interfered with his studies.'[56] When he failed to gain a First in the Schools, the first thing Clough did was to set out on foot from Oxford to Rugby. On arrival, he walked straight up to the School House where Dr Arnold was standing and 'with face partly flushed and partly pale' blurted out: 'I have failed.'[57]

In the Epilogue to his poem *Dipsychus* (1865), written when Clough had achieved a more mature perspective on this moral over-heating, the poet presents a dialogue between a young man and his uncle. The latter quotes a remark of an old friend on the excessive piety of the students of Westminster School. 'It's all Arnold's doing; he spoilt the public schools', says the uncle. Ignoring his nephew's protests, the uncle continues with the assertion that these public school prigs are 'full of the notion of the world being so wicked, and of their taking a higher line, as they call it. I only fear they'll never take any at all.' The nephew prefers to blame the religious movements of the time rather than Arnold for 'This over-excitation of the religious sense, resulting in this irrational, almost animal irritability of conscience'.[58] This lively exchange shows that Clough was well aware of what had happened to him. It is possible that Matthew Arnold, in his later relations with Clough, shouldered some sense of responsibility for what had occurred and slipped naturally into the role of adviser and confidant, in spite of being his junior, as a result of habits begun with the Arnold family at Rugby. Clough was nearly four years older than Arnold but the correspondence often shows the younger man adopting the tone of one who guides, corrects, or admonishes. Clough's side of the correspondence is missing – Arnold was in the habit throughout his life of destroying letters to himself – so we may never quite appreciate the fullness of this relationship.

There was clearly tension between the two young men, from mutual rivalry as poets, and from differences of temper and intellectual preference, but the letters to Clough show an exuberance on Arnold's part that was slowly beginning to disclose, beneath the persiflage, a deeper seriousness. They also bear the mark of their days at Oxford together as a 'little interior company', with elliptical references, in-jokes, and a style of undergraduate camp that contrasts with the clarity and directness that always characterised Arnold's later correspondence. The mythologising of Oxford that was a long-term project of Arnold's begins in the walks in the Cumnor hills around the city with Clough and other friends. But *Thyrsis*, which draws heavily on this sense of Oxford, is not a great elegy like Milton's *Lycidas* whose heavy pastoral dress it shares. It is shot through with Arnold's ambivalent feelings about Clough which, in the end, make it less a great primary cry of grief than an eloquent rendering of the thwarted and discontented friend – 'too quick despairer' – and the aspirations of their shared youth: 'The light we sought is shining still.'

Clough was a more ardent political animal than Arnold and a more innovative poetic technician. He also possessed a more morbid temperament and, in spite of the marvellous ebullience and wit of his long poems which are still, perhaps, not properly appreciated, he was an altogether sadder man. And the ghost of Dr Arnold entered into their relationship. Clough had been a prize pupil at Rugby, although he saw relatively little of Matthew Arnold. The latter eventually entered the school as a fifth former a few months before Clough left on a Balliol Scholarship for Oxford. Their friendship would truly begin at Oxford.

Shortly before leaving Balliol for the summer of 1844 and putting himself in the hands of Clough, Arnold wrote to his mother about the recent appearance of Arthur Stanley's *Life and Correspondence of Thomas Arnold DD*. We have no record of Arnold's feelings about the death of his father when it occurred, or of the nature or extent of his grief, except for a comment that occurs in Rowland Prothero's *Life and Letters of Dean Stanley* (1893) where Arnold is said to have declared on the death of his father that now their 'sole source of *information* was gone'. The emphasis that Prothero reports Arnold putting on the word 'information' is testimony to the way in which Dr Arnold was seen as a moral guide, a source of direction and help, on whom all those around him were dependent, and whose loss would be insupportable. In his letter to his mother Arnold says he is struck by the way in which Dr Arnold in the letters manages to get 'a free full expression of himself' in the discipline of the letter form. 'It often does happen that the rough sketch a man throws off says more about him than the same sketch filled up and transferred in all its fullness into a book', he adds. He concurs with his father's religious views, in particular, his argument 'against the completeness of Newman's system, making it impossible that it should ever satisfy the whole of any man's nature', and notes that 'the sale in Oxford seems to have been very good'. With these pieties out of the way, the letter turns to its real purpose: 'I am in an awful state of want with absolutely only one shilling and sixpence in the world' and although 'the throats of all my great old Debts, Giants Pope & Pagan, are well cut' he has his rooms to settle and asks for his allowance to be paid 'as soon as possible'.[59] He was to write again in the summer asking for '£20 or £25' to enable him to go abroad. He promised that he was going to be in a position next year to save a little, although he blithely adds: 'to save money generally I think wrong, except you have a family to provide for after your death'.[60] Dressing with the dressy men had plainly left him short of funds.

By the middle of July Arnold was in the Lakes, at Patterdale, waiting for Clough to join him from Liverpool. On Sunday 21 July, a party of 'Oxford visitants' arrived, prompting Arnold, after morning service, to invent an excuse to visit Fox How to avoid the 'slowdoms' of this entertainment chore. Clough had already been to Fox How where he had found Mrs Arnold 'somewhat anxious about Mat.'[61] and he now feared that although 'Mat. has done something this week' this 'foolish walk' to Fox How would mean their writing off Monday. Not that Clough did not appreciate a day's respite from his charge, for 'when Mat. is here, I am painfully coerced to my work by the assurance that should I relax in the least my yoke fellow would at once come to a dead stop'. Although Walrond joined them by the end of July and there were several other Oxford men in the area, the house at Patterdale was well out of the way and there were no distractions. The basic problem, however, remained the character of 'Mat.'. Clough wrote: 'he is certainly not the most industrious of students, and I fear has fallen, even now, during the last fortnight, rather under the average of four hours a day'.[62] In spite of a timetable carefully worked out by Clough starting with breakfast at 8 o'clock and a morning session from 9.30 to 1.30 followed by a quick dip and some lunch and then an afternoon session from 3 p.m. until 6 p.m., he was reporting by 31 July: 'Mat. has gone out fishing, when he ought properly to be working, it being nearly 4 o'clock'.[63] Clough and Walrond (who was 'working sedulously at Herodotus') took a self-righteous pleasure in the fact that it had suddenly started to pour with rain and the absent scholar would get 'a good wetting'.

Whether it was this reading of Herodotus or an earlier one that gave Arnold the idea for a poem on *Mycerinus*, the king of Egypt whose story the Greek historian tells, we cannot know. But the subject – a king told by an oracle that he has only six years to live in spite of the fact that he has been a more pious ruler than his father – can be linked to the death of Dr Arnold and Tom's revelation that his brother received a doctor's warning that he, too, was 'doomed'. It suggests the poem was composed at about this time. There is a bitter, and almost atheistical tone, in the speaker's reproach to the Gods for their 'frozen apathy' towards human fate and in his determination to obliterate his doom by throwing himself into a life of pleasure: 'The rest I give to joy.' There is a hint, however, that the joy in feasting was put on and that his surrender to immediate pleasure is a bitter reaction to the knowledge that the gods 'cheat our youth' by marking a limit to life. The temptation is strong to read a personal analogy in this poem, which would partly explain Arnold's youthful dandyism. Such a reading, indeed, may have been endorsed by those who knew him. When the poem was eventually published in book form his sister Mary singled out this poem as an instance of the book's surprising 'knowledge of life and conflict . . . strangely like experience'.[64] We might also note in passing the characteristic potamic 'murmur of the moving Nile' that accompanies the revels.

Other poems composed around this time – like *Stagirius* or *A Question* ('Our vaunted life is one long funeral') – reflect a similar mood of bitter disillusion, or is it no more than a romantic simulation of such feelings? That summer of 1844, before the return to Oxford, Arnold composed his famous sonnet on *Shakespeare*, enclosing it in a letter to K. Famously subject to hostile dissection by the critic F. R. Leavis, this poem reflects the fashionable view of Shakespeare as a lofty, inscrutable genius that was prevalent in the 1840s. 'Others abide our question. Thou art free', writes Arnold of the poet who 'smilest and art still / Out-topping knowledge . . .' and who knew 'All pains the immortal spirit must endure'.

By November all three members of the Lakeland reading party were back at Oxford, starting the term with a 'cocoa-supper' in Arnold's rooms at Balliol. The die was now cast, and on 11 November Clough made a realistic assessment of the situation: 'Matt enters the schools for paper work tomorrow: I think he is destined for a second; this is above his deserts certainly, but I do not think he can drop below it, and one would not be surprised if he rose above it in spite of all his ignorance. However he has had the wisdom I believe to be perfectly candid to his Doctors as to the amount of the disease, and both they and he have been very diligent during the last three weeks.'[65] A week later, after the papers were over, Clough, who had been right before in his predictions of Arnold's academic results, repeated his view that Arnold would get a second. 'May he also tread in my steps next Easter!'[66] he added, hoping that an Oriel Fellowship would be the next step. Ten days later, Clough was proved right and Arnold was awarded a second – 'a worthy addition to our select band'.[67] The general view in Oxford was that Dr Arnold's son should have done better and had only himself to blame. The verdict of Lake was representative: 'He showed us both the strong and weak sides of his character as a scholar, for he was certainly equally brilliant, desultory and idle, and his want of knowledge of his books lost him his "first", when he was obliged, by the strictness of the college rule, to go into the Schools at the end of his third year, his examiners and his tutors being equally disappointed.'[68] Lake remembered Henry George Liddell (co-compiler of the famous Greek lexicon and father of Alice who was the model for Lewis Carroll) expressing his particular annoyance 'that so able a man should have excluded himself from the highest honours'.

4

The question of what Arnold was to do next with his second-class degree was soon resolved. After spending Christmas and New Year at Fox How, where he skated every day for the first week of 1845[69] and stayed until 20 January, Arnold was offered a temporary contract as assistant master at Rugby. Although he was only standing in for a master called Grenfell who was seriously ill, the idea of his becoming a Rugby schoolmaster struck Clough as 'a marvel'.[70] Apparently still an unreformed character, Arnold's diary records that he was frequently late for prayers in chapel and seems to have been playing a great deal of billiards and losing money at whist. But the breathing space enabled him to prepare for the Oriel Fellowship examination which was due to take place on 24 March. This entailed a great deal of serious reading and we have some idea of what books he was deep in from consulting his pocket diary or notebook for 1845. Much has been made by Arnold scholars of the so-called 'notebooks' which were published in a magisterial scholarly edition in 1952. An earlier selection had appeared in 1902 edited by Arnold's daughter Nelly, by then the Viscountess

Sandhurst. The title of the 1952 volume, *The Notebooks of Matthew Arnold*, is possibly misleading, or designed to raise expectations too high by holding out the possibility that the notebooks are workbooks or the discursive records of a mind's encounter with its reading, or off-the-cuff reactions to ideas or people or events. In fact they are culled from the slim, leather-bound, commercially produced diaries that Arnold generally bought every year from Henningham and Hollis, the booksellers at 5 Mount Street, Grosvenor Square. They are the sort of handy diary which a busy man like Arnold, changing trains at Crewe, might quickly slip into his inside pocket. He did not use them in any detailed or regular way as diaries, although sporadically we may be able to plot some of his movements from them. They were most frequently used as repositories for lists of reading, projected or accomplished (we can never always be sure which, and he clearly read a great many books that are not listed) and for quotations culled from his reading.

In spite of these limitations, however, the diaries/notebooks are valuable because they show what a serious reader Arnold was and because the extracts he copies out into the diaries give a hint of what it was that he found significant in his reading. The distinguished Arnold scholar, Kenneth Allott, showed what could be done with this material in an examination of the reading-lists of 1845 to 1847 which were not included in the *Notebooks*. Discussing a list Arnold made at Rugby at the start of 1845 in preparation for the Oriel examination, Allott shows how Arnold – in addition to the billiards and the card-playing – was intending to read Plato's *Republic* and *Phaedrus*, the first part of Kant's *Critique of Pure Reason*, the first two books of Mill's *Logic*, Berkeley's *Siris* and three of his dialogues, Augustine's *In Johannis Evangelicum Tractatus* and Descartes' *Méthode*. Arnold very precisely works out that he has 54 days to get through this demanding list but the reappearance of some of them on a long vacation reading-list for the summer suggests that it may have been too ambitious a programme. What it plainly indicates, however, is that Arnold had a serious interest in philosophy in spite of later disavowals of philosophical pretensions – not to mention T. S. Eliot's sneer that Arnold was, in philosophy and theology, 'an undergraduate'.[71] Allott suggests that what Arnold was trying to do was to 'salvage what he could from the wreckage of his childhood beliefs'[72] because his scepticism was 'always reluctant' and he really wanted to discover some solid philosophic foundation for his religious thought. Tom suggests that already by 1845 his elder brother had lost his faith in orthodox Christianity[73] to such an extent that the publication that year of George Eliot's translation of Strauss's *Leben Jesu* (as usual, Tom gets his dates wrong, it was published the following year) 'found him incurious and uninterested' although it had a profound impact on the belief of so many Victorians. Allott's informed reading of the notebooks shows that they do have undoubted value and that for these years in particular, 1845–7, there is a clear demonstration that the author of the later cultural and religious criticism was straightforwardly descended from the young poet of the 1840s.

In 1900 a writer called Arthur Gray Butler published a barely-fictionalised account of his Rugby schooldays: *The Three Friends: A Story of Rugby in the Forties*, which happily coincides with Arnold's brief spell as a temporary master. It was an interesting moment, as Butler explains: 'We were filled, many of us, with the strong wine of Arnold's [he refers, of course, to Dr Arnold] teaching and example, and the great principles of liberty, then stirring up revolution on the Continent, found a ready hot-bed at Rugby, making us, doubtless, talk great nonsense'. With revolution and Chartism in the air the new headmaster, Tait, was said to have remarked, 'it was easier and safer to be a bishop than a headmaster'.[74] Matthew Arnold, the new teacher, fitted in perfectly with this undeferential mood. In the story he is heard to exclaim: 'Thank Heaven!' when an unexpected half-holiday was announced, 'and the Form cheered him'. When the boys discuss him they conclude that 'There's not a bit of the Dominie about him. He's much too great a swell.' More to the point, he was 'A1 at Fives', a proficiency at bat fives being also attested elsewhere by Tom. On another occasion the boys pay a visit to a master called Fulton who is on the lawn with Arnold. The poet is 'lolling back in an easy chair, with a smile upon his face, seemingly watching the light clouds creeping along the summer sky, as he indolently stroked the head of a great staghound sleeping at his side'. Languidly choosing the largest strawberry from a pile in a dish, Arnold asks flippantly: 'I wonder how much of me would ever come to ripeness if I was a Schoolmaster?' Before anyone can answer, another visitor arrives who turns out to be Clough. The newcomer greets his friend with: 'They have not killed me yet, dear, as you said they would: not even their whole school-days and first lessons.'

Although this portrait is rather crudely drawn and tries rather ineptly to work into Arnold's conversation some of the critical catchwords that were still a decade or more in the future, it shows how firmly established his Oxford image was. That languid flippancy is confirmed in a recollection by Margaret Woods of her father as a young Rugby master sitting down to a breakfast, at which some parents were present, and of Arnold declining the breakfast dishes offered to him with a Jovelike wave:

'No thank you, my darling, I've just bitten off the tails of those three bull-pups of yours, and that does take the edge off one's appetite.'[75] Shortly before leaving Rugby, Arnold wrote to Clough, in the first of the letters in that exuberant correspondence, a confession that: 'I do not give satisfaction at the Masters Meetings.'[76] He gives an example of how the headmaster, Tait, at a staff meeting observed that strict Calvinism devoted thousands of mankind to be eternally – he was about to say 'damned' but shrunk back. The temporary master, however, had no such inhibition about saying the shocking word and promptly supplied it, no doubt to a *frisson* of horror from the staffroom. He then tells Clough that 'it seems not clear why I should stand at Oriel: for wisdom I have not, nor skilfulness – after the Flesh – no, nor yet Learning'. The real question, he continues, in the same tone of part-flippancy and part-seriousness or something between the two, is whether one has force of character. 'For me, I am a reed, a very whoreson Bullrush: yet such as I am, I give satisfaction.' His ironic repetition of the phrase 'giving satisfaction' – hardly what an idealistic young man would be seeking as the world's estimation – suggests it might come from some official report on his performance by Tait. Another letter about this time, which discusses their shared passion for George Sand, also records Arnold's wariness of what he calls 'the strong-minded writer' – by which he seems to mean the sort of writer who has too definite a point of view, too palpable a design on us. Arnold preferred a Keatsian 'negative capability' (or 'a general Torpor with here or there a laughing or crying Philosopher') to the strong-minded writer's tendency to bury self-knowledge in self-assertion or to 'talk of his usefulness and imagine himself a Reformer, instead of an Exhibition'. If George Sand's 'views', for example, were codified into a system her art would be lost. Art should show not tell and even elect spirits like Arnold and Clough 'lovers of one another and fellow worshippers of Isis' knew that they had to remember the 'one-sidedness as doctrine' of their belief in 'the Universality of Passion as Passion' – whatever that high-sounding phrase might mean.[77] These letters strain a little too much for effect but their subjects are serious ones and become more so.

On Saturday 22 March Arnold went up to Oxford and was examined for his Fellowship on the Monday. His diary of 28 March then records tersely: 'Got the Oriel.' On 2 April Clough wrote from Liverpool to his friend J. P. Gell about the election of Arnold 'just thirty years after his father's election'. Arnold was elected alongside John Duke Coleridge's younger brother, Henry. 'I am only sorry that he will be obliged to leave his present duties at Rugby . . . which he appears to have been performing very satisfactorily and with great benefit to himself for the last few weeks',[78] Clough continued. He plainly thought that Arnold was doing something useful at Rugby but he had no choice but to come into residence at Oriel as probationary Fellow. Mrs Arnold was 'of course well pleased' as also, when he heard the news, was Wordsworth, 'the Venble Poet at Rydal, who had taken Matt under his special protection as a 2nd classman'. 'I hope it will do Matt no harm', concluded Clough, 'and he is certainly improved since the disaster of November.'

Arnold immediately wrote to his Uncle Trevenen Penrose pointing out how pleased he was at the coincidence of its being thirty years to the day since his father received a similar honour, at the same college, which would 'delight them so much at home'. Oriel was also the college where Newman had been a Fellow. Arnold admitted that all sorts of practical benefits would now flow: 'it gives me a certain prospect of relieving Mamma of myself' and 'there was much that made it wrong for me to go on after my degree doing nothing for myself'. The Fellowship also retrieved his reputation as a potential tutor. Ever since the disaster of his degree: 'Pupils avoided me as a suspected person.' He had mixed feelings about his six weeks at Rugby: 'tho. the little Boys give me the greatest delight, yet the work is certainly too hard, and I should have made but a very poor school-master'. Perhaps more importantly, the Fellowship had increased his confidence, although Arnold tried to argue that 'the truth is that the Examination was different, not that I had deserved in April much more of a literary success than in November' and that 'in real truth it leaves me, as to my reading, very much where I was before'. The key thing, however, was that it would 'in some measure atone for the discredit of a second class in the eyes of those who felt most the discredit of it'[79] – Arnold's family, that is to say, not the young man himself.

5

For the next two years, until he took up a post in London, Arnold was very much free to do as he pleased since the demands placed on a probationary Fellow of Oriel were not excessive. His notebooks indicate that he continued to read seriously. He also composed more poems such as *In Harmony with Nature*. This was a repudiation of an argument he had heard reported from the lips of an Independent Preacher. Lover of nature and of the poems of Wordsworth that Arnold was, he decided that the injunction to live in harmony with nature was naive pantheistic nonsense: 'Man must begin, know this, where Nature ends; / Nature and Man can never be fast friends'. He seems to have spent the rest of 1845 reading and travelling – to the Isle of Man and Ireland in August and in the Lakes shooting grouse on Wansfell in October. Tom says that his brother spent some time in London between his election to the Fellowship and starting work in earnest in the capital in 1847. For that period of two or three years he had lodgings in Mount Street (where he bought his diaries) over the establishment of a seamstress called Mrs Boag. This enabled him to address letters to his friends from 'Mrs Boag's Baby-linen Warehouse, Mount Street'.[80] We have no other record of these London sojourns and the next we hear is that he is setting off in June 1846 with his cousin John Penrose for France.

Arnold had travelled before to France with his parents but this was his first independent journey and its goal was the country of George Sand's novels. In his essay on the writer in *Mixed Essays* (1879) he describes a summer pilgrimage to her château at Nohant. 'There must be many', he wrote, 'who, after reading her books have felt the same desire which in those days of my youth, in 1846, took me to Nohant, – the desire to see the country and the places of which the books that so charmed us were full.'[81] In particular, he had been reading *Jeanne* (1844) and had made up his mind to see Toulx Ste. Croix and Boussac, and the Druidical stones on Mont Barlot called the *Pierres Jaunâtres*. After visiting the Bodleian to look up Toulx on 'Cassini's great map', he left Oxford on Wednesday 24 June, reaching Paris on the 26th. In the 1840s the railway through the centre of France went only as far as Vierzon where he had to change to a diligence to Châteauroux. On arrival there he had to change again to 'a humbler diligence' which would take him to La Châtre, past the 'plain house by the roadside with a walled garden' where George Sand lived. He dined at La Châtre and changed to 'the humblest diligence of all' to take him on the night journey up the valley of the Indre to Boussac. After this, the only transport available was that ramshackle conveyance the French contemptuously call a *patache*. When day broke they found themselves 'in the wilder and barer country of La Marche'. For the next two days: 'I wandered through a silent country of heathy and ferny *landes*, a region of granite boulders, holly, and broom, of copsewood and great chestnut trees'.

In his description, thirty years on, of this country of 'broad light, and fresh breezes, and wide horizons', Arnold is remembering his youth, the moment of his life when he was most free – his next step was unclear, his emergence as a published poet was still to come and the shades of work and public duty had not closed around the handsome and carefree 23-year-old. At Boussac he wrote Madame Sand a letter 'in bad French' conveying 'the homage of a youthful and enthusiastic foreigner' who had read her works with delight. She must have received 'the infliction' of yet another fan with goodnatured resignation because when Arnold returned on 13 July to the inn at La Châtre a letter from her was waiting to summon him to the château.

Arnold arrived on the *quatorze juillet* to find a large party assembled and still in the throes of a midday breakfast. He entered 'with some trepidation' but the simplicity of George Sand's manner immediately put him at his ease. She introduced him to her guests, including her lover Chopin 'with his wonderful eyes' and he noted that her appearance was quite conventional. There was no sign of the legendary man's clothes. The ardent young Francophile was then made to endure 'the insipid and depressing beverage, *boisson fade et mélancolique*, as Balzac called it, for which English people are thought abroad to be always thirsting, – tea' at the hands of his heroine. She talked to him about Oxford and Cambridge, Byron and Bulwer, and as she spoke Arnold noticed how striking were her eyes, her head, her bearing. But the principal impression she made was 'of *simplicity*, frank, cordial simplicity'. When the breakfast was over she led the way into the garden, asked him about his plans, gathered a few flowers for him from the garden, 'shook hands heartily at the gate' and then bade him farewell. Arnold would never see her again.

We know that he made an impression on her. She later told Ernest Renan how the young poet had struck her as 'un Milton jeune et voyageant'.[82] As she watched him go from the château gates she would have seen what Arnold's niece Mrs Humphry Ward describes as 'The face, strong and rugged, the large mouth, the broad-lined brow, and vigorous coal-black hair'.[83] Mary Ward felt that he did not look like his father or mother 'except for that fugitive yet vigorous something which we call "family likeness"'. She claimed to have seen in Ireland 'faces belonging to the "black Celt" type – faces full of power, and humour and softness, visibly moulded out of the good common earth by the nimble spirit within, which have reminded me of my uncle'. At the same time she was constrained to add that 'nothing indeed at first sight could have been less romantic or dreamy than his outer aspect'. That combination of handsome aspect and solidity comes out in other descriptions of Arnold. His friend George Russell, after quoting a hostile Chicago newspaper account of Arnold, which the poet delightedly chuckled over ('He has harsh features, supercilious manners, parts his hair down the middle, wears a single eye-glass and ill-fitting clothes') concedes that his features were, if not harsh, 'strongly marked'.[84] He goes on:

> His nose was long and mouth wide, but both were well shaped and were exaggerated rather than harsh . . . Arnold's brow, both high and wide, owed nothing of its character to baldness, for his hair, to the very end was thick, glossy, and black as a raven's wing . . . He was tall and strongly built, with a body well framed for exercise, and a natural dignity of bearing. That he looked remarkably unlike one's notion of a poet was due to the fact that, as the American observed, he parted his hair down the middle, which in those days was thought the sign of a fop, and that he cultivated large, black, mutton-chop whiskers, which of all hirsute adornments are the least romantic-looking.

In short, his natural vigour cancelled any hint of the preciousness that the 'Olympian manner' might have seemed to open up.

On 15 July, his mission accomplished, and plans to press on to Switzerland apparently shelved, Arnold returned via Paris to London, arriving on 19 July in time to catch the Comédie Française tragedienne Elisa Félix Rachel – 'the divine Rachel'[85] as he called her thirty years later – performing in Racine's *Andromaque* and two days later in *Phèdre* at St James's Theatre, although his recollection in 'The French Play in London' (1879) was that he had first seen her at the Edinburgh theatre playing the part of Hermione. Perhaps he saw her there on his way to Fox How for the summer. Full of George Sand and full of France, Arnold was not insensible to beautiful women, in spite of the decorousness of his married life and of his marked aversion to 'lubricity' in some forms of French writing. His letters to Clough indicate that women were not entirely absent from their minds and there is even, in the Clough correspondence, a uniquely broad remark about the singer Jenny Lind, whose 'enormous obverse' was commented upon.[86]

By the autumn he was back at Rugby, teaching temporarily there from 3 September to 17 October, but still full of French womanhood and preparing for another assault on Paris. He scribbled a packing-list on the back cover of his 1847 diary: '3 drawers, 7 shirts, 2 collars, 1 nightshirt, 1 [?], 1 waistcoat, 4 socks.' He arrived in the French capital on 29 December and went that very night to see Rachel in *Polyeucte* at the Théâtre Français. For the length of this Parisian trip – which cost him 1,567 francs or about £62 – and which ended on 11 February, he was at the theatre virtually every night. When it was not Rachel in Racine it was the Variétés or the Vaudeville or the Gymnase. He took French lessons, paid his respects to Lady Elgin, attended an Embassy ball and the Opera ball and returned to the rather more staid environs of Oriel College on 14 February. Clough noted in a letter to his mother that day that 'Matt Arnold is just come back from Paris', adding, with a hint that there may have been rather more interest in this trip than we know of, 'his stay at the latter end seems to have been very satisfactory to him'[87] – a brief amour perhaps? A week later Clough was writing to Shairp to reveal the full extent of Arnold's abject Francophilia: 'Matt is full of Parisianism; theatres in general, and Rachel in special: he enters the room with a chanson of Béranger's on his lips – for the sake of French words almost conscious of tune: his carriage shows him in fancy parading the rue de Rivoli; – and his hair is guiltless of English scissors: he breakfasts at twelve, and never dines in Hall, and in the week or 8 days rather (for 2 Sundays must be included) he has been to Chapel *once*'.[88] The possibility that some other transgression more serious than missing chapel might be in question is raised by a query in a letter from Clough to Shairp a few days later: 'What evil report hath come to your ears concerning Matt?'[89]

6

Clearly, Arnold's aimless theatre-going and man-about-town loafing could not go on, for he was now twenty-four and with no visible means of support except for the Fellowship. He could no longer avoid the necessity to work for his living and, thanks to the high regard in which his father was held by the Whig grandee Lord Lansdowne, in April 1847 he was offered the post of private secretary to the Marquis. Although Arnold seems to have discharged his duties well, they were not onerous and for a young poet a sinecure of this kind was an ideal arrangement. It is clear from some of the long letters to Tom which he wrote during working hours at his desk at Lansdowne House in Berkeley Square, that Arnold was not overburdened. He would later write:

> I owe so much to Lord Lansdowne . . . I was for four years and a half with him and during all that time never heard from him one sharp or impatient word: my situation with him gave me, besides many other advantages, comparative leisure for reading at a time of my life when such leisure was of the greatest value to me: he enabled me to marry: and he has treated me with unvarying kindness ever since.[90]

Harriet Martineau, in her *Biographical Sketches* (1869) offers one of the few portraits we have of Henry Petty-Fitzmaurice, third Marquis of Lansdowne. Born in 1780, he was 'an aristocratic gentleman of moderate abilities, and politics which might be called accidentally liberal, being connected with the entire political history of his time by the force of consistency alone'. The picture she paints is of a dull but decent man, on whom, as he once put it, 'all the fiddle-faddle of the Cabinet' fell because of his fondness for what he called 'practical business'. When Arnold sent him a copy of the second edition of his poems in 1854 he promised to read them but added: 'it is true that the stirring events of the day leave one little time even for the general reading that one likes best – & the masses of papers now supplied by red boxes, are of a more than usual absorbing interest'.[91] He entered the Commons in 1802 as Member for the family borough of Calne and although he served in various Cabinets and was Lord President of the Privy Council and chairman of a committee responsible for education grants he never reached the highest office. Harriet Martineau paints him as 'busy doing what he delighted in doing through life, helping people to a position, or fitting people and places to each other'. This picture of Lansdowne as a smooth, aristocratic political fixer is captured in a recollection by Thomas Humphry Ward referring to the period his wife's uncle was employed as Lansdowne's private secretary: 'at that time [he was] one of the chiefs of the Whig party, a man whose great influence in the State was not to be measured by the offices that he held'.[92] Another contemporary observer, Sir James Lacaita, observed that 'Lord Lansdowne is the only real "Grand Seigneur" now living in England, and there is no-one to take his place when he is gone. He is the last of a remarkable generation of statesmen, combining political wisdom with literary accomplishments and high position, and wealth with taste. His is now the only house in London where a distinguished foreigner is sure to be invited, and to meet the most select circle of eminent scientific, literary, artistic and political men.'[93]

When Arnold later came to create his famous division of English culture into three classes, the Barbarians, Philistines and Populace, one imagines him drawing on the image of Lord Lansdowne when describing the strengths as well as the weaknesses of the aristocratic or Barbarian class which, as the course of nineteenth-century history unrolled, watched its political influence wane in the face of rising popular democracy. Lansdowne House in Berkeley Square where Arnold worked had a noted picture gallery and one of the largest private collections of Roman sculpture outside Rome. Lord Lansdowner's country seat, Bowood Park in Wiltshire, was also renowned for its sumptuous style and it was there that he died at the age of 83 from a fall while walking on the terrace. His most notable political contribution was in the field of education as Chairman of the Committee of Council on Education which preceded the creation of an Education Department. When Arnold came to work for him he was serving a second term as President of the Privy Council and he was the man who, in April 1851, appointed Arnold as an inspector of schools.

Lansdowne was clearly fond of his young secretary and only weeks after starting work, Mrs Arnold at Fox How received a letter from the Arnolds' old family friend, the Prussian Ambassador Baron von Bunsen, who explained that he had been talking to Lord Grey, possibly at his club, about the good work that Tom was then doing in the Colonial Office. Lansdowne interrupted the conversation to say: 'And the eldest is with me as private secretary, and does very well.'[94] Bunsen told Mrs Arnold he was very glad to hear this: 'for a confidential place like that of private secretary to Lord L is exactly a place where a young man of talent and acquirements can distinguish himself and find that sort of steady intellectual employment which I always thought so particularly desirable for your eldest son.'

But if the older generation breathed a sigh of relief at Arnold's getting into something more regular and purposeful, his contemporaries were very cool about the appointment. Tom, in a letter to Clough, wrote on Colonial Office notepaper: 'I quite agree with you in disliking the notion of this appointment for Matt.[95] The 'little interior company', which considered itself progressive in politics, disapproved of this yoking of one of their number to the service of a great Lord. But at least he was not a Tory. Clough realised that Arnold was not going to spend much longer at Oriel and saw that a move was inevitable: 'Matt does not seem to dislike the prospect, though he has no intention of making this his permanent line',[96] he told his sister, Anne, adding that: 'It appears that his Mother was very anxious he should have something regular in the way of employment. Quite a mistake, I think, on her part.'

And so Arnold left Oxford in April 1847. Undistinguished as his undergraduate career had been, and eager as he seemed to be to get away from Oriel and establish himself in London, his love of Oxford remained a constant in his life. In the famous passage that concludes his Preface to the first series of *Essays in Criticism* (1865) he paints the first of his dreamy portraits of the city: 'steeped in sentiment as she lies, spreading her gardens to the moonlight, and whispering from her towers the last enchantments of the Middle Age . . . Adorable dreamer, whose heart has been so romantic! . . . home of lost causes, and forsaken beliefs, and unpopular names, and impossible loyalties! . . . Apparitions of a day, what is our puny warfare against the Philistines, compared with the warfare which this queen of romance has been waging against them for centuries, and will wage after we are gone?' Although, in less exalted mood, he could see its shortcomings, such as its failure, in contrast with universities on the Continent, to supply, as an institution of higher education, 'the want of the idea of science, of systematic knowledge',[97] Oxford remained a potent and romantic symbol. The hero of Thomas Hardy's novel *Jude the Obscure* (1896), published several years after Arnold's death, arrives at Oxford carrying his own anticipatory mythology of the place created by, amongst others, Arnold – 'him who has recently passed into silence'.[98] Jude would become disillusioned about the openness of Oxford to the working man at the end of Arnold's century and would turn against its 'stagnant mediaevalism' but Arnold has written, in *The Scholar-Gipsy*, one of the most beautiful and elegiac celebrations in the language of the spirit of Oxford and its environs. How many other Judes have been haunted by 'the line of festal light in Christchurch Hall' which was glimpsed by the alienated gipsy-scholar as a vivid symbol of bright exclusion?

CHAPTER THREE:
A PAIR OF BLUE EYES
[1848–1849]

Stay with me, Marguerite, still![1]

1

1848 was to be a decisive year in Matthew Arnold's emotional development. It was also a year of great political turbulence in Europe. 'The Year of Revolutions' saw the overthrow of Louis Philippe in France and Metternich in Austria and a general movement against Austrian domination in Italy. At home, although Chartism may have been passing its peak, literature was increasingly reflecting the prevailing social unrest. Serious radicalism was in the air and during the year appeared works such as Mrs Gaskell's *Mary Barton*, a story of Manchester in the 'hungry forties' bitterly attacked on publication by the mill-owners and Tory press, Mill's *Political Economy*, and Charles Kingsley's *Yeast*, which touched on the plight of the agricultural labourer and the game laws. And Marx and Engels – no doubt unrecognised by the Oriel Fellows – published the *Communist Manifesto*. On 7 March, caught up in the general euphoria, Arnold gaily addressed a letter to his Oxford friend as: 'Citizen Clough, Oriel Lyceum, Oxford.'[2] As the private secretary to a Cabinet Minister, Arnold was well-placed to pick up the latest political gossip from some of the best sources. He never lost an interest in politics which was strong enough on occasion to draw him to the public gallery of the House of Commons to listen to debates. He described himself always as a Liberal – and swore to the end of his life that he would never vote

Tory – but he was 'a Liberal tempered by experience, reflection, and renouncement'[3] and a thorn in the side of that Party, particularly in his merciless lashing of its bedrock supporters in middle-class Nonconformity and in his criticism of its policies in relation to Ireland.

At the beginning of January, Arnold went to see Aunt Martha Buckland, who was unwell, and the trip gave him the opportunity to indulge in nostalgia for Laleham days. He crossed over on 'the primitive ferry' to Chertsey, a place he called for his mother 'the poetic town of our childhood as opposed to the practical, historical Staines'. Shortly afterwards, Lord Lansdowne, or 'my man' as Arnold described the marquis to his friends, invited his secretary to his country seat at Bowood Park in Wiltshire. Arnold arrived on the London train in time for dinner on 3 January but complained to his mother: 'I do not expect I shall know a soul there.'[4] After this social duty he made his way to Fox How which he still described as 'home'.

By February Parliament was again in session and on the last day of the month Arnold found himself writing to Tom – who in November had emigrated to New Zealand full of high idealistic hopes – from his desk at Lansdowne House, as 'a most musical clock' sounded 1.24 p.m. His desk was situated opposite one of Lord Lansdowne's celebrated pieces of Roman sculpture: 'a marble group of Romulus, Remus and the wolf, the two children fighting like mad, and the limp-uddered she-wolf affectionately snarling at the little demons struggling on her back'.[5] To his left two great windows looked out on to the court in front of the house and one was slightly ajar to let in 'by gushes the soft damp breath with a tone of spring life in it which the close of an English February sometimes brings'. Crocuses studded the green lawn which occupied half the court before it yielded to a gravel walk where nursemaids passed up and down with 'large, still-faced whiterobed babies' in their arms, distracting Lord Lansdowne's secretary from his duties. He could also catch the sound of the world's business out in Berkeley Square: 'the sounds of vehicles and men in all gradations, some from near and some from far but mellowed by the time they reach this backstanding lovely mansion'. All morning another sound, that of the newspaper sellers crying: 'Se—c—on edition of the *Morning Herald* – L—a—test news from Paris: – arrival of the King of the French', reached his ears at which 'every stone in this and other lordly mansions' was made to 'totter and quake for fear'. Eventually, Arnold succumbed and dashed outside for a paper.

Arnold was ideally situated in London to witness the great political stirrings. On 6 March he joined 'the great mob' in Trafalgar Square, which had rioted in the wake of an open-air meeting on the income tax, 'but they did not seem dangerous and the police are always, I think, needlessly rough in *manner*. English officials too often are.'[6] Such early tolerance contrasts with his advocacy, twenty years later, of much more Draconian treatment of rioters. He predicted that, unlike France – where his sympathies, however sanguine, were with the French people not the deposed monarch – there would be nothing more serious than street disturbance in London. But the death-knell of the old order was none the less sounding: 'the hour of the hereditary peerage and eldest sonship and immense properties has, I am convinced, as Lamartine would say, struck'. Presumably, these were notions he did not discuss with his employer. At this time he toyed with the idea of doing some political writing himself but confessed to K that 'in the watches of the night I seemed to feel that in that direction I had some enthusiasm of the head perhaps, but no profound stirring'.[7] Instead he poured out his thoughts to Clough, 'we two agreeing like two lambs in a world of wolves'.

In December 1847 Arnold had sent what he now admitted to be 'a beastly vile note'[8] criticising some draft poems Clough had sent him. A subsequent, apologetic, letter explained that he had been uneasy about Clough's 'apostrophes to duty'[9] and perhaps preferred a less purposeful kind of poetry: 'Yet to *solve* the Universe as you try to do is as irritating as Tennyson's dawdling with its painted shell.' Always ready to tilt at Tennyson, Arnold was, more seriously, wrestling with the problem of how far poetry should be trying to save the world and how far it should just be itself or, as Auden was to put it, 'survive in the valley of its making'. Neither of these two politically aware young writers could condone mere art for art's sake but they sensed just as much the dangers of working to a political agenda. These early letters to Clough show Arnold's critical views in their formative stage and the importance to him of the idea that in the modern world the response of poets was bound to be different from the poets they admired from the past. 'And had Shakespeare and Milton lived in the atmosphere of modern feeling', he insisted to Clough, 'had they had the multitude of new thoughts and new feelings to deal with that a modern has, I think it likely the style of each would be far less *curious* and exquisite. For in a *man* style is the saying in the best way *what you have to say*. The *what you have to say* depends on your age.'[10] The modern age, where there was so much more complexity, so much more to say, presented a greater challenge to the modern poet.

It would have escaped the notice of neither poet that Lamartine, who headed the new Provisional Government in France, was a poet. The same thought had occurred to Lord Lansdowne: 'My man remarks that Poets should hold up their heads now a Poet is at the head of France',[11] he reported to Clough. Although Arnold believed that 'the present spectacle in France is a fine one'[12] he was still holding back a little, as he was always to do, from the glamour of action. He judged that the revolutionary spectacle would appeal more to 'the historical swift-kindling man, who is not over-haunted by the pale thought, that after all man's shiftings of posture, restat vivere'. None the less, he was not prepared to tolerate the way in which *The Times* – another long-term adversary of Arnold's – 'twaddled' about the relations of capital and labour instead of recognising the true extent of the social problem. Arnold saw clearly enough that 'the capitalist understands by *fair profits* such as will enable him to live like a colossal Nob'. It was the openness of the French to ideas, including political ideas, that struck Arnold as the key difference between them and a country whose national organ was *The Times*. 'It is this – this *wide and deepspread intelligence* that makes the French seem to themselves in the van of Europe . . . this is the secret of their power', he told Clough. This was, of course, to be a central tenet of Arnold's later social and cultural criticism and is yet another reminder of how consistent was his thinking. His ideas evolved naturally and many of the seeds of later essays are contained in these early, spontaneous letters.

Meanwhile, under the rubric of *restat vivere*, Arnold was renewing his interest in the London theatre. Towards the end of February he attended a performance of *Othello* at the Princess's Theatre where William Charles Macready and Fanny Kemble had just begun an engagement of eight Shakespeare plays. Arnold wrote to invite Clough to visit him from Oxford but painted such a disagreeable picture of the piece that Clough could be forgiven for wanting to pass it over: 'The squalor of the place, the faint earthy orange smell, the dimness of the light, the ghostly ineffectualness of the sub-actors, the self-conscious-ness of Fanny Kemble, the harshness of Macready, the unconquerable difficulty of the play, altogether gave me sensations of wretchedness during the performance.'[13] Macready himself had confided to his diary during rehearsals that 'I have never seen any one so bad, so unnatural, so affected, so conceited'[14] as Fanny Kemble in the part of Desdemona. None the less, Arnold tried to persuade Clough to give *Macbeth* a try and in the middle of March his friend came to London. The performance they chose, however, was the less highbrow *Sweethearts and Wives* at the Haymarket Theatre, starring a Miss Fortescue.

Alongside their bouts of theatre the two friends continued to exchange letters about literature and politics. Arnold believed that it was the aristocracy and not royalty that should be the target of popular protest and that 'primogeniture – large land and mill owners'[15] was the important issue. Yet if the political agenda was subtly different for England, the example of France was potent – 'if the new state of things succeeds in France, social changes are *inevitable* here and elsewhere . . . the spectacle of France is likely to breed great agitation here', he warned K.[16] Arnold also feared, in a neat resumé of the future argument of *Culture and Anarchy*, that 'the deep ignorance of the middle and upper classes, and their purblindness of vision',[17] by failing to offer moral and cultural leadership to the embryo political movement, would result in mere street anarchy for 'such is the state of our masses that their movements now *can* only be brutal plundering and destroying'. One can see here Arnold's quickened political sympathies struggling with his deeper instinct for the meaning and direction of events. He was very struck at this time (mentioning it to two correspondents) by an article in *The Examiner* by Carlyle which he felt offered some intellectual 'repose' amidst 'the heat and vain words that are everywhere just now'[18] by focusing on the movement's 'ideal invisible character'.

Although he dismissed the English Ambassador at Paris, Lord Normanby, and his 'ineffectual set . . . who, between them all, never had a thought in their lives' and praised the contrasting 'free play of the mind' embodied in a journal like the *Revue des Deux Mondes*, Arnold was not completely seduced by French intellectuality. He felt, characteristically, that it was in a country's imaginative literature rather than in its philosophy that the true source of intellectual influence lay. 'Oh, Comte has been quite passé these 10 years', a fashionable Frenchman said to him. More durable than such ephemeral intellectual fashion statements, the 'applied ideas' of literature could do some lasting good. 'Seditious songs have nourished the French people much more than the Socialist philosophers', he told Citizen Clough.[19]

Excited as he was by the prospect of political change, Arnold was still troubled by the failure of revolutionary politics to feed 'the deepest wants of man'. Clough's total immersion in the political element – 'If it were not for all these blessed revolutions, I should sink into hopeless lethargy'[20] he declared – was foreign to Arnold. He failed repeatedly to interest Clough in the more serene wisdom of the *Bhagavad Gita*. Arnold represented him in *The World and the Quietist* as 'Critias', a man who resented the 'languid' Indian philosophy of quietism with its implied rebuke to those activists 'Who, with such passionate will, / Are what we mean to be.' Clough was never to be convinced, and when he later came to review Arnold's poems in the summer of 1853 in the *North American Review* he attacked their embodiment of a European 'over-educated weakness of purpose' and the failure of the author to escape from 'the dismal cycle of his rehabilitated Hindoo–Greek philosophy'. Clough (who may have been settling an old score with Arnold for greeting his first efforts with the breezy judgement that there was 'a deficiency of the *beautiful*'[21] in them) argued that 'for the present age, the lessons of reflectiveness and the maxims of caution do not appear to be more needful than exhortations to steady courage and calls to action'.[22] Arnold's deepest feelings were always readily engaged – in politics and in love – but passionate, unreflecting commitment and instinctual activism did not come naturally to him. Whether it was a certain coolness of temperament or a purely philosophical delicacy that made him so, Arnold would always be someone who respected the virtues of holding back. Eventually he would come to elevate this to the status of a critical precept.

At about this time he wrote two sonnets which embody that intellectual hesitancy. The first, *To a Republican Friend* (who is, of course, Clough), begins by trying a little too hard to sound convinced – 'God knows it, I am with you' – and proceeds by pretending to share Clough's hatred of 'The barren optimistic sophistries / Of comfortable moles' as well as his friend's thoughts when faced with 'The armies of the homeless and unfed'. Arnold ends bravely: 'If these are yours, if this is what you are, / Then am I yours, and what you feel, I share.' The second sonnet continues the argument without a break but it is already in retreat, signalled by the opening word: 'Yet . . .' When Arnold muses on 'what life is' he is prompted less by excited revolutionary expectation than by 'patience' and the thought that the circumambient 'Mountains of Necessity' spare us 'narrower margin than we deem'. The day of the Millennium – when 'liberated man' stands before his God freed from all social conflict – will not dawn 'at a human nod' is Arnold's moderate conclusion. By July, his 'republican friend' was writing sadly to Tom: 'Matt was at one time really heated to a very fervid enthusiasm, but he has become sadly cynical again of late.'[23] But in April, the month when he met Emerson for the first time (the sage telling him that he had known a European revolution was inevitable) Arnold attended the Chartist convention in London – always keen to witness political events at first hand – and was 'much struck with the ability of the speakers'.[24] In spite of this, however, he told his mother: 'I should be sorry to live under their government – nor do I intend to.' He did not, however, share the general fear of unrest and the 'ridiculous terror' of the public. He was equally independent in his judgement of the Irish Question. In a letter to Clough he expressed his distaste for the role of Lord Clarendon in putting down the Irish revolts and asked what it was the English were trying to uphold in Ireland: '1. a chimerical Theory about some possible dangerous foreign alliances with independent Ireland: 2. a body of Saxon landlords – 3. a Saxon Church Establishment'.[25] The praise of Clarendon 'makes me sick' he told Clough.

In May Arnold wrote to K lamenting the fact that England was 'in a certain sense *far behind* the Continent', an intellectual isolation that arose from 'the sheer habitual want of reading and thinking' and a too exclusive faith in her practical virtues. And then, in one of those moments of far-sightedness that so often characterise Arnold's thinking, he offered a prediction, oddly pertinent to the political climate of Britain at the end of the twentieth century, though derived from Lamartine: '100 years hence the Continent will be a great united Federal Republic, and England, all her colonies gone, in a dull steady decay'.[26] He was also reading Heinrich Heine for the first time but had not yet formed the more positive view of him that he would expound in his first volume of *Essays in Criticism* (1865). He told his mother that Heine 'disgusted' him for trying to imitate Byron without the Byronic social poise. He was reading a life of Goethe, too, and admired his sincerity in 'writing about nothing he had not experienced' like Wordsworth. The difference between the latter and Goethe, however, was immense in terms of their experience, and in a way that was 'not in the Englishman's favour'.[27] Reading another life, this time of Napoleon, had turned him into an admirer of a man who, in the 'astonishing clearness and width of his views' was utterly misunderstood by the English – 'but what foreigner could divine the union of invincibility and speculative dulness in England?'

As well as poetry, politics and pretty actresses, Arnold and Clough were also exercised by religious questions. During the summer of 1848 Clough's religious scruples had mounted to the point where he was about to resign his Oriel Fellowship because of an inability to subscribe to the Thirty-nine Articles. Once again the issue of subscription had come to the fore. Clough was not so much preoccupied with a theological nicety surrounding this or that article as the general notion of being forced to subscribe. His refusal was essentially a stand against ecclesiastical authority over the individual intellect, a matter of civil liberty. He told the Provost of Oriel, Dr Hawkins, that subscription was merely 'a painful restraint on speculation'.[28] Although Arnold did not feel the matter as intensely as Clough, he discussed it with him, gladly furnishing comments on his friend's draft letter of resignation ('perhaps the second paragraph is a little obscure and heavy . . .'[29]) and encouraging him to see his stand as a principled one on behalf of those, like Arnold himself, who found the articles unsatisfactory for the same general reasons: 'to know that there are traitors within the place mightily enheartens the attaquers'. Perhaps this awareness of a shared unorthodoxy, coupled to a similar sense that the destinies of neither had matched their abilities, deepened their fellow-feeling. 'Do not let us forsake one another', Arnold wrote to Clough, 'we have the common quality, now rare, of being unambitious, I think. Some must be contented not to be at the top.'[30]

But Arnold continued to be concerned about Clough. He wrote to K at the end of July, enclosing for her birthday another sonnet inspired by Clough, *Religious Isolation*. The poem urges its recipient to grow up and stop searching his conscience for some inner light that will resolve his doubts. Like the earlier poem that rejected the notion of living in harmony with nature, it argues that doubt will not be banished by the discovery of some natural law: 'Live by thy light, and earth will live by hers!' he enjoins. In this role reversal, Arnold becomes the decisive friend counselling against the very sort of indecision he himself had felt in relation to political action. His covering letter to K explained: 'generally we consider mere individual belief as only opinion and will not act steadily on it – and have to become fanatics, that is to impose one rule on all the world before we can believe it ourselves. I send you as a birthday present a sonnet on this subject addressed to Clough a great *social* fanatic.'[31]

Arnold, in another reversal of role, given Clough's former anxiety to prevent Arnold's academic career from foundering, now tried to encourage Clough to get established in a post after quitting Oriel, fearing that he would not be able to survive on his own. He wrote to Clough in the early summer of 1848 pointing out that Lord Lovelace's son required a summer tutor. He mocked Clough's apparent failure to grasp that 'the Muse willingly *accompanies* life but that in no wise does she understand to *guide* it'.[32] You cannot, in other words, live off your poetry in the changed social conditions of the nineteenth century. Arnold would grasp that necessity all too readily exactly three years later when he grimly assumed the lifelong burden of an inspector of schools.

In February, Arnold's brother William Delafield Arnold, 'Willy', had emigrated to India as an ensign in the Bengal Army of the East India Company, following in the footsteps of Tom who had gone to New Zealand a few months earlier. Willy had the Arnoldian earnestness in far greater quantities than his eldest brother and in 1853 published a novel, *Oakfield or Fellowship in the East*, which E. M. Forster was later to describe as a 'strange, quixotic, disillusioned work'. The 'freedom' of the language in the officers' mess is hated by the novel's hero, Edward Oakfield, who embodies Willy's moral earnestness. He arrives in India with the soon to be disappointed expectation of participating in 'the grand work of civilising Asia' but finds the moral squalor of the British settlers to be the principal obstacle.[33] Arnold probably did not have in mind such an exacting venture for Clough but he wanted his friend to 'Shake yourself . . . For God's sake don't mope . . .' In his next letter, Arnold was forced to apologise for being too nannyish. He explained that he was merely trying to be helpful and prudent 'and do not suppose I make pretensions to *know* you or anybody'.[34] He had also to promise not to tell the world about Clough's resignation plans.

Throughout the summer Arnold kept up his campaign to get Clough decently placed. He found another potential tutorial opportunity with a William Rathbone Greg who lived in the Lake District, and tried to tempt Clough with it. He observed playfully that 'since the Baconian era wisdom is not found in desarts: and you again especially need the world and yet will not be absorbed by any quantity of it'.[35] In spite of such exchanges, they found time to continue their debates about poetry. Arnold conceded that the sincerity of Clough's poems gave them a tighter and more satisfying grip on reality: 'The spectacle of a writer striving evidently to get breast to breast with reality is always full of instruction and very invigorating,' he told Clough, 'and here I always feel you have the advantage of me: "much may be seen tho: nothing can be solved" – weighs upon me in writing.'[36]

Clough had spent May and June in France and had seen with his own eyes the four days of disorder in Paris that marked the disintegration of the poet Lamartine's Provisional Government. In a letter to Tom written when he got back to England and was staying with his family at 51 Vine Street, Liverpool, Clough told the painful story that the newspapers had reported 'in a somewhat shrieky accent'. Although he tried to minimise some of the accounts of Government atrocities he was forced to conclude that Lamartine had proved 'deficient in definite purpose and practicality' and that 'France's prospects are dubious and dismal enough'. He drew the Arnoldian conclusion that the overthrow of Louis Philippe might well have been premature in the sense that the ideas of the revolutionists were 'so far from ripe'. But he stuck to the view that the spectacle overall would 'accelerate change in England'.[37] He also noted how Arnold had become cynical about the political situation. Clough had recently received a letter from him observing bitterly: 'What a nice state of things in France. The New Gospel is adjourned for this bout. If one had ever hoped any thing from such a set of d—d grimacing liars as their prophets one would be very sick just now.'[38] Clough shared, if not to quite the same extent, Arnold's disillusion but was able to point out to Tom that in spite of the political setbacks, for Arnold at least 'I think the poetism goes on favourably.'[39] In less than a year Arnold was to publish his first volume and throughout the 1840s had been writing constantly – a fact that Clough more than anyone would have been aware of. And Arnold was soon to experience an affair of the heart which would bear rich poetic fruit yet at the same time show that the vacillations and deep reserve evident in his political emotions were mirrored in affairs of the heart.

2

In September 1848 Arnold made a trip to Switzerland where, at the Alpine resort of Thun, he met the young woman who became the 'Marguerite' of the poems that form the sequence, much rearranged and retitled by Arnold, which he grouped under the collective title 'Switzerland'. Thun at this time was a picturesque, medieval town on a lake overshadowed by the Bernese Alps and built around a twelfth-century castle. The poet Etienne Pivert de Senancour, whom Arnold admired and about whom he wrote two important poems, brought his romantic melancholy to this region and stayed in Thun around 1790. Arnold would certainly have been drawn to see the spot associated with the author of the novel *Obermann* (1804) whose 'melancholy eloquence' had beguiled him and influenced his reading of the Alpine countryside. Thun was enjoying something of a tourist revival early in the nineteenth century and travellers dependent on Murray's *Handbook* to Switzerland would have been directed there in increasing numbers.

Three brothers called Knechtenhofer had invested their business fortune in exploiting Thun's picturesque medievalism and its perfect position under the Blümlisalp, the Eiger and the Jungfrau. The Victorians were passionate about the Alps – an enthusiasm to which a book like Leslie Stephen's *Playground of Europe* (1871) testifies. Arnold always kept up his subscription to the Alpine Club and regularly took holidays in Switzerland. The lower sites, at the time the brothers started to develop Thun, were underexploited, with Interlaken, for example, being merely an English colony, described by Murray as 'a sort of Swiss Harrogate'. The brothers built their first hotel at Thun in 1830, the Hotel Bellevue, situated on the edge of the hill which rises above the River Aar and the lake. An English church was built and a steamboat was brought in bits from Paris and reassembled on the lake to provide a major tourist attraction. The boat had a mechanical organ which played 'God Save the Queen'. During Thun's golden age of tourism, between 1840 and 1865, the kings of Holland and Württemberg visited the town. Several French families established themselves at Thun, near the hotel, and an avenue of poplars was planted, in the French fashion, at the approach to the town. When Arnold arrived in 1848 the covered bridge across the River Aar had still not been replaced and it appears, along with many other local details, in the Marguerite poems.

We do not know who Marguerite was and almost certainly – barring some remarkable archival discovery – we shall never know. But speculation, inspired guesswork, and attempts at imaginative recreations of the encounter with Marguerite have long flourished. The romantic school of literary biography – which lies under a terrible injunction to invent where no evidence exists – has had a field day with the story of Arnold and Marguerite.[40] In spite, however, of various imaginative flights, the truth was expressed by one of these romantic scholars quite disarmingly: 'Of "Marguerite", who first and last was the passion of Matthew Arnold's boyhood, we know little.'[41]

Perhaps it would be truer to say that we know nothing at all – except what can be deduced from the poems themselves. There are even those who have argued that Marguerite was no more than a fiction. Arnold, in late middle age, when he had become a smiling Victorian pater familias, told his daughters that the lover of his passionate youth did not exist. But there are three compelling reasons why we should interpret this as no more than a piece of judiciously fictive propriety.

The first is a clear statement in a letter to Clough written on 29 September 1848 from a hotel at the Baths of Leuk: 'Tomorrow I repass the Gemmi and get to Thun: linger one day at the Hotel Bellevue for the sake of the blue eyes of one of its inmates: and then proceed . . .'[42] Arnold visited Thun again in September 1849 and the letter he wrote to Clough on that occasion – together with a scrap of verse included in the letter that would later appear in one of the published 'Marguerite' poems – confirms that he was, confusedly and confusingly, in love with someone in that place.

The second argument for a real Marguerite is that Arnold was a poet who placed a very high value on the 'literalness and sincerity' of his poems and who, as we have seen, praised Goethe for his 'thorough sincerity – writing about nothing he had not experienced'. In his essay on *Dante and Beatrice* (1863) Arnold invoked 'the necessary laws under which poetic genius works . . . the inevitable conditions under which the creations of poetry are produced'[43] to rebuke those who would minimise 'the sensible and human element' in a poetic representation. He argued that Dante's Beatrice was no allegorical creation or fiction, that the poet's passion 'was a real passion' for the simple reason that Dante was an artist 'and art abhors what is vague, hollow, and impalpable'. An artist treats as 'indispensable' the basis in the real world of his creations. 'Yes, undoubtedly there was a real Beatrice, whom Dante had seen living and moving before him, and for whom he had felt a passion', asserts Arnold. And in a letter to K he writes: 'The Greeks are eternally interesting because they . . . keep nearer to the *facts* of human life.'[44]

The third argument for 'a real Marguerite' at Thun 'for whom he had felt a passion' lies in the poems themselves. The consistency of the details in the Marguerite poems, the accumulated incidents of the drama they enact, their convincingly authentic emotional truth – their fit with everything we know of Arnold from his letters at this time – persuade me that Marguerite, with whatever poetic enrichment and variation, is drawn from life. In the 1930s two scholars, C. B. Tinker and H. F. Lowry, who were preparing the first scholarly edition and commentary on Arnold's poems, travelled to Thun to see what they could find. The old proprietress of the Hotel Bellevue where the lovers met, who was thought to possess memories of early legends connected with the hotel, had died some months previously, in 1932. The hotel register for 1848 and 1849 had been destroyed, as was the register of Thun Castle where lovers were in the habit of signing their names. There was no record of foreign visitors in the region or signs in the churchyard of foreign names. There is even less chance now of any local evidence coming to light that would place an identifiable Marguerite in Thun at the end of the 1840s.[45]

From the poems, however, we can form a reasonably consistent picture of Marguerite as she existed in the imagination of the poet. She has 'a graceful figure', a 'pliant grace', pale cheeks, ash-blonde hair, blue eyes, and a pleasant, if sometimes mocking smile. She wears her hair in a headscarf, which has led some scholars with a finely tuned sense of caste to speculate that she might have been a chambermaid.[46] Decent gels, runs this particular argument, would wear a bonnet, even in the Swiss mountain country. There is a clear hint of sexual knowingness, or prior experience, a bold physicality, in this 'Daughter of France'. Perhaps her forwardness in this respect was one of the factors that made Dr Arnold's son so hesitant. In the very first 'Marguerite' poem – *To his Friends Who Ridiculed a Tender Leavetaking*, which appeared in his first volume (the remaining Marguerite poems did not appear until his second collection in 1852) and which was later retitled *A Memory Picture* – Arnold had a refrain: 'Ere the parting kiss be dry, / Quick, thy Tablets, memory !' whose explicitness was softened in later editions to: 'Ere the parting hour go by.' The poem has Marguerite predicting that she shall spend the whole year waiting for her lover's return: 'Some day next year, I shall be, / Entering heedless, kissed by thee.' But at the same time, she realises that anything might happen in the interval.

In fact, Arnold did return to Thun a year later in September 1849, after this poem had been published, and the poem *Meeting* records his finding her smiling on the lake shore and waiting for him 'Unalter'd with the year'. In the earlier poem, Marguerite is pictured, as usual with her lilac kerchief, which is tied 'under the archest chin / Mockery ever ambushed in.' Her eyes, as well as being hauntingly blue, and kind, are 'Eager tell-tales of her mind', and have an 'impetuous stress / of inquiring tenderness'. In her frank and tender looks Arnold sees an 'angelic gravity' – her lively beauty has substance and in her spirit dwells an 'unconquer'd joy'. The nine poems which deal with this love affair, written at different times and in different moods, are testimony to the depth of Arnold's passion, and the deep difficulty he had in letting himself go.

In the summer of 1848, Arnold, according to his brother Tom, had conceived a 'romantic passion'[47] for another blue-eyed young woman, Mary Claude, a French Protestant exile staying at Ambleside near Fox How. The coincidence has led some to speculate that she might be the model for Marguerite. But there is no evidence whatsoever to place her in Switzerland that year (although it is true that she had relatives in Geneva). Tom describes her as 'the Cruel Invisible' which suggests that

Arnold's love affairs seldom ran a smooth course. Years later he succumbed to a request from Mary Claude's brother to write an introduction to a collection of her stories, *Twilight Thoughts* and told his daughter, Lucy: 'About her I have a sentiment and her books as I remember them . . . I don't think you know them but I wanted to do her brother a good turn.'[48] The existence of Mary Claude complicates our picture of Arnold's emotional life at this moment in its development but Marguerite remains a mystery.

Young men, when they fall in love, even 25-year-old bachelor Fellows of Oxford colleges in the 1840s, can sometimes get themselves into emotional tangles and be unsure of quite how they feel about this new experience. They can even be in love with more than one woman at once, or discover that they are in love with neither of them. It has always been hard to explain Arnold's irresoluteness in relation to Marguerite and it is at least possible that the presence in his heart of a recent summer romance was at least as powerful a suasion against pursuing his Swiss amour than the explanations usually proffered that Marguerite – one recalls that headscarf again – was unsuitable. Mary Claude – a friend of the family, well brought-up, with literary accomplishments, a fellow Europhile, was the perfect choice for Arnold. But he did not choose to pursue his suit after the rupture with Marguerite in 1849 and instead started to pay court to the daughter of a Belgravian judge.

Such literary detective trails can lead us away from what is truly interesting about the Marguerite poems: how they can help us in trying to understand Arnold at this point in his life. When he arrived in Switzerland in September 1848 he was still unmarried and still without a long-term career (for the post with Lord Lansdowne had the feel of a temporary sinecure). But he knew that he must work for his living and that he was unlikely to be able to survive solely as a writer, for his writing was not of the kind to be truly popular. He was still free and unattached but the way ahead was not clear. The love affair with Marguerite, for all its tenderness and sensual delight, was destined, perhaps, to be a distraction, or a reminder of his restless, transitional state. It was to live with him for the rest of his life, sometimes coming to symbolise for him the idea of freedom and the less hidebound and more expansive spirit of the Continent. But, when it was actually happening to him, it found him confused and unsure of how he should handle the situation.

On 29 September 1848 he sat in the hotel at the Baths of Leuk, before a blazing wood fire, drinking champagne to keep out the cold, and waiting for the arrival of his *café noir*. He pulled out some writing paper and started to write to Clough, in the hope that by putting his thoughts down he could make sense of what was happening to him. He was all alone in the 'vast hotel',[49] penned in by heavy rain and the prospect of frost. Two days previously he had crossed the Simplon Pass into Italy and slept at Domo d'Ossola, where his guide remarked on some 'superbes filles' ('nothing improper', he hastily reassured Clough), but the bad weather had persuaded him to return. The next day he planned to go over the Gemmi Pass once more and stay another day at Thun, for the sake of those blue eyes. He enjoyed talking to the guide and his family, for 'I love gossip and the smallwood of humanity generally among these raw mammoth-belched half-delightful objects the Swiss Alps'. He hated, however, the dirty water caused by the rains because all his life he loved fresh clear water, rivers, and mountain streams, as 'one who looks upon water as the Mediator between the inanimate and man'. In spite of the weather, he had climbed the Faulhorn, 8,300 feet above sea level. His reading matter on this trip was the French poet Pierre-Jean de Béranger and the Stoic philosopher Epictetus. But, tired out by his mountain-tramping, Arnold was in no mood for reading Greek and he was getting bored with Béranger's '*fade*' Epicureanism. 'I am glad to be tired of an author', he told Clough, 'one link in the immense series of cognoscenda et indagenda despatched'.

But it was not only books that left Arnold feeling jaded: 'More particularly is this my feeling with regard to (I hate the word) women. We know beforehand all they can teach us: yet we are obliged to learn it directly from them. Why here is a marvellous thing.' If this was Arnold's attitude the day before rejoining Marguerite it is not surprising that his love made a choppy passage. He quotes some lines of poetry (seemingly his own) which begin: 'Say this of her: / The day was, thou wert not: the day will be, / Thou wilt be most unlovely.' The roaring fire and the bumper of champagne had clearly not warmed this lover's spirits. He ends the letter with a promise to see Clough next at Oxford where we hear from him at the end of October, the month Clough finally took the step of resigning his Fellowship.

The product of Clough's summer was the poem *The Bothie of Toper-na-fuosich, a long vacation pastoral*. Arnold, who was also preparing his first book for the press, had started on the Marguerite poems. Although there is real feeling in these poems, their failure to establish themselves higher in the affection of Arnold's readers is probably due to their being rather uncommon love poems, celebrating neither unalloyed passion nor the conventional tropes of disappointed love. The failure of the affair they dramatise is due neither to a hard-hearted mistress nor to the cruelty of fate. The obstacle to the lover's success appears to be none other than the poet himself. In the first poem, *A Memory Picture*, we encounter Marguerite for the first time as she leans her face towards her lover 'Half refused and half resigned, / Murmuring: "Art thou still unkind?"'. She manages to extract a promise from him to return, but at the time the poem was written – after the first meeting in September but before the publication of the poem in February 1849 – Arnold's second visit was still in the future and hence uncertain. He starts to link the affair to the inevitable transience of human affections: 'Time's current strong / Leaves us fixed to nothing long' and to reflect that all he can do in the face of this is to prize the 'dim remembrance' of joy. What starts to draw these poems away from the brink of such mere poetic commonplaces – common in Arnold's juvenilia – is the vivid sense of the particular in the emotional drama that begins to unfold.

The next poem in the sequence – and here we must jump forward to his second meeting in the autumn of 1849 – is *Meeting*, where the poet arrives to find 'my bliss at hand' but no sooner has he glimpsed her than he is backing off:

> Again I spring to make my choice;
> Again in tones of ire
> I hear a God's tremendous voice:
> 'Be counselled and retire.'

This third quatrain is the theme on which all the subsequent poems in the sequence were to be a variation. Why did Arnold hear this voice and why did he choose to obey it? In part it is a fear of the emotional disorientation that must come to one who believed of the opposite sex that 'we know beforehand all that they can teach us' yet are 'obliged' to learn it from them. Such a priggish fear of engagement is probably not an unusual phase for a young and inexperienced man to go through – and the all-male society in which both Arnold and Clough lived could not have helped to induce a warmer and more spontaneous conception of what relationships with women might turn out to entail – but it is an awkward start for a love poet. By concluding *Meeting* with a plea to that ireful God to direct his warning against 'some more ambitious heart' and 'let the peaceful be', Arnold seems to be claiming some allowance for his emotional coolness.

The next poem, *Parting*, preserves the same tension between the poet's longing for inner calm, symbolised by the majestic snow-capped

Bernese Alps which dwarf the lake of Thun, and the force – or is it a threat? – of passion. He hears Marguerite's beautiful voice on the stair and in the moment of being drawn to her 'lovely lips' hears another voice, that of the autumn storm winds which he imagines sweeping him up to the mountains which are 'unspotted' and where there is 'no life' stirring. The hint of affrighted sexual purity in 'unspotted' quickly becomes more explicit. Like Orpheus, whose transgressive backward look at Eurydice on their ascent out of Avernus, leaves him embracing nothing but air,[50] Arnold reaches out to Marguerite but catches nothing but 'void air' because 'a sea rolls between us'. The nature of that barrier now becomes more explicitly defined as: 'our different past.' Arnold realises that Marguerite has had previous sexual experience and is either frightened of this or is censorious. He sees more clearly the gulf between their respective life experiences and, although he can hardly understand the emotional turmoil into which he has been plunged – 'what heart knows another? / Ah! who knows his own?' – he takes refuge from this sexual tension in contemplation of the cold, prelapsarian purity of the high mountain slopes swept by eternal mists: 'In the stir of the forces / Whence issued the world'.

In *A Farewell*, Arnold describes his arrival at Thun by moonlight and, after following the light of her taper across the roofed bridge, his warm embrace of Marguerite: 'Lock'd in each other's arms we stood In tears, with hearts too full to speak.' But she rapidly discerns that something is wrong and Arnold realises, too, that his love is doomed because of his own 'starting, feverish heart' that cannot give what he believes a woman wants: steadiness and constancy of purpose. His heart, he admits: 'To be long loved was never framed; / For something in its depths doth glow / Too strange, too restless, too untamed.' Although he has longed for 'trenchant force' and 'will like a dividing spear' – images that conjure up the powerful certainties of Dr Arnold – the poet has learnt, as he believes Marguerite will come to learn, that such confident strength is 'far, far less rare than love'. Resigning himself to his fate, Arnold holds out the possibility that one day in the future they will achieve a more satisfactory spiritual harmony. It will be one released from sexual tension, a chastened, and a sadder union: 'A sympathy august and pure; / Ennobled by a vast regret.' His choice of the epithet: 'My sister!' to address her in this exalted, future state at once calls to mind his passionate fondness for K and emphasises the sexless moral utopia Arnold is reaching for – one where he can slake 'The thirst for peace a raving world / Would never let us satiate here.'

The next two poems in the sequence continue plangently to sing of this enforced separation. In *Isolation*, Arnold addresses his own heart which, having kept itself constant to Marguerite, while never descending without remorse to 'the place where passions reign', now recovers its original solitude, admitting that perhaps it might have allowed itself to go too far and be 'self-swayed' without reciprocity from Marguerite. The continuation of this poem was originally entitled in 1852 *To Marguerite, in Returning a Volume of the Letters of Ortis*. This was probably Dumas's translation of the Italian Ugo Foscolo's *Ultime Lettere di Jacopo Ortis* (1802) which had been reprinted in 1847. Ortis was a romantic misfit who, like Goethe's Werther, eventually commits suicide in despair. It seems to indicate that Marguerite possessed some literary taste and would be an oddly specific detail to insist on if this love affair was purely fashioned out of Arnold's head.

To Marguerite – Continued is the most beautiful and heartfelt of the sequence and the most well-known:

> Yes! in the sea of life enisled,
> With echoing straits between us thrown,
> Dotting the shoreless watery wild,
> We mortal millions live *alone*.

The return to an image of the sea separating the two lovers – and more specifically the reference to 'sounds and channels' – emphasises that it was the English Channel that interposed between the poet and his 'Daughter of France'. They might otherwise have been 'Parts of a single continent', as Arnold in his later cultural writing wished the English and the rest of Europe to be. It was the lights of France that Arnold saw when he wrote *Dover Beach* soon after – and some have seen another covert address to Marguerite in that poem's final strophe, although it is ostensibly addressed to his new wife. In the present poem Arnold reintroduces the stern God of *Meeting* as the agent who divided the two lovers: 'And bade betwixt their shores to be / The unplumb'd, salt, estranging sea.'

This poem marks the end of the affair but Marguerite did not depart from Arnold's imagination. She lived again in at least three more poems, two of which Arnold included in the 'Switzerland' sequence, and the third, *A Dream*, which was dropped from many of the later editions of his poems. *Absence* is prompted by the new love which followed quickly on the loss of Marguerite – for Frances Lucy Wightman. In her 'eyes of grey', Arnold suddenly sees the eyes of Marguerite and shivers with remembrance of the love he has lost. He tries to 'struggle towards the light' away from the 'Once-longed-for storms of love' but cannot shake off Marguerite's image. He feels her absence powerfully: 'While yet the night is chill, / Upon time's barren, stormy flow, / Stay with me, Marguerite, still!' *The Dream* is a very vivid picture of the poet and a friend called Martin (possibly his friend of early London days, Wyndham Slade, who seems to have accompanied Arnold to Thun on his second trip in September 1849) sailing down 'a green Alpine stream' on a lovely morning. They suddenly catch sight of Marguerite and her friend Olivia as they emerge on to the carved wooden balcony of a riverside dwelling, dressed in white, straw hats on their heads, and decked with flowers and blue ribbons, to wave eagerly to the two young men. It is the sunniest of the Marguerite poems and the most pictorial but the dream ends abruptly with 'the darting river of life' sweeping their boat away and cancelling the ephemeral vision.

The final poem of the 'Switzerland' sequence, *The Terrace at Berne*, was written ten years later but it completes the Marguerite drama. It recalls her, flushed with 'startled pleasure', running quickly through the oleanders of the Hotel Bellevue grounds, and clapping her hands with an intimate 'C'est toi!' to greet her lover. There is a subtle change in her representation here. She has 'flitted down the flowery track' rather too 'lightly', and there is a corresponding gravity in the poet's demeanour towards her. But he is none the less haunted by the possibility that she might still be there, not having returned to France, nor having changed in 'the crucible of time'. The thought, however, that she might have gone sends him back to the metaphor of the sea of life on which we meet and pass 'like driftwood spars'. This really is the end of the affair – for the past and its encounters cannot be recaptured:

> I knew it when my life was young;
> I feel it still, now youth is oe'r.
> – The mists are on the mountains hung,
> And Marguerite I shall see no more.

3

After the affective drama of Switzerland, Arnold returned to a staider, less expansive – if more emotionally tranquil – England and by the end of October was in Oxford where he stayed with Clough for ten days.

Clough had finally taken the irrevocable step that month of resigning his Fellowship. When Arnold went back to London early in November, after what must have been some very serious discussions between the two men on religious questions (did Marguerite crop up in their conversations?), Clough wrote to Tom (with a painful consciousness of what he was throwing away by leaving Oxford, and what might happen if he were forced to emigrate) that severance from Matthew 'might be added amongst the objections I have stated agst quitting England. Friendships are even more precarious than fraternities . . .'[51] In notes made by the Provost of Oriel after an interview with Clough on 18 October, Hawkins, who concluded that Clough felt he 'could not honestly pursue Truth, whilst under the fetters of Subscription to articles', ascertained that Clough had talked to none of the other Fellows about his doubts, 'he had only spoken of his intention to Matthew Arnold'.[52] If Arnold was the only person Clough could confide in about his profound crisis of belief, it seems unlikely that Arnold would not have reciprocated with some candid revelation of the state of his own mind on his return from Thun.

Settled back in London in November at his desk at Lansdowne House – although his employer was laid up with the gout at Bowood Park – Arnold wrote to Clough to give his reactions to the latter's 'long vacation pastoral'. These were not favourable. Arnold had lost patience while at Oxford with the raving of Clough's friends about the poem. Their indiscriminate praise gave Arnold 'a strong almost bitter feeling with respect to them, the age, the poem, even you'. His reaction is a complex blend of professional jealousy (something never absent from the relationship with Clough), recrimination at his rival's synthetic success with an indulgent in-group, aesthetic disapproval of Clough's poetic style, and despair at the failure of the particular historical moment to live up to the high expectations Arnold had of it. The young poet hated the evidence all around him that he was living in a silver age that made the writing of great poetry difficult if not impossible. His later criticism, with its emphasis on the necessity, for great art to be created, of a coming together of the man and the moment, is foreshadowed here. This feeling was tangled up with his annoyance at Clough for producing such a seemingly trivial poem: 'Yes I said to myself,' he told his friend, 'something tells me I can, if need be, at last dispense with all, even with him: better that, than be sucked for an hour even into the Time Stream in which they and he plunge and bellow.'[53] Some allowance, however, must be made for the special, bantering tone of these letters to Clough. To a certain extent

Arnold was consciously striking an attitude in relation to Clough and 'your Zeit Geist'. He is soon expressing a much more practical interest in the press reception of Clough's poem and its interesting use of hexameter which he reports that 'my people at home could not manage'. The critics were more adventurous than the readers at Fox How, and several noticed the distinction of Clough's metre in the *Bothie*.

Arnold and Clough also discussed the poets of an earlier generation. When an edition of Keats's life and letters came out in the autumn of 1848, Arnold was overwhelmed. When he had time to reflect, however, he offered a more critical view of Keats. He would later elaborate this critique in an essay on Keats in which he would accuse him of lacking 'architectonics' or a structure to support his richness of line. 'What harm he has done in English Poetry,'[54] Arnold declared to Clough. Linking Keats to Browning ('a man with a moderate gift') Arnold argued that both of them were too easily overwhelmed with a 'confused multitudinousness' and, lacking in consequence a proper sense of the overall dynamic of a poem – its sense of going somewhere and having a coherent structure – they were unable to achieve 'the truly living and moving' which Keats, at any rate, knew he ought to be striving for. 'They will not be patient neither understand that they must begin with an Idea of the world in order not to be prevailed over by the world's multitudinousness'. At the same time, Arnold could see that he lacked the ability to swallow his own prescription: 'I have had that desire of fulness without respect of the means, which may become almost maniacal: but nature had placed a bar thereto not only in the conscience (as with all men) but in a great numbness in that direction.'

These remarks are the germ of Arnold's famous aesthetic credo expressed in the Preface to his 1853 *Poems*. They are also an early insight into his literary sensibility – its classical rage for order and its abhorrence of the creative anarchy of the unruly imagination which loads every rift promiscuously with ore, but neglects questions of structure that are crucial to the overall shape desired by a finished work of art. Just as in his social and cultural criticism he would seek to impose a centralising narrative of coherence and a firm cultural authority on the 'multitudinousness' of mid-Victorian England, so in his aesthetic theory he was firmly convinced of the need for a classical architecture in the poem to counter its tendency to run riot, to glut itself on the richness of local detail. Arnold did not articulate his first significant critical statement until he was thirty and writing the 1853 Preface, but his emergent thinking is already on view in the letters to Clough. And in his fear of being 'prevailed over' there is a more personal note. Arnold, although he was slowly to abandon orthodox Christianity, if not a generalised religious belief or questing, was always seeking for a centre of authority, a firm hand to correct intellectual or aesthetic or social indiscipline. Equally, in his first love affair he was frightened by the powerful emotions the experience unleashed and which could not be brought to heel. For all his gaiety, for all his pose of urbanity, he was a man never wholly at ease with himself.

At about this time, Arnold wrote the sonnet *To a Friend* (almost certainly Clough) which begins: 'Who prop, thou ask'st, in these bad days, my mind?' It indicates that in the 'bad days' of social unrest in 1848 Arnold was deriving intellectual support and sustenance from Homer, 'clearest-souled of men', the stoic philosopher Epictetus, newly discovered, and Sophocles, who 'saw life steadily and saw it whole' – an aspiration that Arnold would hold to all his life. In particular, Sophocles possessed, unlike the Marguerite poet, an 'even-balanced soul' that life's business could not make dull 'nor passion wild'. Let down by contemporaries, Arnold focused instead on three ancient Greeks whose wise serenity and equable temper offered an imagined refuge from the *Zeit-Geist*.

4

'At last our own Matt's book', exclaimed Clough in a letter to Tom on 26 February 1849, the publication day of the book that finally marked Matthew Arnold's emergence as a poet. *The Strayed Reveller and Other Poems*, which did not bear his name but merely an initial, 'A', came out from his father's old publisher, Fellowes. It was a small, dark green volume, published in a run of 500. The anonymity was preserved even in the copies Arnold sent to his friends which were inscribed merely as 'From the Author'. Not every recipient was sure of its provenance. Clough had already asked Emerson to look out for the book when he wrote to him on 20 February and expectation amongst Arnold's friends was high. Its publication coincided with another book from Clough's circle, Froude's *Nemesis of Faith* which resulted in Froude following Clough into a resignation of his Fellowship.

There were two significant reactions to *The Strayed Reveller* – from friends and critics, and from the Arnold family. The latter, as we have already seen, were taken by surprise by the volume – both in its seriousness and what they saw as its truth to life. Arnold's sister Mary, the eldest after K, himself and Tom, and later an ardent Christian Socialist, saw a fair amount of her brother during 1849 and occasionally breakfasted with him. When she picked up the volume of poems she felt it 'seemed to make me know Matt so much better than I had ever done before. Indeed it was like a new Introduction to him.'[55] She believed that a reading of the poems would inescapably lead one to expect a great deal from its author as one of those 'who have, in some way or other, come face to face with life and asked it, in real earnest, what it means'. This is a characteristic Arnold family reaction, stressing the moral freight of a literary work, rather than its aesthetic quality. Mary believed that this 'practical questioning' of life in the book showed in her brother 'a knowledge of life and conflict that was *strangely like experience*'. She admitted that, with all his natural gifts, this was not the thing she would have expected to find. She returned to the theme in a letter to another member of the family where, confessing that she did not understand all the poems, she none the less repeated that: 'It is the moral strength, or, at any rate, the *moral consciousness*, which struck and surprised me so much in the poems.'[56]

Similar reactions came from K and Mrs Arnold, who wrote to Tom: 'But the little volume of Poems! – that is indeed a subject of new and very great interest.'[57] His mother noted a growing appreciation of the modestly released book and quoted Arnold's own comments to her about the useful lessons he had taken from people's comments on the book. These persuaded Arnold at this stage to abandon the idea of another collection of short poems and to try to get on with his tragedy *Merope* which he noted 'will not be a very quick affair'. The tragedy – to which Arnold remained doggedly loyal even though it was received without enthusiasm and remains today almost unread, if not unreadable – actually came out nearly a decade later, in 1858, after many more 'short poems', including those to Marguerite. As usual, Arnold affected to be *blasé* about the book. 'I think I am getting quite indifferent about the book', he told his mother. 'I have given away the only copy I had, and now never look at them. The most enthusiastic people about them are the young men, of course.' The young men – such as Benjamin Brodie and John Duke Coleridge, fellow members of the Decade, were enthusiastic, as indeed were the professional critics.

But Arnold continued to be very uncertain about his volume. Six weeks after its publication he was telling his mother that he had not heard much about it that he could pass on to her:

> I don't think, whatever Fellowes says, it *écoules* much: anonymousness – miscellaneousness – and the weariness of modern poetry felt generally are all against it. There is a destiny in these things: I mean a set of circumstances against which a merit twenty times greater than mine would be quite in vain. Sooner or later perhaps: but who can say how much good or *promising fragmentary* poetry time has swallowed though not perhaps since the invention of poetry any great poems. Sometimes I feel disheartened by the universal indifference: sometimes I think it is good for me. However time will show.[58]

This moody, restless, letter shows Arnold's tentativeness about publication and about how he was seen as a poet. His complaint – quite ill-founded – about 'universal indifference' exhibits that pardonable vanity that afflicts all young writers: their hunger for the sort of recognition that validates their ambition and tells them that they are right to think they have a vocation and to pursue it. Arnold wanted to be told that he had made the right choice. In the early part of 1849 his health was not good and he even told his mother that he thought he had symptoms of cholera and in consequence could not make Fox How for Easter (although he managed to get to Oxford on 10 April to take part in an Oriel election). Perhaps this accounts for the air of peevishness in his comments around this time. A letter to his mother written a little later, however, after the receipt of some letters of praise for the volume, shows him in a more equable mood: 'as to praise and appreciations tho' one's vanity might desire instant trumpet-blowing in all the newspapers, yet when one considers the slow growth of the reputations of those poets who composed before the invention of printing, & how little outward acceptance they found (except perhaps in extreme old age) owing to their poetry – one may rest well content with all these kind letters within a month after publication and when one is but 26 years old.'[59]

Early in 1849, as the new book of poems was beginning to make its mark, Arnold drew up in his notebook a list of proposed poems for the coming year and beyond. The list, headed simply, 'Comp.—1849' began with the injunction: 'chew Lucretius'.[60] The poem on Lucretius, whom Arnold had first read in 1845, never appeared, in spite of living in Arnold's mind for more than twenty years as a potential *magnum opus*. A few fragments exist, but the thinking or 'chewing' mostly went into *Empedocles on Mount Etna*. Another entry in this list signals the Switzerland sequence: 'Thun & vividness of sight & memory compared: sight would be less precious if memory could equally realize for us.' He also apparently planned a poem on Narcissus and was showing some interest in the topic of mesmerism. Two letters to K at this time touch on his poetic productivity – one enclosed a copy of the poem *Lines Written in Kensington Gardens* and observed: 'I write a good deal easier than I did tho: not much in quantity.'[61] Another, probably at the end of the year when *The Strayed Reveller* had been well-exposed, reveals: 'I have many poetical schemes, but am fermenting too much about poetry in general to do anything satisfactory. My last volume I have got absolutely to dislike.'[62] The evidence of that 'fermenting' is in the exchanges with Clough.

K was an important reader of his poems. 'I have not heard from you, my darling, since you got my book, which I hoped to have done, seeing your intimacy with it and me',[63] he wrote anxiously. He was hoping for a reaction to the poem *Resignation: to Fausta* which was dedicated to her. The intimacy of Arnold with his eldest sister was very pronounced – although some delicacy in reading mid-Victorian terms of family endearment is necessary to avoid the wrong sort of inference – and he often expressed that intimacy with an extravagance that made the bond on occasion seem equivalent in strength of feeling to the marital one. K reciprocated the love but also played the tutelary role of the eldest sister and was not afraid to criticise her brother. She married an earnest Quaker manufacturer and Liberal politician, William Forster, whom Arnold sometimes expressed misgivings about as a politician in spite of his carefully enthusiastic general praise, for K's sake, of William. She was perhaps the most high-minded of the children of Dr Arnold as a letter to Tom, written on 11 April 1849, demonstrates. She had been to Laleham where, in contrast to her brother's tendency to plunge into nostalgia for his childhood haunts, she had been sharply critical of the 'prosaic' Bucklands and their interest in what she contemptuously dismisses as 'money & interest & good society'.[64] The Bucklands drove her to exclaim: 'Thank Heaven that even the driest prose of life is interpenetrated with a poetry, a loftiness not of this earth – that not the triple bolts & bars of civilised life in the nineteenth century can bar out an ever-present God nor sever the bond of brotherhood in Christ which unites us to the whole human family.' Mrs Humphry Ward called her 'one of the noblest personalities I have ever known'[65] who, when she became immersed after her marriage in London political society, was in that world but never truly of it. 'She moved through it, yet veiled from it, by that pure, unconscious selflessness, which is the saint's gift.' No wonder Arnold was anxious about how K would react to his work.

His letter shows him in one of his more positive moods about the book – he seems to have vacillated constantly in his feelings about it – and he reports that Fellowes says it is selling well 'and from a good many quarters I hear interest expressed about it' although at Oxford there is an objection that the subjects are not interesting enough: 'But as I feel rather as a reformer in poetical matters, I am glad of this opposition. If I have health & opportunity to go on, I will shake the present methods until they go down, see if I don't.' Arnold then delivers himself of a famous critical judgement that shows how deeply he thought about the art of poetry rather than simply making an impression as bright new talent: 'More and more I feel bent against the modern English habit (too much encouraged by Wordsworth) of using poetry as a channel for thinking aloud, instead of making anything.' His own practice in the first volume shows the priority he gave to form, to metrical variety, and to the *art* of a poem. In a letter to Clough early in 1849 he deals more extensively than he had ever done before with the nature of poetic form. He finds Clough's new poems, just published in a two-author volume with Clough's Oxford friend, Thomas Burbidge, under the title *Ambarvalia* to be 'not *natural*'.

In spite of the fastening of the Arnold family on the moral matter of poems, Arnold himself was a true enough poet to recognise that no amount of matter could on its own make a poem and that without the necessary shaping medium of form, content was 'merely a superfluity in the Poet *as such*'.[66] He tells Clough that it is not so much a question of 'congruity between conception and expression' but of the form of a poem striking us as inevitable, of its being expressed in the only way possible and therefore of being 'natural'. In view of the hostility that would come to be expressed towards Arnold's later definition of poetry as 'a criticism of life', it is interesting to see in these wonderfully intelligent experiments in criticism contained in the letters to Clough, a clear recognition of the importance to a poem of sheer creative energy and aesthetic freedom.

In a rebuke to Clough's idea-ruled verse, Arnold says:

I often think that even a slight gift of poetical expression which in a common person might have developed itself easily and naturally, is overlaid and crushed in a profound thinker, so as to be of no use to him to help him to express himself. – The trying to go into and to the bottom of an object instead of grouping *objects* is as fatal to the sensuousness of poetry as the mere painting, (for *in Poetry*, this is not *grouping*) is to its airy and rapidly moving life.'

These comments acquire an extra value if we consider how just such a charge was to be brought by later critics against Arnold himself. He was to be accused of letting his intelligence crush the spontaneous poet in him and, even kill off his poetic talent. Here he sees plainly that aesthetic joy and freedom, a poem's 'airy and rapidly moving life' is the one thing needful and that self-conscious profundity does not make for good poems. 'Not deep the poet sees but wide', is the line from his own poem, *Resignation*, that Arnold throws at Clough. Yet the moral element is not sacrificed entirely. Arnold argues that what is valuable in the case of a poet like Sophocles is his style and 'the grand moral effects produced by style',[67] because style 'is the expression of the nobility of the poet's character, as the matter is the expression of the richness of his mind: but on men character produces as great an effect as mind'. He ends this letter, one of several which make the Clough correspondence as important to the history of English aesthetics as the letters of Keats or Hopkins, with a sad reflection on the context of their intense debates about poetry – how '*unpoetical*' the age and all their surroundings are: 'Not unprofound, not ungrand, not unmoving : – but *unpoetical.*'

The first volume contained twenty-seven poems. Of those not already mentioned, the most interesting were the title poem, *The Strayed Reveller, The New Sirens, The Forsaken Merman,* and *Resignation.* The title poem derives from an episode in the *Odyssey* and is strongly influenced by the German poet Heinrich Heine whom Arnold in a later essay was to describe as having 'an extraordinary delicacy of organisation and susceptibility to impressions'.[68] There is a comparable delicacy here in the fleeting impressions recorded and 'The bright procession of eddying forms' glimpsed by the Youth who, after a night's revelling has collapsed on the portico of Circe's palace. He is greeted by Circe's guest, Ulysses, to whom he describes his rhapsodic, partly hallucinatory vision of what the Gods see as they look down to earth. But the poet who sees must pay a price for his knowledge in suffering: 'such a price / The Gods exact for song: / To become what we sing.' The poem, which runs lightly on a metre probably derived from some idea of a Greek measure, fits with Arnold's conflicting feelings at this time about the role of poetry and the loneliness of the true poet in an unpoetic age.

Resignation is addressed to K, and recalls a two-hour summer walk taken in the Lakes ten years previously. It is a Wordsworthian poem of 'emotion recollected in tranquillity' set in the Wordsworth country. 'Those who have been long familiar with the English Lake-Country will find no difficulty in recalling, from the description in the text, the roadside inn of Wythburn on the descent from Dunmail Rise towards

Keswick: its sedentary landlord of twenty years ago, and the passage over the Wythburn Fells to Watendlath', Arnold wrote in a note added to the 1869 edition of his poems. The poet compares this walk with a more recent one in the company of Fausta/K alone. The sights, set out before them in July sunshine, are unchanged, 'and we, you say, / Are scarce more changed than they'. Unlike the gipsies who are part of this summer scene, Arnold muses, the poet has a loftier view of the passage of time and its meaning for human life.

In contrast to *The Strayed Reveller*, with its emphasis on the suffering visionary artist, he is here advocating a more detached view of life and nature as 'A placid and continuous whole' which the poet contemplates with a 'sad lucidity of soul'. Arnold puts into K's head the thought that the poet 'flees the common life of men' and escapes their 'iron round'. He also sees that the world 'outlasts death' and asks Fausta not to blame the man who, through 'natural insight' sees the vanity of human wishes – on the contrary he should be praised for his wisdom. Recognising that, no more than Fausta, does he share this ideal poet's 'rapt security' from human ambition, Arnold none the less enjoins imitation of the natural world they see around them which seems to 'bear rather than rejoice'. No general benefit would accrue to mankind, he concludes, if they were to try to forget 'in action's dizzying eddy whirled' the brute facts of life, the voice of necessity, the 'something that infects the world'. After K had read the poem in the new volume, Arnold advised her: 'Fret not yourself to make my poems square in all their parts, but like what you can my darling. The true reason why parts suit you while others do not is that my poems are fragments, – i.e. that I am fragments, while you are a whole; the whole effect of my poems is quite vague and indeterminate – this is their weakness . . . the poems stagger weakly & are at their wits end. I shall do better some day I hope.'[69]

In spite of the effort of this poem to exhibit a calm, philosophical resignation, Arnold's Oxford friends were sceptical. Froude, in particular, thought it vaguely preposterous for this sheltered 26-year-old to be putting on display a ripened oriental detachment. His comments, in a letter to Clough, represent the most acute insight into Arnold of any of his Oxford friends, and anticipate the devastating later judgement of T. S. Eliot on Arnold: 'He had no real serenity, only an impeccable demeanour.'[70] Froude, like Eliot, thought that Arnold wasn't very convincing as a man who had looked into the abyss: 'I admire Matt – to a very great extent. Only I don't see what business he has to parade his calmness and lecture us on resignation when he has never known what a storm is and doesn't know what he has to resign himself to. I think he only knows the shady side of nature out of books.'[71] Froude was equally perceptive about the poetry: 'Still I think his versifying and generally his *aesthetic* power is quite wonderful. The merest phantoms he can shape into form and make beautiful till you stretch out your mind to hold and feel them . . . There are some things like the Forsaken Merman, that sound right out of the heart.' Carrying no heavy weight of moral reflection or philosophising, *The Forsaken Merman* is probably the most directly appealing poem in the book. The reviewers liked it. So did Palgrave and Tennyson (whose *The Mermaid* [1830] was almost certainly an influence). 'Everyone likes the Merman',[72] the poet told K. Arnold took the story from Hans Andersen's account of a Danish ballad, *Agnes and the Merman*, about a girl wooed by a merman. She bears five children but one day, hearing the church bells, asks to return to land to attend church. But she does not return, in spite of the weeping of her children and the pleadings of the merman. The attraction of the poem is in its music, the repetitions, the incantatory rhythms, the refrains. And the name of the loved one whom the merman loses is Margaret.

During the year Arnold had been developing a biography habit, consuming throughout the summer lives of Byron, Scott, Napoleon, Goethe and Burns. He also finished the *Iliad* (goaded to it no doubt by finding himself, until he had done so, unable to comment on the worth of Clough's translations) and told his mother that he had during 1849 read through 'all Homer's works, and all those ascribed to him'.[73] He also mentioned to her that there was a sonnet of his in the *Examiner* on 'the Hungarian nation' although he casually dismissed it with an 'as it was not worth much I don't send it'. Never reprinted, the poem contains a phrase about 'that madhouse, France', a reference to the bloody putting down of the insurgents in June 1848. By 1849 Arnold was firmly out of his revolutionary phase, as Clough noted to Tom: 'The millennium, as Matt says, won't come this bout.'[74] During the summer Shairp wrote to Clough to tell him that Arnold was working on a poem about Empedocles, which was 'not much about the man who leapt into the crater – but his name and outward circumstances are used for the drapery of his own thoughts'.[75] Shairp was rather out of sympathy with Arnold's classical obsessions and, like Froude, was unconvinced by his philosophic pose of fatalism. 'I wish Matt would give up that old greek [sic] form but he says he despises all the modern ways of going about the art', he reported to Clough. 'Also I do not believe in nor feel with that great background of fatalism or call it what you will which is behind all his thoughts.'

Shairp also reported: 'He goes in Autumn to the Tyrol with Slade.' Wyndham Slade was a barrister friend of Arnold's, an old Etonian and Balliol man then working in the Inner Temple, who was the means of introducing Arnold into a more elevated kind of London society than he was used to. It was Wyndham Slade who pencilled against the poem, *The Voice*, which has been attributed above to Newman (others still have seen it as referring to Marguerite), 'his father'.[76] Wyndham Slade was beginning to understand his new friend and the role his father played in his make-up. Even if his identification was ultimately wrong he must have had some grounds for a reading which assumed a conscious desire on Arnold's part to resist the seductions of his father's voice. The two friends must have set off some time in September for, by the 23rd, Arnold, who makes no reference to a travelling companion, was in Thun again, exactly a year after his first visit. From there he wrote to Clough a striking letter (written in the highly mannered style the two chose for communications between each other and with a carelessness of normal punctuation).

The letter shows that Arnold's presence again in Thun and the renewal of his relationship with Marguerite had once more thrown his emotions into turmoil. It was also making him weary with his poetry and the relentless demands it made on the inner life: 'With me it is curious at present: all intellectual and poetical performance the impatience at being faussé in which drove me some time since so strongly into myself, and more snuffing after a moral atmosphere to respire in than ever before in my life.'[77] Such thoughts have brought him closer to Clough, who remains, for all the tension and difficulty in their relationship, the only person of their 'untoward generation' to whom he can truly unburden himself. He then tries to explain what is troubling him – a mix of intellectual, artistic, and religious uncertainty all bound together, characteristically, by a desire for control:

What I must tell you is that I have never yet succeeded in any one great occasion in consciously mastering myself: I can go thro: the imaginary process of mastering myself and see the whole affair as it would then stand, but at the critical point I am too apt to hoist up the mainsail to the wind and let her drive. However as I get more awake to this it will I hope mend for I find that with me a clear almost palpable intuition (damn the logical senses of the word) is necessary before I get into prayer: unlike many people who set to work at their duty self-denial etc like furies in the dark hoping to be gradually illuminated as they persist in this course. Who also perhaps may be sheep but not of my fold, whose one natural craving is

not for profound thoughts, mighty spiritual workings etc. etc. but a distinct seeing
of my way as far as my own nature is concerned . . .

If there is a sexual problem, too, being addressed in this struggle
towards self-denial and self-mastery, it is not articulated, but in Arnold's
next comment: 'I am here in a curious and not altogether comfortable
state', the location at Thun, and his desire to 'carry my aching head to
the mountains' the following day, point to a local habitation for his
unease. As always, Arnold links the intellectual and artistic problem to
the wider social and cultural context and the failure of the historical
moment to match up to the aspirations of two idealistic young poets:
'My dearest Clough these are damned times – everything is against one
– the height to which knowledge is come, the spread of luxury, our
physical enervation, the absence of great *natures*, the unavoidable
contact with millions of small ones, newspapers, cities, light profligate
friends, moral desperadoes like Carlyle, our own selves, and the
sickening consciousness of our difficulties . . .' Under the Alps,
Arnold has no desire to return to London and its newspapers, and
the pulse of current affairs, which, however exciting, never stimulate 'a
moral feeling'. That Clough shared his friend's sense of moral gravity is
confirmed by a letter he wrote to Tom, a few weeks later, in which he
asked rhetorically: 'Do we not work best by digging deepest? By
avoiding polemics, and searching to display the real thing? If only one
could do the latter. Emerson is an example, and also Matt.'[78]

Leaving Marguerite for good, and in this confused and dejected
state, Arnold returned home. In a letter to K, Arnold's disillusion with
the 'unpoetic age' is seen extending to the people he sees on the streets
of London. His comments are not wholly attractive but may be the
result of trying to flatter the moral correctness of K. He tells her that
'stupidity and hardness of heart' are the two capital faults of what he
calls 'the great people' he sees. 'Their faults of character seem to me, as I
watch the people in the park, to be the grand impairers of English
beauty.' The men, he finds, express 'a stupid pride' and the women are
'half alive' and equally stupid: 'And a proud-looking Englishwoman is
the hardest looking thing I know in the world.'[79] In spite of valiant
attempts to throw himself back into the social whirl and to play the
metropolitan sophisticate at Fox How – where K was startled by his
impact at the end of November: 'Matt *comes the popular man* so strong
when he is in the valley, that he involves us in all sorts of invitations'[80] –
his inner melancholy was merely being disguised.

That melancholy found an echo – or was partly derived from? – the writing of the French Romantic Etienne Pivert de Senancour (1770–1846) whose epistolary novel *Obermann* had an exceptional influence on Arnold. His attention had been drawn to it by George Sand (who wrote an introduction to the 1840 edition Arnold owned) and Sainte-Beuve. The alienation and *ennui* of Obermann – but perhaps too the location of the novel in Switzerland with all its romantic associations for Arnold – made the writer one of Arnold's lasting passions. In a later essay he refers to Senancour's 'profound inwardness, his austere and sad sincerity, and his delicate feeling for nature'.[81] Arnold located the 'severe sincerity' of the writer in his historical moment, a religious sensibility beached on the Enlightenment, a 'bare and bleak spiritual atmosphere'. He describes Senancour in very pertinent terms as a man who felt that 'in the absence of any real inward basis life was weariness and vanity, and the ordinary considerations so confidently urged to induce a man to master himself and to be busy in it, quite hollow'. Arnold was still susceptible to that melancholy sense of being out of joint and had not yet yielded to the injunction 'to be busy'. Although a lesser figure than many in Arnold's early intellectual pantheon, everything the poet says about Senancour speaks of self-identification: 'He was born with a passion for order and harmony . . . concern for the state and prospects of what are called the masses . . . singular lucidity and plain-dealing.' In November 1849 Arnold wrote his *Stanzas in Memory of the Author of Obermann*. In a footnote he explained that it had been 'conceived and partly composed, in the valley going down from the foot of the Gemmi Pass towards the Rhone'. The poem reveals how much Arnold read the Swiss landscape through Senancour's eyes, meditating on his 'wounded human spirit' as he compares him with Wordsworth and Goethe – two other poets of nature who had their own distinctive vision of the world. But Arnold places himself as a modern with fewer of their consolations: 'Too fast we live, too much are tried, / Too harassed, to attain / Wordsworth's sweet calm, or Goethe's wide / And luminous view to gain.' Senancour seems to express 'the hopeless tangle of our age' and to speak to Arnold's divided condition (exacerbated we can assume by troubled thoughts of Marguerite): 'Ah! two desires toss about / The poet's feverish blood. / One drives him to the world without, / And one to solitude.' Accepting that only those who renounce the world can truly understand it, the poet realises that 'I in the world must live.' Yet, in renouncing Senancour's world-hating exile in the Swiss snows, Arnold knows that he is bidding farewell to a part of himself, to Switzerland, to Marguerite, to Romantic freedom and aspiration – and by embracing the world and stifling a part of his sensibility, he is bidding farewell to his life as a poet.

Arnold's public emergence as a poet in 1849, therefore, seems to have done little to sweeten his spirit. As the decade ended and the 1850s began, he was at his lowest ebb, unhappy in love, unsure in his career, unhappy with his writing, and even feeling let down by the age in which he found himself living.

CHAPTER FOUR:
THE BATTLE OF LIFE
[1850–1853]

Though I am a schoolmaster's son I confess that school
teaching or school inspecting is not the line of life I
should naturally have chosen.[1]

1

Nine months after his abandonment of 'Marguerite' in the autumn of
1849, Arnold was reported once again to be in love. During the winter
– very probably in the company of the barrister Wyndham Slade and
at a reception at the home in Eaton Place, Belgravia, of Sir William
Wightman, a judge of the Queen's Bench – he had met the judge's
daughter, Fanny Lucy Wightman. Clough was the first to report the
affair, sending news to Tom that Arnold would be going to Switzerland
in August, following K's wedding to William Forster, and adding: 'He
is himself deep in a flirtation with Miss Wightman, daughter of the
Judge. It is thought it will come to something, for he has actually been
to Church to meet her.'[2] Arnold was indeed in love – and with a very
different woman from the worldly, knowing Marguerite. Clough's
future wife Blanche Smith would later describe Fanny Lucy as 'nice,
but a little Belgravian'[3], a tart confirmation of Fanny Lucy's eminent
respectability. Clough himself impatiently described her as 'churchy'.[4]
Clough's set rather disapproved at first of such a woman for Arnold –
and certainly resented his being taken away from them by the
infatuation. She was an attractive young woman – described by
Arnold's friend George Russell as 'so small, so delicate, so dainty,

that she looked something like a Fairy Queen and something like a Dresden Shepherdess'.[5] Even Clough conceded that she was 'small with an aquiline nose and very pleasing eyes, fair in complexion . . . she seems amiable'.[6]

Biographers have tended to take up this hint and represent Fanny Lucy as prettily fragile – Mrs Humphry Ward refers cloyingly to 'the dear and gracious little lady whom we grandchildren knew as "Aunt Fanny Lucy" '[7] – but there is no reason to think she was anything other than a robust woman who, after all, bore six children, coped with the death of three of them in childhood, and frequently accompanied her husband on European and American travels. Nor was the life the Arnolds led as comfortable materially as the one she was brought up to. It was probably intellectual snobbery that caused Clough to resist her, for he judged her 'entirely free from the taint of letters'. She was also, unlike the members of the Clougho–Matthean set, 'a zealous and consistent High Churchwoman of the Tractarian School'[8] who listened to the High Church sermons at St Paul's, Knightsbridge. The contrast with Marguerite could not be more complete, yet the love was as strong. From the poems Arnold was writing at this time – *Courage, Self-Dependence* or *Youth's Agitations* – we see the last lingering remnants of regret and the sense that youth, with its 'heats' and 'thwarting currents of desire', is slowly yielding to maturity.

The long poem that appears to dramatise the passage from an old to a new love is *Tristram and Iseult*, the first modern treatment of that legend. It was at Thun – in the pages of the *Revue de Paris* – that Arnold first read the story of the knight Tristram who, mistakenly swallowing a love-potion, falls in love with Iseult, daughter of the King of Ireland – although she is intended for his uncle King Marc of Cornwall – and who eventually is forced to leave and marry instead Iseult of Brittany. As Arnold's source puts it: 'it is in vain that he tries to forget his first love'. It is hard not to see Marguerite and Fanny Lucy as 'the two Iseults who did sway / Each her hour of Tristram's day.' The interesting passage from this autobiographical point of view occurs at lines 112–26 where the poem's narrator reflects on how life 'kills in us the bloom, the youth, the spring', taking away the power to feel 'By drying up our joy in everything'. New feelings – 'call it ambition, or remorse or love' – have the power to change us and make us forget what we once felt, making 'All which we did before, shadow and dream'. Arnold's love for Fanny Lucy was his new passion by means of which he hoped to drive out the memory of the old. At the same time, however, the poem suggests that such passions are 'a diseased unrest' that we would be better off without. Once again, Arnold is pursuing the chimera of emotional detachment and freedom from unsettling passions.

Arnold's first public poetic performance of 1850 was actually the poem written to commemorate the death of Wordsworth on 23 April. Published in the June issue of *Fraser's Magazine*, but written at the end of April at the request of Wordsworth's son-in-law Edward Quillinan, the *Memorial Verses* express rather more of panegyric than of Arnold's considered critical view of Wordsworth. Linking the poet to Goethe – whose inferior Arnold thought Wordsworth was – and to his child-hood poetic model, Byron, Arnold says of this triumvirate that, 'The last poetic voice is dumb.' Though Byron 'taught us little' (the first hint of his famous later criticism of the English Romantics which held that they 'did not know enough') the soul of his contemporaries 'had *felt* him'. Goethe, 'Europe's sagest head', is represented as a spiritual healer who put his finger on every weakness of the age, 'And said: *Thou ailest here, and here!*' Wordsworth, too, was a casualty of 'this iron time / Of doubts, disputes, distractions, fears', yet his power was to restore a sense of the world's freshness and primacy: 'He laid us as we lay at birth / On the cool flowery lap of earth.' Arnold fears that the gifts of Goethe and Byron may find new incarnations, 'But where will Europe's latter hour / Again find Wordsworth's healing power?' Strength and fortitude in a difficult period of historical transition may be found in new writers who will give intellectual strength to resist but 'who, will make us feel?'. Wordsworth's power of expressing spontaneous joy in the natural world – which Arnold saw as the essence of his genius – was far less likely to occur again in the modern world. The loss of moral and intellectual cohesion which is the source of the elegiac tone in poems like *The Scholar-Gipsy* and *Dover Beach*, could only be made good, Arnold implies, by the reappearance of a great natural talent like that of Wordsworth, but the poem does not hold out much hope.

Quillinan was satisfied with the poem, though he would clearly have preferred a more Wordsworthian style: 'It is *very* classical', he wrote to Crabb Robinson, 'or it would not be M.A.'s.'[9] Quillinan had perhaps read a recent review in *The Germ* written by William Rossetti which noted that *The Strayed Reveller* exhibited a predilection 'for antiquity and classical association'. Rossetti also found a lack of passion in the volume and gathered that the author 'avows himself a Quietist'. There was too much in the poetry, he implied, of premature world-weariness. Rossetti also inaugurated the critical tradition of finding fault with Arnold's metre and his ear (while noticing the pervasive influence of Tennyson), arguing that in some cases 'the verse might, generally speaking, almost be read as prose' – sounding very much like a present-day critic inveighing against 'chopped-up prose'. He was also very rude about *To a Gipsy Child by the Sea-shore* which he dismissed as 'drawing room sentimentality'.[10] Meanwhile Quillinan was doubting whether in the memorial verses Byron was 'tall enough' to stand comparison with the other two, but he concluded: 'M. Arnold has a good deal of poetry in him; and it will come out in spite of all the heathen Gods and goddesses that hold him in enchantment.' Arnold wrote to Clough when the poem was published to say that he wanted to see him at breakfast as soon as possible: 'as I have at Quillinan's sollicitation dirged W.W. *in the grand style* and need thy rapture therewith'.[11] The tone of this comment suggests that the poem was rather more of an exercise than Arnold would have cared to admit publicly.

In the same letter Arnold is abruptly dismissive of John Henry Newman's brother, Francis Newman (at this stage oblivious of his future role as Arnold's butt in the lectures on Homer) who had just published a theological work called *Phases of Faith*. At Oxford at the height of the Tractarian Movement Arnold had been utterly bored by theological controversy and now expresses himself even more vigorously: 'One would think to read him that enquiries into articles, biblical inspiration, etc. etc. were as much the natural functions of man as to eat and copulate . . . The world in general has always stood towards religions and their doctors in the attitude of a half-astonished clown acquiescingly ducking at their grand words and thinking it must be very fine, but for its soul not being able to make out what it is all about.' Arnold felt that Francis Newman's petty logic-chopping weakened the religious sentiment 'so much that he quite effaces it to me'. The only solution was to look at religion in a much broader perspective 'in conjunction with the grandeur of the world, love of kindred, love, gratitude etc. etc.'

Arnold's distaste for the fine points of theology was partly a function of his mind's natural impatience with detail but partly, as here, the product of a desire to make religion more attractive and compelling in the modern world. Arnold and Clough saw a great deal of each other (and consequently we have fewer letters) during 1850 and 1851 because they were both working in London. In the period up to his marriage in 1851, for example, they breakfasted together at least twice a week.

All this time Arnold's love flowed no more smoothly than Tristram's and by the summer of 1850 his relationship with Fanny Lucy had reached a crisis. The stern judge was unhappy at the continuance of a courtship of his precious daughter by a poet and man-about-town who had nothing but a slim volume of poems and an income of £72 a quarter (and an Oriel Fellowship that would automatically cease on marriage) to show for himself. The sequence of poems 'Faded Leaves' records the temporary thwarting of Arnold's passion. As Tom put it: 'It was not all prosperous sailing in his love, any more than is the case with ordinary mortals, and of one such counterblast which drove him out of England and towards the Alps the lovely stanzas beginning "Vain is the effort to forget" are the record.'[12] Just before Arnold left for the Continent he wrote to Wyndham Slade about an unsuccessful attempt to meet with 'the young lady' (Slade is so familiar with his friend's case that Arnold has no need to identify her): 'Last night for the 5th time the deities interposed: I was asked specially to meet the young lady – my wheels burned the pavement – I mounted the stairs like a wounded quagga, the pulsations of my heart shook all Park Crescent.'[13] Arnold's eyes 'devoured every countenance in the room in a moment of time' but Fanny Lucy was not there. Her mother had, at the last minute, produced for her some tickets to the opera. With an attempt at self-mockery Arnold tells Slade: 'I suffer from great dejection and lassitude this morning – having shown a Spartan fortitude on hearing the news last evening.' Arnold then discussed with Slade the pair's plans for a foreign trip, ruling out Spain because Arnold has to be back at work by 14 October. He was short of funds and hoped to keep his expenditure on foreign travel down to £60 or £70 this year. Suddenly reverting to his elusive love, he exclaims, in the undergraduate *patois* familiar from the letters to Clough: 'How strange about die unerreichbare [unattainable] schöne! To have met her to have found something abstossend [rebarbative], and to have been freed from all disquietude on her account, voila comment je comprends a matter of this kind. But all the oppositiveness & wilfulness in the human breast is agacée by a succession of these perverse disappointments.'

The poems in the 'Faded Leaves' group articulate those 'perverse disappointments' which once again wakened the emotional confusions of the affair with Marguerite. In his diary at this time Arnold referred to Fanny Lucy as 'F-L', also the initials of 'Faded Leaves'. *The River* was written by Arnold in August 1850 and records a boat-trip up the Thames – the judge kept a house by the river at Hampton – in the company of Fanny Lucy. It is early evening with the mellow August sun setting and, unlike the drowsy boat crew, Arnold is alertly gazing on his love, watching her fingers play with the fringes of her shawl and hoping she will desist in order to reveal 'A lovely strip of thy soft throat

/ Gleaming between it and thy hair'. In a surprising detail, Arnold refers to her 'arch eyes' and 'mocking mouth' – characteristics more appropriate to his descriptions of Marguerite. In his confusion, the feelings of his old love mingle with the new and release the same kinds of apprehension. 'Arch' may be a way of expressing the fear of sexual rebuff, of being 'mocked' should he allow himself to lose control. Crouched in the stern of the boat, the anxious lover – now a self-pitying romantic – pleads with her to smile on him, for: 'My heart is swollen with love unsaid. / Ah, let me weep, and tell my pain, / And on thy shoulder rest my head.'

In the same sultry month Arnold wrote *Too Late*, a short poem even more expressive of the halting lover's anxiety. Noting that death can intervene before the opportunity presents itself for lovers to find 'the twin soul which halves their own' the poet also contemplates the calamity of finding such true compatibility too late. Having lost his first love and now experiencing difficulty with his second (or third, if we recall his 'romantic passion' for Mary Claude), Arnold might well have been feeling that he was doomed to eternal failure in affairs of the heart.

The third poem in the sequence expresses the crisis of *Separation*. The judge has put his foot down and the lovers are forbidden to see each other, although Arnold and Fanny Lucy continued to correspond. Addressing his lover, Arnold forbids her at this moment of 'bitter parting' to talk of the healing power of time. If he is to face the inevitability of learning to forget her, he would rather her image was wiped out now: 'Me let no half-effaced memories cumber!' If then he chances to see her again, the old pain, rooted out, will not be there to torment him and he will simply ask: '*Who . . . is this stranger regards me, / With the grey eyes, and the lovely brown hair?*' Such renunciation, of course, was not possible outside the realms of poetic conceit and Arnold continued to suffer. Although it was not included in the 'Faded Leaves' sequence – it was too candid – *Calais Sands* was written in this same month – one remarkable for its poetic productivity – and it records his brief delay, on the way to the Continent, at Calais, hoping to catch a glimpse of Fanny Lucy as she passed through with her father on the way to holiday on the Rhine. The lovelorn poet, 'mixed with the idlers on the pier', longs to have Fanny Lucy with him to view the historic scene ('Which glows as if the Middle Age / Were gorgeous upon earth again'). Her voice would come to him as exquisite, and the sea-breeze would perhaps 'Shake loose some band of soft brown hair'. Instead, he is compelled to scrutinise the horizon where her vessel will soon be seen – 'Oh, that yon sea-bird's wings were mine, / To win one instant's glimpse of thee!' Unable to come forward and greet her because of Sir William Wightman's edict, Arnold has to be content with a far-off glimpse and the consolation that he will be sleeping that night in the same hotel: 'To-night those soft-fringed eyes shall close / Beneath one roof, my queen! with mine.' Arnold could not let her go and evidently pursued her to 'the storied Rhine' instead of making immediately for the Italian lakes as he had planned to do with Wyndham Slade.

'Vain is the effort to forget', begins the fourth faded leaf, *On the Rhine*, as Arnold accepts that he cannot put Fanny Lucy out of his mind, even if 'an iron knot / Ties straitly up from mine thy lot'. The iron knot was the fact of his relatively low income and uncertain prospects as Lord Lansdowne's secretary which were a complete bar on marriage. Trying to summon up the image of Fanny Lucy – 'Those eyes of deep, soft, lucent hue – / Eyes too expressive to be blue, / Too lovely to be grey' – Arnold once again tries for calm resignation. In nature, in the flow of the Rhine and the solidity of the surrounding hills, he sees a tranquillity that, in its geomorphic history, was once 'restless' and turbulent but now: 'Tamed is their turbulent youthful glow; / Their joy is in their calm.' The frustrated passion in this poem, however, is more convincing than its attempt at solace, its talk of 'calm'. The last poem in the sequence, *Longing*, has some of the directness and physicality of the Marguerite poems and is framed by two identical stanzas whose music is charged with Arnold's frustrated longing for Fanny Lucy:

> Come to me in my dreams, and then
> By day I shall be well again!
> For then the night will more than pay
> The hopeless longing of the day.

Two further poems composed at this time but not explicitly forming part of the sequence, appear to deal with Arnold's feelings for his future wife. *Urania* has, however, sometimes been seen as referring to Marguerite, because of its presentation of a mocking or disdainful love. But such characteristics would fit with Arnold's German epithets for Fanny Lucy in the letter to Wyndham Slade quoted above. The companion poem, *Euphrosyne*, is much more surely about her and contains, in its final quatrain, something like a reproach to Fanny Lucy for acquiescing too readily in her father's ban on their meeting: 'It was not love which heaved thy breast, / Fair child! – it was the bliss within. / Adieu! and say that one, at least, / Was just to what he did not win.'

2

'In 1850 great changes came upon the Arnold family', wrote Mrs Humphry Ward.[14] She is referring to the announcements during the year of the engagements of Tom, Willy and K and their marriages. In contrast to their successes in love, Arnold himself was as far from marriage as ever. Shortly after hearing of K's engagement he wrote her a letter (undated but probably written in the early part of 1850) which shows him in a strange mood of depression and unsettlement probably brought about by his difficulties with Fanny Lucy but somehow exacerbated by K's news. Apart from the mannered correspondence with his Oxford friends, Arnold's letters were always bright and lucid, which makes the dishevelled tone of this letter all the more unusual. The fact that half of the last sheet of the manuscript has been torn away – presumably by a member of the family in subsequent years – indicates that its tenor might have been disapproved of. Arnold tells his sister that he has been 'in a kind of spiritual lethargy for some time past, partly from headache, partly from other causes, which has made it difficult for me to approfondir my matter of feeling'.[15] He promises her that when he comes out of his depression she will be 'truly set right in my mind in respect of your engagement'. He is saying this, not to please her, 'but because I really feel it to be the truth at present my objections are not based on reality, that I feel.' The feeling, and the expression, is rather contorted here but Arnold is plainly unhappy at the news of her engagement. It is not clear whether it is the suitability of her future husband or the effect it will have on their special emotional bond that is disturbing Arnold but he is plainly in some distress, referring to his subjection to what he calls 'these periods of spiritual eastwind when I can lay hold only of the outside of events or words – the material cast wind which now prevails has something to do with it, and also the state of strain and uneasiness in which these days and in London it is hard not to live'. But K has the power to act as a salve to this distress:

> You my darling have been a refreshing thought to me in my dryest periods: I may say that you have been one of the most faithful witnesses (almost the only one after Papa) among those with whom I have lived and spoken of the reality of that abiding inward life which we all desire most of us talk about & few possess – and I have a confidence in you & in this so great that I know you will never be false to yourself: and everything merely fanciful & romantic should be sacrificed to truth.

Here the letter is interrupted. On the reverse of what is left of the last sheet someone is reported congratulating Arnold on the fact that his sister is going to marry their cousin. 'Quelle bêtise', growls Arnold before signing off: 'Adieu, darling!'

By the time of his next letter to K, on 11 May, Arnold has recovered his poise and is talking not of his spiritual eastwind but the familiar topic of the shortcomings of English culture. England, he tells K, 'has fallen so far behind the continent that we cannot expect to see her assisting to carry on the intellectual work of the world from the point to which it is now arrived: for to what point it is arrived not 20 English people know: so profoundly has acting in this country extirpated reflexion'.[16] Against this background Arnold resolves to soldier on 'thankful for the circumstances that have made me alive to the necessity of somehow getting my head above the present English atmosphere in seeking to accomplish anything permanent'. K's actual marriage to William Forster was delayed by a serious illness which necessitated her mother coming to London to be with her. Mrs Arnold wrote to another member of the family during this visit: 'Matt has been with us almost every day since we came up – now so long ago! [Mrs Arnold did not relish a prolonged stay in the capital away from Fox How] – and it is pleasant indeed to see his dear face, and to find him always so affectionate, and so unspoiled by his being so much sought after in a kind of society entirely different from anything we can enter into.'[17]

During one of these social events at which Mrs Arnold would not have been present – a breakfast with Clough on the morning of 24 July – Arnold told his friend of another engagement, that of Tom, who was married later in the year in Hobart, Tasmania, to Julia Sorell. William Delafield or 'Willy' was also married this year at Lahore in the Punjab so Arnold was to see his eldest sister and his two younger brothers achieve the state that seemed denied to him. Willy, who was married in October, wrote to Tom in one of those chaffing Arnold family letters which can bring to mind a modern family of progressive *Guardian* readers teasing each other about supposed lapses from political correctness: 'I wonder whether it has changed you much? – not made a Tory of you, I'll undertake to say! But it is wonderfully sobering. After all, Master Tom, it is not the very exact *finale* which we should have expected from your Republicanism of the last three or four years, to find you a respectable married man, holding a permanent appointment!'[18] K's marriage eventually took place in August, a quiet wedding in Rydal Chapel in Ambleside with the bride, in a simple dress, given away by her eldest brother, Matthew.[19]

After the marriage, and his flight to the Continent, Arnold paid another visit to Rugby. From there he wrote to Clough, trying to disguise by the playfulness of his manner the still unsettled state of his mind. He quoted in German a letter from the correspondence between Goethe and F. H. Jacobi where the latter expresses 'a secret unconquerable disgust with myself'.[20] 'I thought of you', says Arnold airily. He reveals that he is reading Locke's *Essay Concerning Human Understanding*: 'my respect for the reason as the rock of refuge to this poor exaggerated surexcited humanity increases and increases. Locke is a man who has cleared his mind of vain repetitions, though without the positive and vivifying atmosphere of Spinoza about him. This last, smile as you will, I have been studying lately with profit.'

Arnold returned to Fox How in December for his usual Christmas visit. One of the first things he did on arrival was to write to the woman he was not allowed to see. He told Fanny Lucy that he had journeyed through wind and snow, arriving at Fox How early in the morning after the last six-mile stage from Windermere 'like an icicle'. Only Mrs Arnold and Fan were at home and on his first day he listened to family letters being read out, chatted, read Bacon's *Essays*, and wrote a little. At this time he was writing to Fanny Lucy every day and over the next month or two the frequency increased to two or even three times a day.[21]

On Saturday 21 December two visitors came to Fox How: the radical writer and freethinker, Harriet Martineau, and the novelist Charlotte Brontë. Arnold was amused at his neighbour Harriet Martineau's unconventionality and in the account he gave Fanny Lucy reported that she 'blasphemes frightfully'.[22] He succumbed to an invitation to inspect her experimental farm, adding breezily: 'I, who hardly know a cow from a sheep'. Charlotte Brontë, on the other hand, he found to be 'past thirty and plain, with expressive gray eyes though'. The novelist had her own opinions of Arnold, expressed three weeks later in a letter to James Taylor. She conceded that he was 'striking and prepossessing in appearance' but from the perspective of Haworth Parsonage his general demeanour was not approved of: 'his manner displeases from its seeming foppery', she noted. But at the same time 'a real modesty appeared under his assumed conceit, and some genuine intellectual aspirations . . . displaced superficial affectations.'[23] To complete the portrait she noted: 'I was given to understand that his theological opinions were very vague and unsettled.' The basis of Charlotte Brontë's 'regretful surprise' was the contrast of this insouciant young man with his earnest father: 'the shade of Dr Arnold seemed to me to frown on his young representative . . . Most unfortunate for him, doubtless, has been the untimely loss of his father.'

Arnold's letter to Fanny Lucy hints at the change that was to come when he tells her that his old Balliol tutor, Richard Lingen, now Education Secretary, 'and a genius of good counsel to me ever since', says he is going to write him a letter of advice about inspectorships, 'applying to Lord Lansdowne, etc'. The means of Arnold's deliverance – or at any rate the means of his being able to marry – were about to be furnished.

3

Arnold's new year resolution for 1851 was to write to K 'about the end of every month'. His first letter of the year, on 25 January, reflects on how the onset of maturity involves us 'narrowing and narrowing our sphere, and diminishing the number of affections and interests which continually distract us while young'.[24] Arnold was only twenty-eight but he begins to sound like a man starting to bid farewell to his youth and resigning himself to a 'very confined and joyless' state. He was still kicking against this fate, however: 'The aimless and unsettled, but also open and liberal state of our youth we *must* perhaps all leave and take refuge in our morality and character; but with most of us it is a melancholy passage from which we emerge shorn of so many beams that we are almost tempted to quarrel with the law of nature which imposes it on us.' Arnold felt the noose tightening. In order to marry he would have to take up a more secure career which would put an abrupt stop to his bachelor breakfasts, parties, and Continental wanderings. Famous as the Arnold family was, it was typical of the new age in having no independent means or sinecures of the kind that might have supported an earlier intelligentsia. An early member of 'the chattering classes', Arnold knew that he would have to work to sustain his intellectual pursuits and that the life of the man of letters in the nineteenth century was one that could not be pursued as a self-sustaining profession unless one was – what he always insisted he could never be – a popular writer with the rising mass public.

But in accepting the inevitable choices forced on him by maturity,

Arnold was determined, from the first few months of her marriage, not to let them create a gulf between him and K. He set out the problem to her whilst at the same time promising to 'make war' against the tendency it described: 'I am by nature so very different from you, the worldly element enters so much more largely into my composition, that as I become *formed* there seems to grow a gulf between us, which tends to widen until we can hardly hold any intercourse across it.' This letter is quickly followed by another in which he reports that he is burying himself in the literature of the past and rejecting modern literature ('which is all only what has been before and what will be again, and not bracing or edifying in the least'). Nor has he looked at the newspapers for months. Current affairs strike him as 'quite historical' – mere replays of what has already been. He does, how- ever, find time to read Goethe's letters to Lavater which belong to the German poet's 'impulsive youthful time',[25] the time which Arnold sees slipping from his grasp. This pose of rejecting the modern world may well have been another example of Arnold trying to please K and play down, for her benefit, his 'worldly element', for three weeks later he is giving Fanny Lucy a remarkably detailed blow-by-blow account of the difficulties of Lord John Russell's ministry. This administration, which would survive for only another year, had just been beaten by the Radicals in a vote to enlarge the franchise, a failure which made their weakness 'fearfully apparent'.[26] There was no certainty that Lord Lansdowne would survive the political crisis as Arnold judged that 'The old set of Whigs can never come in again.' His position as Lansdowne's secretary might thus appear a little vulnerable. Arnold reported all this political infighting in close detail to Fanny Lucy, which rather makes nonsense of those representations of her as a prettily vacuous 'Tory belle' or Dresden shepherdess. The next month Arnold signed what was one of his last letters as Lansdowne's secretary – a reply to James Penchey, a petitioner to the Lords for the enfranchisement of copyholders, a measure which the secretary was able to assert his employer was 'very favourably disposed towards'.[27] Lord Lansdowne, doing what he liked best, had swung an appointment for his secretary as an inspector of schools that would enable him to marry. After being told the news by Lansdowne, Arnold went to the judge at his chambers on 7 March and 'settled our engagement'.[28] Clough wrote to Tom in New Zealand: 'I am not [married]; nor even engaged; though "the good they fall around us," and the bad too, Matt included.'[29]

Arnold did not actually take up his appointment until 11 October (it had been gazetted on 15 April) and spent the spring preparing for his marriage on 10 June. Twice in the month of May he walked secretly to Eaton Place 'to see Flu at the window'[30] and on the 16th Clough, who was feeling rather left out, reported ruefully to Tom that 'old friends have to make their graceful withdrawal' at such times. 'I consider Miss Wightman as a sort of natural enemy,' he said lightly. 'How can it be otherwise – shall I any longer breakfast with Matt twice a week?'[31] Clough none the less tried to give Tom a fair report of Fanny Lucy: 'Miss Wightman, you will like to know, is small with aquiline nose, and very pleasing eyes, fair in complexion – I have only seen her, however, in her bonnet. I think she will suit well enough; she seems amiable, has seen lots of company and can't be stupid.' From a member of the Clougho-Matthean set, this can probably be taken as high praise.

In spite of Arnold's excited anticipation of marriage to Fanny Lucy, and his moonlit watches in Eaton Place, there was still K to be taken into account. He was upset to hear that she had been unwell, perhaps a recurrence of the illness just before her marriage, and, a month before his own wedding, he wrote to her: 'Seldom as I write to her and cold as my tone often is I never think of my K in weakness or suffering without remembering that she has been to me what no-one else was, what no-one else ever will exactly be again unless indeed we were both to lose what we have dearest and then we should be drawn together again, I think, as in old times.'[32] From someone just about to be married to someone nine months married this is a striking demonstration of the power of their brother–sister love. Arnold goes on to discuss Tom's marriage to Julia Sorell and to speculate about their relations. 'I dare say there is no very deep reaching sympathy between them', he suggests, meaning to point a contrast in his feelings for Fanny Lucy, or as he now starts to call her, in affectionate diminutive, 'Flu'. Shading a little into sentimentality, Arnold tells K: 'Neither Flu nor my much maligned and adamantine self could feel anything but love to you in return for loving her and she is so loveable. I am more inclined sometimes to cry over her than anything else: it is almost impossible to be soft and kind enough with her.' Arnold had much to learn about relations with the opposite sex but the simple primary affection was clearly there.

Four days after the wedding – attended by Arnold's old friends Clough, Walrond, Slade, John Blackett, later MP for Newcastle, Edward Arnold, and some members of the Buckland clan – Clough sent Tom the briefest of chronicles: '. . . Matt is married . . . Nobody cried; Matt was admirably drest, and perfectly at his ease. It rained but we did well enough – they went off before breakfast – where old Croker [the Tory John Wilson Croker, who notoriously savaged

Keats's *Endymion* in the *Quarterly Review* in 1818 and was a long-standing friend of the judge] sat cum Judice. She seems, as Matt calls her, a charming companion.'[33] Judge Wightman was sufficiently won over now to grant the couple £100 a year, a practice he continued, in the shape of quarterly payments, until his death in 1863. Combined with gifts from other relatives, and added to the £700 a year salary as an inspector (made up of a basic salary of £450, travelling expenses of 15s a day, and actual disbursements for railway and carriage fares[34]) the young couple's immediate prospects were good. They had only a brief honeymoon of a few days at Dover before returning to London. The honeymoon proper would start on 1 September.

One moonlit evening, during that brief stay at Dover, Arnold stood at his hotel window and looked out on the calm sea and the lights of the French coast. Flu was with him in the room and came to the window to look at the scene and catch the sweet night air. Arnold's most famous poem, *Dover Beach*, records this moment, although it seems that he first wrote the concluding section which begins: 'Ah, love, let us be true / To one another . . .' on this occasion, adding the earlier lines on his return to London where they were composed on the back of some old notes he had made on Greek philosophy for his poem on Empedocles – not the sort of material he would have brought with him on his brief pre-honeymoon. It is not difficult to see why this is Arnold's best loved poem. Its plain feeling and elegiac music make an immediate impact. In the first few lines we are with him on that warm June night looking out across the English Channel, seeing the intermittent light on the French coast, the cliffs guarding the tranquil bay, and the waves breaking on the 'moon-blanched' shore. Notwithstanding the calm beauty of the scene witnessed by a young man with his new wife at his side, he invests it with a sombre recognition of 'the eternal note of sadness' sounded by the tide's ebb and flow. Like Sophocles looking out on the Aegean, Arnold sees expressed in that note of sadness 'the turbid ebb and flow / Of human misery'. For moderns, the 'Sea of Faith' which once surrounded them no longer comforts, and in consequence all that Arnold can hear is: 'Its melancholy, long withdrawing roar.' The third and final movement of the poem tries to reconcile the beauty of the world with which the poem opened and the melancholy truth into which it deftly led us, by the bridging mechanism of human love. Loving each other is the only certainty we can hold to in a world bereft of faith's traditional sureties. The world itself – so full of surface delight – is actually illusory and when the mask is stripped away there is only anarchy and confusion:

Ah, love, let us be true
To one another! for the world, which seems
To lie before us like a land of dreams,
So various, so beautiful, so new,
Hath really neither joy, nor love, nor light,
Nor certitude, nor peace, nor help for pain;
And we are here as on a darkling plain
Swept with confused alarms of struggle and flight,
Where ignorant armies clash by night.

The poem, with its memorable image of the battle by night (derived from Thucydides' description of the Battle of Epipolae), has come to symbolise the Victorian loss of faith, the sense that what had always been believed had started to disintegrate, and that there was now no sure guide on the way ahead. Although Arnold did appear to lose faith in orthodox Christianity, he remained an unorthodox Christian and a church-goer and a writer on theological subjects for the rest of his life. Two paradoxes about Arnold are suggested by *Dover Beach*. Firstly, here was a young man, happily married, on his honeymoon, with his 'Bliss at hand', alive to the spectacle of the world as 'a land of dreams', yet brooding on the most melancholy and joyless thoughts when he ought to have been full of elation at being with Flu at last. Secondly, the contrast between the plangent sadness of Arnold's poetry and the vivacity and playfulness of his social manner and of his writings in prose could not be more marked. Not only did he fail to introduce into his poetry the liveliness of his other self – he seems to have been constrained by his notions of the appropriate subject-matter for serious poetry – but in his prose he was combative, confident, purposeful, convinced that there were useful things to be said and done. Defeatism or despair were entirely absent from his prose which, throughout the 1860s and 1870s, was to soar at the same time as his poetic gift declined.

Back in London at the beginning of July Arnold wrote to Tom to tell him about his marriage 'which happened on the 10th of last month'. The family had apparently forgotten to tell Tom. He found out about his brother's marriage in a letter from a relative which had arrived in Tasmania with the mails on a prison ship. Arnold was trying to give Tom some career advice, as usual, and warns his brother about coming home in the expectation of getting a teaching job at Oxford. The only place where he could imagine Tom getting a place would be as a Rugby master – 'the most hideous and squalid of occupations'.[35] In fact, Arnold reveals that he is rather envious of Tom and would himself like to have tried the colonies. He explains why he was 'obliged to get something permanent' in order to marry but he is clearly not enthused about his inspectorship: 'I should greatly have preferred to go to the colonies myself – that is to the warm ones – not the American or Australian ones – as colonial secretary or some such thing: but if it had been possible, the young lady's father would not have allowed it.' Arnold does not manage to name 'the young lady' in this studiedly offhand account of his marriage but adds: 'They will have told you from Fox How who she is, but hitherto only Susy [the seventh Arnold child, later Mrs Cropper] has seen her. We are living at present up at Hampstead.' Arnold was still with Lord Lansdowne in spite of the appointment and was not due to receive the inspector's salary until his period of service as private secretary was completed in the summer.

Before starting on his new career, Arnold and his wife now embarked on a proper honeymoon, leaving on 1 September for France, Switzerland, and Italy. The only record we have of this is the poem *Stanzas from the Grande Chartreuse*, written some time later, but prompted by a visit to the Carthusian monastery of the Grande Chartreuse in France on Sunday 7 September. The poem describes the couple's autumnal ride up to 'the Carthusians' world-famed home' where, in the quiet cloisters 'ghostlike in the deepening night, / Cowled forms brush by in gleaming white'. Arnold was always intrigued by Catholicism, in spite of teasing Tom about his 'Popish practices' when the latter converted, and showed none of the hostility towards it that so animated his father. But here he feels alienated from the traditional sanctity of the Carthusian monks: 'For rigorous teachers seized my youth, / And purged its faith, and trimmed its fire, / Showed me the high, white star of truth . . .' In other words, he is emancipated by new developments in thought from traditional Christianity. Yet he is fascinated by the continuation of the monastic tradition, its anachronistic survival. His own, more complex, modern fate is to be: 'Wandering between two worlds, one dead, / The other powerless to be born, / With nowhere yet to rest my head.' Arnold felt strongly this limbo state of having shaken off outmoded ways of thinking but not yet having seen the new clear way. Nor was the emancipation yielding its expected dividend of unburdened calm – 'Say, is life lighter now than then?' Arnold's melancholy, 'sciolists say, / Is a past mode, an outworn theme' but it lives with him none the less. A future generation might enjoy the fruits of enlightenment but those in a state of transition pay an inevitable price and cannot be wholly free so: 'while we wait, allow our tears'. Arnold is also feeling the tension between the attractions of the contemplative life and the insistent call to the active life that the Victorian age made to him and that his new career, which he would be starting in barely a month, would come to symbolise.

Four days after he started work as an inspector – covering much of Wales and the North West and the Midlands – Arnold wrote manfully from the Oldham Road Lancasterian School in Manchester to Flu: 'I think I shall get interested in the schools after a little time.'[36] All tender melancholy put behind him, Arnold's first comments on his new job show a practical understanding of the schools and a sense of the context of his activities. In contrast to his father, whose career as an educational reformer was confined entirely to one major public school educating a small upper tier of the privileged members of his society, Arnold's work as an inspector and a writer on educational matters was exclusively concerned with the cause of universal compulsory State education. In his first week, therefore, he told Flu that the effects of the new elementary schools (which had started to receive public money only since 1833) would be 'immense' and their future effects in 'civilising the next generation of the lower classes, who, as things are going, will have most of the political power of the country in their hands'[37] would be so important. He admired the commitment to education of the Manchester cotton manufacturers and their egalitarian approach 'not confined, as in the schools of the richer classes, to the one or two cleverest boys'. But at the same time Arnold recognised that he had taken on a tough assignment after the undemanding years with Lord Lansdowne. Like many a young writer he dreamed of the success that would free him from the drudgery of desk work. 'We shall certainly have a good deal of moving about; but we both like that well enough, and we can always look forward to retiring to Italy on £200 a year', he bravely told Flu, adding: 'I intend seriously to see what I can do in such a case in the literary way that might increase our income.' Brave, but forlorn, for Arnold never won that emancipation and was a Government official for the rest of his life.

What exactly did Arnold do as an inspector of schools for those thirty-five years? Apart from three separate overseas missions to report on how things were done differently in Continental schools, Arnold's principal activity was visiting elementary schools which, since 1839, had required inspection as a precondition of their grants being maintained. In 1846 the Committee of the Privy Council which was responsible for education had established a system of training 13- to 18-year-old pupil-teachers which meant that an inspector would carry out oral and written tests of pupils and pupil-teachers. The inspector also supervised qualifying examinations for pupil-teachers at training colleges and Arnold spent a week every December administering these examinations at colleges like that at Borough Road, in North Southwark. When Arnold was appointed there were about twenty inspectors covering between them about 4,000 schools. Church of England and Catholic schools were inspected by clergymen of those denominations so Arnold saw only pupils at the Nonconformist Wesleyan and 'British' schools, although after the 1870 Education Act, all schools were subject to State inspection. In view of the outspoken views Arnold was later to express on English Dissent it is worth noting that his strictures, fair or not, were derived from first-hand experience.

Arnold's initial territory as an inspector was large but over the years it narrowed until he was left with a very convenient area of central London. He seems not to have been a terribly rigorous inspector, according to Sir Joshua Fitch, the Chief Inspector of Training Colleges who in 1897, twenty years after Arnold recruited him as Principal of the Borough Road Training College, wrote a study of the influence on English education of Arnold *père et fils*. 'If he saw little children looking good and happy, and under the care of a kindly and sympathetic teacher, he would give a favourable report', wrote Fitch, 'without inquiring too curiously into the percentage of scholars who could pass the "standard" examination.'[38] Arnold was less interested than he might have been in the minute detail of the curriculum or in what we would now call educational theory.

There was a flavour of enlightened amateurism about his excursions into the schools. 'He valued the elementary schools rather as centres of civilization and refining influence than as places for enabling the maximum number of children to spell and write, and to do a given number of sums without a mistake', noted Fitch. Partly for this reason he was bitterly opposed to the later Government policy of 'payment by results' where narrow and rigid testing for each pupil was applied by inspectors to the detriment, as Arnold saw it, of the broader aims of a school. Just as his father saw schools as factories for the production of 'Christian gentlemen' so Arnold saw the end product of the State elementary school as the cultured citizens of a new democracy. The curriculum was a detail.

In later years, Arnold acquired an assistant, Thomas Healing, whose help he valued greatly, not least because Healing did not share his impatience with specifics. 'He never pretended to be an oracle in methods of instruction', observed Healing, 'and therefore never attempted to prescribe to teachers the precise methods they should use'.[39] Ready as he was to give teachers free rein in their methods,

Arnold could be severe in his criticism of textbooks. Many such elementary school books, according to Thomas Healing, were rewritten as a result of Arnold's strictures.

In a speech made on his retirement, Arnold recalled these first days as an inspector: 'My wife and I had a wandering life of it at first. There were but three lay inspectors for all England. My district went right across from Pembroke Dock to Great Yarmouth. We had no home; one of our children was born in a lodging at Derby, with a workhouse, if I recollect right, behind and a penitentiary in front. But the irksomeness of my new duties was what I felt most, and during the first year or so this was sometimes almost insupportable.'[40] What made this ordeal more supportable was growing to know at first hand the teachers – who worked harder and were paid less than him. 'I saw them making the best of it; I saw the cheerfulness and efficiency with which they did their work, and I asked myself again, How do they do it?' Chastened by these reflections, Arnold developed the habit of putting himself in their place and tried to 'enter into their feelings, to represent to myself their life'. He claimed that this effort of identification made him both fair and sympathetic to the teachers, and from them, it is fair to say, we have only positive reports. 'Seeing people once a year is not much, but when you have come into sympathy with them they do not fade from your mind', he told his audience of teachers. Arnold developed long-lasting friendships as he went around the country and his arrival was often keenly anticipated by a school. The Welsh MP William Jones, who started his career as a schoolteacher, recalled in 1913 Arnold's inspectorial visits and their talks together about literature.[41] On these occasions Arnold enthused about William Hale White who wrote, under the pseudonym Mark Rutherford, novels that, from within the tradition of English Dissent rather than from Arnold's position of mocking vantage, anatomised that culture of English provincial nonconformity that Arnold knew but could never learn to love.

On 2 December 1851, Arnold wrote to Flu from the Queen's Hotel, Birmingham – a city which he thought 'next to Liverpool, the finest of the manufacturing towns'. He complained to his wife: 'I have had a hard day. Thirty pupil teachers to examine in an inconvenient room, and nothing to eat except a biscuit, which a charitable lady gave me'.[42] In spite of the oppression to his spirit of these early inspecting days he was responding a fortnight later to Clough's request for help in getting a similar post. Arnold had already written him a glowing, if not hyperbolic, reference for the post of head of a college at Sydney in

Australia[43] the previous week and now he urged him to get on with making his approaches for an Inspectorship: 'We are growing old, and advancing towards the deviceless darkness: it would be well not to reach it till we had at least tried *some* of the things men consider desirable'.[44] The year came to a close with a family visit to Fox How where Arnold wrote a few *Stanzas in Memory of Edward Quillinan*, Wordsworth's son-in-law, who had just died.

4

If Tom had been late getting the news of Arnold's marriage he was equally late in getting to hear of his brother's progress in his new career. Seizing on a reference in a Fox How letter to Arnold's being off on an inspecting tour, Tom asked: 'Tell me; has he renounced literary aims? does he regard his Inspectorship as a permanent role? or what does he hope for and look forward to?'[45] We do not have Mrs Arnold's reply to these highly pertinent questions but we can say with confidence that he had not 'renounced literary aims'. In spite of the pressures of work, Arnold was still writing poetry.

On 4 January 1852, the last day of the Christmas and New Year break at Fox How, Arnold took a solitary walk along Rydal Water and Grasmere, while the others were at afternoon service. The following day he would be in a train bound for Crewe to start a heavy schedule of duties in the Midlands but for now he relished the 'windy, bright day'[46] and the opportunity to savour the Lakes for a few more hours. From his diary entry – 'finished Wordsworth; pindaric' – we know that on this day he finished *The Youth of Nature*.

The poem recalls a visit Arnold made to the Lake District in June 1850 with Wyndham Slade. The pair stayed in a little inn at the end of Wastwater,[47] only a matter of weeks after the death of Wordsworth. The poem begins, characteristically, with water and moonlight, and is a reflection on Wordsworth and the endurance of the natural features he described: 'For he lent a new life to these hills.' Arnold does not disguise the facts of Wordsworth's increasing political reaction and hatred of democratic reform – 'He grew old in an age he condemned' – and compares him in this to 'the Theban seer' Tiresias. Although

Arnold, like his father, did not share Wordsworth's latter-day High Tory politics he regrets that the 'sacred poet' is gone who was 'a priest to us all'. Arnold asks whether the natural beauty that surrounds him is a function of being described by a poet or whether it is intrinsic, needing no poet's words to move those who witness it. Nature replies that the latter is the case and even a great poet like Wordsworth is 'less than his themes', particularly when, towards the end, he had lost much of his poetic power. The poet cannot recreate the actuality of nature – the living presence, for example, of Marguerite who seems hinted at in nature's challenge: 'Canst thou paint the ineffable smile / Of her eyes as they rested on thine?' Succeeding generations have thought they could fix nature in some artistic medium or make it their own but now: 'They are dust, they are changed, they are gone! / I remain.'

A little later in the year Arnold composed a companion piece, *The Youth of Man*, altogether more sombre and reflecting Arnold's growing sense that his youth was fading – and with it his poetic gift. Nature is now a backdrop to the fact of human mutability and Arnold pleads with it not to leave him to 'grow old in darkness and pain'. The second half of the poem – later printed separately as *Richmond Hill* – is set in the garden of Judge Wightman's house at Hampton-on-Thames where Arnold was a frequent visitor with Flu. Children are playing on the lawn and their parents, on this summer evening, are stirred in watching them by 'Airs from the Eden of youth'. They glimpse, in a chastened moment of self-knowledge, the 'weary, unprofitable length' of their 'faded, ignoble lives'. This is a bleak poem which can end only by urging youth to 'Yearn to the greatness of Nature' and 'Rally the good in the depths of thyself' before succumbing to the inevitable sterility of age. Arnold was still only twenty-nine but he seems to have reached a Stoic acceptance that his youth was over.

The Monday morning after completing *The Youth of Nature*, Arnold was at the railway station at Windermere on his way to Crewe. On Tuesday he started to inspect a school at Audley, and for the rest of the month visited Boston-on-Humber, Derby, Wednesbury, Cheadle, Shrewsbury, Edgbaston, Birmingham, Burslem, Burton-on-Trent, Loughborough, Melton Mowbray and Nottinghamshire. School managers greeted him at Dissenting schools with names like The New Jerusalem Church Day School, the Graham Street Protestant Dissenting Charity School or the Church of the Saviour School. He must have had plenty of cause to try to rally the good in the depths of himself that January as he rattled about the wintry railway towns of Victorian middle England.

Back in London in March, Arnold took Flu to a box at the Lyceum Theatre, where they met Clough briefly. The following night, before setting off again on an inspecting tour in the morning, they met Clough again at the Blacketts'. That night Clough wrote to his fiancée Blanche Smith complaining at this small ration of his old friend. 'Considering that he is my most intimate friend (or has been) it is not a great deal to have seen of him during the ten days that he has been here and hereabout, – to have spent an hour with him at a theatre last night; with perhaps a couple of hours more this evening at a party?'[48] Perhaps Arnold simply wanted to see as much as he could of Flu, after those wretched solitary hotel rooms. She accompanied him on some of his early inspecting tours but, already pregnant with her first child due in July, it is unlikely that she had done so on this occasion. Arnold in fact wrote to Clough on 9 April from Cheltenham claiming that he was the one being neglected. Clough had apparently failed to turn up to an occasion at the judge's house in Eaton Place and 'I did not know what had become of you.'[49] With a playfully assumed dictatorial manner, Arnold instructed Clough to come and see him at Derby – which seems to have been a frequent base for Arnold's inspecting activities – saying that he would foot the bill.

The mandatory levity did not conceal a note of resignation in Arnold's new life. 'I have a real craving to see you again', Arnold told Clough – for their friendship recalled youth and poetry and freedom, not the demands of Bradshaw's railway timetable. 'How life rushes away, and youth,' he exclaimed. 'One has dawdled and scrupled and fiddle faddled – and it is all over.' Yet behind this slightly premature world-weariness was emerging a more attractive and practical wisdom. Writing to Clough from one of his schools at Edgbaston in early June, Arnold tried to give Clough some more career advice – the job at Sydney not having been given to him – and reflected that 'a great career is hardly possible any longer – can hardly now be purchased even by the sacrifice of repose dignity and inward clearness'.[50] Arnold said that he was more and more convinced that 'the world tends to become more comfortable for the mass, and more uncomfortable for those of any natural gift or distinction' – adding, in anticipation of such an observation sounding rather arrogant and Olympian, that 'it is well perhaps that it should be so – for hitherto the gifted have astonished and delighted the world, but not trained or inspired or in any real way changed it – and the world might do worse than to dismiss too high pretentions, and settle down on what it can see and handle and appreciate'.

Arnold was at once coming down to earth and writing a practical manifesto for himself. 'I am sometimes in bad spirits', he told Clough, 'but generally in better than I used to be.' None the less, he saw in 'the air of the present times' a lack of proper sustenance and was convinced that 'we deteriorate in spite of our struggles – like a gifted Roman falling on the uninvigorating atmosphere of the decline of the Empire'. Summoning up all the energy of his best self, Arnold concluded: 'Still nothing can absolve us from the duty of doing all we can to keep alive our courage and activity.' This is an unconventional heroism – the word seems a just one – for the attempt to play a practical part in life yet at the same time to sacrifice none of one's artistic or intellectual ambitions, forcing them to survive in an uncongenial climate, is easily undervalued. Arnold was not a sufficiently popular writer to be able to play the part of the poet full time, but in spite of the demands of his job he did not give up. He produced, the hard way, a major body of work. He is the patron saint of those who have struggled to do serious intellectual work at the same time as holding down a conventional job.

On 6 July Flu gave birth to their first child who was christened Thomas, after his famous grandfather. The birth coincided with a general election and Arnold, who was inspecting schools in North Lincolnshire, was 'much amused by talking to the farmers, and seeing how absolutely necessary all the electioneering humbug of shaking hands, clapping on the back, kissing wives and children, etc., still is with these people'.[51] Arnold always loved 'the smallwood of humanity'[52] and, if his polemical writing sometimes lashed aspects of provincial life, he seems to have had a genuine feeling for its particular flavours and tints. In August, Arnold wrote to his mother on her birthday to say that she was 'such a mother as few sons have'.[53] Although he sometimes achieved a mode of oblique candour in his family letters, Arnold was just as likely to slip into an elevated Arnoldian tone. 'The more I see of the world', he intoned to his mother, 'the more I feel thankful for the bringing up we had, so unworldly, so sound, and so pure.'

Attentive though he might have been to his mother, Arnold was continuing to neglect Clough. The latter wrote to Blanche Smith to tell her: 'I dine with Arnold but do not stay long, because of "Fanny Lucy", who wants him to be with her'.[54] The nocent inverted commas around Fanny Lucy's name are eloquent. Arnold wrote to his wife from Rugby where he had stayed the night during his tour of inspection in the Midlands: 'It would be such a pleasure to go over with you the places I knew from the time I was eight till I was 20.'[55]

Just before this Arnold had been inspecting his Welsh schools for a fortnight. Notes scribbled on the fly-leaf of his 1852 diary show that he toured the country, stopping at Bridgend, Carmarthen, Llanelli, Pembroke Dock, Llandovery, Swansea, Cardiff, Neath, and many other Welsh towns. At the end of the Welsh trip, for the last few days of which he was joined by Clough, Arnold was anxious to see Flu again and the baby. She was much better although still 'delicate' and the baby, Thomas, was a delight, 'though he was not very gracious, as he had been kept awake to see his Papa'.[56] Soon they were off for a month to Fox How where they met Henry Crabb Robinson. The latter, who told a correspondent that 'The Arnolds have had an overflowing house for many weeks', found that the eldest son 'has a nice little wife in the daughter of Justice Wightman'.[57]

Arnold had some work to do while at Fox How – writing up the last of his reports on the schools in his district visited in July and August. On 28 September he despatched these to the Secretary of the Committee of Council on Education with an apology for the delay which blamed the managers of one or two of the Welsh schools for their tardiness in forwarding the requisite forms.[58] At the end of each school year Arnold wrote a general report on his inspections. These reports were always lucid and vigorously expressed and showed none of the characteristics of official prose. He reported in 1852 on 104 schools, carefully noting that the omission of Church of England and Roman Catholic schools made the picture slightly unrepresentative, and regretting that one visit to each school hardly amounted to an 'intimate acquaintance'. He did not mince his words in accusing the managers of the Wesleyan schools of in effect running private schools because they charged 2d to 8d per week, thus excluding the poor. 'It is evident that schools of this kind have not the first claim to assistance from public funds, which are designed to promote the education of the poor',[59] he wrote.

He was equally controversial in his comments on the Welsh schools which taught in the medium of the Welsh language. Conceding the arguments about preserving the language 'on grounds of philological or antiquarian interest', Arnold argued, characteristically, that it was the duty of the Government to insist on breaking down barriers between parts of 'its dominions' and thus it ought to use the lever of grant-aid to force Welsh pupils to acquire the English language 'which is socially and politically desirable for them'.

Turning to the pupil-teachers, Arnold found their heads stuffed full of facts but their general culture in a lamentable state. Their literary skills were minimal and Arnold felt this was precisely the side of education which 'chiefly forms the character' and which the classical training of the public schools tended to strengthen. Arnold wanted the poorer pupils to enjoy the full advantages of pupils at the more privileged schools and thought that the study of 'portions of the best English authors, and composition' was the means to 'elevate and humanise' the teachers. It would have the added advantage of 'tending to bring them into intellectual sympathy with the educated of the upper classes'. These brief comments show clearly how Arnold saw education both as a moral activity, in an individual and a social sense, and a political one in that it served to bind together the various classes of society in a common aim of humanistic cultivation.

After the summer break – of 'splendid weather and many days of wandering'[60] – Arnold and Flu set off again on tour. From the Boys' School in Milford Haven at the end of October Arnold wrote to Clough who was just about to emigrate to the United States. He returned to his favourite theme of the need for modern poetry to 'use great plainness of speech' and not to make the error of Keats and Shelley in trying to reproduce the exuberance of the Elizabethans. The critics encouraged these tendencies by assuming the object of poetry to be 'to produce exquisite bits and images' whereas, for Arnold, 'modern poetry can only subsist by its *contents*'. Like the poetry of the ancients it should include religion as part of itself and in its general style it should be 'very plain direct and severe: and it must not lose itself in parts and episodes and ornamental work, but must press forwards to the whole'.[61] In these comments Arnold is edging slowly towards the famous 1853 Preface which set out his view of what poetry should be. Arnold ended the letter by urging Clough to keep in touch 'as with all our differences we agree more with one another than the rest of the world'. He admitted he was not in terribly good spirits, although he was surviving: 'what a difference there is between reading in poetry and morals of the loss of youth, and experiencing it! And after all there is so much to be done, if one could but do it.'

For all his seriousness about the art of poetry, Arnold was oddly tentative about his own productions. In a letter to Wyndham Slade on 22 October he announced, as it were in passing: 'I have published some poems, which, out of friendship, I forbear to send to you; you shall, however, if you are weak enough to desire it, have them when we meet.'[62] This was Arnold's second volume, *Empedocles on Etna, and other Poems* and, like his first, was published anonymously as 'by A'. He was later to claim that it had sold only 50 copies. The volume contained, for the first time, most of the Marguerite poems and the 'Faded Leaves' sequence as well as *Tristram and Iseult*.

The title poem had been planned ever since he scribbled the injunction 'Chew Lucretius' in his diary in 1849. He derived the story of the life of Empedocles, a fifth-century BC Sicilian philosopher who wrote *On Nature* and *Purifications*, from an 1838 publication by S. Karsten, *Philosophorum Graecorum Veterum*. It was on the back of his notes from this book that Arnold drafted part of *Dover Beach* in 1851. Arnold's notes show that he saw Empedocles as a peculiarly modern spirit who lacked 'the religious consolation of other men' yet saw 'things as they are – the world as it is'. At first he could derive joy from this clear-sightedness and share it with his friends but eventually his friends die and he becomes isolated in the possession of these great truths and loses 'his spring and elasticity of mind'. He becomes 'clouded, oppressed, dispirited, without hope and energy'.[63]

Arnold's identification with Empedocles' *ennui* – which was also the reason why he was to drop the poem from the next edition of his poems – is clear enough. Exhausted by his inspecting duties, out of sympathy with the intellectual and aesthetic climate, disillusioned with politics, yet still convinced that he had something to say, Arnold found a metaphor for his own unease in the life of Empedocles. The poem also drew on his philosophical reading of the 1840s and 1850s, Karsten being supplemented by Lucretius, Epictetus, Marcus Aurelius, Carlyle, Senancour and Spinoza. It is described as 'a dramatic poem' yet Arnold worried that increased reflectiveness and self-consciousness on the part of the mature poet could undermine the ability to create an objective dramatic representation. In a passage in one of his notebooks he wrestles with this problem:

> while the outward appearance & manners of men can be absolutely rendered; the requisites for such rendering being lively curiosity & vigorous senses on the part of the poet: so the inward being of men, which is unseen, can never be absolutely rendered: but the poet, endeavouring to put himself in the place of the person represented, tries his own soul in certain situations, and reports accordingly: a great opening being here left for the subjective & arbitrary.[64]

The poem, however, is not a solipsistic failure and begins beautifully with Callicles the harp-player savouring the misty loveliness of early morning on the lower slopes of Mount Etna: 'One sees one's footprints crushed in the wet grass, / One's breath curls in the air . . .' He hopes that Pausanias the physician has hit on the perfect cure for Empedocles' condition – 'half mad / With exile and with brooding on his wrongs' – in this scene of natural beauty. Callicles' hope that Empedocles will be charmed by his harp-playing is rooted, perhaps, in Arnold's fear that his own intellectual preoccupations might be threatening his poetry. 'I cannot conceal from myself the objection . . . that the service of reason is freezing to feeling . . . & feeling and the religious mood are eternally the deepest being of man, the ground of all joy and greatness in him,'[65] Arnold wrote in his notebooks. As Callicles and Pausanias discuss the predicament of Empedocles the former rejects the suggestion that their friend has some external cause to be gloomy: 'There is some root of suffering in himself, / Some secret and unfollowed vein of woe, / Which makes the time look black and sad to him.' Arnold's friends must sometimes have thought this of him – his outer life must have struck them as happy and reasonably fortunate but the 'vein of woe' was real enough.

In the second section of the poem Empedocles tries to make Pausanias a little less credulous, enjoining Stoic acceptance of things as they are in place of a belief in miracles. Feeling 'the burden of ourselves' we should try to look within ourselves for the cure: 'Once read thy own breast right / And thou hast done with fears.' If Pausanias could grasp that he had 'no right to bliss' then he would have taken the first step towards accommodation with reality. This necessitates the recognition that 'we are strangers here; the world is from of old'. But we too often rail against Fate or the Gods instead of learning acceptance. And in spite of the fact that we cannot dream of some bliss to come we can at least make the best of the life we have: 'Because thou must not dream, thou needs't not then despair!'

The final section of the poem has Empedocles facing the fact that 'something has impaired thy spirit's strength'. He hears in Callicles' song the truth that: 'The brave, impetuous heart yields everywhere / To the subtle, contriving head.' This deepens his despair and his sense that the times are out of joint. Among his last words before he hurls himself into the volcanic crater are: 'Slave of sense / I have in no wise been; but slave of thought?' In this poem Arnold expresses his sense that the 'contriving head' had expelled his own spontaneous joy. But he did not follow Empedocles in his despair. In place of the tragic beauty of this poem, its willingness to live with difficult truths, he put the compromise of purposeful activity, of sorting out the world rather than continuing to represent, with anguished beauty, the 'root of suffering'. If we wanted to be harsh with Arnold we would accuse him here of evasion. Several decades as a writer, active and productive, lay ahead, but in turning away from the struggle of Empedocles he had started to bid farewell to poetry.[66]

Other poems of interest in the 1852 volume include *Lines Written in Kensington Gardens*, written probably in the spring of 1852, a celebration of the quietude of *rus in urbe* where 'amid the city's jar' the poet asks for calm: 'Calm, calm me more! nor let me die! / Before I have begun to live.' *A Summer Night* recalls the period of his engagement to Flu in May 1851 when he stood secretly outside her window 'In the deserted, moon-blanched street'. Another poem of coming to terms with life's limitations, in it the poet is addressed by the moon who asks whether he still possesses 'the old unquiet breast' that is 'Never by passion quite possessed / And never quite benumbed by the world's sway'. This moment of self-knowledge – 'never by passion quite possessed' – shows that Arnold perhaps glimpsed the inadequacies of the Marguerite poems or the concluding apostrophe of *Lines Written in Kensington Gardens*, just quoted. They are passionate utterances in form but the poet is somehow insufficiently unmastered. His sadness is always truer, more convincing, than his passionate assertion.

In *The Buried Life* the poet, in the course of some playful banter with his love, realises that even lovers do not always reveal themselves fully to each other. He represents our true self as an 'unregarded river' that flows mostly out of sight but which, from time to time, we accidentally rediscover. Often in the din of the city: 'There rises an unspeakable desire / After the knowledge of our buried life'. Holding his lover's hand (and perhaps elements of Marguerite and of Fanny Lucy are entwined here), the poet may sometimes glimpse that buried life with its promise of true felicity: 'A bolt is shot back somewhere in our breast, / And a lost pulse of feeling stirs again. / The eye sinks inward, and the heart lies plain, / And what we mean, we say, and what we would, we know.' In the possession of that moment a man thinks he knows: 'The hills where his life rose, / And the sea where it goes.' Here, by discovering the metaphor of the river (flowing water having such a hypnotic effect on his imagination), Arnold achieves a more moving expression of his feelings than in the many sententious, prosy, or sub-Wordsworthian shorter pieces which form the remainder of this volume, and which sometimes fail to come to life.

Reviewing this volume and its predecessor in the *North American Review*, Clough found in *Empedocles* 'a plainer and simpler and less factitious manner and method of treatment'. Clough, who did not allow his friendship to get in the way of some trenchant criticism, urged: 'Not by turning and twisting his eyes, in the hope of seeing things as Homer, Sophocles, Virgil, or Milton saw them; but by seeing them, by accepting them as he sees them, and faithfully depicting accordingly, will he obtain

The earliest photograph of the young Arnold at 33, less than five years married and an inspector of schools, and the year before he became Oxford Professor of Poetry. The date (10 September 1856) and the time have cleverly been incorporated in the photograph taken at Field Foot about 500 yards from Arnold's family home at Fox How in the Lake District. (*Master and Fellows of Balliol College*)

The earliest piece of writing from Arnold's hand: a page from his *Pilgrim Love* written at the age of seven, from the manuscript in Balliol College. (*Master and Fellows of Balliol College*)

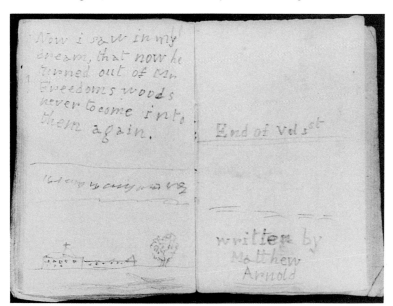

Portrait of Arnold's father, Dr Thomas Arnold, Headmaster of Rugby, after Thomas Philips RA, oil in Oriel College. (*Oriel College*)

Sketch by Arnold's sister Jane ('K') done at the time of a visit by the Queen Dowager to Rugby in 1839 and showing Dr Arnold in headmaster's gown on the school field. (*Rugby School*)

Cardinal John Henry Newman, the central figure in the Oxford Movement, towards the end of his life in 1889. Arnold always thought of Newman as a potent influence and admired especially his 'intellectual delicacy'. (*Trustees of the National Portrait Gallery*)

The School started by Thomas Arnold and his brother-in-law John Buckland at Laleham-on-Thames where Matthew Arnold was born.

Above left: Mrs Mary Arnold, Matthew Arnold's mother to whom he wrote long, detailed letters every week of her life. (*Moorman Collection*)

Above right: Frances ('Fan') Arnold, Matthew's youngest, unmarried sister who lived on at Fox How after her mother's death until the autumn of 1923 dying just short of her 90th birthday. Here she is 25. (*Moorman Collection*)

Right: Jane Martha Arnold, the eldest child of Dr and Mrs Arnold and Matthew's favourite sister, always addressed by her childhood nickname, K. She married the Liberal MP John Forster in 1850. (*Moorman Collection*)

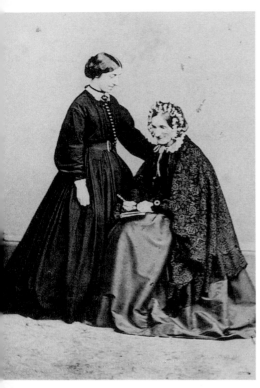

Left: Fan with her elderly mother, Mrs Arnold, with whom she lived at Fox How, from where they both, sometimes anxiously, followed Matthew Arnold's career. (*Moorman Collection*)

Below left: Arnold's younger brother Tom just before he left for New Zealand in 1848. (*Moorman Collection*)

Below: Arthur Hugh Clough, the poet, former Rugby pupil of Dr Arnold, and intimate Oxford friend of Arnold whose death is lamented in *Thyrsis*. From the 1860 painting by Samuel Rowse. (*Trustees of the National Portrait Gallery*)

Written in Kensington Gardens.

In this cool open glade I lie
Screen'd by dark trees on either head:
While at its head, to stop the eye,
Those dark-topp'd red-bol'd pinetrees
stand.

The clouded sky is still and grey,
Though silken rifts soft pierce the Sun:
Light the clear-foliag'd chestnuts play,
The massier elms stand grave and dun.

The birds sing sweetly in these trees
Across the girdling City's hum.
How green under the boughs it is!
How thick the tremulous sheep-cries come.

Fox How today – a private residence not open to the public.

Another early portrait of Arnold in a pose befitting the nickname accorded to the author of *Culture and Anarchy* by the *Daily Telegraph* in the 1860s, 'the elegant Jeremiah'. (*Trustees of the National Portrait Gallery*)

Arnold's wife, Fanny Lucy *nee* Wightman, or 'Flu', who was married to the poet in 1851, two months after he was appointed an inspector of schools. (*Moorman Collection*)

the object he desires.'[67] While Clough was drafting this review, Arnold wrote to him in the United States from a training school in Battersea with the confession that: 'As for my poems they have weight, I think, but little or no charm.'[68] He now felt that he had a better sense of his poems' defects, 'but I doubt whether I shall ever have heat and radiance enough to pierce the clouds that are massed round me'. Nevertheless, he was able to report on some good reviews and asked Clough what Emerson thought of the poems. Arnold seems to have thought that he had achieved something by analysing 'the modern situation in its true *blankness* and *barrenness*, and *unpoetrylessness*'.

At the end of November Arnold and Flu and Thomas were settled in the Midland Hotel at Derby, 'the best of all possible hotels where the people know us and show the greatest possible kindness to Baby'.[69] Arnold was anxious about the baby, having noticed some 'singular palpitations'[70] which made him fear that the hereditary Arnold heart disease might be starting to show itself. He had gone out from his Derby base to Lincoln where he found the cathedral peculiarly soothing and in visiting the vicinity of Fledborough the country people were 'astonished' at his knowledge of the topography of his mother's early home. His recollections of Fledborough, he told her, 'are the only approach I have to a memory of a golden age'.[71] In another letter from Derby, Arnold had told Wyndham Slade: 'You are to come and see me fighting the battle of life as an Inspector of Schools some day.'[72] As the year ended he wrote a miserable letter to Flu from the trenches at Battersea. 'This certainly has been one of the most uncomfortable weeks I have ever spent', he complained. The road was so execrable and the rain so incessant that he spent the day floundering through the mud. But at least there was the consolation of spending until 20 January in London working on papers before setting off again for the Huntingdonshire schools.

5

The reception of *Empedocles on Etna and Other Poems* turned out to be less enthusiastic in the long run than its immediate impact had seemed to suggest to Arnold might be the case. He paid a flying visit to Palgrave just before Christmas, 'looking as pleasant as ever' but grumbling about his duties. 'He finds one great nuisance in his Inspecting work, in that it cuts him off from congenial spirits and from congenial books',[73] Palgrave reported to Clough. 'Empedocles has fallen I fear on evil days', Palgrave added, 'having been scarcely reviewed at all – but when reviewed, generally favourably.'

Arnold's district changed a little in 1853 with South Wales and Bristol being replaced by the eastern counties (he retained for the time being North Wales). He was also given about twenty schools in London to inspect. Writing to Flu from the Bull Hotel at Cambridge at the end of May he referred to 'a long, tiring day' and the relief he would feel at getting the eastern counties out of the way. He was now receiving invitations 'on my father's account' from schools to come and inspect them and he felt it hard to refuse. The impression he gives Flu is of a busy, harried man, dashing about and only just managing to catch trains. 'At the station here I had just time to eat a bun and book for St Ives',[74] he told his wife. Two days later he was in Cambridge – which was impressive but operated under the disadvantage of not being Oxford. 'I feel that the Middle Ages and all their poetry and impressiveness are in Oxford and not here', he told Flu. He was missing her on these lonely, gruelling excursions: 'I want you sadly to go about with me; everything would be just doubly as interesting.'[75]

A sequence of letters written throughout March from the eastern counties tour show how miserable he was and how 'peculiarly oppressive just now' he found inspecting. 'All this afternoon I have been haunted by a vision of living with you at Berne, on a diplomatic appointment, and how different that would be from this incessant grind in schools', he told Flu, pulling himself back with a sardonic: 'but I could laugh at myself, too, for the way in which I went on drawing out our life in my mind.'[76] The hospitality of various well-to-do Quakers – one of whom had his walls covered with a 'ghastly' collection of stuffed birds – did little to make the task more bearable and he reported to Flu that at the end of one day in March: 'About four o'clock I found myself so exhausted, having eaten nothing since breakfast, that I sent out for a bun, and ate it before the astonished school.'[77] A day or two later he was still 'too utterly tired out to write' and still dreaming of Flu joining him – 'the only thing that could make this life anything but positive purgatory'.[78] Flu was keeping house at 23 Grosvenor Street West, another temporary lodging, and after the eastern tour Arnold returned there.

He immediately wrote to Clough, tactfully avoiding a comment on his friend's *Amours de Voyage* which he did not like, by concentrating instead on Charlotte Brontë's *Villette* which he deplored as a 'hideous undelightful convulsed constricted novel . . . one of the most utterly disagreeable books I ever read'. He still retained a disagreeable impression from having met her and described her as 'a fire without ailment . . . one of the most distressing barren sights one can witness'.

Relieved no doubt to be talking about books again instead of inspecting school books, Arnold continued to pour out to Clough his views on various writers. Relations between them had improved after an exchange of letters a month previously where Arnold had to defend himself against a charge from Clough that he was growing cool towards him. In that letter Arnold, evidently unsettled by Clough's criticism, wrote: 'I am past thirty, and three parts iced over – and my pen, it seems to me is even stiffer and more cramped than my feeling.'[79] Confessing that his preoccupation with Flu had made him 'as egoistic and anti-social as possible', Arnold ruefully admits that 'being in love generally unfits a man for the society of his friends' but promises that he had only feelings of 'attachment and affection' towards his old friend. It is a frank and generous letter that shows how deeply Arnold was attached to Clough, in spite of their intellectual differences. 'I cannot say more than that I really have clung to you in spirit more than to any other man', he told Clough. He was exhausted after inspecting and found writing difficult. Taking up the letter the next day he returned to the issue:

> I am and always shall be, whatever I do or say, powerfully attracted towards you, and vitally connected with you: this I am sure of: the period of my development (G–d forgive me the d–d expression!) coincides with that of my friendship with you so exactly that I am for ever linked with you by intellectual bonds – the strongest of all: more than you are with me: for your development was really over before you knew me, and you had properly speaking come to your *assiette* for life.

Arnold did concede some criticism of Clough, however, telling him that 'you are the most conscientious man I ever knew: but on some lines morbidly so, and it spoils your action.' In the meantime they agreed to continue to write to each other – Clough was now in America – and Arnold agreed that '*congestion of the brain* is what we suffer from – I always feel it and say it – and cry for air like my own Empedocles . . . *Arid* – that is what the times are.'

In the letter he wrote to Clough from Grosvenor Street West, Arnold revealed that he had enjoyed Thackeray's *Henry Esmond* (1852), 'one of the most readable books I ever met', although he regarded the author as 'a first rate journeyman . . . not a great artist'. He had also read *Uncle Tom's Cabin* by Harriet Beecher Stowe whom he assumed to be 'a Gorgon'. Both this judgement and that on Charlotte Brontë show that Arnold readily took against women writers with a strong point of view, excepting only George Sand whose characters were judged to be 'heaven-born' and not the common terrestrial stuff of Thackeray's imagination. After mentioning the poems of Alexander Smith, Arnold concludes: 'I am frightfully worked at present. I read Homer and toujours Homer.'[80] He was indeed 'frightfully worked' and, by some kind of miracle, was still managing to write poetry. *Sohrab and Rustum* was beginning to take shape.

His friends, however, were not all impressed by his second volume. Shairp shrewdly analysed its defects in a letter to Clough where he observed: 'I fear Mat's last book has made no impression on the public mind. I'm not much in the way of hearing but I've seen no one, except a few Oxford Rugbeans who have even read it.'[81] For Shairp the problem was that though it had 'great power' that power was thrown away on a 'false and uninteresting' view of life. 'Anything that so takes the life from out things must be false . . . Mat, as I told him, disowns man's natural feelings, and they will disown his poetry. If there's nothing else in the world but blank dejection, it's not worth while setting them to music.' Shairp's insight was a profound one, for the gradual waning of Arnold's powers as a poet was now not far off. And it was his 'view of life' that, at least in part, was to make the loss of his gift appear as a self-inflicted wound. Shairp returned to the theme in a letter to Clough in May where he said: 'The terrible want of fresh heart spoils Mat. to my taste. I can't read much of his last book without pain . . . There's not one skylark tone in them.'[82]

It became clear during the spring and summer of 1853 that Arnold had not been completely successful in easing the strain in his relations with Clough. More letters were exchanged which are valuable – in their candour – in shedding more light on the relationship. On 1 May Arnold wrote to Clough:

> I do not think we did each other harm at Oxford. I look back to that time with pleasure . . . I am nothing and very probably never shall be anything – but there are characters which are truest to themselves by never being anything, when circumstances do not suit. if you had never met me, I do not think you would have been the happier or the wiser on that account: though I do not think I have increased your stock of happiness. You have, however, on the whole, added to mine.[83]

Arnold was in North Wales in July and wrote to Clough from the Penrhyn Arms at Bangor commenting on his recent writing and suggesting that 'we leave the past to itself'.[84] Clough was now back from America and working for the Education Office like Arnold. A few days later Arnold wrote from Barmouth where he mentioned that Froude had joined him and Flu at Beddgelert where they had planned, over dinner, an ascent of Snowdon in a fortnight's time.

As usual Arnold and Flu spent August and part of September at Fox How. Arriving there in late August, Arnold confessed to Clough that he was 'nearly stupefied by 8 months inspecting' but in better health as a result of 'knocking about in open cars in Wales' in July.

Arnold offered Clough his views on their superiors at the Education Office saying that Francis, later Lord Sandford, was 'a far better fellow than Lingen and has real geniality . . . Lingen I think a bore.'[85] William Ralph Lingen, who had been a Balliol Fellow when Arnold was an undergraduate there, was made Education Secretary in 1849 and Arnold frequently clashed with him. He offered another piece of advice to Clough on the subject of conformity to the Thirty-nine Articles, recommending conformity on the grounds that it freed one from the 'unnatural and unhealthy attitude of contradiction and opposition'.[86]

After the summer holidays Arnold returned to work, basing himself again at Derby for six weeks. He had finished the Preface to his new volume which was about to be published. In spite of the arduous nature of his inspectorial work he had managed to keep writing and reading. The new volume would be testimony to that achievement in the teeth of circumstance. It was also to mark a new phase in his life because for the first time, in the Preface, he would give evidence of his abilities as a prose critic.

CHAPTER FIVE:
THE EMERGENCE OF THE CRITIC
[1853–1860]

<hr>

How difficult it is to write prose.[1]

1

The publication of a third volume – albeit one that reprinted poems from the earlier collections and added only a few entirely new poems – showed that Arnold was not allowing the pressure of work to stifle his writing. The two most important new poems in the new collection entitled *Poems: A New Edition*, and published by Fellowes (at Arnold's expense) at 5s.6d., were *The Scholar-Gipsy* and *Sohrab and Rustum*. The latter was written during the arduous first year as an inspector in which Arnold worried that his mode of life was not conducive to the composition of a sustained long poem of this kind. In April 1853 he had written to K saying: 'I am occupied with a thing that gives me more pleasure than anything I have ever done yet, which is a good sign; but whether I shall ultimately spoil it by being obliged to strike it off in fragments, instead of at one heat, I cannot quite say.'[2] A little later he told his mother that he had spent all his spare time on the poem and it was 'by far the best thing I have ever done' and that he hoped it would be generally liked. 'I have had the greatest pleasure in composing it – a rare pleasure with me',[3] he told her. Having speculated about the authorship of the *North British Review* article on his poems – he had no idea it was by Clough – he declared: 'I never felt so sure of myself, or so *really* and *truly* at ease as to criticism, as I have done lately.' He was also boosted by a reported comment by Lord John Russell that had filtered back to Flu: 'In my opinion Matthew Arnold is the one rising young poet of the present day.'[4]

As the summer wore on, however, Arnold was beginning to show some doubts about *Sohrab and Rustum*. In August he told Clough that, having written it out, 'I like it less.'[5] Composition 'in the painter's sense – that is the devil', he insisted. This was a variation on his theme that poems needed structure, and involved a belief on Arnold's part that, just as contemporary painters could not *compose* – 'though they can show great genius' – so in poetry it was inevitable that in composition 'the awkward incorrect Northern nature should shew itself' even if 'we may have feeling – fire – eloquence – as much as our betters'. He had the same feeling reading Shakespeare – he had just started on *The Tempest* – remarking: 'How ill he often writes! but how often too how incomparably!'

The new book finally came out from Fellowes – the first book actually to carry Arnold's name 'instead', as Clough put it, 'of that meagre anatomy of an initial A'[6] – in November. Letters from friends started to pour in and Arnold replied to them on tour from Derby and Lincoln. John Duke Coleridge had some criticisms – and didn't like the preface – but Arnold was happy to acknowledge the Miltonic influence on Sohrab: 'Milton is a sufficiently great master to imitate'.[7] Clough was sufficiently impressed to write to the Harvard scholar Charles Eliot Norton in America asking whether Ticknor and Fields would be interested in publishing it there – 'or is my friend too terribly European in his mind, matter and manner to bear crossing the salt water?'[8]

Clough was still uncertain about *Sohrab*, complaining that it was Tennysonian. Arnold asked him to read Tennyson's *Morte d'Arthur* and then follow this immediately with *Sohrab* 'and you will see the difference in the *tissue* of the style of the two poems, and in its *movement*'.[9] The similarities, thought Arnold, were due to their both having imitated Homer. He also suspected that Clough was being perverse again – 'I think you are sometimes – with regard to *me* especially – a little cross and wilful.' This was a shrewd guess because Clough would later tell Charles Eliot Norton that he had taken against the poem largely 'out of a spirit of contradiction'.[10] Arnold conceded that the poem did not have that quality in Homer that he thought so characteristic, rapidity, but he hoped it had fluidity, something that would make it unTennysonian.

Composing poems, notwithstanding the difficulty of doing so given his mode of life, 'seems to keep alive in me a *cheerfulness*,' he told Clough, 'a sort of Tüchtigkeit [capacity], or natural soundness and valiancy, which I think the present age is fast losing – that is why I like it'. John Blackett liked *Sohrab*, as did Froude, although Lingen wrote a letter of four sheets 'on behalf of sticking to modern subjects'.[11] Arnold began to calculate how the various reviewers would react and hoped for a repetition of *The Times'* praise of *Empedocles on Etna* the previous year which had produced the astonishing result of putting it on the railway bookstall at Derby.

Arnold found the story of Sohrab, he later told the French critic Sainte-Beuve,[12] in one of the latter's *Causeries du Lundi* where Sir John Malcolm's *History of Persia* (1815) was being referred to. Arnold took Sainte-Beuve and the *Iliad* on his honeymoon of autumn 1851 but probably started to write the poem at the end of 1852 and the early part of 1853. It tells the story of the Persian leader Rustum's encounter with the champion of the Tartars, Sohrab, who is actually his son – a fact that Rustum discovers only when his son lies mortally wounded after their single combat. This scenario has led some commentators to see encoded in the story some of Arnold's feelings about his father – a suppressed resentment at how his way in life was hampered by having to grow up in the shadow of a famous and powerful personality, and how his father, oblivious, had crushed some of the life in him accordingly. Suggestive as this interpretation is, it has no biographical endorsement: there is no evidence that Arnold actually saw the poem in this way, although there is plenty of evidence that behind his pious family references to his father's memory he was aware of his parent's shortcomings.

The poem is written in blank verse and in an epic style that owes much to Arnold's reading of Homer. It begins and ends with the image of the River Oxus – all his best poems are refreshed by flowing water or breaking waves, often bathed in moonlight and stillness, these being the ingredients of his imaginative ideal of harmony and beauty, the elusive tranquillity he sought in the restless and disjointed modern world. The memorable coda of the poem makes the movement of the 'majestic river' imitate the flow of human life – another Arnoldian theme – so that the 'shorn and parcelled Oxus' is now, after its youthful exuberant flow, 'a foiled circuitous wanderer', trimmed by circumstance and necessity, forgetting its former 'bright speed', destined to reach 'the longed-for dash of waves' on the Aral Sea.

Froude wrote to Clough that the poem was to his taste '*all but* "perfect"',[13] but he felt that Arnold had 'overdone the plainness of expression which he so much studies'. There were also too many repetitions which, however Homeric, grated on the English ear: 'I don't think he studies enough the effect to be produced by the *sound* of words. But the essentials, the working up of the situation – faultlessly beautiful.'

The other major new poem in the collection was *The Scholar-Gipsy*, perhaps Arnold's best-known poem after *Dover Beach*. Long-planned, the poem was probably written in the early summer of 1853. The story of the 'Oxford scholar poor' who joined the gipsies is derived from a seventeenth-century book by Joseph Glanvill, *The Vanity of Dogmatizing* (1661) which Arnold bought in 1844. The popularity of the poem is due to its gentle Romantic melancholy, its beautiful regret at the loss of spontaneous joy and wholeness in the divided modern psyche, and the sad English pastoral mode in which it is cast.

For Arnold and his friends it gained an extra dimension from being in part an elegy for their youth of wandering as undergraduates in 'the Cumner country' around Oxford – the city itself a romantic symbol of the survival of things that mattered in a hostile modern world. In a letter to Tom written on 15 May 1857 when Arnold was canvassing support for his Oxford Professorship of Poetry, he recalled

> that life at Oxford, the *freest* and most delightful part, perhaps, of my life, when with you and Clough and Walrond I shook off all the bonds and formalities of the place, and enjoyed the spring of life and that unforgotten Oxfordshire and Berkshire country. Do you remember a poem of mine called 'The Scholar Gipsy'? It was meant to fix the remembrance of those delightful wanderings of ours in the Cumner hills before they were quite effaced – and as such, Clough and Walrond accepted it, and it has had much success at Oxford, I am told, as was perhaps likely from its *couleur locale*.[14]

That local colour is a little harder to recapture in present-day Oxford with its tangled traffic and tourist coaches. Taking a walk today from the village of Cumnor to the old ferry at 'the stripling Thames at Bablock-hithe', giant electricity pylons bestride the landscape, and at the ferry-point (where the Thames, probably as a result of recent water-engineering in the Thames Valley, could hardly now be called a 'stripling') there is an ugly caravan park, a pub with tables and bright umbrellas, and a thatched car-port concealed behind the trees. The ferry, which was in operation as late as the 1920s as a chain ferry, is now disused. But it is still possible – in the vicinity of North and South Hinksey, Bagley Wood, and the bridleway past Chilswell Farm – to get some feel of this gently sloping country that looks down on the Oxford spires, although one has to risk the encounter with some amusing fictions of the local tourist industry such as 'Matthew Arnold's Field' and 'Matthew Arnold's Tree'.

The poem – which owes something of its richness and stanzaic mode to Arnold's *bête noire*, Keats – captures the beauty of Victorian Oxfordshire and Berkshire, the sights and sounds which fill 'All the live murmur of a summer's day', and local landmarks like the Fyfield elm around which 'maidens' from the 'distant hamlets' come to dance in May. The scholar-gipsy – whose solitariness is most ungipsylike – is not merely a romantic wanderer glimpsed at the edges of ordinary life but, what he becomes in the second half of the poem, the symbol of spiritual wholeness – 'Thou hadst *one* aim, *one* business, *one* desire' – of a kind that the modern mind is denied by the fact of change – 'For what wears out the life of mortal men? / Tis that from change to change their being rolls'. Energy is drained by the repeated shock of the new and 'the elastic powers' are numbed. Two centuries separate the scholar-gipsy from the modern world with its 'sick fatigue' and its 'languid doubt'. He waits for 'the spark from heaven' but it is unlikely to fall on Arnold and his contemporaries – 'Light half-believers of our casual creeds, / Who never deeply felt, nor clearly willed'. Life is seen pathologically as 'this strange disease of modern life, / With its sick hurry, its divided aims' whose 'infection' and 'feverish contact' the scholar-gipsy is urged to flee. Otherwise he would succumb to the radical uncertainty, weakened resolution, and mental sickness of the modern world: 'And then thy glad perennial youth would fade, / Fade, and grow old at last, and die like ours.' Once again, the thirty-year-old poet is lamenting the loss of his youth.

This time Clough was impressed. 'I myself think that the Gipsy Scholar is best', he told Charles Eliot Norton. 'It is *so* true to the Oxford Country.'[15] Arnold wrote to Clough, however, with some doubts: 'I am glad you like the Gipsy Scholar – but what does it *do* for you? Homer *animates* – in its poor way I think Sohrab and Rustum *animates* – the Gipsy Scholar at best awakens a pleasing melancholy. But this is not what we want.'[16] What the mass of men want, Arnold believed, was 'something to *animate* and *ennoble* them – not merely to add zest to their melancholy or grace to their dreams. – I believe a feeling of this kind is the basis of my nature – and of my poetics.' The moralist, as usual, was at war with the poet. Yet compared with sententious poems like *Morality* or *Progress* in the same volume, Arnold managed in the longer poem to blend his intellectual content with feeling, and pictorial skill, and things to delight the senses. Perhaps he was attending to his own injunction in an isolated quatrain he composed around this time but which was not published until 1867, *A Caution to Poets*: 'What poets feel not, when they make, /

A pleasure in creating, / The world, in *its* turn, will not take / Pleasure in contemplating.' A feeling for the music of a poem rather than its high moral content makes for two more notable successes in this volume, *The Neckan* and *The Church of Brou*.

The 1853 volume came also with a Preface which, when he had completed it in October, Arnold felt had 'a certain *Geist* in it'.[17] 'How difficult it is to write prose', he told Clough, 'and why? because of the *articulations of the discourse*: one leaps over these in Poetry – places one thought cheek by jowl with another without introducing them and leaves them – but in prose this will not do.' Whatever the merit of this remark, Arnold's Preface shows him to be already a master of discursive prose. Henceforth, he would demonstrate that mastery with increasing confidence. Lucid, supple, and witty at its best, Arnold's prose could admittedly, at its worst, be repetitious. This happened when he came to rely too heavily on certain key concepts whose introduction yet again into a particular essay or address gave the fatal impression of a man increasingly quoting from himself, rather than minting a new and happy expression in the heat of the moment. It is, however, the content rather than the style which made the Preface controversial and which saw it rejected by friends like Clough. Perhaps the most unsettling thing about it was that it constituted an argument for his not reprinting one of the best poems in the 1852 volume, *Empedocles*, which, succumbing to pressure from Robert Browning, he did eventually reprint in a collection of 1867.

The Preface sets out a view of what poetry should properly be (although, following Aristotle, his strictures are really applicable to epic and dramatic rather than lyric poetry) and introduces several of the key phrases which were to be the hallmark of his subsequent criticism. Arnold believed with Schiller that art should be joyful and therefore the disillusion and despair of Empedocles were not a fit subject for poetry. They were insufficiently uplifting. By the time of the historical Empedocles, Arnold argued, the best characteristics of the Greeks had been eclipsed: 'the calm, the cheerfulness, the disinterested objectivity have disappeared; the dialogue of the mind with itself has commenced; modern problems have presented themselves; we hear already the doubts, we witness the discouragement, of Hamlet and of Faust.'[18] Arnold inveighed against the 'morbid' art which represents situations 'in which the suffering finds no vent in action; in which a continuous state of mental distress is prolonged, unrelieved by incident, hope, or resistance; in which there is everything to be endured, nothing to be done.' This sounds more like a moralist speaking than a poet. Arnold insisted that the suppression of Empedocles was nothing to do with the argument that poets should write about modern subjects – a notion he certainly rejected – it was to do with the need to select 'an excellent action' as the subject for a poem. 'Poetical works belong to the domain of our permanent passions', he asserted and the key difference between the ancients and the moderns was that they were principally concerned with 'the poetical character of the action in itself', whereas we fix our attention 'mainly on the value of the separate thoughts and images which occur in the treatment of the action'. Although the Greeks were the masters of 'the *grand style*' their expression drew its force directly from their matter. In an interesting image Arnold describes the Greek dramatic poet as working like the light on a dim group of statuary – gradually illuminating something already there. By contrast, modern critics looked for local felicities – 'bursts of fine writing' – and neglected the grand design, the 'architectonics' which even Goethe and Shakespeare lacked – not to mention Keats!

Arnold actually uses the words 'higher poetical duty' to describe what the poet must be at if he is to avoid these pitfalls. 'What he wants is a hand to guide him through the confusion', writes Arnold in what is in effect a plea for an aesthetic headmaster like Dr Arnold to impose a continent regime on the 'caprice' – a key term in Arnold's criticism – of contemporary poetry. The fear of freedom, of 'anarchy', sent Arnold into the arms of the ancients – for no living poet or critic could suffice – in his search for an ideal of order and discipline and exalted nobility. In terms like 'poetical duty' or 'conscientious rejection of superfluities' or 'wholesome regulative laws' Arnold was deploying ethical jargon to analyse the art of poetry. The ancients understood that the choice of subject was all and that they would get nowhere by 'inflating themselves with a belief in the pre-eminent importance and greatness of their own times . . . of their mission, nor of interpreting their age', Arnold believed. The blend of contemporaneity and conservatism was highly characteristic. Finally, a degree of impersonality or humility would help: 'let us, at least, have so much respect for our art as to prefer it to ourselves'. The Preface is of the highest importance in understanding Arnold the critic. It contains *in nuce* much of his later thinking and it introduces many of his key concepts – 'the dialogue of the mind with itself', 'the grand style', 'caprice', and so on, which however can become so tedious when repeated endlessly on the lips of academic 'Arnoldians'. We get closest to Arnold when we give these sonorous phrases the slip and catch his mind in its more spontaneous and flexible performances.

Three letters written to K at this time show that in private Arnold was a little less categorical than he appeared to be in his authoritative Preface. K had evidently expressed puzzlement at some of the poems. 'Fret not yourself to make my poems square in all their parts, but like what you can, my darling', he reassured her. 'The true reason why parts suit you while others do not is that my poems are fragments – i.e. that I am fragments while you are a whole . . . the poems stagger weakly & are at their wits end.'[19] His next letter was a 'scrap' for which he apologised – he was writing from a school – and lamented how 'the cares of life deepen about one; after 30 one understands why the ancients, with their strong, practical sense, talk so perpetually about Cura – it is a better word than sorrows and miseries and all the modern more sentimental expressions. Cares is just what it is.'[20] The following letter confesses that: 'I seem to want to see you and be with you more than anyone when my Poems are making their way, or beginning to make it. You were my first hearer – you dear K – and such a sympathising, dear – animating hearer, too.'[21] He told her that he would like nothing more just now than to go to Rome and 'live for some months quite quietly there' to get away from the noise about his poems. 'It does me no good hearing the discussion of them – yet of course I cannot help being occupied by it. I intend soon to try and make some strong resolution in this respect – and keep it.'

In spite, however, of his attempts at getting above the critical reception of his poems, his comments to K show that he was monitoring it all. *The Spectator* attacked him but he was 'very anxious' to see *The Examiner* which was taken seriously by people like Lord Lansdowne. Arnold was sufficiently proud of his book to send it to Mrs Gaskell whose books gave him such 'sincere delight' and who had told his mother she liked his poems. Although he had never met Mrs Gaskell he sent the book with the hope that 'you will not be repelled from the first poem of the collection by its Eastern names; for I think you will find the story a very human one'.[22] Another recipient of the poems was Sainte-Beuve himself. Arnold sent the book on 6 January 1854 and, in May, Sainte-Beuve replied graciously that he was honoured to have been the occasion of bringing forth such a poem. By now critical opinion was sifting down in a manner summed up by Clough in a letter to Charles Eliot Norton: 'The critics here have been divided into two sets – one praising Sohrab highly and speaking gently of the preface; the other disparaging the preface and the general tone, and praising Tristram.'[23]

2

Arnold's inspection district changed again in 1854 and his connection with Wales was finally severed, North Wales being replaced by an area in south-east and south-central England. In spite of the preoccupation with his poems and their critical reception, Arnold was not neglecting his role as an inspector. His annual report for 1853 had shown a keen anxiety about the exclusion of the very poor from the elementary schools because of the fees charged. Two decades before the 1870 Education Act he asserted: 'It is my firm conviction that education will never, any more than vaccination, become universal in this country, until it is made compulsory.'[24] He was also concerned at the 'embarrassing' inadequacy of the textbooks used in many of the schools. His general report for 1854 was chiefly concerned with the need to establish uniformity and consistency in the method of inspecting and for reports to be 'unvarnished and literal'. But it also demonstrated how sensitive Arnold was to the people he inspected and to the peculiar difficulties they faced – particularly those schoolmasters 'of weak health and purely studious habits' who came to teaching thinking it the best way of keeping up their studious interests but often finding 'alas . . . there are no pursuits more irreconcilable than those of the student and the schoolmaster'.[25] Arnold knew all about the difficulties of reconciling study and a career.

In July of 1854 Arnold went to Dover with Flu for work purposes but, tempted as always by the proximity of Europe, dashed across the Channel for a few days in Brussels ('a white, sparkling, cheerful, wicked little place'[26]), Ghent and Antwerp – where he was impressed by the Reubens collection – spending £15 on the trip. He told Wyndham Slade afterwards that he and Flu had 'recorded a solemn vow, if we live, to spend at least seven weeks abroad next year'. Arnold loved Dover, however, and they came back for three weeks there in August to lodgings at 6 The Esplanade. 'It is a real pleasure to see the landings, day after day', wrote Arnold, frustrated at not being on those boats 'perpetually steaming off under one's nose' for Europe where he had found pleasure and freedom in his youth and which remained a potent symbol of release from his daily round and the constrictions of English culture.

Dover was his base for inspecting in Kent and Sussex and he spent a few days in Brighton with Flu's brother-in-law Henry Benson who commanded the depot of the 17th Lancers. Arnold stayed at the barracks and was up until one o'clock in the morning playing cards and drinking champagne and claret with the young 'nincompoop' officers. Eventually they sailed back to London on a coastal vessel to prepare themselves for the real holiday of six weeks at Fox How. But that was over too quickly and by October Arnold was soon heading once more for his schools, this time in the Oxford area, with only Hesiod and Kingsley's *Hypatia* to console him on the journey. Flu had gone with Thomas and Trevenen, who this month was one year old, to Liverpool to stay with Arnold's sister Susy and her husband John Cropper at Dingle Bank. 'We have had such a happy time at Fox How', he told Flu sadly. 'Then, too, I have had time for employment that I like, and now I am going back to an employment which I certainly do *not* like, and which leaves me little time for anything else.'[27]

Just before he left Fox How, Arnold wrote to K saying how much he had enjoyed her holiday letters from Switzerland which brought his poems to mind: 'there is no-one and never will be any one who enters into what I have done as you have entered into it, dearest K, – and to whom I so want to communicate what I do.'[28] He told her he had just finished a poem – almost certainly *Balder Dead* – that was better than Sohrab 'though here I think they do not consider it so'. Fox How was never an indulgent critical forum for Arnold. After he had left and was back on tour, Oxford was some consolation. He was able to spend a few days at Walrond's rooms at Balliol, marvelling that it was thirteen years since he had left. The pair went off to revisit the Cumnor country and one day Arnold 'got up alone into one of the little coombs that papa was so fond of, and which I had in my mind in the "Gipsy Scholar", and felt the peculiar *sentiment* of this country and neighbour-hood as deeply as ever'.[29] He was less impressed with the intellectual atmosphere of Oxford and its scholars, feeling they had both suffered from the loss of Newman's influence. Perhaps, he speculated to Flu, the influx of the sons of Dissenters 'of that muscular, hard-working, *unblasé* middle class' might stiffen Oxford's sinews a little, however high a price in their 'abominable disagreeableness' must be paid. Reading the newspapers with accounts of the growing domination of the Euro-pean Alliance by France, Arnold felt more depressed with England and exclaimed to Flu: 'How I should like to live quietly in Switzerland with you and the boys!'[30]

In December Arnold published his *Poems by Matthew Arnold*, second series (although it bore the date 1855) which reprinted earlier poems with the addition of the new poem *Balder Dead*. As usual, choice of subject was important to Arnold and he derived it from P. H. Mallet's

Northern Antiquities (1847) which contained a translation of the Scandinavian *Edda* but he had been reading Homer again during the period of its composition and the poem has an epic aspiration. Or as Clough put it, the poem was 'on the Scandinavian Apollo, Balder, in blank verse, in the *neo*-Homeric manner'.[31] It recounts the story of Balder the Good from Norse legend whom the Gods try to recover from the kingdom of the dead after he is slain by trickery using one of their own number as agent. Apparently mocked by some contemporaries as 'Balder Dash', the poem is in fact remarkably successful. It has some of the qualities that Arnold desired of epic – swiftness and economy – and the narrative moves easily. It is also punctuated by some delightful epic similes that draw on Arnold's keen observation of the natural world (although there is more of Westmorland than the Scandinavian wastes in their detail). It demonstrates how Arnold's imagination was more effectively stimulated by Northern and Celtic myth than by the classical models he so desparately wanted to emulate. The new book contained a very brief Preface which refined the previous one of 1853, insisting that he was not wishing to confine poets to classical subjects. 'Nor do I deny that the poetic faculty can and does manifest itself in treating the most trifling action, the most hopeless subject.'[32] But he stuck to his belief that study of the classical writers of antiquity was therapeutic: 'They can help to cure us of . . . the great vice of our intellect . . . that it is *fantastic*, and wants *sanity*.' Study of the ancients cures us of 'caprice and eccentricity'.

Arnold, sending six copies of the new book to his mother, with a request that she give one to Mrs Wordsworth for the sake of the *Memorial Verses*, was sanguine: 'I think this book will hold me in public repute pretty much at the point where the last left me, not advance me and not pull me down from it.'[33] He hoped that he would 'make something by the poems' but the length of time since most of them were written and his preoccupation (like Clough who on 12 June had married Blanche Smith, a cousin of Florence Nightingale) with the Crimean War now at its height left him oddly indifferent to their fate. Added to this, he had been unwell and was worried that he had not been doing his inspecting work very well recently. He told K, however, that he thought *Balder Dead* would consolidate his reputation, although 'many will complain that I am settling myself permanently in that field of antiquity, as if there was no other'.[34] He doubted that the book would attract much attention with everyone's mind on the war – 'the one cry being for newspapers' – but he predicted resignedly that the book would 'dribble away in a year's time or so'.

Perhaps some of this limp self-esteem was due to the lack of enthusiasm from his family for the volume.

Arnold was to go on writing poems for another decade or so but the only poem of real interest that lay ahead was *Thyrsis*. The slow transformation of Arnold from poet to writer of prose was beginning. His old friend Arthur Stanley, however, claimed that Arnold was 'in good heart' about the poems. He told Tom: 'He is also – I must say so, though perhaps I have no right to say so – greatly improved by his marriage – retaining all the genius and nobleness of mind which you remember, with all the lesser faults pruned and softened down.'[35]

3

Clough began 1855 full of gloom at finding 'the Tories in once again'. He lamented to a friend: 'When they last came in, they drove me from England into New England.'[36] Arnold, however, was preoccupied not with the arrival of Palmerston but the removal of an asphalt floor at a school presided over by a Miss Rosella Pitman.[37] He was also inspecting 500 students a week. A scribbled note in his diary for this year shows that he inspected 117 'institutions', 173 schools, 368 pupil-teachers, and 97 certificated teachers. One bright prospect, however, appeared to be the proposal for taking a lease at 11 Belgrave Street for five months from March to July. The Arnolds had led a peripatetic life since their marriage, living with parents-in-law, and in hotel rooms, temporary lodgings, and short-lease properties. This would continue until the start of 1858. In the end, however, the Belgrave Street lease was not taken and the Arnolds took instead the house in Grosvenor Street West which they used for three consecutive years as their London base – with tours of inspection, and summer in the Lakes, they seem to have spent relatively little time in London at this stage in their life. In April he was able to combine inspecting in the Cotswolds ('one of the richest and most beautiful parts of England'[38]) with a trip to Oxford where he and Flu stayed with the Provost of Oriel, Dr Hawkins, who seemed to Arnold 'very worn and thin'.

This taste of academic life was a welcome contrast to the daily grind which he had recently described in a letter to Tom, worth quoting as an insight into a typical London-based working day:

My school for today [28 March 1855] was at Waddesdon — a village on the Bicester Road, six miles from Aylesbury. I got up in a yellow, foggy morning, at a quarter past 7, leaving Flu in bed — breakfasted alone at 8 and was off, having seen the two children in their beds, in a cab for Euston Square at a quarter to nine: started by the Express at a quarter past 9 and was at Aylesbury (43 miles) at a quarter before eleven — turning off the old Birmingham line which you remember so well at Tring: at Aylesbury I got into a fly and drove to Waddesdon — got there about 12 — went to lunch with an old Wesleyan farmer and his wife at their farmhouse among the fields . . . then the school, a very small one, at 1: recommended the managers to come to terms with the clergyman, get their children into the National School and shut up their dissenting one — and at 2 got into my fly and was at Euston Square again at a quarter to 5. Having had no walking I walked from there to the Cumberland Gate end of Oxford Street carrying my plaid and portfolio in my hand — then got into a hansom and drove here . . . When I got home I went & sate in the nursery, both the children having bad colds, till it was time to dress for dinner — and then took Tom down with me, who ran about the room and put my things in order while I dressed — There is a history![39]

This was one of the lighter days when he at least had time to eat and when the actual inspection was brief. On another occasion, inspecting trainee teachers at the Borough Road Training College, Arnold let slip to Flu an uncharacteristically dismissive remark about women: 'I am much struck with the utter unfitness of women for teachers or lecturers',[40] immediately adding the qualification that it was probably 'no natural incapacity, but the fault of their bringing up'.

Meanwhile, April saw the publication in *Fraser's Magazine* of the *Stanzas from the Grande Chartreuse*. Arnold wrote to acknowledge the cheque: 'I assure you I consider the latter liberal payment for the short poem I sent you.'[41] He was later to adopt a more aggressive posture with his publishers. Shortly after publication Arnold wrote again to Parker at *Fraser's*: 'You will think I flood Fraser with my verses — but I am about a thing in memory of poor Charlotte Brontë which I think may suit you when it is done and which I should like to appear at no great distance of time from her death.'[42] He promised to send it by the 23rd or 24th of April, adding: 'it will be in irregular metre . . . which many people consider objectionable'. Arnold was keen to offer a fairer assessment of Charlotte Brontë, who had died on 31 March, than that produced after their meeting on 21 December 1850. 'I am glad to have the opportunity to speak of her with respect at this time, and for merits which she undoubtedly has',[43] he told his mother. The poem recalled the 1850 visit accompanied by Harriet Martineau who was now, Arnold thought, mortally ill. In fact she recovered and lived for another twenty years. Later versions of the poem had to be amended accordingly. The Arnold family were not pleased at the eulogy of Miss Martineau, the author of the *Philosophy of Comte*, and Arnold was forced to write to K to defend himself, arguing that notwithstanding her 'antipathetic' progressive views her character was 'a fine one' and 'her independence and efforts to be sincere with herself worthy of admiration'.[44]

The poem itself, *Haworth Churchyard*, published in the May issue of *Fraser's*, repeats this praise of Harriet Martineau's spirit and intellectual courage. Arnold had visited Haworth, inspecting schools, on 6 May 1852, but did not apparently visit the church, because his poem represents Charlotte's grave as joining those of Emily and Anne out in the open. Charlotte and Emily were, in fact, buried inside the church in the family vault, and Anne's grave was at Scarborough. On publication Mrs Gaskell wrote tactfully to point out the error ('I hardly know whether to tell you'[45]) but also to say how much Charlotte would have appreciated his praise of Emily in the lines: 'whose soul / Knew no fellow for might, / Passion, vehemence, grief, / Daring, since Byron died.' Arnold replied: 'I am almost sorry you told me about the place of their burial. It really seems to put the finishing touch to the strange cross-grained character of the fortunes of that ill-fated family that they should ever be placed after death in the wrong, uncongenial spot.'[46] Mrs Gaskell felt of *Haworth Churchyard* that 'the poetry of it seems above my praise'.

Dignified and eloquent as the poem is, however (apart from a representation of the Yorkshire miners, which inevitably strikes the modern reader as faintly comic, as the 'rough, grimed race') it has some of the faults of *Rugby Chapel* which it resembles, in being a little too prosy and earnestly gravid and finding too little opportunity to take poetic flight in memorable images. Arnold worried only about the irregular metre and about defending himself from the charge of indulgence to Harriet Martineau. He told his mother that he knew nothing of her creed 'only her boldness in avowing it'. In a vehement defence, he told her that he would not side with the attackers of a woman who tried to 'deal perfectly honestly and sincerely with herself'. Besides: 'The want of independence of mind, the shutting their eyes and professing to believe what they do not, the running blindly together in herds for fear of some obscure danger and horror if they go alone, is so eminently a vice of the English, I think, of the last hundred years'[47] that he was right to take her part.

These remarks show that the future author of *Culture and Anarchy* was beginning to limber up. Whether it was this run-in with his family, or frustration at not being able to write more poetry, Arnold told K: 'I

am not going to write any more for the magazines. I have not time.'
The death of K's husband's mother and of the Wightmans' doctor at
Hampton just at this time reminded Arnold of his mortality: 'How the
days slip away, and how little one does in them!' he exclaimed to K.
But his growing family was a great consolation – his letters are
frequently punctuated with accounts of their doings and sayings.
'They are dear little men', he told his mother, 'and with them and
one little girl I should have all the family I wish for. I wish you could
see the boys – Tom playing the Marseillaise on a paper knife and Budge
[the nickname for Trevenen] dragging the litter basket around the
room to the tune of Cheer Boys Cheer.'[48]

The failure of Judge Wightman to get the North Wales Circuit –
which would have enabled Arnold once again to earn a much needed
£75 acting as the judge's marshal – meant that the family would go to
Dover for a few weeks in the summer before Flu's confinement at Lady
Wightman's house for the birth of her third child in the autumn – Dick
was eventually born on 14 November. K, meanwhile, was planning a
trip to Northern Italy which gave her, she felt, the sense of where her
brother's poetry came from. However, he replied that she would
perceive it more in the Auvergne: 'The country has such beautiful
forms and such a southern air.'[49] During the summer Tennyson's *Maud*
was published and in a semi-business letter to Clough, who was busy in
the Education Office, Arnold seized the opportunity for another
disparaging remark about the poet: 'Altogether I think this volume
a lamentable production, and like so much of our literature thoroughly
and intensely *provincial*, not European.'[50] Arnold's own poetic project
was now 'a tragedy of the time of the end of the Roman Republic'[51]
which he told Wyndham Slade would take at least two years to
compose. In fact it never saw the light of day and his next poem
was to be the tragedy *Merope*, which he was already at work on in 1856.

In 1856 Arnold received the sum of £39.10s.1d. from Longman from
the sale of his *Poems* (first and second series) which no doubt convinced
him that his poetic income was never to be Tennysonian. 'My poems
are making their way, I think, though slowly,' he wrote to K, 'and
perhaps never to make way very far. There must always be some people,
however, to whom the literalness and sincerity of them has a charm . . .
The fact is that the state of mind expressed in many of the poems is one
that is becoming more common . . . I think I shall be able to do
something more in time, but am sadly bothered and hindered at present
. . . To make a habitual war on depression and low spirits, which in
one's early youth one is apt to indulge and be somewhat interested in, is

one of the things one learns as one gets older.'[52] These gloomy reflections were made worse by the death of his close friend John Blackett: 'I had lived so much with him that I felt mixed up with his career, and his being cut short in it seems a sort of intimation to *me*.'

The income from Arnold's poems would barely cover his annual subscriptions to the Alpine Club and the Athenaeum. Membership of the latter club in Piccadilly filled Arnold with special delight. At the end of 1855 he started to lobby William Forster about being made a member on the strength of his literary reputation rather than his establishment credentials – or, as he put it to William, 'as a literary adventurer without ballot'.[53] By the middle of February he received the news at Edgbaston where he was inspecting that he had been elected and looked forward 'with rapture' to the use of the library. 'It is really as good as having the books of one's own – one can use them at a club in such perfect quiet and comfort',[54] he wrote enthusiastically to K. In another letter to Willy he described the scene at the club: 'I am writing now, at half past 12, in the day, writing at a window in the great Drawing Room with only two other people in the room – every side of this magnificent room covered with books and the room opening into others also full of books . . . I look out upon the facade of the Senior United and the open place in front between that club and ours, and on the roofs and colonnade of the old Italian opera – and the Park below the Duke of York's column is full of people waiting for the guns to fire for the peace was signed yesterday'.[55]

Arnold was feeling the need of a quiet retreat from the three young children and the press of educational business. He had another retreat, too, in the rooms of Wyndham Slade who, out at court during the day, allowed Arnold to seek sanctuary at 101 Mount Street 'from the everlasting going in and coming out of Eaton Place.' Here, like Epicurus, he could 'hide his life' and join those who escape 'the malicious pleasure the world takes in trying to distract them till they are as shatter-brained and empty-hearted as the world itself'.[56]

Henceforth many of Arnold's letters and articles would be written from the Athenaeum. Publishers' messengers would cool their heels in the lobby waiting to collect handwritten essays urgently needed for the press. And when Arnold later had the use of an occasional overnight room nearby owned by his publisher George Smith he could spend even more time at the club when living in Surrey. 'This Athenaeum is a place at which I enjoy something resembling beatitude', he told K a month after being elected. In this first letter written from there, he gave his reactions to Ruskin's *Modern Painters*, just off the press: 'Full of excellent *aperçus*, as usual, but the man and character too febrile, irritable, and weak to allow him to possess the *ordo concatenatioque veri*.'[57] Pre-eminently among London clubs at this time, the Athenaeum was a meeting place for a kind of intellectual freemasonry of writers, bishops, judges, senior civil servants as well as those members owing their eminence more to social or class distinction.[58] As Arnold's fame grew in the 1860s and 1870s he would increasingly find the club a place where he was recognised and fêted – and in consequence prevented from working – even when he retreated to the quieter North Library which was also a retreat from the gaslight he disliked in the main library. But in the early years it was a blessed retreat.

In a letter to Willy, Arnold shared with his brother what he called 'the absurdity and disadvantage of our heredity connexion in the minds of all people with education'.[59] Everywhere they went the ghost of Dr Arnold attended them but his son was always fighting the temptation to say: 'My good friends, this is a matter for which my father had a specialité, but for which I have none whatever.' It was still a struggle for Arnold to summon up enthusiasm for his work and he felt that any conventional career – even politics – would have had the same result: 'so I am glad my sphere is a humble one and must try more and more to do something worth doing in my own way, since I cannot bring myself to do more than a halting sort of half-work in other people's way'. The prospect of a job as colonial secretary for Mauritius now came up, with a salary of £1,500 a year. But his present salary of £900 was likely to increase and a more favourable inspection territory in London was beckoning. In addition, his friends advised him not to go, so he abandoned the idea. But the climate of Mauritius would have been 'heavenly' and he could have taken the children – 'I should have sate all day on a coral rock, bathing my legs in the Southern ocean.' Another offer this year was to go for four months abroad as secretary to a Commission to inquire into foreign military education which would have involved enviable travel to Paris, Berlin, Vienna and Turin, but it fell through.

A welcome diversion in the summer of 1856 was another stint as marshal for Judge Wightman on the circuit. In spite of an inauspicious start, Arnold developed a good relationship with the judge who, according to the *Dictionary of National Biography* was 'an exceptionally sound and clear-headed lawyer' and had 'great humour, considerable literary gifts, and was widely read in English letters' – the latter qualities rather surprising in view of his treatment of Arnold. But a letter he wrote to his son-in-law in 1859 at the age of seventy-five from the Pyrenees revealed a cordial side to his nature: 'I have sadly wanted you to be with me in the wild romantic regions we have lately visited', he wrote from Pau.[60] The judge's party had let him down with various illnesses and he wanted a more active companion such as Arnold, whom now he could only regale with descriptions, urging him to look up the places he mentioned in the indispensable handbook to France of 'Murray (in whom we place implicit confidence)'.

On the present occasion, in 1856, Arnold accompanied him to the Welsh Marches. 'All the country from Shrewsbury to Gloucester was new to me', he told Wyndham Slade, 'and Ludlow and Herefordshire are well worth seeing.'[61] He also went down the Wye to Chepstow but was frustrated by the weather in his attempts to fish. The only drawback was the food on circuit – invariably 'greasy and ill-served' so he looked forward to spending most of August at 'our old quarters' at No. 6 The Esplanade, Dover, followed by September at Fox How. The Arnolds were deliberately husbanding their resources so that they could have a proper six-week holiday in 1857 'without borrowing or forestalling'. Tom was at Fox How and reported afterwards to Clough that 'putting out of sight the whiskers (which considering their bushiness it is difficult to do) I consider the old boy very little changed'.[62]

Back at work in the autumn, Arnold met the secretary of the Manchester Mechanics Institute who informed him that his poems were greatly read in the Library of the Institute. More than this, the Secretary had recently read *Sohrab and Rustum* aloud to a hushed Mancunian audience of two or three hundred working men who had 'all been melted by it'.[63] Equally remarkable was a report that filtered back to Arnold that Tennyson had told a friend, a Mr Sellar, that 'if anything happened to him I ought to be his successor'.[64]

4

Early in January 1857 Arnold decided on some new year resolutions:

- not to be *in* bed later than 8¼
- when at home not to be later than 11 in getting to *work* after breakfast
- to work one hour before dinner
- to work one ½ hour before bed (when either of these two hours is interrupted, to make up the time at some other part of the day).[65]

His own annotation suggests that these were poorly observed rules but they indicate how much he felt the pressure of circumstance to be working against his intellectual performances. The children, who seemed plagued with illness, cannot, however, have helped such codes of discipline. Four days after drafting these rules for himself Arnold was fretting about his youngest boy, Dick, now fourteen months old, who was being dosed with calomel. Tommy, the eldest, had just come in to his father saying of Dick: 'He's in the nursery – he's very ill – he's had a fit – he's dead – where shall we put him?'[66] The third boy, Budge, was fast asleep 'with a new boat which his grandmother Wightman has given him on the pillow beside him, with one of his fat hands resting upon it.' To the pram in the hall was added a quarrel between the housekeeper and the nurse – for whom Arnold and Flu had that very day done service as godparents. 'I am aghast sometimes when I think of bringing them up', Arnold told his mother, 'but then I think of Papa, and the mountains he managed to move so easily.'

With the spring came a renewed desire to see the Alps. Arnold explained to K that there were 'two or three things I have in hand which I cannot finish till I have again breathed and smelt Swiss air'.[67] He added grimly: 'I shall be baffled, I daresay, as one continually is in so much.' He remembered Goethe: 'Homer and Polygnotus daily teach me more and more that our life is a Hell, through which one must struggle as best one can.'

The struggle was a little assuaged by their latest temporary lodging, a pleasant house at Hampton on Arnold's beloved Thames – 'the only *riant* part of England'. From here Arnold conducted his quiet campaign – we have no record of his discussing it with anyone before this point – to be elected as Oxford Professor of Poetry. Arnold's proven distinction as a poet, the respect paid to him by his peers such as Browning, Tennyson, Rossetti, Swinburne and Clough, his gradual emergence as a critic with something urgent and timely to say about the art of poetry, and his intimate connection with Oxford, made the decision to stand a very plausible one. Between noon and five in the afternoon on Tuesday 5 May 1857, members of Convocation arrived at Oxford to cast their votes. Arnold was pitted against the Reverend John Ernest Bode, author of *Ballads from Herodotus* and described as 'a thoroughly orthodox divine'.[68] Although it was clear which of the two was the establishment candidate, Arnold won decisively with a majority of 85 votes. On the election day Arnold, Flu and the three boys went across from Hampton to the telegraph station at Charing Cross and received the first telegram about four in the afternoon from Walrond: 'Nothing is known, but it rumoured you are ahead'.[69] The family then filled in a little time shopping for toys in the Lowther Arcade where Tom and Budge insisted on an identical colour for the horses pulling their toy waggons while Dick was given a musical cart. At five they returned to the telegraph office to receive another message: 'Nothing declared, but you are said to be quite safe. Go to Eaton Place.' To Eaton Place, the home of Judge Wightman, they went and a little after six the judge burst joyfully into the room with news of the victory which he had collected from the telegraph office on his arrival at Paddington Station.

The salary was not large – £130 a year – but the duties were minimal – three lectures a year, a Latin oration to be delivered every alternate year, and the adjudication of undergraduate prize poems such as he himself had written in his youth. Arnold's Professorship was marked by two innovations: he was the first holder of the post since its inauguration in 1708 not to be a clergyman of the Church of England (no Poetry Professor has ever been a clergyman since) and he delivered his lectures not in Latin but in English. His predecessor had been John Keble who once observed that if English were to be adopted: 'I think Latin would suffer more than Poetry would gain.'[70] Keble was also of the opinion that it would be to let down the office to make the lectures 'opportunities for delivering merely brilliant essays, which find their not inappropriate future in fashionable series' – which is exactly what came to pass from Arnold's day to Seamus Heaney's. Keble had some eccentric notions about poetry which he saw as 'a vent for overcharged feelings'. The job of the critic was to 'account for' the various classes into which poets fall 'by reference to the various objects which are apt to fill and overpower the mind, so as to require a sort of relief'. The decision to deliver the lectures in English was a decision to enlarge the scope of the Professorship and to use it as an accessible public platform for critical debate about poetry rather than as an opportunity to talk to a smattering of dons about Latin and Greek poetry in a dead language. 'There is no direction in the Statute as to the language in which the lectures shall be', Arnold pointed out to Tom, 'and the Latin has so died out, even among scholars, that it seems idle to entomb a lecture which, in English, might be stimulating and interesting.'[71]

In a letter to his mother telling of his success, Arnold made the obvious connection with his father who in the early 1840s had occupied the post of Regius Professor of Modern History all too briefly: 'in my well-doing you may truly feel that the memory of Papa helps so much as to give you a yet closer and clearer connection with it than most mothers, ever, have with their sons' well-doing. I am never tired of thinking how he would have rejoiced in his son's thus obtaining a share in the permanence and grandeur of that *august* place which he loved so much . . . how there could hardly perhaps have been conferred on me a distinction, of those conferred by men, which he would have so much prized.'[72] The Arnold connection celebrated with such self-satisfaction here was not lost on Dr Arnold's old enemies. Conservative Oxford rallied behind the author of the ballads from Herodotus but Arnold rejoiced in their rout – with two hundred more people having voted than ever before as a result of the high-profile contest. 'It is a great lesson to Christ Church, which was rather disposed to imagine it could carry everything by its great numbers', he reported to his mother.[73] The High Church party, in other words, had been scattered by Arnold's 'immense victory', with many votes being cast on the strength of his father's memory. Even Keble voted for him in the end, along with Archdeacon Denison, Canon Millar (who called him 'that son of a great and good man') and two members of 'the high Tory party', Sir John Yarde Buller and Henley the jingoist poet. Although the victory was gratifying and promised Arnold an important new platform – 'you will do great good there',[74] Froude wrote – he remained sanguine about the general shape of his career, telling his mother sardonically that one of the pleasures of the Professorship was 'its finding me in a profession which admits of no rise and no distinction'.[75]

In spite of the excitement of the Oxford election in May, Arnold was soon back at work. Later in the month he was visiting the King Edward British School in Albert Street, Mile End, in London's East End. He scribbled directions in his diary – the frequently shaky handwriting suggests that he made notes on the train – which indicated that his destination was 'behind Whitechapel work-house'[76] – a far cry from the Oxford high table. His anxiety about the passage of time which occurs frequently in his letters at this time, coupled to his worries about the palpitations in little Tom's heart – a possible sign that the hereditary Arnold heart disease was claiming another victim – made Arnold very conscious (although he was only thirty-four) of his mortality. He pencilled a list on the inside cover of his 1857 diary of the dates of death of various writers – Dante, Voltaire, Rousseau – which suggests a morbid preoccupation.

It was time for a holiday, and that summer, after a brief stay at Dover, he and Flu crossed the Channel for a trip through Paris, Basle, Lucerne, the Titlis Alp ('for Obermann's sake'[77]), Zermatt (to rendezvous with Wyndham Slade and his family) and Geneva. He was now working exclusively on his tragedy *Merope*, though he confessed to K that 'between indolence and nervousness I am a bad worker'.[78] By the autumn the work had been announced, 'a tragedy (to rival Voltaire's)',[79] Clough described it to Charles Eliot Norton.

But first he had to deliver his inaugural lecture at Oxford as Professor of Poetry on 14 November in the Sheldonian Theatre. His subject was *On the Modern Element in Literature*. It was meant to be the first of a series but although Arnold delivered six lectures between November 1857 and 19 May 1860 all but this – which was not published until eleven years later – have been lost and were never published. Audiences diminished after the first lecture and the remaining five of this first series were delivered at the smaller Taylor Institution. When the inaugural lecture was reprinted in 1868 in *Macmillan's Magazine* Arnold conceded that the style was 'that of the doctor rather than the explorer . . . a style which I have long since learnt to abandon.'[80] He was conscious of the shortcomings of the lecture's 'generalizing mode of treatment' and its attempt to lay down the law. 'He seems to lust after a system of his own', complained William Wordsworth (the poet's grandson) in a letter to Henry Crabb Robinson, adding: 'I do not know whether it is the result of a general law or not, but it seems to me that these young gentlemen who are as melancholy as night, and kick under the burden of life – seem sufficiently resigned and prosperous when one meets them.'[81]

Arnold began the lecture by characterising modern ages as those which make a demand for 'intellectual deliverance'. The present age offered a bewildering variety of new things to comprehend so a 'true point of view from which to contemplate this spectacle' was required. As usual Arnold was not content to permit the disorder of multiple impressions and diverse points of view – he would have been appalled by today's post-modernist theory – and was keen to offer authoritative instruction and guidance – although, in fairness, he praised the ancient Greeks (who constituted his ideal) for 'the growth of a tolerant spirit' as a central constituent in their culture. The most 'adequate' interpretation of an age, he believed, was to be found in its poetry and the age that would offer true 'deliverance' would be one which was marked by 'the simultaneous appearance of a great epoch and a great literature'. It would also value the critical spirit and judge matters by 'the rule of reason, not by the impulse of prejudice or caprice'. One reason why Sophocles was such a perfect model of 'adequacy' was that he was free from prejudice and caprice and was scrupulously objective and disinterested: 'he saw life steadily and saw it whole'. By contrast to this sunny, sane Greek wholeness, the modern age is fragmented and divided – as the poet of *The Scholar-Gipsy* had already asserted.

'Depression and *ennui*; these are the characteristics stamped on how many of the representative works of modern times!' Lucretius was an early example of this 'modern spirit'. Because he was 'over-strained, gloom-weighted, morbid' – one seems to see Clough here – he could be 'no adequate interpreter of his age'. By this standard Virgil and Horace also fall because they did not form part of 'a commensurate literature', one that properly matches up to its age without flinching, without letting its personal and capricious inadequacies get in the way.

None of this is unfamiliar to anyone who has read Arnold's letters to Clough or the Prefaces of 1853 and 1854. It raises many of the same doubts: on the one hand Arnold is expounding an apparently reasonable ideal, on the other hand it is one which, since it appears unattainable – certainly unattainable by Arnold, whose best poetry is 'modern' in this sense, and whose poetic practice contradicts his critical arguments constantly – can lead only to despair. In many ways one of the most acutely aware poets of his age – in the sense of thinking through the implications of the great age of transition which was the nineteenth century and what it meant for poetry – Arnold was haunted by a sense that the best had been and that the modern could only be a falling off. Yet at the same time he looked to the future. Unlike many of his contemporaries who merely theorised about the state of the nation, Arnold was out and about, travelling across the new railway network on his way to inspect at first hand the actual social conditions of Victorian England – a man who propagandised for new forms of education and new cultural standards. Even in this lecture he argues a kind of intellectual Darwinism when he says that: 'The human race has the strongest, the most invincible tendency to *live*, to *develop* itself. It retains, it clings to what fosters its life, what favours its development, to the literature which exhibits it in its vigour . . .' Arnold was simultaneously a progressive and a man nostalgic for a land of lost content. He was a conservative radical of a recognisably English kind.

5

The tragedy of *Merope* was finally published in December 1857 but on its title page it bore the date of 1858. Arnold listened to the critics of this poem but remained steadfastly loyal to it, even dreaming that it could one day be performed. Even one of Arnold's most informed and sensitive scholarly readers has called it if not unreadable then 'dead'.[82] The dutiful biographer who has trekked across its frozen wastes can only return with the confirmation that this is an eminently fair judgement and that it is indeed 'a cardboard imitation of Sophocles' *Electra*' although some critics have responded more favourably to its blank verse. It is unlikely that anyone reads it today. Yet it ought to have been the triumphant embodiment of Arnold's poetic theories, an 'adequate' composition that answered, in the way he sought, the demands of the age. Were Arnold's critical theories and moralising tendency now combining to kill off his spontaneous poetic power – that instinctual imaginative energy and free creative range that makes for real poetry rather than a lifeless academic exercise written to a theoretical programme prompted by the head not the heart? One recalls Auden's line: 'He thrust his gift in prison till it died.'

The poem is about the revenge of Merope's youngest son, Aepytus, for the death of his father Cresphontes whom Polyphontes murdered, subsequently marrying, against her will, Merope. It has moments of poetic life, as when Aepytus in disguise pretends to describe his own death to Polyphontes during a stag hunt. The description of the Arcadian landscape and the hunt are vividly done but of course worked up from books. Arnold wrote to the classical topographer William Leake, enclosing a copy of the poem, and admitting how dependent on his work he had been: 'you will perceive but too clearly that I have never been in Greece . . . but . . . I have found no other author except Pausanias himself from whose works on this subject I have derived so much instruction'.[83]

The poem was published with a long Preface in which Arnold sought to justify his classical form and subject and to explain why he had rejected the idea of translating a Greek tragedy or taking a theme already treated by a Greek dramatist: 'No man can do his best with a subject which does not penetrate him: no man can be penetrated by a subject which he does not conceive independently.'[84] He also reviewed other treatments of his subject by other poets and explained the attraction that 'severe' Greek forms had for him where balance is always restored before the end of the drama, however turbulent it has been: 'the final sentiment in the mind must be one not of trouble, but of acquiescence'. Arnold ends the Preface somewhat edgily with an admission of his incapacity to the task, and wishing that someone better equipped than himself had been able to attempt to enrich English literature, 'to extend its boundaries in the one direction, in which, with all its force and variety, it has not yet advanced'. If *Merope* was a failure, it was a noble one.

Arnold's letters at the time were full of explanation and self-justification. Sending his mother the first batch of reviews he observed: 'They have lost no time in opening cry . . . The bane of English reviewing and newspaper writing is, and has always been, its *grossièreté*.'[85] Two weeks later he sent her some more reviews, 'none of them exactly favourable',[86] and assured her that he had 'no intention of producing, like Euripides, seventy dramas in this style, but shall now turn to something wholly different'. Another important reader was K – 'I never think a performance of mine is fairly launched until I have your opinion of it',[87] he told her, and was gratified that she and William claimed to admire it. In a comment that shows the worrying deficiency of his dramatic sense, he added: 'You must remember that this form of drama is above all calculated for the stage – a sort of opera stage – and that as much as the Elizabethan drama loses by being acted the Greek drama gains.'

Arnold had no grasp of Elizabethan stagecraft and was frequently left cold by Shakespeare in performance. In a letter to Tom – in which he struggled to adopt a detached view of the criticism coming at him from all quarters – Arnold accepted that if he was right about *Merope* being 'nothing without the stage'[88] then his lack of time and means 'to establish a school of actors . . . and to provide a stage for them – to do in fact in England in my own way what the great classical school did in France in their way' meant that he could do no more in this vein. By the beginning of February he was telling his sister, Fan, that he was 'dead sick of criticism'.[89]

Many of his critics, he felt, were objecting to *Merope* because they saw it as an attempt to 'substitute tragedies *à la Grecque* for every other kind of poetical composition in England' and accordingly they swung into 'violent resistance' to such a project. He wanted readers to catch something of the 'power, grandeur, and dignity' of Greek dramatic art. 'But the British public prefer, like all obstinate multitudes, to "die in their sins", and I have no intention to keep preaching in the wilderness.' His view of that public was that 'one has oneself to consider as well as the public and one cannot always give them what they ask for'.[90] His mounting exasperation was softened by the fact that the book was selling well but he was shrewd enough to see that this was largely 'curiosity', the poem now having become a talking point in literary society. In a letter to Fanny de Quaire (sister of his recently deceased friend the MP John Blackett) Arnold explained that the poem was 'calculated rather to inaugurate my Professorship with dignity than to move deeply the present race of *humans*'.[91] He claimed that his 'real love for this form and this old Greek world' enabled him to 'infuse a little soul into my dealings with them which saves me from being entirely *ennuyeux*, professorial and pedantic'. This did not stop the poem being reviewed everywhere 'very civilly, but very expostulatingly'.

Throughout January Arnold struggled to field these criticisms while marking examination papers for pupil-teachers seeking certificates. 'I am up to my eyes in examination papers', he complained to his old boyhood tutor, Herbert Hill, 'the revision of these is the most tedious part of my yearly business.'[92] Yet somehow he managed to keep reading: 'I am reading Dante in *Italian* for the first time. O what force!'

As far as friends were concerned, Max-Müller delicately combined criticism and tact to go to the heart of the matter – 'may not a poet be classical, and yet modern and English?'[93] He saw that only 'a few carefully educated men' would appreciate the poem, which is disastrous for a poet – 'Sophocles wrote for his Athenian fig-eaters'. Max-Müller admired 'the breeze of fresh pure Greek air – and yet I would wish you some English clouds – ay some London smoke – on the blue sky of your classical soul'. Clough told a friend: 'I cannot say that I received much natural pleasure from it.'[94] The choruses also seemed to him 'indiscreetly long, and tedious even to the classical amateur'.[95] Lowell wrote to Clough from Cambridge, Massachusetts to say gruffly: 'I don't believe in poems that are arguments and require prefaces.'[96] Froude – always ruthlessly honest and illuminating about Arnold – said he could not feel the poem was 'adequate to your powers'.[97] He conceded it was 'the best reproduction' of Greek tragedy he had seen but therein lay the problem. To reproduce Greek tragedy, when the intervening centuries had fundamentally changed human sensibility, was to risk inevitable falseness: 'The problem of life presents itself to us differently . . . We are conscious of something in ourselves more subtle & more complicated of emotions to which the reproduction, at least of Greek poetry can give no vent'. Arnold failed either to match the silent grandeur of Sophocles or to show us his own heart. The verdict of Arnold's friends, however tactfully or obliquely they expressed themselves, was that the poem was an unmitigated disaster – and need not have been so had he not been perverse enough to devote so much extraordinary labour to a project misconceived from the outset.

Arnold – now a poet and professor of renown – was starting to be found at the dinner tables of hosts like Lord Granville where he listened eagerly to the political gossip. He always enjoyed a good table and good wine – the latter a constituent of 'the agreeableness of life'[98] and as his public eminence grew so did the business of his social diary. His most important piece of news in the letter to Fanny de Quaire was the announcement that the Arnolds had at last taken a more or less permanent house, at 2 Chester Square, Belgravia. 'It is a very small one', he told Fanny (the 'small' house still stands and a ten-year lease on a comparable property in the square in the 1990s would cost one and a quarter million pounds), 'but it will be something to unpack one's portmanteau for the first time since I was married, now nearly seven years ago.' The lease was for ten years (although in fact they stayed only until May 1866) and the judge came up with £800 to furnish the house.

Things were now looking a little more rosy for the Arnolds financially. Arnold's accounts for this year show a total income of £2,238.6s.9d made up of his emolument from the Professorship, the allowance from Judge Wightman (in addition to the furnishing bill), his salary, and his income from acting as marshal to the judge on circuit. Arnold's constant complaint about lack of funds is a little surprising given this very large income in mid-century terms. Flu, of course, was used to living in some style and had very active accounts at Fortnum & Mason and the Army and Navy. She would occasionally try to push her husband into applying for more lucrative posts – although his few attempts were to prove unsuccessful – and they remained comfortably off but never as rich as the Wightmans. And they loved the house: 'I cannot tell you how perpetual a pleasure our house is to us',[99] he told his mother. Another important domestic development at this time was the arrival of the robust and competent housekeeper, Mrs Tuffin, who was to stay with the Arnolds for many years. The two older boys were thrilled because her husband had been a dragoon and promised to tell them stories about soldiers. Mrs Tuffin was abetted by the nursemaid, Charlotte, and two other servants, Mary and Jane.

In May Arnold gave his second lecture at Oxford – neither the subject nor the text has survived – and he reported to his mother: 'I had a good many people, but not so many as the first time – hardly any undergraduates – and the theatre was, to me, depressingly too big for us.'[100] He wondered if the real reason for the falling off was the unfashionable task he had set himself: 'the one grand idea of these introductory lectures is to establish a formula which shall *sort* all literature: an attempt which so far as I know has not yet ever been made in England.' The question of Arnold's ability as a lecturer –

which was to cause such difficulties much later in America – had not yet become an issue, although *The Times* did report that his Latin oration in June at the annual Encaenia – the Crewian Oration – was problematic: 'Unfortunately, Mr Arnold was unable to make himself heard.'[101] His report on the third lecture was that: 'Flu liked it better than the second – and I always find that she thinks as a great many people think.'[102] He added, in a throwaway line: 'I breakfasted with Gladstone the other day.'

Mrs Arnold came to see the new house in Chester Square in June, and after setting off on circuit with Judge Wightman in July – leaving Flu horribly sick from the chloroform applied to have two teeth removed – Arnold was off to the Continent for the summer with Walrond. He wrote to K from Martigny about Froude's comments on his poems, observing that: 'if the opinion of the general public about my poems were the same as that of the leading literary men, I should make more money by them than I do'.[103] Arnold recognised that popularity was not just about making money but about providing the stimulus of an audience 'to produce my best – all that I have in me, whatever that may be – to produce which is no light matter with an existence so hampered as mine is'. Free for a few weeks with his old friend, Arnold could reflect on the price that had been paid for his secure married life and growing career as a public man. In a comment to K that shows how Arnold was in effect resigning his claim to true poetic originality, he wrote:

> People do not understand what a temptation there is, if you cannot bear anything not *very good*, to transfer your operations to a region where form is everything. Perfection of a kind may there be attained, or at least approached, without knocking yourself to pieces, but to attain or approach perfection in the region of thought and feeling, and to unite this with perfection of form, demands not merely an effort and a labour, but an actual tearing of oneself to pieces which one does not readily consent to (although one is sometimes forced to it) unless once can devote one's whole life to poetry.

These are desperately sad words. We are witnessing Arnold giving up, because he now knows he cannot properly live the life of a poet, any ambition other than for academic exercises ('perfection of a certain kind'). His desire for perfection, to be 'very good', far from issuing in beautiful poetry such as he had written in his twenties, had become a sort of straitjacket. His theories and his critical strictures, coupled to the demands of his public life, were killing off the poet. His critical mind attacked Keats (although he was subtly influenced by him) but the earlier poet once wrote that 'if Poetry comes not as naturally as the Leaves to a tree it had better not come at all'.[104] In place of such spontaneous growth, Arnold's poetry seemed to be withering on the bough. Only Goethe, Arnold felt, had managed to write great poetry while having to contend with an '*existence assujettie*' but he, too, could have done more poetically 'had he been freer'. This was something to do with the age. Had Arnold lived in a time of happy poetical abundance like that of the Elizabethans it would all have been so much easier. In such an epoch: 'It is natural, it is the bent of the time to do it; its being the bent of the time, indeed, is what makes the time a *poetical* one.' Arnold had told Clough when they were younger that they lived in 'an unpoetical age'. For a poet as conscious of the historical moment as Arnold not to live in a vigorous poetic climate was ultimately disabling.

The journey taken by Arnold and Walrond took them to Geneva, Zermatt, the Grand St Bernard, Dijon and Paris. It was invigorating but Arnold was missing Flu as a travelling companion 'more than I could have believed possible, and will certainly never travel again for *mere pleasure* without her'. He wrote her several long detailed letters describing his trip, recalling their previous trips together, and aching for her to be with him – 'I cannot tell you how I wished for you',[105] he wrote from the Alps. If the Muse was deserting him his love for Flu was constant. On his return he went straight to Fox How where she joined him with the three boys. He considered that without his annual visit to Fox How the year would have 'a great blank'[106] in it.

Back inspecting in October he was able to stay a few days at Oxford, finding Froude – now reconciled with the University by making appropriate noises about the Thirty-nine Articles – reading in the Bodleian 'as pleased as a child with his restored cap and gown'. He also went to hear the radical orator John Bright at a public meeting in Birmingham – 'an orator of the highest rank'[107] – before continuing to inspect. Arnold was popular with the Banbury schools and was showered with grapes and Banbury cakes by the pupils which made him long for his own children in the nursery at Chester Square. He told Fan that he took some time to get over 'the profound disgust'[108] at the loss of the country which coming back to London from Fox How always implanted. He had been inspecting a school at Hammersmith where the November sun shone but by the time he got back to Belgravia an 'impenetrable fog' had descended. He immediately sent Budge and Dick out into Hyde Park with the nurse for better air. The previous day a society lady had ordered her carriage to stop in the park so that she could inspect the delightful child and demand to know who Dick was.

The house was very pleasant, even if Arnold would have preferred to be twenty miles out of London and its fogs. He had fitted a huge bookcase in the study to receive his library. He had also just bought a print of Papa at Colnaghi's which was placed over the mantelpiece in the dining room for the edification of the frequent diners at 2 Chester Square. In December Flu was just about to give birth to her fourth child (Lucy was born on Christmas Day) but Arnold had to leave her to go on circuit with the judge again. This was a bore but 'the £75 of the Western Circuit Marshalship is a boon not to be refused'.[109] Tom, too, was unwell and the Arnolds' enthusiastic doctor, Hutton, was dosing the little boy with port wine and water to revive him, adding 'hot fomentations' on his chest for his heart, and, to finish off, his feet were placed in mustard and water. Arnold was at work on his third and fourth lectures (on 'the feudal state of society and the scholastic philosophy' and 'Dante, the troubadours and the early Drama' respectively) and was feeling pleased with the overall results: 'when the course is finished and published it will form a body of doctrine, true, as I of course think, but very novel and strange in England'.

6

Arnold spent six months from March to August 1859 as a Foreign Assistant Commissioner to France, Belgium and Switzerland to report for the Education Commission on the system of elementary education there. It was a dream posting, as he admitted to Fan: 'I cannot tell you how much I like the errand.'[110] It would, of course, mean some separation from Flu and the four children but as he began the year 'overwhelmed with grammar papers'[111] and having 'a hard time of it at present' it must have seemed a bright prospect. He blithely admitted to K that he had 'no special interest in the subject of public education'[112] but was looking forward to getting free of the routine work 'of which I sometimes get very sick'. He found foreign life very 'liberating' although he knew that his unfinished business with the English meant that he would 'work best in the long run by living in the country which is my own'.

On 15 March, three days after Arnold's fifth Oxford lecture, the whole family set off for the Continent. On 28 March he wrote to his mother from the Hotel Meûrice in Paris, anxious about Tom's heart trouble. The boy was so ill they feared the end had come. On the previous day he and Flu had walked to the Crémerie Imperiale which was supplied with milk from the Empress's farm in the country, 'and there we got the most delicious milk for him'.[113] The famous French doctor, Armand Trousseau, who was costing a ruinous £20 a week, looked down at Tom and murmured: 'Pauvre chat, pauvre chat' and prescribed atropine. Arnold reluctantly took the boy into his bed because he was 'as you know, a bad sleeper'. In spite of this, their first few days in Paris were marked by a box at the opera by courtesy of the Rothschilds, and meetings with Guizot and Mme de Staël. 'This society is still the first in the world, sorely tried as it is', Arnold decided. Paris was also a good place to be to learn about the Franco-Austrian conflict, a subject on which Arnold was planning a pamphlet – 'the moment is certainly most interesting and agitating',[114] he told Flu. By now she and the children had returned to London. Arnold's income of £18 a week from the Commission wasn't even enough to cover the doctor's bills so the decision was inevitable. Alone in Paris, he received news of the death of Willy at Gibraltar on 9 April, returning from India.

Arnold's travels about France were reported in detail in letters to Flu. He was particularly interested in the Druidical monument at Carnac in Brittany and told his mother that he thought of her Trevenen descent when seeing the Breton surnames of Cranic and Trevenec everywhere. His enthusiasm for the Breton peasantry made him think that 'the profoundly democratic spirit which exists among the lower orders'[115] made 'the revival of an aristocratic society impossible'. He also noted, while in Bordeaux, that: 'The Revolution has cleared out the feudal ages from the minds of the country people to an extent incredible with us.'[116] At Nîmes he was struck by the classical remains and their 'immense superiority to the Teutonic middle age'.[117]

After France, Arnold was in Holland, a small taste of which he told Fan, was sufficient. He hated the climate and the feeling of 'mortal ennui'[118] among the people. 'It is the Norman element in England', he suggested, 'which has kept her from getting stupid and humdrum too, as the pure Germanic nations tend to become for want of a little effervescing salt with their magnesia.' Arnold was delighted to return to France: 'Paris', he told Fan, 'like London, has always immense life and movement in its streets.'[119] He was more than ever determined now to write his pamphlet. He met a British diplomat, Lord Cowley, who gave him a long briefing on the issue. He was generally in good spirits and beginning to wish that he was not so lazy, 'but I hope and believe one is less so from forty to fifty, if one lives, than at any other time of life. The loss of youth ought to operate as a spur to one to live more by the head, when one can live less by the body.'[120]

Arnold had just read John Stuart Mill's latest book, *On Liberty*, and was enthused. 'It is worth reading attentively, being one of the few books that inculcate tolerance in an unalarming and inoffensive way', he told Fan. In addition to the general impact on Arnold of this classic statement of the virtues of toleration, one cannot help noticing, in Mill's warning against the absorption by government of the critical energies of the independent intelligentsia, the use of the word 'machinery'. Arnold was to make this one of the key terms in his social and cultural criticism. It was the vice of too many of his contemporaries, he felt, that they worshipped machinery – meaning formal and pedantic arrangements – as opposed to the free play of thought, such that the British Constitution had become 'a colossal machine for the manufacture of Philistines'.[121] Mill's placing, in the closing paragraph of his essay, of 'the perfection of machinery' in opposition to 'the vital power' of free citizens represented a duality Arnold understood. For all his powerful advocacy of the role of the State, Arnold knew that society depended on the inner life of the individual to provide the energising force of its culture. Or as Mill put it: 'The worth of the State, in the long run, is the worth of the individuals composing it.'

Arnold's advocacy of flexible intelligence and the 'Hellenic' virtues, owes a great deal to his reading of Mill. One section of British society which exemplified Arnold's and Mill's critique was the aristocracy. 'What pains the English aristocracy seem to be taking to justify all I have said about their want of ideas!'[122] he exclaimed to K from Geneva. Arnold sometimes admired the nobility of the English aristocracy but he could never respect their intellect. His comments on the recently defeated Prime Minister Lord Derby, the fourteenth Earl, are typical: 'But the true type of the British political nobleman is Lord Derby – with eloquence, high feeling, and good intentions – but the ideas of a schoolboy.'[123] He also told K that he had been elected a member of the Alpine Club 'though entirely undeserving of such an honour'. Flu had come out from England once more to be with her husband, although this time the children had been left behind.

Switzerland did Flu good: 'At Chamonix she has ridden nearly up to the top of the Breveut, and is getting quite sunburnt and strong',[124] he reported to his mother. But by the end of July, they were both missing the children and longed to be back in England.

They returned in August – a planned trip to see George Sand not having taken place in spite of Arnold's bearing a letter of introduction from the historian Jules Michelet. Perhaps his youthful enthusiasm was waning – 'she is so unfrench and so taciturn that it is quite possible I might not get much out of her',[125] he told his mother. For the first two weeks in August the family took lodgings at 1 Wellesley Terrace, Dover. The pamphlet, *England and the Italian Question*, had been rushed out and Arnold was keen to collect reactions to it, particularly those of K: 'You and Clough are, I believe, the two people I in my heart care most to please by what I write',[126] he told her. 'Clough (for a wonder) is this time satisfied, even delighted . . .' Another friend, however, Francis Turner Palgrave, told Clough he thought the pamphlet 'degrading twaddle'.[127] Gladstone, however, was more sympathetic and in a letter acknowledging his praise, Arnold stressed how what he had said was based on 'solid experience'[128] and that it was justified because: 'In the last few months I have visited nearly every part of France and seen all classes of society from archbishops and Prefects to village schoolmasters and peasants'. The pamphlet also went down well in France.

During this brief interlude at Dover the whole family went out one afternoon to the beach, by the piles which supported the railway, and the children ran into the sea to bathe: 'They take to the water like ducks', the doting parent told his mother, 'and you should have seen that lovely little figure of Dick's laid down flat on the bright shingle with his sweet face upwards and his golden hair all floating about him waiting for the wave to come up and wash over him.'[129] This was a far cry from the Dover beach which, eight years earlier, had prompted poetic meditations on the loss of Faith. Mrs Tuffin, too, was fond of Dick and asked if she could take him to see her sister who was also in service at Canterbury.

Back in Paris by the middle of August, Arnold dined with Sainte-Beuve: 'I stayed with Sainte-Beuve until midnight', he told Flu, 'and would not have missed my evening for all the world. I think he likes me, and likes my caring so much about his criticisms and appreciating his extraordinary delicacy of tact and judgement in literature.'[130] On his return to London at the end of August, Arnold wrote to Fan to say how much he felt he owed his new success as a pamphleteer to his father: 'It is the one literary side on which I feel myself in close contact with him, and that is a great pleasure. Even the positive style of statement I inherit.'[131]

By now Arnold had discovered a new distraction from writing – military drill. He had enlisted with the Queen's Westminster Rifle Volunteers and spent two hours, two or three nights a week, on the parade ground. 'I like the drilling very much; it braces one's muscles, and does one a world of good',[132] he told Fan. But Clough reported to Tom rather sarcastically that his friend was 'learning "the goose step" and other soldierly accomplishments as Member of the Queen's Volunteers or Pimlico Rifles, who drill thrice a week in Westminster Hall.'[133] Arnold dismissed the idea put forward in 'the cheap Radical newspapers' that this was a dangerous exercise in 'arming the people' by pointing out that it was only the responsible middle and upper classes who were taking up the rifle. The only real drawback was 'the hideous English toadyism with which lords and great people are invested with the commands in the corps they join, quite without respect of any considerations of their efficiency. This proceeds from our national bane – the immense vulgar-mindedness, and, so far, real inferiority of the English middle classes.'

What Arnold should really have been engaged with at this time was his report on the French schools, not square-bashing. 'I am always very stupid at providing anything by a given time or for a special purpose',[134] he admitted to his old Balliol friend, Edward Walford, in a letter written from the judge's lodgings at York where a period as marshal just before Christmas was adding to his distractions. Notwithstanding these, he even toyed with the idea of going back to Paris – 'winter society having begun there, and everybody being alive and gay'[135] – to compare notes with a French educational inquirer, Cousin.

The year ended with Arnold looking ahead to composing his Oxford lectures on Celtic literature during 1860 (in fact they would be delivered in 1865 and 1866 and published in 1867). He told K how much he was indebted to the French scholar Ernest Renan for his ideas on Celtic literature. 'I have long felt that we owed far more, spiritually and artistically, to the Celtic races than the somewhat coarse Germanic intelligence readily perceived, and been increasingly satisfied at our own semi-Celtic origin, which, as I fancy, gives us the power, if we will use it, of comprehending the nature of both races',[136] he wrote to K, recalling their Cornish ancestry. On the last day of the year Arnold wrote to his mother, describing a visit to the zoo with Dick, Tom, Budge and Lucy, who were rewarded with the lion 'growling magnificently'. He also noted with regret the death of Macaulay: 'But the *Times*' leading article on him is a splendid exhibition of what may be called the *intellectual vulgarity* of that newspaper.'[137]

Arnold had now published his first independent prose work and was poised to begin a new career as a prose polemicist of great vigour and style. He would henceforth do battle with the English Philistines and their 'intellectual vulgarity'. He was to write very little poetry from now on – perhaps only *Thyrsis* of the poems to come was of any real distinction – and his energy was to be thrown instead into controversy in prose and into criticism. Various suggestions have been made above to account for this change of direction but there is no simple, comprehensive explanation for Arnold's desertion by the Muse, nor could there ever be. The pressures of his career, his Arnoldian sense of public mission, his emasculating theories about poetry, his private domestic tragedies, his keen sense of what was lost with the loss of youth, all played their part in the Muse's desertion. But he did not despair and his work as a critic was done with relish and panache, leaving us a body of work in prose of great value, easily equal to what he achieved in poetry, but impossible to contemplate without at least some sense of regret.

PART TWO

The Triumph of the Critic

CHAPTER SIX:
THE NICEST MODERATION
[1860–1865]

It is not, it seems to me, freedom, not energy, not even honesty that is at the present time wanting in England, but intelligence . . .[1]

1

Amongst the annual clutch of quotations assembled in the blank pages of Matthew Arnold's pocket diary for 1860 is one that has an obvious autobiographical resonance. It is from George Sand's *L'homme de neige* (1858): 'I too have been a little frivolous: and then, after having spent my best years a little negligently, I picked myself up and I now press forward . . . Throw yourself into your studies.'[2] Arnold's correspondence during the year shows him consciously screwing himself up to greater effort in response to the great intellectual challenge that he felt the age was throwing down to him.

England and the Italian Question had been his first prose work and, in a way that would be characteristic of so much of his work to come, its real interest lay not so much in its ostensible subject – the military conflict between Austria and a Sardinia backed by her ally Napoleon III of France – as in its preliminary rehearsal of some leading Arnoldian ideas about the English aristocracy. In particular, Arnold represented the aristocracy as innately conservative and unable to entertain new ideas because of its imprisonment in the status quo. Compared with the lively polemical style of his later criticism, this is a restrained work with only the briefest rhetorical flourish – a reference to Napoleon's confidence that he could violate the treaties of Vienna 'though a hundred Cassandras in the English Upper House bewail them with dishevelled hair'.[3] The pamphlet is charged with the spirit of progressive liberalism, confident in 'the triumph of the modern spirit' and the inevitability of change.

Arnold spent the first few weeks of the year, when he had got back from Fox How, working on his report on French schools, doing much of the work in the British Museum, now greatly improved as a place to work in, he felt, following work carried out in 1857. He planned to enlist Flu as a helper in copying out extracts. As he pored over the material on France, Arnold's respect for Napoleon – 'that astonishing man'[4] – grew. He admired the way in which Napoleon 'held the balance between old and new France in reorganising things'. A similar caution about the pace of change is evident at this time in Arnold's views about America. In a letter to Fan he suggested that – notwithstanding his attacks on the English aristocracy – the *'national character'* of the Americans was giving cause for concern: 'It seems as if few stocks could be trusted to grow up properly without having a priesthood and an aristocracy to act as their schoolmasters at some time or other of their national existence.'[5]

In spite of these official preoccupations, Arnold was not entirely neglecting his poetry. On 1 June he wrote to John William Parker, publisher of *Fraser's Magazine*, offering him some lines which he had only just found time that morning to write out. *Saint Brandan* was eventually published in the magazine's July number and its subject derives from an essay on Celtic poetry in a recently published book by Renan, *Essais de Morale et de Critique* (1859). Saint Brandan, the Benedictine Abbot of Clonfert, Galway, according to legend made a seven-year voyage in search of the Land of Saints in the course of which, in the polar regions, he encountered Judas Iscariot, released from the fires of hell for one hour a year at Christmas – thanks to an act of generosity in his lifetime when he gave his cloak to a leper. Arnold, in this last of his narrative poems, was trying to achieve that balance of the magical and the realistic which Renan saw as the essence of the Celtic aesthetic, but he seems not to have been satisfied with the poem. It confirms how deeply interested Arnold had become in Celtic poetry, an interest which would culminate in the lectures on Celtic literature in the middle of the decade. His imagination responded to this material and in dealing with it he let himself go a little more freely than his customary classical sense of restraint allowed.

In the same letter to Parker, Arnold mentioned some stanzas written the previous May at Carnac in Brittany on the death of 'my poor brother William'[6] which he had thought to send him but had now decided to keep for a later collection of his poems (the poem would eventually be published in the 1867 edition of Arnold's poems). Willy, as noted above, had died at Gibraltar on his way home from India and the poem – which describes the ancient Druid shrine at Carnac – regrets his failure to reach these 'Cool northern fields'.

Probably at the same time as this poem, Arnold started work on another, *A Southern Night*, which also dealt with 'high-souled' Willy's death. Like the Carnac stanzas, it plays on the contrast between the tropical and the Mediterranean climates where Willy worked and died, and the cold, busy, Northern world where he originated: 'In cities should we English lie, / Where cries are rising ever new, / And men's incessant stream goes by'. The 'spent ones of a work-day age' lie incongruously by the 'waters of romance'. Mingled with the regret for Willy is a regret at the kind of prosaic world of business in which Arnold increasingly now found himself. Another moonlit night recalled in the poem, when the poet would 'Wander unquiet, and my own / Vexed heart deplore', is perhaps one of those which Arnold spent in secret vigil outside Flu's house in Belgravia at the time her father forbade them to meet. 'But now that trouble is forgot', writes Arnold briskly, now a hampered public servant having to write up a report on foreign schools.

During the early summer of 1860 Arnold exchanged several letters with Harriet Martineau. He seems to have sent her sections of his report for comment and they also discussed the political situation: 'We are on the eve, I believe, of great changes', wrote Arnold, 'and a theory of government which did very well when only a small part of the nation took part in governing, will no longer serve when democracy enters into proportion. At least I have never read of any democracy which truly succeeded except by entering into that alliance with the best intelligence and virtue within itself and submitting to that guidance from it which autocratic and oligarchic governments manage to get on without.'[7] We seem to hear in these words Arnold drafting a job description for himself.

It is not clear when Arnold finished his report – which was published early in 1861 – but he had probably finished the main sections by the summer when the family went on a trip to the Continent. They stayed for three weeks at Viel Salm in Belgium, in a hotel that was good value at four francs a day for Arnold and his wife, and three francs for Mrs Tuffin and Charlotte the nurse, and one franc for the three boys and baby Lucy. Arnold had brought his gun and his rod with him and he delighted in the astonished reaction of the locals to his use of a fly to catch the abundant trout. He was thoroughly enjoying himself, in spite of the weather, and wrote to Fan: 'Flu treats me as her great schoolboy, to whom she is giving his holiday'.[8] Fishing, and shooting snipe and hare, and falling asleep after dinner, Arnold could forget about the world's cares, although he did see a Belgian newspaper containing summaries of *The Times* which he noted 'blunders intrepidly on as usual'.[9] He also wrote to Tom, one of many letters urging his brother to get a grip on his affairs. He had already written to him from Dover, exasperatedly: '. . . my dear Tom, it is one of your few weaknesses, that you *cannot* look your position in the face and *force* yourself, *and others* to adapt themselves to it.'[10]

Eventually this delightful holiday came to an end and the family mounted 'the great omnibus' to Spa, bearing an enormous basket of peaches and nectarines from their hosts. They stayed at the Hotel de l'Europe at Liège, sampling urban pleasures again, and at the Hotel Bellevue at Brussels ('a consolation to my party for the simplicity and solitude of Viel Salm'[11]). After early church on the Sunday Arnold took Flu with him to the battlefield of Waterloo which fascinated him. Their guide was the same man who had taken Byron to the site in 1816. They returned to the 'dear little house' at Chester Square at the start of October and for a week Arnold was unable to pluck up the courage to tackle the pile of papers from the Council Office which had built up in his absence.

In addition to the office work, tidying up the last details of his report, and inspecting at Banbury, Arnold had to prepare his latest Oxford lecture. He explained to his mother that his aim was to 'lay down the true principles on which a translation of Homer should be founded'.[12] Strictly speaking this was an additional lecture given 'partly because I have long had in my mind something to say about Homer, partly because of the complaints that I did not enough lecture on poetry'. It was eventually delivered on 3 November and grew to two more delivered on 8 December and 26 January 1861, the series being published in January 1861 as *On Translating Homer*. He was thus extremely busy in the autumn but, as he put it, perhaps rather bitterly, to his mother: 'With the limited sphere of action in outward life which I have, what is life unless I occupy it in this manner, and keep myself from feeling starved and shrunk up?' A few weeks later he told her that he was still 'very hard at work' on the second lecture and contemplating a third. 'I feel very sure of my ground in these lectures', he added, 'and that makes me do them, no doubt, all the better. I hear from Oxford that people were greatly pleased and interested by the first of the set.'[13]

The sense of satisfaction made the hard work bearable and Arnold was clearly feeling at the height of his powers: 'I have not been in better case for a long time,' he told Fan, 'and I attribute it entirely to making greater demands on myself. If you only half use the machine it goes badly, but its full play suits it; and if I live and do well from now to fifty (only twelve years!), I will get something out of myself.'[14] He was planning, once the Homer lectures were completed, to be 'well plunged into the Middle Age'. But it was not until 1864, with the Oxford lecture on *Pagan and Christian Religious Sentiment* that anything like the fruit of a study of the Middle Ages actually appears. Arnold said he strongly disliked the 'irrationality' of the period and the 'utter folly of those who take it seriously and play at restoring it' but it still had 'poetically the greatest charm and refreshment possible for me'. He added: 'There is something magical about it, and I will do something with it before I have done.' Tennyson, Arnold believed, had failed utterly to capture 'the peculiar charm and aroma' of the Middle Ages in his *Idylls of the King*, partly because he was 'deficient in intellectual power, and no modern poet can make very much of his business unless he is pre-eminently strong in this'.

Arnold's prejudice against Tennyson was remarkably consistent. It is not easy to discern why the animus was so strong, because Tennyson himself – although he once replied to a suggestion that Arnold be a dinner guest with the observation that he 'didn't much like dining with Gods!'[15] – does not seem to have responded in kind. On another occasion he told his son Hallam Tennyson: 'Tell Matt not to write any more of those prose things but to give us something like his Forsaken Mermaid [*sic*] & Gipsy Scholar.'[16] Not wholly injudicious advice, we might feel. Perhaps the consciousness of the gap between the 'popular' and the unpopular poet sharpened Arnold's response to Tennyson. (When Clough was convalescing on the Isle of Wight early in 1861 and being befriended by Tennyson, he was told by Arnold to convey to Tennyson that he would have 'great pleasure in sending him anything of mine he wants to see',[17] which shows that Arnold had that ambivalent anxiety to please lurching into a readiness to condemn that is often the keynote of literary jealousy.) Perhaps, too, he thought the poet's success was too easily bought, and resented in some way the displacement of his idol, Wordsworth, by Tennyson's popularity in the mid-century, a phenomenon referred to in his later selection of the

Lake poet's work. Whatever the reason, Arnold seldom passed over an opportunity to disparage the more famous poet. In 1860, however, the Oxford Professor of Poetry was cautious about voicing his views on Tennyson outside his private correspondence 'though gradually I mean to say boldly the truth about a great many English celebrities, and I begin with Ruskin in these lectures on Homer'.[18]

On the last day of the year Arnold wrote to his mother at Fox How giving an account of his workload – grammar papers from the student teachers to be marked, a study of Greek accents in connection with his Homer lectures to be completed, his annual report to be done, and the French schools report to be prepared for the press. Much as Arnold complained, however, of the press of business he once told Clough, during a languid summer at Fox How: 'I for my part find here that I could willingly fish all day and read the newspapers all evening, and so live – but I am not pleased with the results in myself of even a day or two of such life.'[19]

2

Arnold's lectures on the translation of Homer are his first major essay in criticism and they remain today lively and pertinent explorations of his theme: the right way to translate Homer ('the most important poetical monument existing'[20]). Arnold recognised that 'the study of classical literature is probably on the decline' and therefore translation would increasingly become the gateway to the classical poets for most people. All the more reason, therefore, to get it right. He was concerned, he said, not to get involved in theories of translation but to give 'practical advice' to the translator. He dismissed previous Homeric attempts by Pope and Chapman because, in his view, they got the spirit of Homer wrong – Chapman because he was an Elizabethan and therefore, according to Arnold's critical reading of that period of literature, subject to fancy and caprice and unable to discipline himself sufficiently to represent Homer's plain thought. In consequence, he '*tormented*' it. Arnold's central argument was that the translator must 'reproduce the effect' of Homer not create something else that suited his or her purpose. His ideal translation would allow the reader to get as close as possible to the experience of those who read it in the original language. It was an argument that the translator should be self-effacing.

In the first lecture Arnold introduced the contemporary translator Francis Newman (brother of John Henry Newman and Professor of Latin at University College, London, whose translation of the *Iliad* had appeared in 1856) and proceeded to have great sport with him. Arnold's characteristically *ad hominem* approach to intellectual debate – which added considerably to the entertainment value of his criticism – was not adopted out of malice. He would sometimes be surprised by the reaction to his sallies and would revise subsequent editions of his work accordingly. Like many high-spirited writers who discover in themselves a talent to deride, Arnold came to enjoy the exercise of his gift for ridicule – too readily, perhaps, forgetting that the world is often not so easily amused. In the case of Newman, Arnold believed that the translator had simply got Homer wrong, treating him as a sort of old-fashioned balladeer with a quaint style to match ('O brother thou of me, who am a mischief-working vixen', says Newman's Helen to Hector).

Arnold believed that Homer was distinguished by four essential qualities: 'Homer is rapid in his movement, Homer is plain in his words and style, Homer is simple in his ideas, Homer is noble in his manner.' Taken together, these qualities constituted 'the grand style' which was, for Arnold, the distinguishing mark of the truly great poet. He felt that translators who failed to recognise Homer's nobility were condemned to misrepresent him and that Newman, who was 'quaint, garrulous, prosaic, low', was a particularly unfortunate example of this. He rejected the currently fashionable analogy for Homer's style – the ballad – and argued that the *Iliad* had 'a great master's genuine stamp and that stamp is the *grand style*'. The rapid, clear, flowing nobility of Homer's style was more than moving, Arnold argued, 'it can form the character, it is edifying'. Artists who work in the grand style 'can refine the raw natural man, they can transmute him'.

Arnold concluded the second lecture by saying that the arbitrariness and eccentricity of these English translators – and here he echoed his 1853 Preface – were part of what was wrong with English literature in the mid-Victorian period. It explained why 'regarded not as an object of mere literary interest but as a living intellectual instrument' contemporary English literature 'ranks only third in European effect and importance among the literatures of Europe; it ranks after the literatures of France and Germany'. Of these two other literatures, Arnold believed, 'as of the intellect of Europe in general, the main effort, for now many years, has been a *critical* effort; the endeavour in all branches of knowledge, – theology, philosophy, history, art, science – to see the object as in itself it really is'. This latter phrase, introduced here for the first time, was to become one of Arnold's perhaps too frequently reiterated phrases in the critical essays that lay ahead. The absence of proper criticism in England, he went on, meant that translators were often lacking in 'simple lucidity of mind'. Character-istically, Arnold had moved from a specific literary topic to a general indictment of the shortcomings of the contemporary English intelli-gentsia when compared with what he judged to be the larger and more critical spirit of their equivalents in Europe.

It was not until the third lecture that Arnold really came down to specific detail – announcing to Clough that he intended to 'lay down a little positive doctrine having negatived enough'[21] – by stating that the best way of rendering Homer in English was through the English hexameter. This is a poetic measure which has always enjoyed a bad press in England, in Arnold's day and our own, but which, as Clough demonstrated, can be an attractive and supple metrical form. Arnold praised the effort to translate Homer into hexameters made by Dr Hawtrey, the Provost of Eton, and argued that the hexameter possessed both 'a natural dignity' and 'a loose grammatical style' that were up to the job of rendering Homer. Tentatively, Arnold even offered some Homer in hexameters of his own, conceding quickly that they probably possessed 'an air somewhat too strenuous and severe'. But he was trying to achieve the essential '*moderation*' of Homer, so alien to the 'boisterous, rollicking' way in which the English often talked about him. 'For Homer's grandeur is not the mixed and turbid grandeur of the poets of the north, of the authors of *Othello* and *Faust*; it is a perfect, a lovely grandeur.'

3

A week before Arnold delivered his last Homer lecture (at the end of which he would be cheered by his Oxford audience) he noted in his diary, on 19 January 1861, that he had 587 papers to mark. To make matters worse he was afflicted by an eye infection which had him dabbing with a mixture of rosewater and zinc, eyes which felt 'as if you had a basket of sand in them'.[22] His health remained poor for the next two months and he gloomily reported to his mother at the end of February: 'I have more to do than I can well manage, but have been employing these good-for-nothing days in school-reports and a quantity of drudgery on which it is a shame to throw away a brighter time.'[23] At the beginning of March he told Clough: 'I dare say for the next week or so I shall lead the life of a dog.'[24] The children were ill, too, with measles. And as well as the exam papers he was being harried by Longman who wanted to publish his *Popular Education of France* in a separate edition. This eventually appeared in May only a few weeks after its appearance in official form as part of the report of the Newcastle Commission. This instant recycling – or what he described as 'de-officialising' – was done at Arnold's expense. He was alarmed, however, to receive a bill of over £80 from Longman in October 1862, the book having failed to cover its costs by that amount. This was more than all he had received in total in over thirteen years as a writer. Arnold had already reported rather haughtily to Clough, in relation to his Italian pamphlet, that Longman was 'as regards books, a thorough *tradesman*'.[25]

As well as the writing of his introduction to the French report, January was dominated by proof-reading the Homer lectures (made more difficult by all the Greek quotations), composing his annual inspector's report, and yet more marking. One day, having had enough, he went out in 'execrable weather' to Battersea with Dick and Budge to see if they could get some skating. But the ice was too rough and he had to carry Dick back on his shoulders. The same night he picked up Thomas from a children's party 'rolled up like a ball in two plaids and put away in a corner of the brougham'. There was a lively family debate just now on whether the boys should be sent away to school but Flu used the argument of her imminent confinement to keep them at home, fearing that any mishap in the birth might mean she would never see them again.

After the Homer lectures were published one of the first reactions was from K who accused her brother of being too dogmatic. He defended himself by saying that the tone of a lecturing professor could not be the same as that of a periodical writer and that he was bound to speak formally and *ex cathedra*. None the less, the charge registered with him, for he always took K (who was now looking for a house in London after William Forster's election as MP in Bradford) seriously. 'There are few people of whom I so often think as of you',[26] he had told her the previous month. But in a letter to his mother he referred to K's accusation and tried to defend himself by saying that 'when one is on the side of *common sense* much pointedness is forgiven'.[27] A few weeks later he told her: 'What takes people in my lectures is the stress laid on what is *tonic* and *fortifying* in Homer. This sort of thing always attracts attention from English people, however barbarous they may be.'[28] The birth of Eleanor, who was always called Nelly, on 11 February, however, overshadowed such concerns. For the first few days, Arnold, who was out all day inspecting at Sydenham, only saw the new baby ('a very large, fine child') when she was asleep in her cradle.

A week later Arnold wrote to his old tutor, Herbert Hill, who had apparently attended one of his Oxford lectures. Arnold was sorry to miss him, he said, 'though for my part a lecture has so few attractions for me that I am always a little surprised to find anybody present at mine. This comes, in me, from a peculiar dulness in learning *orally* – that which I listen to quite languidly and inattentively if I hear it spoken I often read with great interest when I get it under my eyes in peace and quiet'.[29] He also told Hill that he had no plans to translate Homer himself – it had been rumoured that he might and, when sending a copy of the lectures to Gladstone, Arnold had been forced to repeat the disclaimer. He informed Hill, however, that Clough was thinking of doing so. Arnold felt that 'the immense labour' required to translate Homer could not be justified unless he was certain that the hexameter would work. He was still uneasy about Clough's experiments with the hexameter: 'I think he is cumbering himself with mechanical rules of making his lines scan *quantitatively* instead of by accent, which will take the naturalness out of his work.'

Arnold was receiving many letters now about his lectures and 'almost every one contains a protest against the hexameters'.[30] Arnold confessed to Hill: 'I don't mean to publish any more poetry till I am past 40 – and I still want two more years of that time. I go on doing what I can but it is a hard life for us all, and it is only while we are strongly exciting ourselves that we lose the sense of its hardship.' For all Arnold's bravado about the stimulus of hard work, making the machine operate at full throttle, and so forth, these remarks make clear that he knew costs were being incurred. The actual inspecting work was not heavy – it was the combination of it with a range of other intellectual tasks, each pulling Arnold in a different direction, that created the pressure. He even admitted to his mother that 'Inspecting seems mere play when I have nothing else to do beside it.'[31] That was a condition in which he almost never found himself.

Partly out of a desire to give the children a healthier environment after their winter attacks of measles, the Arnolds decided to take out a short rental of a house at 11 Regency Square, Brighton from 18 April to 19 July, sub-letting the house at Chester Square for the duration. Writing to his mother from Lewes while acting as a marshal again, Arnold told her of the reprinting in translation of his poem on Obermann in Sainte-Beuve's new book on Chateaubriand. He realised that the praise of Sainte-Beuve – 'the first of living critics' – was valuable 'because it carries one's name through the literary circles of Europe in a way that no English praise can carry it'. Moreover, it was administered 'with a delicacy for which one would look in vain here'.[32] His diaries were filled this year with quotations from the French critic, whose influence on Arnold was enormous.

The appeal of 'delicacy' was strong for Arnold just now and, while on an inspecting trip to Oxford – where he gathered orchises and bluebells in the Maytime Cumnor hills – he noticed how much more intense the intellectual life of Oxford was now. This was leading to envies, hatreds and jealousies in the academic community of a kind which he was anxious to avoid, 'convinced as I am that irritations and envyings are not only negatively injurious to one's spirit, like dulness, but positively and actively'.[33] Arnold's polemical zest perhaps hid the fact that he was capable of being hurt by controversy. He could well have been unsettled by the dissension engendered by his Homer lectures.

His new book, *The Popular Education of France*, was published in the first week of May. In recommending it to Gladstone, Arnold had singled out the introduction, on 'Democracy', which is certainly the most interesting part of the book and which, recognising its importance, Arnold later abstracted as an essay with that title for his collection *Mixed Essays* (1879). Just as the 1853 Preface launched some primary critical ideas that were later to be expanded and developed into something like a body of critical doctrine, the essay on democracy contains the first outlines of his cultural criticism. It also shows how clearly and firmly he envisaged a role for the State and how unimpressed he was by the middle-class cries for a more laissez-faire approach to government.

Arnold argued that 'The growing power in Europe is democracy.'[34] He believed democracy was both inevitable and desirable and that the contemporary impulse towards it was 'identical with the ceaseless vital effort of human nature itself'. It was a matter of 'affirming one's own essence', a concept which meant 'to develop one's own existence fully and freely, to have ample light and air, to be neither cramped nor overshadowed'. Arnold's passion for equality – which was the foundation of his later notion of culture as something that depended crucially on being universally diffused if it was to have any meaning – was never so vigorously expressed as in this essay. 'Can it be denied', he asked, 'that to live in a society of equals tends in general to make a man's spirits expand, and his faculties work easily and actively; while, to live in a society of superiors, although it may occasionally be a very good discipline, yet in general tends to tame the spirits and to make the play of the faculties less secure and active?'

France was a democracy, organised so as to give all her people the opportunity for 'full and free expansion'. England was not because of her aristocracy: 'At epochs when new ideas are powerfully fermenting in a society, and profoundly changing its spirit, aristocracies, as they are in general not long suffered to guide it without question, so are they by nature not well fitted to guide it intelligently.' But at the same time Arnold was anxious that English society should not become 'Americanised' or vulgarised by having achieved democracy yet finding herself with nothing to aspire to. 'The difficulty for democracy is, how to find and keep high ideals', he suggested. His answer to that dilemma was for the State to act and for a critical national culture to be forged, not the culture of the nineteenth-century English middle class 'with their narrow, harsh, unintelligent, and unattractive spirit and culture', which, by failing to impress the masses beneath meant that 'society is in danger of falling into anarchy'. Drawing on Burke, Arnold defined the State as 'the nation in its collective and corporate character', something that could draw people towards a finer, shared ideal. He admitted that he was on dangerous ground for 'the great middle classes of this country are conscious of no weakness, no inferiority'.

Arnold was to spend the rest of his life trying to puncture that complacency, to open his fellow countrymen to ideas, to awaken in them a more critical spirit. In this sense, T. S. Eliot was right when he described Arnold as 'a propagandist for criticism',[35] for Arnold saw himself as needing to recommend the activity itself quite as much as to deliver himself of particular critical judgements. At such a transforming epoch, he believed that 'openness and flexibility of mind' were the one thing needful. The closing paragraph of the essay makes explicit the religious source of Arnold's secular prescriptions for culture – a crucial dimension of his thought that is too often overlooked. He recalls Christ's injunction: 'Be ye perfect', to introduce the notion of spiritual perfection that pervades later works like *Culture and Anarchy*. 'Perfection will never be reached', Arnold admits, 'but to recognise a period of transformation when it comes, and to adapt themselves honestly and rationally to its laws, is perhaps the nearest approach to perfection of which men and nations are capable.'

4

In the spring of 1861, Arnold was increasingly worried about K. She was now living in London because her husband William Forster was an MP, but she was unhappy, and, as Arnold explained to his mother, 'she is so much alone'.[36] One day towards the end of May he took her with him to a school in Somers Town and on another, coming home from a school in the afternoon and finding her despondent, he took her off to the Botanic Garden in Chelsea. This made him late for dinner at Eaton Place 'which was vexatious as you know the Judge's punctuality, and, I may add, his fidgetiness' he explained later to his mother. He added that K 'says her shyness she does not get over and not having a carriage, and being a good deal alone her afternoons must often be long. Then the remoteness of the place where they live is terrible.' Perhaps K contrasted her own life with that of her brother and his happy, growing family – she remained childless until she adopted the four children of Willy who were given the surname Arnold-Forster.

'Children . . . are a great pleasure, or at least I find mine so', Arnold wrote to his mother from Brighton where he and the two eldest boys had been bathing from a bathing-machine on the shore. His presence in Brighton prevented his accepting an invitation from a new friend who would become increasingly important in his life: Lady Louisa de Rothschild whose seat at Aston Clinton happily fell within Arnold's inspection district. Sounding the note of witty gallantry that would characterise this relationship, he wrote to her: 'Advancing years make me an encumbrance in a ballroom, but had I been in London I should have braved the waltzes to have the pleasure of seeing you.'[37] A few days later Arnold wrote what was to be his last letter to Clough, advising him against leaving his steady job in the Education Office: 'The mental harass of an uncertain life must be far more irksome than the ennui of the most monotonous employment',[38] wrote his friend from a depth of experience. Tackling his own 'mental harass', Arnold wrote some more rules in his diary: 'At least one case reported daily till finished. One canto of Dante daily. One half chapter of Guizot's memoirs daily.'[39]

Soon, however, he was on circuit again in Norfolk and the midland counties, staying at Cambridge, where he lodged with the judge at Trinity, and Bedford where a wealthy clergyman was their host. Of his two 'charming' daughters, one was married and 'The other is still unmarried and quite delightful',[40] Arnold noted. On this circuit Arnold met a number of former Rugby men and many others who had known his father. 'I find people are beginning to know something about *me* myself, but I am still far oftener an object of interest as his son than on my own account',[41] he reported to his mother. He also mentioned to her the anonymous attack on his Homer lectures in the latest edition of the *Saturday Review* – it was in fact written by James Fitzjames Stephen (the uncle of Virginia Woolf) who described the clash with Newman as 'a good stand-up fight'[42] but reacted stiffly to the levity of tone: 'We are quite sure that they are not the sort of things which an Oxford Professor ought to deliver officially before the University.' Stephen castigated Arnold's 'contemptuous and insulting language', his 'personal abuse' and his 'low buffoonery' and poured scorn on Arnold's own Homeric versions and his concept of Homer's nobility. He also objected to the constant references by Arnold to himself: 'The whole of the lectures are one constant I – I – I.'

Arnold admitted that when he first read an attack of this kind he was annoyed, 'then I think how certainly in two or three days the effect of it upon me will have wholly passed off; then I begin to think of the openings it gives for observations in answer, and from that moment, when a free activity of the spirit is restored, my gaiety and good spirits return, and the article is simply an object of interest to me.'[43] Reading between the lines, however, we can sense that Arnold was quite taken aback by the criticism and he was genuinely concerned at the upset to Newman's feelings 'which I am really sorry to have hurt'. He planned a final lecture to set the record straight. But he also gained some consolation from Thackeray – another victim of the *Saturday* – who pointed out that the charge of conceit from such a source was rather rich. In the Athenaeum, Goldwin Smith, the Regius Professor of Modern History at Oxford, pulled up a chair next to Arnold's and assured him: 'I wish you to know that I had nothing to do with that article on you in the *Saturday Review*.'[44]

Still smarting, however, he wrote to K on her birthday, with a sage reflection on the significance of having reached the age of forty: 'how undecided and unfinished and immature everything seems still, and will seem so, I suppose, to the end.'[45] A fortnight later, in a letter to his mother, the sense of time passing had not diminished: 'Tell Fan I must finish off for the present my critical writings between this and forty, and give the next ten years earnestly to poetry. It is my last chance. It is not a bad ten years of one's life for poetry if one resolutely uses it, but it is a time in which, if one does not use it, one dries up and becomes prosaic altogether.'[46] This was poor prophecy, for there was to be no ten-year poetic renaissance in Arnold's life and, if he was to 'dry up' poetically in the 1860s, the 'prosaic' Arnold was to triumph – for a true poet no recompense, but a substantial achievement none the less.

In October Arnold visited the Isle of Wight where he saw the Arnold family graves at Whippingham and his father's childhood home at Slatwoods – at that time being carved up for development by a building society. The visit renewed his family feeling – something never far below the surface in the Arnolds – and he wrote from Gosport to Fan: 'After all, one likes one's own family about one better than anything in the world, whether one is married or single – and except Flu and the children Mamma and you are what I have now the sense of being my own family more than anything in the world.'[47] The approach of middle age intensified such feelings – and then, suddenly, came the death of Clough at Florence on 13 November to mark the end of his most intense youthful friendship.

The news came when Arnold was inspecting in Oxfordshire and neighbouring counties – playing croquet with the Rothschilds on their beautiful lawn at Aston Clinton. Arnold's reaction to Clough's death was eloquent but subdued – and certainly not demonstratively grief-stricken. His feelings about Clough were as complex and ambivalent as they had always been. He told his mother that the loss was one 'which I shall feel more and more as time goes on, for he is one of the few people who ever made a deep impression upon me'.[48] He added: 'People were beginning to say about Clough that he never would do anything now, and, in short, to pass him over.' He foresaw, however, that there would be a change and that attention would now be fixed 'on what there was of extraordinary promise and interest in him when young'.

But Arnold had declined an invitation to write a memoir of him for the *Daily News* and felt that he could make no immediate response in print, 'but I shall some day in some way or other relieve myself of what I think about him'. With this hint the way to *Thyrsis* was prepared but the poem would not be written for at least another four years. Perhaps his most heartfelt (yet subtly honest) tribute was in a letter he wrote to Mrs Clough. 'Our friendship was', he wrote, 'from my age at the time when it was closest, more important to me than it was to him, and no one will ever again be to me what he was. I shall always think – although I am not sure that he would have thought this himself, – that no one ever appreciated him – no one of his men friends, that is – so thoroughly as I did; with no one of them was the conviction of his truly great and profound qualities so entirely independent of any visible success in life which he might achieve'.[49]

A more immediate task for Arnold than writing a public obituary of Clough was the preparation of the final Homer lecture which was delivered at Oxford on 30 November. It did, however, contain a reference to his friend. In the lecture – published in March the following year as *Last Words* – Arnold made a handsome apology to Francis Newman: 'Any vivacities of expression which may have given him pain I sincerely regret.'[50] He noted 'the baneful effects of controversy' and how it 'always checks the free play of the spirit'. Perhaps he had in mind the disabling effect on his father of his angry and bitter polemical engagements with a variety of adversaries. At the same time he contrived to argue that: 'I never have replied, I never will reply, to any literary assailant', suggesting that what he was offering Newman was an 'explanation'. It was certainly not a full retraction.

Arnold lamented that there was not an Academy in England, 'a public force of correct literary opinion' that would have provided a court of appeal in his case against Newman. Pining as ever for an intellectual police force that would discipline the 'chaos of false tendencies' endemic in English culture, Arnold declared that 'somewhere or other . . . there is a final judgement on these matters'. He also made clear that his objection to contemporary translations such as that offered by Francis Newman was that they sank beneath the weight of eccentric theories and inappropriate scholarship such that ignorance was almost a virtue in those seeking a better way. 'The critic of poetry should have the finest tact, the nicest moderation, the most free, flexible and elastic spirit imaginable; he should be indeed the "ondoyant et divers," the *undulating and diverse* being of Montaigne.'

This is Arnold's critical testament. Reading it today we observe how far removed it is from the all too prevalent modern notion of the critic as a hanging judge rather than a taut listener out for sounds. For Arnold criticism was 'vague and impalpable', abhorring 'obduracy and over-vehemence in liking and disliking, – a remnant of our insular ferocity to which English criticism is so prone'. Elsewhere he said the critic was not 'an abstract law giver'.[51] His critical practice generally lived up to this principle – although, like most great critics, he had his eccentric judgements and oracular pronouncements (such as that on the poetry of the age of Pope and Dryden) which have not worn well.

In an injunction that one would like to nail above the desk of many a present-day critic he asserted that the critic's first duty was '*to welcome everything that is good*', an openness and generosity of perception that is all too rare. 'In poetical criticism the shade, the fine distinction, is everything', he went on. For this reason a cautious pragmatism was the best aid: 'I dislike to meddle with general rules.' He tried, none the less, to answer his critics who accused him of failure to define what he meant by the grand style: 'the grand style arises in poetry, *when a noble nature, poetically gifted, treats with simplicity or with severity a serious subject*'. The grand style simple was Homer's, the grand style severe was that of Milton. The former was the better of the two because it was more 'magical'.

Arnold ended his last lecture on Homer with a handsome tribute to Clough who possessed, he said, 'two invaluable literary qualities, – a true sense for his object of study, and a single hearted care for it . . . His interest was in literature itself; and it was this which gave so rare a stamp to his character, which kept him so free from all taint of littleness.' Fresh from his wrangle with Newman, Arnold added: 'In the saturnalia of ignoble personal passions, of which the struggle for literary success, in old and crowded communities, offers so sad a spectacle, he never mingled . . . that in him of which I think oftenest is the Homeric simplicity of his literary life.'

No sooner had Arnold delivered his lecture at Oxford than he was off with the judge on the North Eastern circuit. As soon as he could, he began to explore the surrounding countryside of Durham where they were lodged. He found its views even better than his beloved Cumnor country: 'The country, too, has a strong turbulent roll in it which smacks of the north and of neighbouring mountains, and which greatly delighted me.'[52] He even stayed to listen to some music in the cathedral and risked his only recorded criticism of an art to which he always confessed himself wholly insensitive: 'I should say the Durham music was greatly overrated had I not heard one anthem, which was really superb.' When he got back to London in the second week of December, Thomas was ill again but the other children were a delight – 'a couple of pickles' he described Lucy and Dick to his mother after he overheard Lucy in the passage as he dashed out to a school one morning saying: 'Won't we do a piece of mischief now, Wichard.'[53] That night he dined with Froude to discuss the project of publishing Clough's literary remains. His own poem, *A Southern Night*, was now published in an anthology called *Victoria Regia* and he spent the guinea fee for it on a collection of Cowper's poems which he was coming more and more to admire. The poem was liked at Fox How and by K 'my first reader (or hearer), and who perhaps has even now the first place in my heart as the judge of my poems . . . No one had seen or heard a word of it, not even Fanny Lucy.'[54] Arnold also told his mother that he was 'less and less inclined to show or repeat' his poems – 'although if I lived with K I daresay I should never have got out of the habit of repeating them to her'.

On the wider stage, the American Civil War was raging and it made Arnold yield to one of his occasional spasms of wishing harsh treatment to be meted out: 'I myself think that it has become indispensable to give the Americans a *moral lesson*, and fervently hope that it will be given them.'[55] This devout wish was in part because the Americans were 'a parody of the English middle classes, with all their energy, acuteness, self-confidence, narrowness of soul, and vulgarity'.[56] Christmas at Chester Square, however, was overshadowed by more domestic worries with Thomas giving them 'a terrible fortnight' at the end of December. Lady de Rothschild sent a present to the sick boy, prompting a letter from Arnold regretting that the illness meant he could not go to Paris but must solace himself instead with a new book by Sainte-Beuve on Chateaubriand which he recommended to her, since she was 'one of the few people who still read anything'.[57] He wrote to Sainte-Beuve expressing his appreciation and enclosing a copy of his old friend Palgrave's best-seller, the *Golden Treasury* anthology, which had already sold over 10,000 copies.

5

Throughout 1861 Arnold had been preoccupied in his official capacity with a controversy over the means of providing State aid to schools. The Education Department had been established in February 1856 under the control of the Privy Council Committee on Education. A

Vice-President was provided from the Commons – in Arnold's time as an inspector it was Robert Lowe – and the Secretary was first Sir James Kay-Shuttleworth then Ralph Lingen. In the summer of 1861, Lowe tried to introduce a new system for grant-aiding schools which would help to reduce public spending by tying grants to the results of testing each pupil in the three 'Rs'. The slogan 'payment by results' was attached to the policy and Arnold immediately positioned himself in the opposition camp, alongside the school managers and the teachers who saw this Revised Code as a reversal of the whole basis on which State support for schools had hitherto been made.

A pamphlet war broke out, one in which, had it not been for his preoccupation with the Homer lectures, Arnold would have entered earlier. In spite of being a public servant, and with some apprehension, he managed to get away with publicly attacking Government policy. In March 1862 his article on *The Twice Revised Code* (the title an allusion to the fact that Lowe was forced in the Commons to trim his original proposal) appeared anonymously in *Fraser's Magazine*. 'It is a ticklish thing to do as I must blame the Office and it is sure to be soon guessed who the article is by',[58] he reflected. When it appeared it was immediately reprinted as a pamphlet. 'As to the article making a *sensation*', he told his mother, 'that I by no means expect. I never expect anything of mine to have exactly the popular quality necessary for making a sensation, and perhaps I hardly wish it. But I daresay it will be read by some influential people in connexion with the debate which will soon come on.'[59] He added: 'I think my comments on his [Lowe's] proceedings will be found vivacious.' He wanted the Government to take a larger view of its role in education and was pleased that his fellow-opponents of the Revised Code in Parliament took the view 'that the State has an interest in the primary school as a *civilising agent*, even prior to its interest in it as an *instructing agent*'.[60]

The essay argued that payment by results would lead inevitably to cutbacks which would 'lower the standard of popular education'[61] at a time when schools were beginning to make progress in their wider aim of compensating for deprived educational backgrounds. By focusing on a narrow cost-cutting yardstick the proposal treated a school as 'a mere machine for teaching reading writing and arithmetic' rather than 'a living whole with complex functions, religious, moral, and intellectual'. Arnold wanted to meet 'the strong desire of the lower classes to raise themselves' by giving them the means to acquire a full share in cultural life rather than just a few basic skills. At the same time he recognised the inauspicious political climate of the early 1860s when the 'tide of reactionary sentiment against everything supposed to be in the least akin to democracy . . . is now sweeping over Europe'. In essence 'a great deal of money would have to be spent in maintaining inspectors which would be better spent in maintaining schools' and the inspectors would be turned into 'a set of registering clerks'. Philosophically, the proposed Code

> severs all vital connexion between the State and popular education, substitutes for the idea of a *debt* and a *duty* on the State's part towards this, the idea of a *free gift*, a gratuitous boon of *prizes*; for a supervision of the whole movement of popular education, – its method, its spirit, and its tendency, – a mechanical examination of certain scholars in three branches of instruction.

In a powerful closing paragraph, Arnold lambasted his traditional enemies – *The Times*, the 'extreme Dissenters', the 'selfish vulgar of the upper classes', the 'clever and fastidious' – who, from their various perspectives, formed an unholy alliance aimed at blocking a progressive move towards bringing education to the working class.

On 25 March Arnold, who was at this time on circuit as marshal in the eastern counties, trying to keep up with the controversy, wrote an anonymous letter (signed 'A lover of light') to the *Daily News* in which he graphically restated the problem: 'In London, in a school filled with the children (not infants) of poor weavers of Spitalfields, every child will under the Revised Code be examined by the Inspector. Great numbers of them will fail: so backward are they, so long neglected, so physically feeble.'[62] In passages like these Arnold's compassionate feeling for the poor working-class children with whom he was regularly in contact around the country spills over. It is worth noting that his more famous cultural criticism was informed by an egalitarian desire to bring the full benefits of civilisation to as many people as possible (although ironically it has been his fate frequently to be misrepresented as a cultural élitist) but it is in less lofty, more practical, passages like these – when Arnold is speaking out on behalf of the ragged, barefoot children of the Victorian working class in the teeth of opposition from the complacent Parliamentarians (many of whom he had just been meeting on circuit, along with the Conservative 'county gentlemen'[63]) and their organs of opinion – that his progressive spirit is glimpsed most clearly. In the end, he was on the side of 'the little ploughboys'[64] who had the right, but at that time no means, to receive a proper education as citizens of a modern democracy. And he came close to risking his job – and certainly any hope of future promotion – for their sake.

In the Commons Lowe was pushed on to the defensive and the Code was revised in such a way as to be a partial victory for its opponents. 'The Goddess of Unreason counts many votaries in that august assembly',[65] Arnold wrote of the House of Commons, the controversy sharpening his style and expanding his reserves of mockery and invective. Payment by results, however, did survive and was not abandoned until after Arnold's death. In a further essay for the *London Review* in May Arnold defined that policy – which he believed had been undermined at least in principle – as meaning 'that the right way to make a bad scholar better is to cripple the school which teaches him'.[66] He looked forward to the eventual collapse of payment by results though 'the *Times* will thunder, the *Telegraph* whistle, the *Star* scream'.

Involvement in the controversy had greatly added to the pressures on Arnold. 'My hand is so tired I can hardly write',[67] he had complained to his mother in February, insisting that (in spite of appearances, we might feel) he had 'rather live in a purer air than that of controversy'. He was actually referring to the clash with Newman not with Lowe but, after a couple more controversial pieces, he planned to retire from the fray: 'I mean to leave this region altogether and to devote myself wholly to what is positive and happy, not negative and contentious, in literature.' This was to prove a forlorn hope. Another pressure was also being exerted on Arnold's busy schedule – dining out. This increasingly became a social duty as his renown and public profile grew. Through K's husband, William Forster MP, he met many political figures, and notwithstanding his pleasure in good food and drink (and K's company) he affected to complain to his mother: 'I have more dining out than I care for, and more eating and drinking.'[68] On 2 February he wrote in his diary: 'From this day – on every week-day to work 4 hours, besides inspection: one day may make up another. (24 hours a week). To have prayers every morning at 1/4 before 9.'[69] The other entries for this year frequently centre on the need to work, to conquer laziness or procrastination, and to achieve a degree of unworldliness. A characteristic entry is an excerpt from a letter by Mendelssohn whose published correspondence he was reading at this time: 'when I have composed a piece just as it sprang from my heart, then I have done my duty towards it; and whether it brings hereafter fame, honour, decorations, is a matter of indifference to me'.[70]

The growing family also added to Arnold's worries and at the beginning of the year they came close to taking on on a half-French manservant called Edouard Achard, but this eventually fell through. Mrs Tuffin continued to be a tower of strength, even if sleepless nights nursing the baby led to her to nod off gently in the nursery during the day. Arnold struggled with his articles and his 'detestable papers' and 'horrid' school work. 'I am up to the elbows in Xmas bills, and headachy besides',[71] he complained to his mother. Everyone, however, said how well he looked: 'But the gray hairs on my head are becoming more and more numerous, and I sometimes grow impatient of getting old amidst a press of occupations and labour for which, after all, I was not born. Even my lectures are not work that I thoroughly like, and the work I do like is not very compatible with any other. But we are not here to have facilities found us for doing the work we like, but to make them.'[72] Arnold was expressing his sense that business was getting the upper hand over art in his life: 'I hate this sort of occupation',[73] he said of the letter to the *Daily News*. But in a letter to his mother about the educational pamphlet he said that even if writing it lost him his job as an inspector he owed it to 'a cause in which I have now a deep interest, and always shall have, even if I cease to serve it officially'[74] – hardly the words of a man who lacked commitment to his non-literary life.

Going on circuit – yet another theft of creative time – did, however, have its compensations. In court at Lewes with the judge at the end of March, Arnold was amused by the case of a stuffer of birds who was bringing a case against the Brighton Railway Company for injuries suffered in a railway accident. The bird-stuffer argued that he had a 'genius' for his craft whose loss could not be made good by the assistance of his wife (whom Arnold noted was 'good-looking') and family. Arnold, as he sat scribbling in the courtroom, reflected on the 'indecipherable something'[75] that was genius and, no doubt, on the now fitful visitations of the poetic manifestation of that quality.

Arnold returned to London briefly before setting off for Oxford on Saturday 29 March to give a lecture on Dante to a 'capital audience'[76] which included the Vice Chancellor. He had been too busy to write out a fair copy of the lecture and delivered it from his rough copy. The debate on the Revised Code continued and he hoped that Lowe's failure to get all of what he wanted would precipitate the end of his tenure as Vice-President of the Education Department. 'I for my part will not be satisfied till we get rid of Lowe',[77] he told his mother shortly before the Commons debate on the issue on 5 May. He was inspecting in Kent after Easter and particularly enjoyed Ramsgate: 'I like the neighbourhood of the Continent with all its life and interest, on the South East coast; in the West you look only towards the melancholy solitudes of the Atlantic.'[78] He also squeezed in a visit to Oxford, where he stayed at All Souls, having promised Clough's widow that he would take with him some lines of the dead poet she had sent 'and there, among the Cumner hills where we have so often rambled, I shall be able to think him over as I could wish. Here, all impressions are half-impressions, and every thought is interrupted.'[79]

The interruptions were largely domestic. The house at Chester Square was being redecorated and he and Flu made an 'expedition' to Heal's to buy a new bed for Thomas. Shortly afterwards Flu had two teeth removed and it took her two days to recover from the chloroform. 'What she does is astonishing', he reported to his mother, 'her only shortcoming is in not being down in a morning and in being too late in going to bed; but the number of things she sees to in the day is surprising . . . It is touching to see what a comfort and companion little Tom is to her.'[80] He resolved to buy a chess-set for them to play together. Flu had been with him at Oxford, and their hosts were attentive, but he managed to get away on his own one afternoon: 'I got down into the meadows below Iffley, and filled my hands with fritillaries, half of them white ones; and I had a beautiful walk from Faringdon Road station to Wantage in the early morning on the first of May, getting a handful of cowslips and wild apple blossom with all the dew still on them. I am going back on Tuesday but I shall hardly get the time for meditating among the Cumner hills which I want. Nor do I see much prospect of liberty in London before the autumn.'[81]

Arnold would have been turning over in his mind his response to the death of Clough and trying to begin the composition of *Thyrsis* – the elegy for his friend which would be so bound up with remembrance of the Cumnor landscape. Wild flowers remained a constant passion in Arnold's life – he corresponded regularly with a Mr Gibson in Saffron Walden, whom he had met on a tour of inspection, on questions of identification – and in the middle of May he took the whole family to Darent Wood in Kent to look for wild lilies. He hoped to fill the empty sandwich basket after lunch with the plants. He was also dreaming of his other passion, and planned to take Dick with him to Tavistock on Dartmoor for some fishing. Filleted into this springtime relaxation was the preparation for his lecture at Oxford on 13 June on Heinrich Heine and the longer-term project of *A French Eton* which would be his next prose work. While staying with some friends in Bromley he picked up Stanley's life of his father one rainy afternoon and was struck by the 'bourgeois' character of the account of his death 'whereas the characteristic thing about Papa is the loftiness and fine ardour of his spirit and life, as in the great men of antiquity, and Plutarch's heroes'.[82]

Just before Arnold went in to dinner with Flu one evening, he was struck by her 'new green silk dress and appleblossom wreath, looking wonderfully young and pretty'. There was, in fact, much wining and dining during the early summer. Struggling to compose a formal Latin oration at Oxford – the Creweian – Arnold reported to his mother a string of engagements with the Forsters, Froude, Thackeray and others: 'I do nothing except my inspection, eat and drink much more than I wish to, and long for the circuit to bring me a little country air and peace . . .'[83] He was still hoping to get some work done during the summer, including a notion of translating the Book of Job, a project which came to nothing. In fact he spent a lazy time at Fox How – after which he sent Fan 'a pretty little copy of *I Promessi Sposi*[84] to help revive her study of Italian – and three weeks at Dover (including a brief excursion across the Channel to see Viel Salm again and try some fishing).

After the summer break Arnold was back at work on his next lecture which was due on 15 November – *A Modern French Poet* – on Maurice de Guérin. Harried by inspection duties which seemed to prevent him writing letters or reading he reported to his mother a new strategy for getting work done: 'I must force myself to write at nights when I go to bed – though this is very much against the grain with me.'[85] During November, however, he was managing to finish inspecting by 2 p.m. which meant he could work regularly at the Athenaeum until 6. This revived his productivity and enabled him to say to his mother: 'Either in Fraser or Macmillan I hope to have something (prose) every month till June inclusive'[86] – these were the essays which would eventually form the first series of *Essays in Criticism* (1865). Having completed the Maurice de Guérin lecture, and prepared for its publication in December's *Fraser*, Arnold observed to his mother: 'I think it will be found an interesting piece of criticism, but I never feel quite sure how far there is really at present in this country a public for criticism or indeed for any literary work except novels and religious books.'[87] His output was steady, however, and, after reeling off his projected list of essays to his mother, he revealed: 'I am making money to take me to Rome, and I have, I am happy to say, written so little that I have at least ten subjects which it has long been in my mind to treat and which, but for some stimulus, I should never have set about treating.'[88] Arnold was discovering the dynamics of Grub Street – that the pressure of editorial demands and deadlines greatly stimulates output – but no poems were being written.

When he was not writing he was dining. Robert Browning – 'a quite remarkably agreeable converser' – came for Sunday lunch and they were often at the Wightmans' table. On a typical night, Arnold returned from Eaton Place at 10.15 p.m., wrote a school report, two or three letters, 'read about a hundred lines of the *Odyssey* to keep myself from putrefaction'[89] and went to bed at midnight. The Arnolds themselves now acquired a new cook who 'introduced much reform in the lower regions where I believe there was a good deal of waste'[90] – creating a below-stairs revolt in the process. The Arnolds' servant William took umbrage and had to be talked into retracting his notice.

As the year came to a close, Arnold, who had been unwell frequently during 1862 with repeated minor colds and flu, and had taken periods of sick leave, was able to declare: 'I am very well . . . and in full work and vigour.'[91] His article on Bishop Colenso, *The Bishop and the Philosopher*, was finished and due for *Fraser* in January. He conceded that the tone of it was 'a little sharper than I could wish, but the man is really such a goose that it is difficult not to say sharp things about him'. He added: 'I worked very hard last week, passing some 6 or 7 hours each day in reading over and over the authors I am going to deal with and in setting my mode of treating the subject, and now I am writing away at great speed.' Increasingly, Arnold was trying to learn to live with his divided existence as a public servant and a man of letters. 'I find the increasing routine of the office work a good balance to my own increasing literary work', he explained to his mother, 'but unless I throw myself into the latter, the irrationality of the former would worry me to death.'[92]

6

At the end of 1862 Arnold celebrated his fortieth birthday at Chester Square. Once again he listed on the inside cover of his diary for the new year of 1863 the ages at their death of a selection of great men (Dante, Shakespeare, Spinoza, Michelangelo, Leonardo da Vinci, Raphael). Whether it was that quiet background note of apprehension about his own mortality – the knowledge that he had inherited the Arnold weak heart – or the sense that he had reached the milepost of forty and must ask what he had achieved, Arnold was, in some sense, taking stock. He was now a public figure, an acknowledged critic, a guest at the most elevated dinner tables of the capital – 'the eating and drinking is too incessant',[93] he complained – a leading controversialist, and a poet of repute. Yet at the same time, he was aware that much of his work was, in the eyes of many of his contemporaries, at odds with the spirit of the times. Early in 1863 he wrote defiantly to his mother in defence of the study of a writer like Spinoza whose views may not necessarily have coincided with his own: 'But what the English public cannot understand is that a man is a just and fruitful object of contemplation much more by virtue of what spirit he is of than by virtue of what system of doctrine he elaborates.'[94]

As well as defending the open mind, Arnold defended his vigorous treatment of unfashionable subjects: 'I long ago made up my mind that if one had to examine views not current and popular it was indispensable to enounce them in at once the clearest and the most unflinching style possible.' But that very 'unflinching' boldness – when launched at an unprepared public opinion – sometimes landed him in trouble. The essay on *The Bishop and the Philosopher*, which had just appeared in *Macmillan's Magazine*, did precisely that. *The Examiner*, which Arnold described as 'the organ of the regular English liberal of the Miss Martineau type',[95] was 'furious' at the essay, accusing him of treating the majority in society 'as pigs'. Whether it was the urbanity of his manner, or the originality of his positions, Arnold frequently upset the conventional wisdom, and even up to the present day, has often been misinterpreted and misrepresented – sometimes to the extent of being accused of arguing the exact opposite of what his words can be found to declare. In this instance he observed philosophically to Fan: 'The newspapers, which exist for the many, *must* resent a supposed insult to the many.'[96] But he clearly had no intention of trimming his sails: 'One cannot change English ideas so much as, if I live, I hope to change them, without saying imperturbably what one thinks and making a good many people uncomfortable. The great thing is to speak without a particle of vice, malice, or rancour',[97] he told Fan.

The flow of articles at this time, coupled to the Oxford lectures and the inspecting, did not prevent Arnold from planning to write 'one or two short poems'[98] and he told his mother: 'After the summer I mean to lie fallow again for some time, or to busy myself with poetry only.' He added that his great advantage was that he was not casting about for subjects to write about – which would 'drive one mad' – but treating in every case subjects 'that I have long reached in my mind, read and thought much about, and been often tempted to write of'. During a brief stay at Oxford at the end of April, Arnold tried and failed to get his poem 'about the Cumner hillside, and Clough in connection with it'[99] started, but 'I have been accumulating stores for it'.

Back in Oxford in June to deliver his lecture on Heine, he reflected that his audience, 'chiefly composed of ladies',[100] was not the ideal one. Looking out on the 'dead bones' in front of him he realised that, notwithstanding his ability on this occasion to raise some laughter from his 'wooden' listeners with some examples of Heine's wit, it was the readership in the periodical press to whom his lectures were really addressed.

On 26 June 1863, Arnold finished inspecting in Spitalfields in the morning and popped into the Athenaeum for lunch. At 4 he returned home to dress and await a carriage which would take the family to Lady de Rothschild's children's party at Kingston House. It was thus a characteristic day in Arnold's variegated life, beginning in the poverty of the East End and ending in the drawing room of a Baroness. The June garden parties were 'incessant' and Flu had already attended two balls at Miss Burdett-Coutts'. 'Yesterday evening', reported Arnold to his mother, 'we had *such* a party on Clapham Common! Flu, I, Mrs Tuffin – & Dick, Lucy & Nelly and 3 donkeys. You never saw such happiness as that of the 3 children – racing and shouting. Clapham Common with its trees, ponds, fern and gorse is very beautiful . . . By the new rail from Victoria we are only 7 minutes from it.'[101]

Arnold's joy in his family seemed at its most intense in these years. His regular letters to his mother are crammed with detail about the doings and sayings of the children. One July afternoon in Kensington Gardens Lucy asked her father how she could catch the sparrows and thrushes that surrounded her. 'By putting salt on their tail,' he replied. She paused for thought then, spotting what her father judged to be 'a dirty little white dog', announced that she wanted to have it. The only way to do that, however, her father told her, was to marry its owner. 'Can I marry him?' she asked. 'Of course you may not,' Arnold replied. 'But couldn't I marry him *if I put salt on his tail?*' she asked sweetly.

But more serious tasks called him that summer. His next book, *A French Eton*, was wanted for the press and he was struggling to finish it. He managed to complete the first part for September's *Macmillan's*, with a second part to follow in October or November. He was now very much aware that he had an audience and a means to reach it, with the editors of the leading periodicals eager for every new essay from his hand. From now on all his books would be composed of material that had first been launched in the periodical press. The medium of the critical essay was one that he began to perfect. 'It is very animating to think that one at last has a chance of *getting at* the English public', he told his mother. 'Such a public as it is, and such a work as one wants to do with it!'[102] But Arnold did not want to abuse his power, recognising that 'everything turns upon one's exercising the power of *persuasion*, of *charm* . . . Even in one's ridicule one must preserve a sweetness and good humour.'

The recipients of Arnold's 'charm' did not, however, always quite see it in such cordial terms. And in this anxiety to do good things with the English public there was more than a hint of Dr Arnold – something his son did not fail to recognise: 'I certainly feel, even while treading ground he did not tread, how much he influences me and how much I owe him.'[103] For the more popular press such as the *Telegraph* and the *Star* ('that true reflexion of the rancour of Protestant Dissent in alliance with all the vulgarity, meddlesomeness, and grossness of the British multitude'), and its public, Arnold had little respect. 'Happy people, in spite of our bad climate and cross tempers, with our penny newspapers!'[104] he exclaimed sarcastically after reading their accounts of the Lord Palmerston scandal.

But Arnold was very much part of the newly expanding 'higher journalism' which was narrowing the gap between the popular press and the rarified world of the Athenaeum intellectual. A graphic illustration of this was the experience of Flu who found herself walking the length of Regent Street in November 1863 behind a sandwich-board man advertising her husband's latest essay on Marcus Aurelius in the *Victoria Magazine*. Arnold tried to see the lighter side of his mission, sardonically describing to K the risk he ran 'if I cannot charm the wild beast of Philistinism while I am trying to convert him, of being torn in pieces by him; and, even if I succeed to the utmost and convert him, of dying in a ditch or a workhouse at the end of it all.'[105] To his mother, however, he confessed some anxiety that all this critical work was becoming too much. Next year, he said, 'I hope to do some poetry and ripen.'[106] It was none the less central to Arnold's thinking that poetry and the critical intelligence were mutually supportive and necessary to each other. 'I do not at present very much care for poetry unless it can give me true *thought* as well,' he added. 'It is the alliance of these two that makes great poetry, the only poetry really worth very much.'

At the end of November he wrote to George Smith, publisher of the *Cornhill Magazine*, offering *Heine's Grave*, 'as a sort of pendant to my prose article on that worthy', adding, 'it is in an irregular unrhymed metre, in which several of my poems are composed'.[107] The poem had been written earlier in the year and finished, according to Arnold's diary, on 19 April. He had visited Heine's grave in the cemetery at Montmartre on 14 September 1858 and had at any rate started the poem before January 1862 where his diary records the injunction to himself: 'finish "Heine's Grave" '. The elegy for Heine embodies the critical strain in poetry that Arnold identified as vital to the art's success. He refers to Heine's scathing view of the English and concurs with it, arguing that his country has forgotten the poetic triumphs of its past and 'Stupidly travels her round / Of mechanic business, and lets / Slow die out of her life / Glory, and genius, and joy.' Drawing on details of Heine's journey to the German woods of Hartz 'from hot / Paris drawing rooms' in his poem *Die Harzreise*, Arnold imagines Heine achieving a sort of pantheistic identification with 'the Spirit of the world' and wishes that he, too, could achieve a 'rapture of peace' such as Heine seemed denied in his 'strange' and 'bitter' life. It is a prosy, over-reflective poem which ends rather vapidly and hardly vindicates Arnold's argument that thinking poetry is 'the only poetry really worth very much'.

During 1863 – between May and June – Arnold also composed *The Terrace at Berne*, already noticed above, which had more personal feeling, as a result of its nostalgia for lost love. He also composed during the summer of 1863 and the early part of 1864 as many as fourteen Italian sonnets (see, for example, *A Picture at Newstead*) which reveal little but the decline of his poetic gift – their indifferent quality in pointed contrast to the growing confidence and accomplishment of his critical writing at this time. The only sonnets of the group which have any real interest are those forming *Rachel*, written in July on the death of the actress whom he had watched eagerly in his youth in Paris. He transcribed into his diary copious extracts from de Barrera's *Memoirs of Rachel* (1858) which he was just reading. In the same mood of emotional nostalgia which informed *The Terrace at Berne*, Arnold recalls 'Rachel's Switzerland, her Rhine' – locations of Arnold's love for Marguerite and Flu respectively. The poem shows that he had lost none of his adulation of Rachel, 'this radiant Greek-souled artist', whose 'intellectual power'[108] was the source of her strength as an actress.

Early in December, Arnold slept at Mentmore, the home of the Meyer de Rothschilds ('it is like fairyland') and was next to Lady Louisa de Rothschild – 'my unapproached favourite'[109] – at dinner. The relationship between Arnold and Lady de Rothschild was a source of delight to both of them and was based as much as anything on intellectual sympathy. Arnold wrote her many lively letters which are witty and animated but hardly flirtatious. Years later, when she read his published letters she wrote in her diary that the letters recalled 'the affectionate, modest, simple nature of the man'.[110] Louisa was almost the same age as Arnold, pretty with blue eyes, and, like him, both high-minded and vivacious. He encountered her first when inspecting Aston Clinton school and they formed a fast friendship. She sent Christmas presents to his children and game from the estate. Something of the likely fellow-feeling between her and Arnold is indicated by her account, in a letter to her daughter Constance, of a meeting with General and Lady Booth in 1881: 'O what a queer individual the former is! . . . I felt rather rubbed up the wrong way by the Salvation Army and defended *parsons* and *smoking*.'[111] She also had her own perspective on the intellectual rigidity of the English to add to Arnold's, for as a young woman she attended the Lords debate on 30 May 1848 on the Jew's Bill and wrote afterwards in her diary: 'The speeches against the admission of Jews into Parliament were intolerant and bigoted and calumnious.'[112] At her home, Aston Clinton, Arnold met many famous contemporaries, attracted by a hostess who, in the recollection of Algernon West, 'fully appreciated conversations on intellectual literature, in which she was fully capable of holding her own'.[113]

On his birthday on 24 December Arnold wrote to his mother expressing his shock at the sudden death of Thackeray (which came hard on the heels of the death of Judge Wightman on 11 December), and making a rare allusion to his own sense of living on borrowed time: 'Today I am forty-one, the middle of life in any case, and for me, perhaps, much more than the middle.'[114] He felt that he was 'ripening', however and felt 'I rejoice to say, an inward spring which seems more and more to gain strength, and to promise to resist outward shocks, if they must come, however rough.' It had been a busy year, and he told Tom that he was hoping soon to ease up a little. 'One should not be always before the public and I have executed a vigorous sortie and may now keep quiet a little.'[115] There was little sign of that silence in 1864 which saw the publication in June of *A French Eton*. The book was based on his French visit for the Newcastle Commission in 1859 and it is an indication of how busy Arnold had been that it took so long to take shape. The inquiry of the Clarendon Commission into the public schools had given it a further impetus. *A French Eton or Middle-Class*

Education and the State is an important precursor to *Culture and Anarchy* and is essentially a plea for State involvement in education.

It introduces his theme of the three classes – aristocracy, middle class and populace – and talks about culture as growth and liberation and something that depends crucially on being diffused throughout society rather than being confined to 'a small upper class only'.[116] He insisted that he was addressing the middle class and had its true interests at heart. 'To convey to Eton the knowledge that the wine of Champagne does not water the whole earth, and that there are incomes which fall below £5,000 a year, would be an act of kindness towards a large class of British parents, full of proper pride but not opulent.' The 'French Eton' of the title was the Toulouse Lyceum which Arnold described, together with the College at Sorèze, arguing that it offered a viable model for an education that was 'at once reasonably cheap and reasonably good'. He was vigorous in his defence of State intervention but his real object in the essay is to address the wider intellectual deficiencies of English middle-class culture. 'Before the English middle class can have the right or the power to assert itself absolutely, it must have greatly perfected itself', he argues. He wants it to become 'something higher, ampler, more gracious' and dreams of a great future based on a new universal system of State education. The book closes with an inspiring address to the 'children of the future, whose day has not yet dawned'. They will not understand how 'progress towards man's best perfection' was so reluctantly undertaken, 'how it should have been for years and years retarded by barren commonplaces, by worn-out claptraps . . . and the shrill querulous upbraiding from publicists in their dotage'.

The whole essay derives its force from a combination of practicality – Arnold had a close day-to-day knowledge of how schools worked – and breadth of vision about the shortcomings of English culture and the future it could have if it chose. 'I have written, to my own mind, nothing better',[117] he wrote to his mother. He told the publisher, Alexander Macmillan, to send copies to various important people and himself sent a copy to Emerson, informing him that 'I can never forget the refreshing and quickening effect your writings had upon me at a critical time of my life.'[118]

At the end of January 1864, Arnold visited Aston Clinton in response to pleading from Lady de Rothschild who wanted him to meet Disraeli and the Bishop of Oxford. At the end of a long day that had begun with a school at Bethnal Green in the East End, Arnold found himself in a room full of titled people sitting opposite Dizzy, who was looking 'moody, black and silent'. Recognising Arnold from a literary dinner several years before, he leaned forward and said: 'At that time I had a great respect for the name you bore, but you yourself were little known. Now you are well known. You have made a reputation, but you will go further yet. You have a great future before you, and you deserve it.'[119] He then went on to say that he himself had given up literature because, as Arnold put it, 'he was not one of those people who can do two things at once'. Arnold's success in doing at the very least two things at once would have been familiar to his hostess to whom he frequently wrote about the difficulties of finding time to write under the pressures of his official career.

During May and June the Arnolds rented, during the ill-health of its vicar, the Rectory in Woodford, Essex to get away briefly from London. 'I am living in the country but I am not yet the rector of Woodford and in orders',[120] he joked to George Smith. One June morning Arnold plucked a rose in honour of the day, thirteen years previously, that he and Flu had married. 'I have not seen her so cheerful for years',[121] he wrote to his mother. The domestic finances were in good order as a result of Arnold's industry and some extra work which included a week as an examiner for the Indian Civil Service applicants. 'My receipts for this quarter very nearly reach £550,'[122] he reported in July.

In August they went to stay at Llandudno, Wales being 'a country which has always touched my imagination'.[123] He told his mother a week later: 'The charm of Wales is the extent of the country which gives you untouched masses which the tourists do not reach, and then the new race, language, and literature give it a charm and novelty which the Lake country can never have.'[124] He and Flu explored Caernarfon, Llanberis and Penmaenmawr and when he came to deliver his lectures on Celtic literature the following year this visit would be recalled. Describing the holiday to Lady de Rothschild he admitted to 'a great *penchant* for the Celtic races, with their melancholy and unprogressiveness'.[125] He told Fan: 'The poetry of the Celtic race and its names of places quite overpowers me.'[126] After the Welsh trip, the Arnolds went on to Fox How, from where Arnold wrote to the scholar and biographer of Coleridge, James Dykes Campbell, elaborating his reasons for deprecating Tennyson, who had just published *Enoch Arden*: 'I do not think Tennyson a great and powerful spirit in any line . . . and unless a poet, especially a poet at this time of day, is that, my interest in him is only slight, and my conviction that he will not finally stand high is firm.'[127] But Arnold drew back from public criticism on the grounds that to do so would risk 'odious motives' being attributed to him – apparently because it would be seen as mere rivalrous comment. 'I do not really set much store by him, in spite of his popularity', [128] he wrote to Lady de Rothschild. Such delicacy was not exhibited towards Arnold himself, however, and a furious attack by Fitzjames Stephens again in the *Saturday* on his essay *The Function of Criticism at the Present Time* which had been published in the November issue of the *National Review* elicited another, not wholly convincing, assertion by Arnold that he disdained personal controversy.

Arnold's account of his method of argument seems almost naive in its assessment of how his words would be taken: 'my sinuous, easy, unpolemical [*sic*] mode of proceeding has been adopted by me, first, because I really think it is the best way of proceeding if one wants to get at, and keep with, truth; secondly, because I am convinced that only by a literary form of this kind being given to them can ideas such as mine ever gain any access in a country such as ours.' [129] As always, Arnold was highly conscious of the fact that the medicine he was prescribing would be found bitter-tasting by his fellow-countrymen. He was already turning over in his mind a piece that would eventually appear a year later as *My Countrymen* – 'a thing half serious, half playful' [130] – which would continue his sprightly campaign against the British Philistine. This was more the sort of role he wished for and he was more than relieved not to be chosen at the end of the year to be on the Commission on middle-class education, a body he felt hobbled by being packed with people already opposed to the principle of State intervention. The Commission 'like all else which happens, more and more turns me away from the thought of any attempt at direct practical and political action and makes me fix all my care upon a spiritual action, to tell upon people's minds, which after all is the great thing, hard as it is to make oneself fully believe it so.' [131]

CHAPTER SEVEN:
THE ELEGANT JEREMIAH
[1865–1869]

I see more and more what an effective weapon, in a
confused, loud-talking, clap-trapping country like this,
where every writer and speaker to the public tends to say
more than he means, is *irony* . . .[1]

1

During the summer of 1864, Matthew Arnold had been discussing
with his publisher Alexander Macmillan the idea of putting together in
one volume all the essays and lectures that had been pouring from his
pen since the latter part of 1862. 'About Christmas or the beginning of
the new year would do very well, wouldn't it, for the book to appear',[2]
he suggested. In fact, it was published in February and at six shillings –
the same price as Tennyson's recent *Enoch Arden*. But first Arnold had
to settle on a title. 'I had thought of "Essays of Criticism" in the old
sense of the word *essay – attempt – specimen*',[3] he mused to Macmillan,
'but perhaps this will hardly do. What do you think of "Essays *in*
Criticism"?' The title stuck. Arnold now broached what he called 'a
most desirable novelty in English publishing' (though this was quite
normal in France) to bring it out 'in *paper* instead of those ordinary
boards'. This, however, was too revolutionary an idea for Macmillan
and it duly appeared in conventional hardback format. 'I am the most
unpopular of authors but I think this volume will pay its expenses',
Arnold continued. 'If not I shall retire into a monastery and try this
infernal English public no more.'

The book, however, turned out to be a success – so much so that it was also published in June in America by Ticknor and Fields in an edition which added *A French Eton* and *On Translating Homer*. The book had a lively and provocative Preface (too much so for the sober drawing room at Fox How) leading into *The Function of Criticism at the Present Time* which had started life as a lecture at Oxford on 29 November 1864, and had then been published in Walter Bagehot's new *National Review* in November. While drafting it Arnold had told Lady de Rothschild: 'I have said what must, I fear, give offence, but I am not sure whether my horrible cold and sore throat this last week have not left a *nuance* of asperity in my manner of saying it which need not have been there. I shall try and get rid of it, however, in correcting the proofs.'[4]

The Preface, according to Henry James (who reviewed the American edition in July, having read it with 'rapture', lying all day on a sofa clutching the page proofs and finding himself 'somehow transported, as in a shining silvery dream, to London, to Oxford, to the French Academy, to Languedoc, to Brittany, to ancient Greece'[5]), enabled Arnold to take 'a delicate literary vengeance on his enemies'.[6] The combative style rather alarmed Flu, who was 'always thrown into a nervous tremor by my writing anything which she thinks likely to draw down attacks on me',[7] and it was received 'in solemn silence' when it was read to Fan and Tom. Arnold turned with relief to the one person who would appreciate its animation and zest – Lady de Rothschild – gratefully lapping up 'the refreshment of your sympathy'.[8] His confidence to his mother that: 'The Preface will make you laugh',[9] was to prove unfounded but he was able to reassure her of the proper seriousness of his intent. He explained that the moment was right for a collection of essays of this sort and that if it succeeded 'the way is the more clear for my bringing in my favourite notions yet further . . . all my efforts are directed to enlarge and complete us by bringing in as much as possible of Greek, Latin, Celtic authors. More and more I see hopes of fruit by working steadily in this direction.'[10] This echoed his remarks to K about his desire to stimulate the intellectual life of England 'and to make her feel how many clogs she wears, and how much she has to do in order to run . . . as her genius gives her the power to run, is the object of all I do.'[11]

Arnold's missionary intent was, fortunately, less apparent than the liveliness of the style in the Preface. Written almost on the eve of publication, it was highly topical, making reference to his continuing dispute with the translators of Homer, to one of whom he apologised for a phrase that had in it 'too much vivacity'. This word – which in Arnold's day implied a sort of vivid impertinence – was frequently used against him by his critics, who looked for more decorum in an Oxford Professor of Poetry. Yet Arnold insisted that he was not speaking here *ex cathedra* but as 'a plain citizen of the republic of letters'. The *North British Review* duly scolded him for those 'vivacities'[12] but he dismissed it breezily by observing that 'it is a Scotchman who writes'.[13]

In the Preface Arnold threw down the gauntlet of his playfulness: 'My vivacity is but the last sparkle of flame before we are all in the dark, the last glimpse of colour before we all go into drab, – the drab of the earnest, prosaic, practical, austerely literal future. Yes, the world will soon be the Philistines'!'[14] The Preface we generally read today is not the original one, which Arnold wisely pruned of some of its more arch and self-regarding passages, its heavy-handed satire. Reading those suppressed passages now, we can see that the cuts were judicious ones.

Arnold had made his target in the essays clear – the self-satisfied English middle-class Philistine – and his irony, in the Preface, rises to a crescendo. He is trying, he explains, to 'pull out a few more stops in that powerful but at present somewhat narrow-toned organ, the modern Englishman' whose nation, having 'searched all anchorages of the spirit . . . has finally anchored itself, in the fulness of perfected knowledge, on Benthamism'. Referring to a notorious recent murder on the North London Railway, Arnold mockingly pretends that the transcendental philosophy imputed to him by the *Saturday Review* has succeeded in insulating him from the anxiety of his fellow passengers on the Woodford Branch of that railway line. He tries to persuade 'a portly jeweller from Cheapside' – the very model of the Philistine he has in his sights – that the latter's death would in the overall scheme of things mean very little: 'All was of no avail. Nothing could moderate, in the bosom of the great English middle class, their passionate, absorbing, almost blood-thirsty clinging to life.' Arnold pretends that the portly jeweller wishes so devoutly to stay alive because he desires to see the final apotheosis of Benthamism and is in truth not on his way to his shop but on 'a pious pilgrimage, to obtain from Mr Bentham's executors a secret bone of his great, dissected master'.

These passages of mocking irony – read with frosty bewilderment by the Arnolds – show how keen an observer of contemporary *mores* Arnold was, what a sharp-eyed satirist, whose Philistine enemy was not a polemical abstraction but an all-too-palpable flesh and blood reality – a fellow commuter, a pompous school manager, a sober-suited official of the Education Department. Unlike the more abstract and rhetorical

Victorian sages such as Carlyle, Arnold's social criticism was always leavened by specific observation. But he allowed himself a more wistful ending to the Preface by contrasting his 'puny war with the Philistines' with the eternal values of Oxford, romantically apostrophised: 'spreading her gardens to the moonlight, and whispering from her towers the last enchantment of the Middle Age . . . Adorable dreamer whose heart has been so romantic! . . . home of lost causes, and forsaken beliefs, and unpopular names, and impossible loyalties . . .'

Taken as a whole, the first collection of *Essays in Criticism* (the second, in 1888, would contain his more famous critical essays) does not quite live up to Arnold's aim of putting criticism in touch with the 'main currents' of the age. Some of the authors chosen, particularly the French ones, are minor, and the book hardly amounts to a comprehensive account of the most significant French writing of the mid-century, particularly given Arnold's insistence that his fellow-countrymen had much to learn from France. There is no mention of Arnold's exact contemporaries Flaubert or Baudelaire, no Gautier, no Leconte de Lisle. No modern literary scholar would regard his essay on Heine, for example, as the last word on its subject. Yet at the same time the collection displays the full range of Arnold's critical ideas, his notions of cultural centrality, his critique – rising in the case of Heine almost to rage – of the English Philistine. And he always quotes well – if sometimes at too great length.

The greatest twentieth-century inheritor of Arnold's tradition of literary, cultural and social criticism (though he did little but disparage his precursor) – T. S. Eliot – called Arnold, as has already been noted, 'rather a propagandist for criticism than a critic'[15] and believed he 'wasted his strength' engaging in battles with the Philistine, an activity that could have been carried on more effectively by a newspaper pundit. Eliot's mandarin disdain for the sorts of activity in which Arnold engaged – he would certainly not have lost any sleep over the absent educational opportunities of the children of poor Spitalfields weavers or the 'little ploughboys' – vitiates some of his criticism of Arnold. But in the main his exploration of a man whose concerns were profoundly unsympathetic to him, remains valuable. It is certainly true that Arnold's most impressive criticism is often found in essays where he is operating primarily as 'a propagandist for criticism'.

The best example of this is *The Function of Criticism at the Present Time*. The most important essay in the 1865 collection, it starts from a recognition that, although the critical faculty is lower than the creative, there are moments when criticism has vital work to do in the interests of creativity, in 'rendering it possible'. Arnold, with characteristic emphasis, argued that 'the elements with which the creative power works are ideas' and that the most creative literary epochs are those in which there is 'a national glow of life', making for an 'epoch of concentration' when 'the power of the man and the power of the moment' come together triumphantly. An intelligent, critical culture, alive to the excitement of ideas, and fully receptive to them, Arnold believed, would be one in which the highest art could flourish. The critic's function was to prepare the ground, to ensure that 'a current of true and fresh ideas' flowed easily and naturally around the creative artist and his or her audience. Opposed to this was the culture of the 'portly jeweller from Cheapside' who believed himself to be living in the best of all possible worlds, and in no need of opening his mind to anything other than his own delight in his material success. Arnold lashed out at 'the absorbing and brutalising influence of our passionate material progress . . . our railways, our business, and our fortune-making'.

Here he was launching his extended criticism of those 'Victorian values' which were to have a fitful after-life in the world of English political rhetoric in the 1980s. The function of the critic, he insisted, was 'to keep a man from a self-satisfaction which is retarding and vulgarising' and which made 'spiritual progression' impossible. Arnold was not alone in the nineteenth century in trying to formulate a 'spiritual' critique of the cult of material progress and the machine – quite apart from fellow English writers such as Carlyle (who a generation earlier had inveighed against 'Mechanism' in *Signs of the Times* [1829]), one thinks of his exact contemporary, Fyodor Dostoyevsky, raging in *Notes from Underground* (1864) (published as Arnold was finalising this collection of essays) against the facile utopianism of Chernyshevsky's *What is to be Done?* (1863) that reduced man to a programmable, perfectible creature who need only apply a scientific formula in order to be able to act in his own best interests. Dostoevsky's rejection of the notion that man was a mechanistic 'sprig on the cylinder of a barrel-organ' matches Arnold's critique of such symbols of Victorian progress as the railway explosion. He was a direct beneficiary of such technological advances, and his own social thought exhibited the characteristic progressive drive of nineteenth-century liberalism, but he was at war with the self-satisfaction that rested in such achievements rather than in the contemplation of what remained to be done on the spiritual plane.

In a famous passage in this essay Arnold, characteristically drawing an example from current events, seized on a newspaper report of a wretched girl named Wragg in a Nottingham workhouse who, in despair, had murdered her illegitimate child. The stark newspaper phrase 'Wragg is in custody', striking Arnold just after he had read a politician's eulogy of the English as the finest race imaginable, prompted him to the reflection: '*Wragg!* . . . what a touch of grossness in our race, what an original shortcoming in the more delicate spiritual perceptions, is shown by the natural growth amongst us of such hideous names, Higginbottom, Stiggins, Bugg!' But in spite of the immediacy of Arnold's criticism – the ease with which (unlike, say, T. S. Eliot's) it found its matter in the particularity of contemporary, and often trivial, events – he also valued the critic's role of standing back a little, of being 'disinterested'. To this end, he argued, the criticism should keep out of 'the region of immediate practice' and focus on its proper business which is 'simply to know the best that is known and thought in the world, and by in its turn making this known, to create a current of true and fresh ideas'.

That phrase, 'the best that is known and thought in the world' – launched for the first time in this essay and destined to enjoy a long and fruitful life of repetition, later in the slightly altered form 'the best which has been thought and *said* in the world'[16] – has been responsible, more than anything else Arnold wrote, for his being misrepresented in popular debate as an 'élitist', particularly at the nadir of his reputation in the 1960s when use of the word 'best' was considered unfortunate by would-be progressive thinkers.

It was exactly the English deification of practicality that Arnold was opposed to and would return to in *Culture and Anarchy*. For now, he saw it as a national vice embodied in the English constitution 'with its compromises, its love of facts, its horror of theory, its studied avoidance of clear thoughts . . . a colossal machine for the manufacture of Philistines.' This also explains his ardent Europeanism. The criticism he yearned for would be 'a criticism which regards Europe as being, for intellectual purposes, one great confederation, bound to a joint action and working to a common result'.

Criticism, Arnold believed, was concerned with advancing knowledge rather than with handing down verdicts, the true critic being more 'a sort of companion and clue' than an 'abstract law-giver'. The essay on the function of criticism ends on a relatively pessimistic note. Arnold saw that he was not living in the age of Aeschylus or Shakespeare when the 'national glow of life' guaranteed great art (we recall his youthful letters to Clough regretting that they lived in 'an unpoetical age'). The perfect world for which his perfect critic was legislating would not be realised in his time – 'that promised land it will not be ours to enter, and we shall die in the wilderness' – but the struggle must continue.

Another important essay in the collection, *The Literary Influence of Academies*, explored another of Arnold's central themes by asking: 'What are the essential characteristics of the spirit of our nation? Not, certainly, an open and clear mind, not a quick and flexible intelligence.' This led to another question – might a literary academy, a 'high court of letters', be the cure for English eccentricity, a corrective to 'the note of provinciality'. Arnold canvasses the possibility that a body which enforced a more rigorous intellectual standard and offered 'the fitness, the measure, the centrality, which is the soul of good criticism' might correct the shortcomings of English culture, but, in the end, he backs off. Arnold realised that such a body as the French Academy would simply not work in England. The battle against 'the provincial spirit' and 'all mere glorification by ourselves of ourselves' would have to be waged in a different way, by the propagandists for criticism continuing to warn of the dangers of intellectual complacency and arbitrary standards of taste.

Although such broadsides can suggest an irascible or conservative critical temperament, Arnold was in fact always trying to look forward. He characteristically praised Heinrich Heine in his essay on the German poet for being 'a great modern poet . . . not conquered by the Middle Age'. In the most radical essay of the book, Arnold described Heine as 'a soldier in the Liberation War of humanity' who joined Goethe as one of the 'dissolvents of the old European system'. Critic of self-satisfied materialism Arnold may have been, but he was also a man of his time who believed implicitly in Progress and could praise a poet like Heine – although he chose to concentrate on Heine the critic – for 'bringing all things under the point of view of the nineteenth century'. Like his father, Arnold never doubted the necessity of the French Revolution (his admiration of Burke did not prevent him from regretting the latter's stance on the Revolution) and of the collapse of the old aristocratic order in Europe. This essay also includes one of Arnold's most attractive attempts to define the nature of poetry. 'Poetry is simply the most beautiful, impressive and widely effective way of saying things, and hence its importance', he wrote.

Reviewing these essays, one is struck both by the consistency of the arguments and the recurrence of certain key themes, one of which is the notion of centrality. Even if we allow that Arnold meant simply to indicate by this term the highest and most stringent standards being applied — he feared that, without some authoritative centre, more capricious and eccentric standards might establish themselves to the detriment of the highest possible achievement in literature — which is what he meant by castigating 'provinciality' — one might still register some unease. Arnold had inherited from his father a tendency to sanction at certain moments — for all his eulogies to 'sweetness and light' (the phrase from Swift's *Battle of the Books* which he noted in his diary at about this time and which he was later to appropriate in *Culture and Anarchy*) — an abrupt and draconian use of the power of 'centrality'.

Some of Arnold's modern critics have detected a coercive streak in his criticism. It is certainly true that he offers little comfort to present-day multiculturalists who argue for cultural pluralism, for the right of sections of society to resist assimilation. But if that debate (to which Arnold offers much food for thought) is not entirely closed, his willingness to sanction political strong measures is less easy to condone. There is a disturbing passage in the essay on *Marcus Aurelius* which justifies the Roman emperor's persecution of the Christians by arguing that, to him, they seemed 'philosophically contemptible, politically subversive, and morally abominable' and therefore he 'incurs no moral reproach' for his actions in putting them down. The State, Arnold argued, had in such cases 'the duty to suppress'. It is an ugly phrase. Even if we set against it Arnold's frequently sensitive comments on, for example, the Irish Question, it has to be faced that there was a repressive streak in his vaunted liberalism which — admittedly only rarely — could come to the surface.

2

Essays in Criticism did well — although Arnold asked Alexander Macmillan not to include 'the newspaper panegyrics'[17] in advertisements because he had 'an inexpressible dislike to it'. Although he planned in future editions to leave out some of the more provocative material in the Preface, Arnold was convinced that the book was being well received, and in the right places. 'I think the book will reach and influence the writing and literary class', he told his mother, 'not the great reading class whom the *Country Parson*, for example, reaches: for reputation this is all very well but for sale and profit it is, of course, not so well.'[18]

But Arnold's attention was soon drifting towards a new project of visiting France as a member of the Schools Inquiry Commission. He was enormously excited by the prospect of six months' leave on the Continent. 'Of course, I do not like leaving Flu and the children', he wrote to his mother, 'but it is a great satisfaction to me, as you and Fan well know, to be going on this errand.'[19] One advantage of the trip was that it would give him a breathing space from current pressures which were forcing him to get up at 6.30 a.m. to write and prepare his lectures. 'I am pestered with applications to write for new periodicals',[20] he complained. His planned departure on Monday 3 April was delayed, however, because Lingen made an objection to his normal salary being paid while he was away and the matter had to be resolved. Lady de Rothschild gave him some useful contacts at Frankfurt and he promised: 'I shall often think of you.'[21] In the end, after a 'captious unfriendly letter',[22] Lingen climbed down and Arnold was allowed to keep his salary as well as the expenses for the trip.

By the second week of April he was in Paris, booked in to a third-floor room in the Hotel Meurice in the Rue de Rivoli – a sumptuous hotel, with its heavy chandeliers and ornate gilt mirrors – overlooking to the present day the Tuileries gardens. Paris was just about to erupt into leaf but Arnold was not impressed by the changes since his last visit six years ago: 'They make Paris, which used to be the most historical place in the world, one monotonous handsome Belgravia.'[23] He had been so overworked just prior to leaving that his normal pleasure at travelling had not yet reawakened. Moreover, as he wrote to his mother: 'I miss Flu and the children dreadfully.'[24] This unusual lack of excitement persisted for some days such that he told Flu: 'I have sometimes thought of putting myself into the train and coming back to you.'[25] But eventually the official visits and social engagements began to draw him in. At the salon of the Princess Mathilde which he attended in the company of Sainte-Beuve who had called for him at his hotel, he was informed by her that his knowledge of France and his literature made him a 'Français'.[26]

In between his official engagements Arnold was working on the lectures on Celtic literature that would eventually be delivered at Oxford at the end of the year. He was also writing to his other publisher, George Smith, of Smith and Elder, about plans to write for the latter's *Cornhill Magazine*. After Paris, Arnold went to Italy, settling in the middle of May in the Hotel de l'Europe in Turin. Then he passed through Florence (where, in spite of his poorly developed feel for visual art he managed to spend an hour in the Uffizi) and Rome ('It is a glorious place but it overwhelms me'[27]) and Naples which, he told Flu, was 'brilliant and lively as Paris only in a natural, popular sort of way'.[28] To K, however, he opined that the Italians 'want backbone, serious energy, and power of honest work'[29] – a view originally expounded by 'Papa' which his son was happy to endorse. Germany, he found 'the most *bourgeois* of nations'[30] and concluded: 'all I see abroad makes me fonder of England, and yet more and more convinced of the general truth of the ideas about England and her progress, and what is needful for her, which have come to me almost by instinct, and which yet all I see keeps confirming.'[31]

Arnold was now in Gernsbach in the Black Forest for a month and, to his delight, Flu and the children had joined him. There was plenty of fishing, with Dick carrying his father's landing-net and following him for hours 'deeply interested in all my proceedings'.[32] He told his mother after they had gone that Dick and Nelly had such a good effect on his spirits 'that it is almost impossible for me to be depressed when they are with me'.[33] At the end of the summer Arnold wrote to George Smith, in the playful spirit he generally adopted with him, that he had not written a line for months 'and how good is that for us all!'[34] He added that he was getting too old for travelling and planned on his return 'to remain quiet, if I live, for years, solely occupied in doing good to my enemies by recalling them from numerous bad courses'.

By the start of November, Arnold was back in England and had plunged straight back into the maelstrom of work in the shape of 'a forest of documents'.[35] He was soon suffering from tiredness and headaches and complained to his mother that 'our engagements are beginning to thicken which I do not like as I can do nothing in the evening if I dine out'.[36] He was sustained, however, by sympathetic readers. In a letter to Lady de Rothschild, thanking her for a brace of pheasant from the Aston Clinton estate, he wrote: 'I never am at work, as I am now, on anything I have to write, without thinking of you as one of the regular readers whose judgement I am anxious to satisfy and to whom it is a genuine pleasure to me to give pleasure.'[37]

Towards the end of the year, Arnold was reading the privately printed selection of letters and journals of Clough edited by his widow. It brought his friend vividly back to him. 'The loose screw in his whole organisation is, however, much more evident to me in reading this book than it was in consorting with him in life', he wrote to his mother, 'and then the rigid overtaxed religiousness of his early life was a surprise to me – of his whole Rugby time, I mean. I first knew him, really knew him, some five years later.'[38] Arnold felt that Clough's best years were between 1845 and 1847 and that the book didn't do justice to these. Also, the questionable influence on the sensitive young man of Dr Arnold was plain to Arnold: 'certainly Clough appears to have felt him *too much*, and yet it is curious how down to the very end of his life he is eager to repel the charge against Papa, of over-stimulating, prematurely developing. This is most striking. Poor dear Clough. I have long had a design, in some part already fulfilled, of making some memorial in verse of what I saw of him and felt, and feel about him.' *Thyrsis* was near to being completed and would appear the following March.

3

Although Arnold was now a regular contributor to the periodical press and much in demand in its pages – and receiving on average twenty-five pounds per article in the *Cornhill*, many of which were recycled Oxford lectures – his money worries did not seem to lessen. In 1866 he wrote to his mother asking her to write to the Archbishop of Canterbury nominating Dick for a charitable place at Charterhouse 'as a grandson of Papa's'.[39] Fees at Rugby at this time were £150 a year and day fees at Westminster £30. £50 was also needed for the governess for Lucy and Nelly 'and how am I to find another £150 for Dick's public school?' His mother lent him an unspecified amount of money and gave some to the children who immediately opened Post Office accounts. They accompanied their father to make their deposits, solemnly coming up to the counter one by one, until the postmistress declared: 'Why, *how* many little Master Arnolds are there?'[40]

Arnold knew that the only solution to his financial problems was work and he threw himself once again into his writing. At the end of 1865 he had delivered at Oxford two lectures on Celtic literature which would duly appear in the *Cornhill* in March and April, and he began 1866 by working on his third Oxford lecture on the same topic –

not to mention a mass of 'abominable'[41] examination papers which had him complaining to Tom: 'I have had a hard time of it lately.'[42] Before snatching a short break at Fox How in mid-January, Arnold had borrowed the quiet of K's house at 80 Eccleston Square in order to work without interruption. 'I can only work at home early and late', he explained to his mother, 'at this time of year I never work early, and the two hours I get after the children are gone to bed is not enough.'[43]

In spite of the hard work, however, Arnold spent January assuring all his family and friends that a piece on which he was also working for the *Cornhill* would amuse them. Unfortunately the vivacity of this piece – *My Countrymen* – was received at Fox How with little more enthusiasm than the Preface to *Essays in Criticism* had been, although Arnold could report to his mother: 'The article is immensely read and I hear of it wherever I go.'[44] Carlyle was so impressed that he invited Arnold to visit him. By way of defending himself against the disapproval of Fox How, Arnold told his mother that the times had changed and that he had to write in the manner he did in order to secure an audience. He was now beginning to suspect that the audience existed and that he was getting through to it: 'A certain curiosity is slowly awakening, I think, about the things I publish; a suspicion that the way I am going, at any rate, we all must go if we are to get forward',[45] he told Macmillan, but with the sardonic coda: 'Still, I shall no doubt die in the wilderness.'

One result of Arnold's growing exposure was that he was now courted by the fashionable intelligentsia: 'But we are getting to know too many people', he complained, 'and though it would be pleasant enough if one had double one's present income I more and more am coming to the resolution to break away from it, and to live the next ten years, at any rate, somewhere in the outskirts of London, going in for the evening once a week.'[46] His friends at the Council Office now tried to persuade him to apply for a vacant Charity Commissionership. He was attracted by the £300 a year salary, the greater independence it would give, and the promise of being able to use the position to advance 'some great and sound education scheme'.[47] But after having 'wasted a week' applying he was unsuccessful. 'I see nothing but a Secretaryship for Middle Class Education which would really suit me',[48] he told his mother as he plunged back into the awesome task of completing his report on the Continental educational mission which somehow had to be accomplished alongside all his other tasks and distractions.

At the end of March Arnold received a cheque from Macmillan for £25 – 'the best pay I have yet had, and I have no doubt, as the curiosity about my things increases, they will bring me a little money'[49] – for a poem published simultaneously in the April number of *Macmillan's Magazine* and the *Atlantic Monthly*. It was to be Arnold's last major poem and was the elegy, five years after his death, on Clough, entitled *Thyrsis*. Although less emotionally charged than *The Scholar-Gipsy* – because it admits Arnold's mixed feelings about Clough – it inhabits the same landscape. 'It had long been in my head to connect Clough with that Cumner country',[50] he wrote to his old friend Shairp. He admitted that 'not enough is said about Clough in it' but added that Clough '*had* this idyllic side, too; to deal with this suited my desire to deal again with that Cumner country: any way, only so could I treat the matter this time'. The romanticisation of the 'Cumner country', Arnold seems to be admitting, was a kind of evasion of the duty of an elegist to say precisely what he feels about the man who has died.

The poem is beautiful but it fails to give an adequate account of Clough. It concentrates more on the sense of change in the landscape, where the meadows of wild flowers they both knew as young men have been ploughed up, and represents the Cumnor country as a land of lost content. The 'Fyfield elm', the poet records, still stands, as a symbol of perpetuity. The scholar-gipsy also is still present in spirit in the landscape to symbolise freedom, creativity, a readiness to think against the grain. The two images establish Arnold's emotional co-ordinates in the poem and govern its shifting uncertainty of tone. Arnold's emphasis on the rareness now of his visits to the 'Cumner ground' voices his recognition of the rareness now of visits by the Muse to the harried school inspector, paterfamilias, Grub Street hack, controversialist, lecturer and dinner party guest.

One of the most important stanzas in the poem is that beginning: 'A fugitive and gracious light he seeks / Shy to illumine; and I seek it too'. It embodies Arnold's sense of being a prophet without honour, pursuing unfashionable truths (probably more effectively than Clough) and sustained by his own light: 'Yet on he fares, by his own heart inspired.' Clough himself is represented as one who left Oxford out of an awkward, unaccommodating sense of principle, and was too scrupulous, too easily overcome by self-doubt and agony of conscience – 'Too quick despairer'. Clough was also a poet whose art was not properly appreciated (although Arnold cannot quite pass over the opportunity to hint, in the phrase 'cut a smoother reed', at a judgement on Clough's poetry and its shortcomings): 'But Thyrsis never more we swains shall see; / See him come back, and cut a smoother reed, / And blow a strain the world at last shall heed.' The last lines of the poem suggest that Arnold must continue what he and Clough originally dreamed of on their walks together around Oxford as young men. The imagined injunction delivered by Clough: 'Roam on! The light we sought is shining still', brings to a close an elegy which is as much a lament for the lost dreams of youth as it is a lament over a friendship which was always compounded of complex undercurrents of feeling, of mutual criticism and reserve, of impatience and disagreement, as much as love.

'I have heard nothing about the poem', Arnold reported to his mother at the end of the first week in April: 'It is probably too *quiet* a poem for the general taste, but I think it will stand wear.'[51] He also stressed to her that 'the images are all from actual observation . . . The cuckoo on the wet June morning I heard in the garden at Woodford.' When he wrote to Shairp, who liked the poem, Arnold declared, 'It will not be popular'[52] and went on to concede that 'the whole *prophet* side' of Clough had not really been dealt with by the poem. He was so concerned at his failure to say enough about Clough in *Thyrsis* that he resolved not to send it to Mrs Clough.

The Arnolds decided to get out of London for the summer and let Chester Square for the whole of May and June and the first half of July. They rented a farmhouse at West Humble near Dorking in Surrey and loved the surrounding countryside. On 10 June Arnold wrote to his mother from there in high spirits: 'This is our wedding day. We have been fifteen years married, and it seems as if it was only last week. Certainly I feel no older, and that is one great benefit of going on reading and thinking, one's sense of a freshness and newness in things remains.'[53] He wrote to Tom on the same day: 'My dear old boy, how I wish you were going to dine with us and drink our health and happiness in Champagne.'[54] The joy, however, was tempered by the looming prospect of a Latin oration for the Oxford Commemoration ceremony to be delivered that week. Arnold told his mother that getting rid of this chore – 'a trouble to prepare and a nuisance to deliver'[55] – would be the chief reward of giving up the Professorship which was now coming to an end. Arnold tried to tempt visitors to West Humble, telling George Smith that it was within a mile of Box Hill station and the last train back to London was at 10 p.m., and to Lady de Rothschild – with whom he was always lively and facetious – he playfully alluded to the place name which 'as you see, perfectly suits the occupant's nature'.[56]

By mid-July Arnold was back in London wrestling with his official report which 'hangs like a millstone round my neck and prevents my doing anything else'.[57] To complete it he took refuge in the Athenaeum, 'the only place where I can get any real work done'.[58] He was to spend the rest of the year at the task. Dedication to a task in hand, however, did not mean that Arnold cancelled all other work entirely. On 21 July, in the *Pall Mall Gazette*, appeared the first of the satirical letters woven around his comic invention Arminius, Baron von Thunder-Ten-Tronckh, later to be collected in Arnold's funniest book *Friendship's Garland* (1871).

These letters – which make us regret that he did not pour more energy into indulging his gift for satire rather than, say, his penchant for essays on religious subjects – purported to be an account by Arnold of Arminius' views and, through his mock-distancing from the censorious Prussian's perception of the English and their alleged lack of intellectual culture or 'Geist', he was able to take aim at his customary targets with even more playfulness and zest than usual. 'My letter on Geist has been a great success, and I hear of it wherever I go',[59] he reported to his mother, adding in anticipation of her distaste for its vivacity: 'I understand what you mean by my graver and gayer manner, but there is a necessity in these things, and one cannot always work precisely as one would.' Mrs Arnold was closer in feeling to *The Spectator*, which a few months previously had taken issue with the Olympian mockery of Arnold's essay *My Countrymen* in the following terms: 'An essay by Mr Matthew Arnold on the narrow and dimsighted views of the English middle class is like the visit of an intellectual angel, not unconscious of angelic graces, to the dull and earthly sphere of our political literature.'[60] It went on to mock his 'dogmatic mock humility, his airy scorn' and imagined him disappearing into the upper air having delivered his 'useless but beautiful messages' to the unheeding Philistine. There are, it must be conceded, some palpable hits in this criticism.

On 19 August Arnold's sixth and last child, Basil, was born at 12.45 a.m.: 'a great thundering boy . . . Nelly is much annoyed at the new arrival and requests everyone to take it away'.[61] Flu took more time than usual to recover from the birth and his planned trip to Scotland to fish on the estate of his old friend Grant Duff (later Sir Mountstuart Grant Duff, Secretary of State for India) had to be postponed until the beginning of September. Arnold fished a great deal (a Banffshire paper's report of his capture of a salmon was picked up by the *Morning Star* in London) and regretted missing Lady de Rothschild who was also in Scotland. When he got back he told her that he had actually avoided getting in touch 'as I wished to be kept out of temptation'[62] and that the weather had been awful. In addition, he had 'missed all the birds and four-footed things at which I fired'.

Scotland was followed by three weeks at Fox How, but although Westmorland in the first fortnight of October had 'perfect colouring'[63] he was harassed by the foreign schools report which he had brought with him to try and finish. He complained to Macmillan that he couldn't enjoy the Lakes with this task hanging over him and that 'when I am in hard work I would almost sooner be in town'.[64] When he did eventually return to town he had to fight off his publishers, telling George Smith that he was too 'report-laden'[65] to contribute anything to the *Pall Mall Gazette*. 'My work spreads and spreads before me',[66] he complained to his mother. During the summer he had told her that he was really through with these reports on education: 'However, the English world is visibly beginning to move my way on the whole question of state-action so it is worth keeping at work and doing all one can to prevent checks and stoppages.'[67]

As the year drew to a close the report was still not finished and a new distraction presented itself. The Arnolds had a new cook called Walsh who seemed to be performing well at dinner parties – which was just as well, Flu remarked, 'because men are such pigs about their dinner'.[68] But Walsh developed severe bronchitis and was just on the point of going into St George's Hospital for a treatment of vapour baths when her busybody sister turned up at Chester Square to announce that hospitals, as Arnold reported exasperatedly to his mother, 'were always full of groaning and dying people and that no-one ever comes out of them alive'.[69] Walsh now refused point blank to go to St George's and was moved down instead from her attic room to the housekeeper's room in the basement which contained a fire – a move that created friction below stairs. She did not recover and was dead within the week. 'Walsh, poor thing, looked quite handsome in the calmness of death',[70] Arnold reflected. He was desperately busy with the report after all this domestic upheaval and sent Mrs Tuffin and the servants to the funeral at Brompton in his place. Arnold always took a deep interest in the domestic staff and treated them as individuals. The care was reciprocated, with Walsh having said that Chester Square was the first place where she had ever been happy.

As Christmas approached, Arnold yearned to be rid of his report. 'No words can say what a relief it will be to me to get done with it',[71] he told his mother. But even if he succeeded in finishing it he would be immediately required to fulfil a promise to the *Cornhill*, not to mention 'those terrible examination papers' which always came around Christmas. He was hoping again to borrow the tranquillity of K's home at 80 Eccleston Square to work in because the Athenaeum, so recently seen as a welcome haven, was becoming impossible as a result of Arnold's growing celebrity. 'This club is getting to be no working place for me', he told his mother, 'I know too many men: since I have been here today I have talked to Frederick Maurice [the Christian Socialist], Herman Merivale [the literary scholar and playwright], Richmond the artist, Freeland (whom William knows too well), Frederick Pollack, Pitt Taylor, George Lefevre, old Crawford, Richards the Speaker's counsel, Arthur Stanley and John Coleridge. This is not conducive to work.' Perhaps for these reasons, the report did not meet its target and the general summing-up would still remain to be done in January.

Arnold gladly gave himself up to Christmas with the family. They had to tackle four pheasants and two hares sent by Lady de Rothschild from her estate and a turkey from Flu's relatives, the Bensons, in Swansea. Arnold's birthday, coming as it did at the very end of the year, invariably led him into reflections on the passage of time or stock-taking before the start of the new year.

> Forty-four is indeed an age at which one may say 'The time past of our life may suffice us' . . . I more and more become conscious of having something to do, and of a resolution to do it; and if, as John Duke Coleridge wished for me the day before yesterday, I double my present age, I shall, I hope, do something of it, but whether one lives long or not, to be less and less *personal* in one's desires and workings is the great matter . . . [72]

4

Having failed to complete his foreign schools report by Christmas, Arnold began 1867 in poor humour, suffering from a prolonged attack of neuralgia and coping with weather so bitterly cold that the jug in his dressing room one January morning was full of ice and the sponge was frozen to the marble of the washstand. A few days later he was in the warmth of the North Library at the Athenaeum (the only one of the club's three libraries that had no gas – which Arnold hated to read or write by) writing to his mother with another complaint about the interruptions he suffered at the Athenaeum. 'I shall be obliged to give up working here, and take to the British Museum',[73] he told her. He also mentioned his finances which were a little healthier than usual, owing in part to Macmillan's proposal to buy outright the next edition of his essays.

Arnold up to this point had published 'on my own account' as he put it, which meant that he published at his own risk instead of selling the rights to the publisher for a fixed sum regardless of sales. For the time being he kept to this arrangement for his poems. From the mid-1860s until his death Arnold was published chiefly by two houses – Macmillan and Smith & Elder. He had a particularly close relationship with George Smith (publisher of the *Cornhill* and *Pall Mall Gazette*, founder of the *Dictionary of National Biography*, banker, underwiter and shipper) and they often played billiards together and lunched in Soho over champagne and oysters. Alexander Macmillan had a more formal relationship with Arnold although it was also more intellectually serious. Arnold did not make Macmillan rich – he averaged less than ten pounds a year profit on the *Poems* between 1869 and 1877 – but as a thoughtful man he valued his relationship with Arnold.[74] Smith, too, recognised that Arnold was a valuable property – from his name and his capacity to stir controversy.

Arnold's second son Trevenen ('Budge') was now at Rugby so he needed to think seriously about his income (Thomas, the eldest, was too delicate in health to be sent away to school). 'I am frightened at what I hear of the increased expense of Rugby – at least £150 a year now',[75] he told his mother. He and Flu were trying to keep down their expenses but even a planned retrenchment for the three months of February to April involved them in dining out three times a week. Flu was not always thrilled by these dinner parties where politicians, poets and periodical writers mingled. In her 1867 diary (the only one, unfortunately, that survives) she wrote on 6 April: 'Matt & I dined at the Clarendon Hotel with Mr and Mrs Smith. Large party of literati. Not pleasant.'[76]

Even after the wretched report was finally finished in February, Arnold's next project – publication of the lectures on Celtic literature that he had delivered at Oxford between December 1865 and May 1866 and which had already appeared in issues of the *Cornhill* throughout 1866 – was unlikely to be a money-spinner. George Smith, who was relieving Arnold of the financial risk of publishing the book himself, was sanguine about its likely profitability. Arnold reported to his mother Smith's view that 'it is hardly the sort of book a

British parent buys at a railway bookstall for his Jemima. But I daresay it will pay its expenses.'[77]

On 1 March Arnold decided to approach George Smith with what he frankly admitted was 'an audacious request'[78] to borrow £200. He explained that having been tied up for ten months with the foreign schools report ('which I hope will be useful, but for which I do not receive one farthing') he had been unable to earn any money from writing. 'I make literature put my boys to school, and literature failing me, I want £200', he announced briskly. To borrow it from an insurance company would entail buying life insurance so he proposed that Smith should lend him the money at 5 per cent and be repaid £100 this time next year and £100 the same time the following year. He had come to Smith, he explained, 'because you have treated my productions with a liberality the poor things were not accustomed to before' and because Arnold could offer him an exclusive deal whereby he would write for noone but the *Cornhill* so long as the debt was unpaid. Seeing the advantage of this, Smith agreed the same day and the money went into Arnold's bank, Twinings at 215 the Strand, in a matter of days. He explained to Smith that now the report was out of the way he had 'all sorts of things in my head' and that the book on Celtic literature was ready for the press – 'but I am afraid it is not with a book on Celtic literature that £200 is to be made'.

With the Oxford Professorship now over Arnold was a little freer to look around for more lucrative work (he had received over £200 at the end of 1866 for his Professorship). The schools report had been arduous and unprofitable and his current work as an 'unpopular author' did not look like bringing in much income. Conscious that Flu wanted to see her husband earning more money, Arnold decided to apply for another public appointment – the Librarianship of the House of Commons. He wrote directly to Gladstone, a shrewd letter that made the very valid point that his career as a practical public servant had given him 'more experience of business than usually falls to the lot of a literary man . . . so that I have, perhaps, more of the aptitudes and information required for the post . . . than might at first thought be expected from a Professor (who is very soon going to be an ex-Professor) of poetry.'[79] Arnold also solicited the help of Disraeli – not yet Prime Minister at this time but Chancellor of the Exchequer in Lord Derby's Cabinet – through the agency of Lady de Rothschild. Dizzy wrote back to her courteously: 'I have no idea I can do anything in the Librarian business, but I will try, & shall be very glad to assist your friend, Mr Arnold.'[80] Arnold was delighted when she forwarded the letter to him: 'There is, on the whole, no Member of the House by whom I would so soon be recommended as by Mr Disraeli, for there is no member who interests me so much, in spite of all drawbacks, and there is no-one to whom I should with so much pleasure owe his intercession as to you.'[81] In spite of these, and other eminent persons' testimonials, Arnold was unsuccessful and probably undisappointed since he had already told his mother: 'I do not myself think the Speaker will give it me, and I do not much care whether he does or not, for I do not thoroughly fancy the place.'[82] His friends came up to him afterwards one by one to tell him that it wouldn't have suited him: 'The freedom of my present life is considerable, and that is a great thing',[83] he told his mother.

The Arnolds decided to leave London for the spring again and to go to Brighton for three weeks from 1 May (from which base Arnold would carry on inspecting) and then for eight weeks from 22 May to West Humble once more – a move about which the children were 'wild'[84]. The rent was high but 'the country is so delicious and so incomparably superior to anything else reachable from London'. There was a newly opened railway line to London and good grammar schools at Dorking and Leatherhead for the boys within a quarter of an hour by train from West Humble. Arnold longed to be done with dining out, although he had recently met and dined a couple of times with a new friend, Thomas Huxley, the scientist, Darwinian apologist, and foe of Christianity. The two men, in spite of later public disagreements culminating in Arnold's *Literature and Science* lecture, were great friends, plainly sharing a lively sense of humour and fondness for intellectual iconoclasm. Given Arnold's sequence of religious works throughout the 1870s when their friendship was at its liveliest, the rapport is all the more remarkable.

It was from West Humble that Arnold wrote to George Smith promising that he would have his last Oxford lecture, *Culture and Its Enemies* for the July *Cornhill* – 'so keep a place for it'.[85] He had recently told his mother: 'I more and more have the satisfaction of seeing that what I do produces its effect, and this inspirits me to try and keep myself at my best, in good temper and clear spirits, and in that variety of activity which is, in my opinion, necessary for producing a fruitful effect in a country like this.'[86] But his immediate business with George Smith was the publication of *On the Study of Celtic Literature* as a book. With his customary playfulness, but possibly stiffened by a hint of genuine anxiety, Arnold quipped: 'Is it possible that you will find any one to give 8s/6d for a knowledge of my ignorance of Celtic literature?

My best hope is that the Welsh . . . may purchase me out of pure patriotism.' Arnold's misgivings were understandable. He had no obvious qualification for writing about Celtic literature, spoke none of the Celtic languages, and was disarmingly forthright about his ignorance. The book was printed with last-minute annotations by the Celtic scholar, Lord Strangford, which Arnold described to Smith at the proof stage as 'one or two alterations on points of etymology – points where I have no doubt I am fearfully shaky'. In fact the footnotes often contradict flatly points that Arnold gaily dilates on in the text.

Although it was a reading in 1860 of the French scholar Ernest Renan's essay *Sur la poésie des races celtiques* which had put Arnold on to the study of the subject, and which strongly influenced his treatment, his specific enthusiasm for Welsh culture was first sparked by his visit to the Eisteddfod at Llandudno during a summer holiday in the resort in 1864. It was a letter to *The Times* on the subject of *eisteddfodau* that provoked one of the 'young lions of the *Daily Telegraph*' to mint the famous epithet 'the elegant Jeremiah'[87] for Arnold. The anonymous article, which appeared in September 1866, was actually written by James Macdonnell, a young journalist hired, as young journalists are today, to write noisy controversial copy. Writing in the rumbustious, heightened style which Arnold deplored in the *Telegraph*, Macdonnell sneered at the Eisteddfod and the spectacle of 'people leaving their shops for a week to recite songs, and sing ballads, and read essays, and talk patriotism, and eat leeks'. He mocked Arnold's argument that the spiritual delicacy of the Celts could reform middle-class Philistinism by 'the founding of a Celtic chair at Oxford – and the singing of bits of ballads'. Arnold was dubbed 'the high-priest of the kid-gloved persuasion' and 'a literary coxcomb' who needed to be reminded that 'There is no analogy . . . between a prophet and a fop.' It was good, rollicking journalism but, ironically, Macdonnell was later to admit privately that he admired Arnold as a critic. Such contradictions are still part of British journalism.

In spite of the knocking-copy of the *Daily Telegraph*, the lectures were influential and probably instrumental in the Celtic revival which led to the establishment of a chair of Celtic literature at Oxford at Jesus College in 1877. Its first incumbent was John Rhys, one of the 'flock of young Celts'[88] who had attended Arnold's Oxford lectures at the behest of the Jesus Principal, Charles Williams. The latter was heard to declare at the close of the fourth and final lecture on 26 May 1866 on *The Celtic Element in English Poetry*: 'The Angel ended.'[89]

Although Celtic scholars might today walk warily around *On the*

Study of Celtic Literature – where they are not openly hostile to Arnold's views on the Welsh language – it still has value on a number of counts. It helped to make the serious study of Celtic literature possible and prised it as a discipline out of the grip of the romantic antiquarians. It also provided – for Arnold always had the gift of telling quotation – a sort of running anthology of the imaginative riches of this tradition which is still calculated to send its readers hurrying off to read texts like the *Mabinogion*. But it was also, like so many of Arnold's works, a critical Trojan Horse out of whose flanks poured the anti-Philistine army. Long before its completion he was telling George Smith of an invitation to speak at the Chester Eisteddfod of 1866 (it was the decision instead to write a letter on the topic to *The Times*, that gave Macdonnell the opening for his invective in the *Telegraph*). Arnold was tempted to take up the offer as a means of 'doing a stroke of work for the conversion of the Philistines'[90] – not perhaps the most immediate task suggested by a contemplation of Celtic literature.

But Arnold yet again saw a fresh way of coming at the central theme of his criticism. 'I believe there is a Celtic element in the English nature, as well as a Germanic element',[91] he wrote, characterising the latter by the 'slowness and clumsiness of the language, the eternal beer, sausages, and bad tobacco, the blank commonness everywhere' which the traveller saw in Northern Germany. The Celt seemed to embody rather more of those virtues of sweetness and light on which Arnold placed such a high value. In his analysis of the Celtic temperament there is a strong sense of self-portraiture: 'it may be seen in wistful regret, it may be seen in passionate, penetrating melancholy; but its essence is to aspire ardently after life, light and emotion, to be expansive, adventurous and gay . . . He loves bright colours, he easily becomes audacious, overcrowning, full of fanfaronade.' But he is also 'soon up and soon down', because 'keenly sensitive to joy and sorrow'. In a prefiguring of his later distinction between the Hellenic and the Hebraic, in *Culture and Anarchy*, Arnold contrasts the unworldliness and spirituality of the Celt with the stolid virtues of the Saxon: 'Doors that open, windows that shut, locks that turn, razors that shave, coats that wear, watches that go, and a thousand more such good things, are the invention of the Philistines.' This ironic catalogue leaves us in no doubt of which sensibility Arnold leans towards – the one whose poetry is characterised by 'natural magic', not the dreary materialism of the Victorian consumer.

Arnold's conclusion, which combines this binary distinction with his strictures about the need to study Celtic literature with more scientific rigour than has been the norm, explicitly connects his argument with the problems of contemporary Ireland. In his Introduction he had quoted a comment from *The Times* (of a kind that has by no means vanished from English journalism) disparaging Welsh culture. He exhibited the paper's 'asperities' as a symptom of the British Establishment's attitude to its component nations: '*Behold England's difficulty in governing Ireland!*' The conclusion of *On the Study of Celtic Literature* returns to the same theme: 'let it be one of our angelic revenges on the Philistines, who among their other sins are the guilty authors of Fenianism, to found at Oxford a chair of Celtic, and to send, through the gentle ministration of science, a message of peace to Ireland.'

In spite of this rare tenderness for the Celtic nations, however, Arnold was of the opinion that 'the fusion of all the inhabitants of these islands into one homogeneous, English-speaking whole, the breaking down of barriers between us, the swallowing up of separate provincial nationalities, is a consummation to which the natural course of things irresistibly tends . . . The sooner the Welsh language disappears . . . the better.' Arnold the school inspector in Wales had made similar observations in his annual reports. It is entirely consistent with his view that culture was a binding, unifying agent and it shows how utterly uncomprehending he was of the view that national cultures have legitimate claims to proclaim their identity. Arnold's trenchantly stated and uncompromising stance still causes anger in Wales and a recent Welsh historian has called him 'perverted, destructive and utterly opposed to all sound educational principles'.[92]

Arnold's lecture on *Culture and Its Enemies* – the germ of *Culture and Anarchy*, which would not appear for another two years – was published in the *Cornhill* in the same month as his book on Celtic literature. It seems to have given him some difficulty, however, which Flu's diary records: 'Matt up to his eyes with his lecture . . . Matt up at 3 am to finish his lecture . . .'[93] The report on foreign schools, however, was still lowering over Arnold and the pressure of work, he confided to George Smith, made him 'miserable and bilious'.[94] He finished the lecture in the small hours of 7 June, delivered it at 2 p.m. at Oxford, and went fishing the next day with Dick at Wotton to celebrate. It was his last lecture as Oxford Professor and he wanted to go out in style, although that made it, as he put it 'Oxfordesque', necessitating some re-editing for the periodical public. 'The lecture was my *last*,' he told Smith, 'and having often trod on the toes of Oxford and yet having a sincere affection for her, I wanted to make my last lecture as pleasing to my audience and as *Oxfordesque* as I could. I succeeded, and finished my career amidst a most gratifying display of feeling.'[95] Flu's diary records that it was received with 'Gt applause at the end & altogether very successful'.[96]

Part of that success may have been due to Arnold's growing confidence as a public speaker, a confidence which probably grew from a low starting point (his performances in the larger, more difficult lecture halls of America were later to prove disastrous). 'I now nearly speak my lecture, though it is all written', he explained to his mother, 'but the attention of my audience animates me to speak rather than read what I have written.'[97] The content of the lecture when it was published attracted 'many attacks and answers . . . but the great thing is to drag the dissenting middle class into the great public arena of life and discussion, and not let it remain in isolation'.[98] He planned to follow its *Cornhill* appearance with another called *Anarchy and Authority* for the August number, but during June he began to pick up various 'murmurings' and suggested waiting a little in order to make use of them. Alexander Macmillan, who had just published in his magazine Henry Sidgwick's *The Prophet of Culture* (a shrewd analysis of Arnold's argument in the essay that, although in some measure sympathetic, was unhappy with his definitions of culture and accused him of being in 'an access of dilettante humour'[99]), wrote to Arnold regarding the murmurings: 'I am sure these discussions do great good & the country owes you much. Your critics and opponents increase your influence for good.'[100]

As well as doing good to the public, Arnold had been contemplating a new book of poems – 'but this will be a labour of love',[101] he explained to his mother. As early as March he had been in correspondence with Alexander Macmillan to mention that he had nearly finished a poem that would conclude the volume. This was *Obermann Once More*. Arnold accepted Macmillan's suggestion that it be called *New Poems* (although much already published material filled out the book) and corrected the proofs at West Humble while surrounded by all his prose tasks of the early summer. It was published in July (Arnold reverting to his old practice of publishing at his own risk) and Macmillan now said that he had read it with 'great admiration', adding: 'Empedocles is a noble poem. I had only a dim remembrance of it, and thought of it as obscure. I did not find it so this reading. I really think you should succeed.'[102] The rehabilitation of *Empedocles on Etna* (as a result of the constant advocacy of Browning who dined frequently at the Arnolds' during these years, although Swinburne also claimed some credit for persuading Arnold to take pity on the poem) was the most important feature of the volume (although it published for the first time *Calais Sands*, *Dover Beach*, *Growing Old*, *Rugby Chapel*, *Heine's Grave*, and the *Epilogue to Lessing's Laocoön* as well as a crop of workaday sonnets).

The last poem was sparked off by the eighteenth-century German critic and dramatist Lessing's work of critical theory, *Laocoön*, which took issue with the argument of Horace in his *Ars Poetica* that a poem is like a painting (*Ut pictura, poesis*). In the poem Arnold asks an unidentified friend with whom he is walking in Hyde Park why it is that the other arts seem to have more individual successes than poetry. Reflecting on the busy scene of people at their leisure in the park, Arnold argues that the poet, unlike the painter whose art captures a single intense moment, works through the progressive imitation of an action: 'he must life's *movement* tell! / The thread which binds it all in one, / And not its separate parts alone.' For this reason, Arnold concludes, poetry is superior to the other arts for it captures more of the pathos and power of life, and poets have the brightest glory 'for greatest hath their labour been'.

Obermann Once More was begun while Arnold was on his foreign schools mission in 1865, although not finished until the volume was nearly ready for the press. It deals with the central premise of his religious writing of the 1870s that Christianity, though vitally necessary, must adapt its message to a changing world if it was to survive and to continue to offer something meaningful to the modern world. It takes as its epigraph a question put by Senancour's Obermann: 'Savez-vous quelque bien qui console du regret d'un monde?' The poem revisits the Switzerland of Arnold's youth twenty years before and recalls Obermann – 'Thou master of my wandering youth' – and his words: '. . . serene, / Yet tinged with infinite desire / For all that *might* have been.' Obermann then comes to Arnold as an apparition to ask: 'And from thy world, with heart oppressed, / Choosest thou *now* to turn?' Obermann seems to express surprise at Arnold's reappearance as a wandering contemplative at a time when there are grounds for hope in the intellectual climate for religion, comparing it with the early, animated days of Christianity.

Although Obermann believes that he himself lived in an unsympathetic time, he urges Arnold not to follow him in despair. It is true that the modern poet comes to his task shorn of some of 'the joy, the bloom, the power' that should be his and that Arnold has now reached middle age and 'spent thy youthful prime', but Obermann urges him to devote his remaining years to attaining the goal of seeing 'One common wave of thought and joy. / Lifting mankind again.' Waking from this apparition, Arnold looks out on the beautiful Alpine scenery to catch the morning suddenly breaking – a symbol of the birth of Christianity – and the poems ends on a note of hope and optimism. It bears the mark of Arnold's religious thought at this time – his notebooks for these years are filled with religious aphorisms, biblical quotations and uplifting saws – and serves to underline the importance to him of religion, an aspect of his mind often overlooked partly as a result of too literal a reading of a poem like *Dover Beach*. That poem, so often taken as a representative expression of the Victorian loss of faith, is in fact not Arnold's farewell to belief but his heartfelt regret at the contemporary loss of certainty. There is confusion on the darkling plain of nineteenth-century belief but there may be a way forward none the less. Arnold was to spend a decade trying to find it.

He wrote a long letter to his old tutor at Oxford, Henry Dunn, on *Obermann* which concluded: 'That Christ is alive is language far truer to my own feeling and observation of what is passing in the world, than that Christ is dead.'[103] In *Obermann Once More*, Arnold has managed to introduce some of the purposeful optimism of his prose into the normally resigned and regretful medium of his verse. For a glimpse of that other mood, *Growing Old* in this volume is a chastening example.

By the end of August the volume had done reasonably well, selling between 400 and 500 copies. By the beginning of January 1868 Macmillan wrote to say that only 150 copies remained and that Arnold should come in and talk about a reprint. There were relatively few reviews, however, in the first months. Swinburne put his finger on a possible cause: 'For some years the immediate fame of Mr Matthew Arnold has been almost exclusively the fame of a prose writer.'[104] Yet Swinburne urged that 'the most memorable quality about him was the quality of a poet . . . as a schoolboy . . . the songs of Callicles clove to my ear and memory'. Arnold wrote to his brother Edward that Browning's insistence that he reprint *Empedocles* 'was really the cause of the volume appearing at all'.[105] He was pleased with Swinburne's review – which appeared in the *Fortnightly Review* – and wrote to thank him, particularly for his judicious selection of extracts from the poems. Swinburne's reply – which admitted that the anonymous French critic he had introduced into his review to praise Arnold was in fact an invention – suggested that French readers would appreciate his poems better than the English. Later in the year Arnold and Swinburne met and dined together, the latter having 'turned out very well behaved and interesting'.[106] 'His praise . . . has inclined the religious world to look out in my writings for a crusade against religion',[107] Arnold reported, together with examples of crass readings of *Empedocles* by the Dissenting journals which fixed on certain passages to observe gravely: 'Mr Arnold here professes his pantheism' or 'Mr Arnold here disowns Christianity'.

Arnold sent a copy of the poems to Emerson, pointing out that he was so much in his debt 'that I consider myself almost bound to make an offering to you of any production at all considerable which comes from me; since you are sure to have had some part in it'.[108] But Arnold had to wait until the end of October for a review in a mass-circulation paper. In the lobby of the Athenaeum he thanked someone from *The Times* where a good review had just appeared with the words: 'Well you have done your best to put £50 into an unpopular poet's pocket.'[109] By November 1,000 copies of the collection had sold. Almost at the same time a witty criticism of *Culture and Its Enemies* appeared in *The Fortnightly* written by Frederic Harrison, a young critic and follower of Comte who would figure in the pages of *Culture and Anarchy*. Arnold always enjoyed a joke against himself and was tickled by parodies and spoofs of his work. He described Harrison's *Culture: A Dialogue* to Lady de Rothschild as 'in parts so amusing that I laughed till I cried'.[110] Arnold's enjoyment of polemic (in spite of his regular, unconvincingly serene, attempts to represent himself as being above the fray) was clear in the terms in which he described the proposal to write *Anarchy and Authority* for the Christmas *Cornhill*: 'It will amuse me to do it, as I have many things to say; and Harrison and Sedgwick, and others, who replied to my first paper, have given me golden opportunities.'[111]

5

During the summer, Arnold reported to his mother that the boys were doing very well with a private tutor at West Humble and that this was a good argument for educating boys at home. He was beginning to have doubts about the public school system. 'I am not sure that the old English public school system, with its almost unlimited freedom and leaving the boy to himself, has not served its time and come to need replacing.'[112] He returned to the theme later in the year, reporting that

Budge was doing very badly at Rugby: 'he is at the very bottom of his class . . . he is prodigiously fat, and wants, I cannot help thinking, quite another system.'[113] The headmaster of Rugby, William Temple, no doubt sensible of the bad publicity which would be caused by Dr Arnold's son pulling out his child from the school, tried to persuade him keep Budge at Rugby. Arnold was not easy to persuade: 'It is curious how I am destined to receive through my own child a confirmation of my instinct that the old English school system has served its time,' he told his mother. He thought of sending him either to a school in Paris or a new progressively minded school called Spring Grove in London, one of whose governors was his new friend Thomas Huxley ('a man of great ability'[114]).

Partly in order to find better schools, the Arnolds decided after their return to London at the end of the summer to try and find somewhere to live outside the city and chose Harrow which was convenient for London and for Arnold's inspecting district, and which would enable the boys to attend Harrow School daily. He was able to take advantage of a foundation that would bring the cost of fees down to £45 a year for the three boys together, although he hesitated at first out of a fear that his enemies would make capital out of an educational reformer being seen to get public school education on the cheap. His friends, however, assured him that there was no reason to hesitate. 'I am just giving up my house in London – driven into the wilderness by those young ravens, or cormorants, my sons',[115] he joked to Swinburne. Harrow, Arnold told Lady de Rothschild, was 'real country, though ugly country, like the neighbourhood of Rugby where I lived so long'.[116]

It was to be the end of March 1868, however, before the Arnolds, dismissing endless shoddily built suburban villas, moved into Byron House, a spacious house with an acre of garden and a good kitchen garden, half-way up Harrow Hill. The spring violets were already out and 'we gave orders about planting lettuces, as we are such great salad people'.[117] There were mature figs and vines trained against the wall, apricot trees, and asparagus beds. 'I cannot tell you how the old countrified Middlesex look of the house pleases me, and how the physiognomy of one of the modern villas with their patch of raw garden depresses me',[118] he told his mother.

Arnold's domestic preoccupations, however, did not prevent him from observing with alarm the contemporary political scene. He watched politics with a degree of detachment, and, while a lifelong sympathiser of the Liberal Party, was highly critical of the performance of the Liberals in power. He does not seem to have lamented the fall of the Liberal administration of Gladstone (a fellow Greek scholar to whom he had sent his lectures on translating Homer in 1861) over the 1866 Reform Bill and was concerned at the growth of agitation during this period – the Hyde Park riots of July 1866 and further disturbances following Disraeli's second Reform Bill in 1867. These events sparked Carlyle's dark anti-democratic pamphlet *Shooting Niagara* which appeared in *Macmillan's* in August 1867. Arnold's liberal humanism, his faith in democratic government, was never tempted to the rant of a Carlyle – the 'apostle of equality' had no time for the cult of the strong man – but he was certainly not indulgent to mass agitation. His anxiety at social 'anarchy' conditioned the mood of his next great prose work.

Dining at the Garrick on 13 December 1867, Arnold's meal was interrupted by the arrival of a guest whose hansom cab had nearly been knocked down by a string of cabs stuffed with policemen dashing to Clerkenwell Gaol which had just been blown up by the Fenians. When he later read the newspaper accounts Arnold concluded that a Government which did not deal firmly with rioters 'simply opened the flood-gates to anarchy'.[119] He added: 'Who can wonder at these Irish, who have cause to hate us, and who do not own their allegiance to us, making war on a State and society which has shown itself irresolute and feeble?' As the year drew to a close, Arnold told K: 'We are in a strange, uneasy state in London', but he believed, as always, in the inevitability of progress, in 'the loosening of all old prejudices, respects, and habits as is beginning, and cannot be stopped, for it is the course of nature'.[120]

He was aware, too, of his growing status as a commentator, pointing out to his mother that his name was always in the newspapers and that: 'I constantly hear of the way my things are working, and people say to me that I am "a power"; I am sure there is great need of a power in our present troubled condition, if the power can but make or keep itself a good one.'[121] In a cutting comment, however, on K's husband William Forster MP, Arnold said that there was a growing public awareness of the need for politics to be better-informed:

> and if they do not take care even men like William Forster, who entirely give up real study and think they can keep qualified for public affairs by mother-wit, going into Bradford [Forster's constituency], reading newspapers, going to the House, going to the Cosmopolitan, will be left behind . . . whoever lives ten years will see great changes, not only in these respects, but in our very centre of movement, which has long been the House of Commons, and bids fair to be so no longer, but the real mind of the nation.[122]

Just before Christmas, Arnold was coming out of Cannon Street railway station when he stumbled on the steps of the portico and crashed forward, breaking two teeth in the front of his mouth (next to one broken years previously when bathing near Fox How) and bleeding profusely. He resolved to sue the railway company for the bill from Kahn, his dentist, because they 'ought either to shut up their gates when their trains have ceased running, or, if they keep their gates open and their stations accessible, to keep the lamps in along their portico'.[123] The solicitor handling his personal injury claim, later pointed out that his case was like that of 'an illiterate man' falling into a reservoir because he did not read a notice, an analogy which delighted Arnold. A more worrying domestic development, however, was the state of little Basil. Flu's diary charts the progress throughout December of the baby's illness and the attempts of Dr Hutton to rally him with camomile injections.

At the end of the year Arnold's foreign schools report, *Schools and Universities on the Continent*, was finally ready for the press. Arnold also sold 'a sort of schoolbook on Greek poetry' to Macmillan for £300. 'This is the first money of any importance I have made by literature and I hope it will help to set us straight',[124] he told his mother. It did not materialise, however, and after endless correspondence, Arnold paid back the advance. *Schools and Universities on the Continent* finally appeared in March 1868. Of interest chiefly to historians of education, the key elements of the book for an understanding of Arnold are in Chapters 22 and 23 where he sets out his ideas on the purpose of education: 'to enable a man to know himself and the world . . . To know himself, a man must know the capabilities and performances of the human spirit'.[125] Arnold stressed the 'equipollency' of science and the humanities and, interestingly for such a traditional classicist, argued that the study of literature rather than grammar was of key importance. With his customary prescience he forecast the decline of Latin and Greek in the school curriculum. For the rest, he used the example of Continental educational practice once more as a stick with which to beat the English who were told to overcome their 'denial or . . . ignorance of the right of mind and reason to rule human affairs' and he praised the municipal organisation of those countries. Arnold was always a strong advocate of local government. The book was well reviewed and sold out its entire edition of 750 (*The Popular Education of France* had sold only 300 copies).

Although *Anarchy and Authority* appeared in January 1868, its publication was dwarfed by a private sadness as, on the 4th, Basil,

Arnold's youngest child, died. He was buried at Laleham on 11 January. Arnold had stayed up till four in the morning with him, reading examination papers, and, as he looked at him in death 'with his hands folded and a white camellia Georgina Wightman brought him lying on his breast, he is the sweetest and most beautiful sight possible'.[126] They photographed the dead child and Mrs Tuffin told them that it made Basil look as if he were trying to tell them: 'I am so comfortable – don't disturb me.'[127]

The turn of the year, coinciding as it did with Arnold's birthday on Christmas Eve, always prompted reflections about where he had reached in his life. Once again, to K who would understand the nuance, he hinted at his own sense of not being able to rely on a long life because of his inherited condition, when he wrote that 'the departure of youth, cares of many kinds, an almost painful anxiety about public matters' reminded him of the biblical phrase he had used before 'the time past of our life may suffice us'. This, he told his sister, was 'true for all of us, and for me, above all, how full of meaning and warning'.[128]

This sense of the fragility of human existence no doubt tempered Arnold's pleasure at realising how much in demand he was now as a writer, and how influential he was becoming.

'Altogether I am in request just now',[129] he told his mother, 'everywhere I see signs of my notions bearing fruit and awakening thought.'[130] He was able to refuse an offer to write for his *bête noire*, the *Daily Telegraph* and he noted Lord Lytton's observation that 'all the writing world have a kind of weakness for me, even at the time they are attacking me'. In particular, the classification of society into Barbarians (the aristocracy), Philistines (the middle class) and Populace which was to be the cornerstone of *Culture and Anarchy* when it was published in January 1869 was already, through the *Cornhill* articles, in common currency. At the home of Lord Cowper in June Arnold reported: 'I should think I heard the word *Philistines* used at least a hundred times during dinner.'[131] To Lady de Rothschild he joked: 'I hope you laughed over the *Barbarians*.'[132] To his mother he predicted: 'I think *Barbarian* will stick.'[133] Joking aside, Arnold was upset by a review in *The Spectator* which talked of 'my contempt for unintellectual people. It is not at all true, and it sets people against one.'[134]

The Arnolds were now settled in Harrow at Byron House, having taken out a rental until 1 June 1873. In their second week the couple went for a walk in a lane off the Sudbury road where they immediately found themselves in a wilderness of fields with primroses, dog violets, cowslips, wood anemones and wild hyacinths. In Arnold's diary, preserved in the library vault at the Beinecke Library at Yale, a tiny dried flower, possibly a forget-me-not, still marks the pages of this early spring. He and Flu spent most of April walking in the countryside around Harrow and even on an inspection in Suffolk, when his train broke down and the passengers were compelled to make use of a navvy's trolley to get to the next town stop, he was delighted by the cowslips growing on the railway embankment. It was clear that the house, though a little costly, was going to be a success. There would be savings on school fees and an escape from relentless metropolitan dining out so they were very pleased with their new base. 'Champagne and fizzing stuff of all kinds I have cut off absolutely, and this will save not less than £20 a year',[135] he announced.

In spite of all the bustle of settling in, however, Arnold found time to reply to a letter from Harriet Martineau in which he expressed the hope that *Schools and Universities on the Continent* was a little less dogmatic than his previous reports: 'As one gets older one gets, I hope, less and less disposed to lay down the law', he wrote. 'I hope with time to convince people that I do not care the least for importing this or that foreign machinery, whether it be French or German, but only for getting certain English deficiencies supplied . . . the longer I live the more thankful I am for the education I have had, with all its shortcomings, and I doubt whether my children, in this time of unsettlement and transition, will have as good a one.'[136]

Although able to refer to the 'shortcomings' of his education in this way, Arnold was increasingly prepared to acknowledge his father's influence. Writing to his mother on 13 June 1868, Dr Arnold's birthday, he observed: 'The nearer I get to accomplishing the term of years which was papa's, the more I am struck with admiration at what he did in them.'[137] He judged that Dr Arnold would have approved of his son's work and seen it as 'indispensable' although he would certainly not have shared his interest in Hellenism. He confessed himself 'astonished' at the favourable reception his writing was receiving and saw it as proof of 'how ripe people's minds are for a change in some of their fixed notions in these matters'.

Thus encouraged, Arnold spent the summer finishing his *Anarchy and Authority*, with breaks to dine with the Barbarians, one of whom, Lord Houghton, introduced him to the poet Longfellow, who had told Macmillan that Arnold was one of three people in England (with Tennyson and F. D. Maurice) he had most wished to see. Longfellow, who had a very simple and pleasing manner, got on very well with Flu over lunch at Harrow. Arnold took Lucy to the Eton and Harrow cricket match at Lord's and with the whole family attended one of George Smith's opulent garden parties at his mansion in Hampstead where the children were delighted with 'the grand entertainment with the champagne ices and hothouse fruit afterwards',[138] after which Smith put them into his open barouche and they were taken in style to Kilburn station.

In spite of such distractions, Arnold finally finished his *Cornhill* paper at the end of July, 'to my great relief'. He confessed that: 'I am too much harried for my peace, but perhaps the paper has the more *verve* and flow from having been written so rapidly.'[139] One small detail in the paper worried Arnold. In a passage that has earned him much posthumous rebuke, Arnold quoted with approval his father's opinion that there was only one way of dealing with social disorder: 'As for rioting, the old Roman way of dealing with *that* is always the right one; flog the rank and file, and fling the ring-leaders from the Tarpeian Rock!'[140] Arnold was quoting from memory out of one of his father's letters and asked his mother to verify it for him if she could find the original letter. Stanley thought the phrase was 'Crucify the slaves' not 'Flog the rank and file' but Arnold, ironically in view of the opprobrium that this illiberal spasm has brought down on his head, decided that the phrase he used was better because 'milder'.[141]

Shortly after the family returned from summer at Fox How, Arnold's eldest boy, the frail Thomas, who had fallen from his pony in Westmorland, became very ill. He never recovered and eventually died on 23 November after exhibiting, in Arnold's judgement, 'heroic self-control' by saying just before he died: 'Don't let Mamma come in.'[142] Flu was deeply distressed by the loss of 'the occupation of her life', the second of her boys to die in one year, and one she had nursed through frail health for sixteen years. Thomas was buried at Laleham next to his little brother, Basil, and Arnold reported to Clough's widow: 'Mrs Arnold got through the long, endless day better than I could have hoped.'[143]

All this came at a time when the Arnolds were at their happiest. Arnold almost began to feel that the Middlesex countryside he had originally disparaged might come to equal the Cumnor country in his affection. The domestic pleasures and routines of Byron House, coupled to the success of his public writing, made his life at this period as happy as it was ever to be. 'A morning of work here, lunching with the children at 1, walking in the afternoon with Rover, dining very late and playing patience with Flu afterwards is the sort of day I like best',[144] he wrote to his mother. They had acquired a pig and planned to build a cow-shed next to the pony's stable to accommodate an Alderney cow. 'These are some of the soundest refreshments and pleasures of life, after all',[145] he reported comfortably to his mother. But the loss of his two boys lent to his customary birthday stocktaking on 24 December a more than usually serious tone. He was conscious that he was now almost the same age as his father had been when he died. 'Everything has seemed to come together to make this year the beginning of a new time to me',[146] he wrote to his mother, 'the gradual settlement of my own thought, little Basil's death, and then my dear, dear Tommy's. And Tommy's death in particular was associated with several awakening and epoch-marking things . . . All these things point to a new beginning, yet it may well be that I am near my end, as papa was at my age, but without papa's ripeness, and that there will be little time to carry far the new beginning.'

6

Tommy's death cast a shadow over Arnold's last-minute revision for the press of what was to be published in January as *Culture and Anarchy*, his best-known prose work. He sat writing the Preface on the day Tommy died, sitting in the boy's room on 'that mild, rainy dim afternoon'[147] of Sunday 23 November. He then went out for a walk with Rover, thinking of Tommy, and could not bring himself to continue the playful mood of the Preface: 'there was some persiflage in what I had written and I could not go on in that strain'. Certainly the Preface, with its religiose conclusion, is more sombre than the Introduction, which is written in Arnold's most 'vivacious' manner. Picking it up again at the end of the year, however, and reviewing the book's components, Arnold reflected that they now amounted to 'a well-looking and useful body of doctrine'.

Although always disdaining any pretensions to systematic thinking, Arnold presents in this book, in its most coherent form, his view of culture and how it related both to his philosophy of life (although he would protest that he had no such thing) and what he saw as the needs of his society at a very particular historical moment. It is thus personal, topical, and deeply serious – whatever its manner of delivery might suggest. It is also, paradoxically, at once the best read and the most misrepresented of Arnold's prose writings, for the notion of culture it expounds is wholly at odds with the popular view of Arnold entertained, and regularly disseminated, by many present-day cultural commentators.[148] 'Matthew Arnold' seems to have become a sort of easy shorthand for such writers, standing for a notion of cold cultural arrogance, an élitist disdain for mass culture, rightly rejected in a democratic age. Any disinterested reader who gets no further than the first couple of pages of the first chapter of *Culture and Anarchy*, will quickly perceive how untrue to Arnold's actual thinking such caricatures are. Given, however, the terminological, philosophical and political confusions in current debates about the competing merits of 'high' and 'low' culture (distinctions which did not really concern Arnold who was interested in what culture could do, not how it could divide) the failure to understand Arnold should not really surprise.

In his Preface he states: 'The whole scope of the essay is to recommend culture as the great help out of our present difficulties; culture being a pursuit of our total perfection by means of getting to know, on all the matters which most concern us, the best which has been thought and said in the world; and through this knowledge, turning a stream of fresh and free thought upon our stock notions and habits . . .'[149] For Arnold, therefore, culture was socially useful because it made people think freely and creatively rather than thoughtlessly accepting a *status quo* which was itself visibly breaking up in the Britain of the 1860s. But at the same time it was 'inward', a pursuit of individual perfection, expressed explicitly in religious terms, although *Culture and Anarchy* tends to work today primarily as a secular argument. Arnold was to spend much of the next decade in writing books which attempted to fashion an accommodating, liberal theology. *Culture and Anarchy* was his secular prologue. His targets are already familiar: the Philistine, the provincial Nonconformists, who having made obsessive dissent their *raison d'être* have failed to develop their humanity to the full and are 'not in contact with the main current of national life', the worship of machinery, the self-satisfaction of the middle-class Liberals, and the roaring of 'the young lions of the *Daily Telegraph*'.

Culture, Arnold argued, is far broader than the mocking definition he quotes from Frederic Harrison, the 'very clever writer' who saw it as no more than 'a desirable quality in a critic of new books' rather than 'disinterestedly trying, in its aim at perfection, to see things as they are'. Harrison, the young barrister and disciple of Comte, the founder of 'positivism', whose *Culture: A Dialogue* had so amused Arnold when it was published in the *Fortnightly* in November 1867, mocked the failure of Arnold to define what he meant by culture and his silence about the practical means to achieve it. Although Harrison's dialogue borrows Arnold's satirical creation, Arminius von Thunder-ten-Tronckh, he did not have Arnold's skill as a satirist. He does, however, raise some valuable objections and in a later essay *A Few Words about the Nineteenth Century* (1882), which is a powerful critique of Victorian materialism, shows that he was not wholly at odds with the writer he mocked.

In his opening chapter, 'Sweetness and Light', Arnold assigns four very clear characteristics to his notion of culture: (a) it is not élitist ('an engine of social and class distinction, separating its holder, like a badge or title, from other people who have not got it') or a status symbol; (b) it is socially useful since it is motivated not just by the love of pure knowledge 'but also the moral and social passion for doing good'; (c) it is dynamic not static ('Not a having and a resting, but a growing and a becoming'); and (d) it is profoundly democratic and inclusive rather than the preserve of a favoured few ('perfection, as culture conceives it, is not possible while the individual remains isolated'). His culture was indissolubly linked to what he called 'the social idea' – the egalitarian passion for spreading the riches and benefits of culture to everyone: 'the men of culture are the true apostles of equality. The great men of culture are those who have had a passion for diffusing, for making prevail, for carrying from one end of society to the other, the best knowledge, the best ideas of their time'. True culture, Arnold passionately believed, needed to be open to all, to be made 'efficient outside the clique of the cultivated and learned'. This notion of Arnold as a contributor to the English egalitarian tradition, which his detractors on the Left would find hard to swallow, has been recognised by at least one prominent member of the British Labour Party, former Home Secretary Roy Hattersley, who in 1995, during a debate about his Party's current ideology, defined his own 'view of socialism' by a perhaps surprising triumvirate of influences: 'Arnold, Tawney and Crosland'.[150]

Arnold also calmly demolished another nostrum of present-day cultural debate, which holds that commercialised or popular mass-media culture is more 'democratic' than 'high' culture, by putting his finger on the patronising and manipulative nature of so much putatively 'popular' culture: 'Plenty of people will try to give the masses, as they call them, an intellectual food prepared and adapted in the way they think proper for the actual condition of the masses', he noted scathingly.

Arnold had no time for those who condescended to or talked down to the masses. He wanted them to enjoy the riches he himself enjoyed. This is not to say that he is beyond criticism, even from those who share his passion for 'diffusion'. Harrison was right to say that he needed to be more specific about how his cultural utopia was to be built,[151] and, more immediately, Arnold's manner of debate sometimes led him into denunciations of social groups that we (and, no doubt, they) might see as lacking in the characters of sweetness and light. Arnold may have had a legitimate point about the narrowness of Nonconformist culture but to put it in the following terms risked the charge of arrogance and priggishness: 'Look at the life imaged in such a newspaper as the *Nonconformist*, – a life of jealousy of the Establishment, disputes, tea-meetings, openings of chapels, sermons; and then think of it as an ideal of a human life completing itself on all sides, and aspiring with all its organs after sweetness, light, and perfection!'

In the book Arnold also returned to his theme of the inadequacy of merely 'doing as one likes' as a rule of life (extending his condemnation to sporadic working-class protest) and defended the role of the State. He set out in the fullest terms yet his tripartite division of society into Barbarians, Philistines and Populace. Mockingly placing himself in this scheme, Arnold acknowledged: 'I myself am properly a Philistine' – albeit one who had, for the most part, 'broken with the ideas and the tea-meetings of my own class'. In fact: 'I never take a gun or fishing-rod in my hands without feeling that I have in the ground of my nature the self-same seeds which, fostered by circumstances, do so much to make the Barbarian; and that, with the Barbarian's advantages, I might have rivalled him.'

Using his concept of the 'best self' which can transcend these instinctive class reactions, Arnold argued that there were, in all classes, those who could break free and whom he called 'aliens', or 'persons who are mainly led, not by their class spirit, but by a general *humane* spirit, by the love of human perfection'. In his anatomy of mid-Victorian England, the monarchy – whose Prussian counterparts he had approved for supporting educational innovation – were little more than a sort of 'grand advertising van' acting as cheerleader to the projects of English Philistinism.

The book also expounded for the first time Arnold's famous distinction between 'Hebraism and Hellenism'. He summed up the distinction by saying: 'The governing idea of Hellenism is *spontaneity of consciousness*; that of Hebraism, *strictness of conscience*.' It requires little effort to see which side of this equation attracted Arnold and which summed up the sins of the Philistine. He believed both were essential components of human culture but that Hebraism had for the moment got the upper hand in England and it was time for a strong dose of Hellenism: 'To get rid of one's ignorance, to see things as they are, and by seeing them as they are to see them in their beauty, is the simple and attractive ideal which Hellenism holds out before human nature . . . and human life in the hands of Hellenism, is invested with a kind of aerial ease, clearness, and radiancy . . . full of what we call sweetness and light.'

Hebraism, by contrast, is the philosophy of English puritanism, strict in conscience and in obeying the law, but deaf to the music of freedom and spontaneity, the disinterested love of truth, any kind of spiritual delicacy. In the penultimate chapter Arnold tells the story of Mr Smith whom the newspapers reported as having committed suicide because, as they put it, he 'laboured under the apprehension that he would come to poverty, and that he was eternally lost'. Arnold took Mr Smith as the epitome of the middle-class Philistine whose life was reduced to two imperatives only: 'the concern for making money, and the concern for saving our souls!' Although Arnold was writing very consciously about the present and trying to address its immediate needs, he also claimed the right not to get involved in the area of immediate practice, to refuse, as he put it 'to lend a hand at uprooting certain definite evils'. In the face of those who saw this as the weakness of the effete man of culture who did not wish to get his hands dirty and who was thus guilty of 'provoking the earnest lovers of action', Arnold maintained that culture – by encouraging the free play of thought, the disinterested attempt to see things as they really were – would in the long run do more good than the rush to short-term palliatives which, because they were not thought through and were the product of mere 'stock notions and habits', would have little effect.

In his final chapter he runs over some current Liberal political initiatives – including the Bill to enable a man to marry his deceased wife's sister which became a bee in Arnold's bonnet and a symbol for him of the Nonconformists' 'double craving so characteristic of our Philistine . . . the craving for forbidden fruit and the craving for legality'. Inevitably, Arnold's detached treatment of such issues made him seem a little Olympian and disdainful – Leslie Stephen said that Arnold in his oracular mode, liberally (and perhaps sanctimoniously) deploying the pronoun 'we', set his teeth on edge.[152] The effect on some of his readers of an assertion like 'we seem to minister better to the diseased spirit of our time by leading it to think about the operation our Liberal friends have in hand, than by lending a hand to this operation ourselves' can be imagined. But Arnold would say that the mere repetition of the nostrums of the practical man was no more effective in 'uprooting certain definite evils'.

He explicitly juxtaposes passages from *The Times* extolling the material glories of Victorian commerce (and briskly dismissing the 'inevitable' poverty of the East End) alongside his own experience in the East End – 'whither my avocations often lead me'. The ineffectual man of culture pointed out that to live – as *The Times* complacently did – with the belief that the poverty of the East End was a fact of nature, its 'multitude of miserable, sunken, and ignorant human beings' necessary to ensure middle-class prosperity, was a failure of humanity. Remembering what he saw as he walked the streets of Bethnal Green, Arnold declared: 'Individual perfection is impossible so long as the rest of mankind are not perfected along with us.' It is at moments like these, when Arnold is indicting 'the Thyestean banquet of clap-trap which English public life for these many years past has been' – rather than when he is crudely invoking draconian measures to repress 'anarchy' as he does in the book's Conclusion – that he is at his most persuasive and appealing as a social critic of probing and humane intelligence.

The book was received, understandably enough, with a marked lack of enthusiasm by those sections of the media whom Arnold had attacked in it. The appearance of its parts in periodical form had made everyone familiar with its arguments and, as the *Saturday Review* put it: 'We all of us know pretty well by this time what to think of Matthew Arnold.'[153] Macmillan, however, told Arnold: 'On the larger and more important questions I think you have done a good deal to make matters clear where you have been understood imperfectly.'[154] Huxley, who had been teased by Arnold in the Preface, invited him to the annual dinner of the Geological Society, and made very positive references to it in his speech as President. Arnold wrote to his mother and Fan at Fox How saying he would not send them a copy of the book 'because neither of you sincerely liked it and it is of no use giving a book under such circumstances'.[155] He also wrote to Lady de Rothschild asking her to send a copy of the book to Disraeli: 'And now I have done with social and political essays for a long time to come.'[156]

Arnold frequently announced such abstentions and with comparable frequency failed to sustain them but it is true that he was now working on his abortive anthology of Greek poetry and arranging for another collected edition of his poems which would appear in June in two volumes, the first 'Narrative and Elegiac' and the second 'Dramatic and Lyric'. The edition contained no new poems but the £300 paid for it by Macmillan (Arnold had finally accepted Browning's advice that it was better to sell the edition to a publisher rather than bear the risk himself) helped to ease Arnold's money worries which were acute at this time (he noted with interest that the second-hand bookseller, Pickering, was now asking 18 shillings for a copy of the out-of-print *The Strayed Reveller*).

The Arnolds took in at about this time a lodger, the teenage Duke of Genoa, Prince Thomas of Savoy, which provided income and a welcome breath of the European. 'Flu takes kindly to him because his name is Thomas,'[157] Arnold reported to his brother. Arnold took the Prince with him to the vulgar Barbarian pile of Lord Lytton at Knebworth ('a strange mixture of what is really romantic and interesting with what is tawdry and gimcracky'[158]), where the elegant Prince wrinkled his refined nose at what he saw: 'The Prince, with his Italian tastes, finds this place Gothic and oppressive', Arnold reported.

Byron House – whose menagerie now included a cow – was still a picture of domestic bliss. Daffodils from Fox How bloomed, the apricot trees were in blossom, and Arnold bought a guinea's worth of vegetable seeds from Carter's in Holborn to plant in the kitchen garden: 'Hardly a day passes without our having either cauliflower from it or Brussels sprouts or Jerusalem artichokes – of all of which I am very fond.'[159] There were still trips to London, however, and in April Arnold went to the private view of the Royal Academy exhibition, and dined afterwards between Frith, the painter of *Derby Day* and Lord Leighton, the painter of classical subjects, who was particularly struck by Arnold's notion of Hellenism. He also joined an exclusive society of forty members – including the Bishop of Oxford, Lord Salisbury, John Duke Coleridge and a good sprinkling of Barbarians – called the Literary Club which cost two guineas a year and dined, in the rooms of the Dilettante Society in London, on the first Monday of the month. 'It will be a very pleasant way of keeping up one's hold on what is pleasantest in London society', he told his mother. Addicted as he was to the domestic *rus in urbe* of Harrow, Arnold retained his taste for metropolitan life. And for fishing. At the end of May 1869 he went to fish at the Duke of Bedford's estate at Chenies. He went up two days before Flu in order to fish in 'perfect seclusion', staying at the Bedford Arms where he breakfasted on honey and cream. When Lord Charles

Russell and Flu arrived to interrupt his bliss, he proudly displayed on the table of the little inn in three enormous kitchen dishes his catch, the largest of which was two and a half pounds in weight, with several between one and two pounds.

Arnold's poems came out on 4 June and, in a letter to his mother the following day, he made a much-quoted declaration about his poems which shows how clearly he thought about his poetic mission and its significance and how acute his understanding of his relative position was:

> My poems represent, on the whole, the main movement of mind of the last quarter of a century, and thus they will probably have their day as people become conscious to themselves of what the movement of mind is, and interested in the literary productions which reflect it. It might fairly be urged that I have less poetical sentiment than Tennyson, and less intellectual vigour and abundance than Browning; yet, because I have perhaps more of a fusion of the two than either of them, and have more regularly applied that fusion to the main line of modern development, I am likely enough to have my turn, as they have had theirs.[160]

He was conscious, too of his wider intellectual influence as a prose critic and his letters increasingly testify to his conviction that he was effecting a real change in thought. Having made his mark in the fields of poetry, literary criticism and cultural debate, Arnold was about to carry his standard into a new field of battle and to deal directly with religious subjects.

CHAPTER EIGHT:
RELIGION AND THE ZEIT-GEIST
[1870–1877]

And it is because I am sure that the belief in miracles must go as the belief in witches and hobgoblins has gone, and that I see how terrible will be the blank and bewilderment in England when it has gone, that I wish and strive, while there is yet time, to accustom people's minds to a conception of the Bible in which its truth and power shall no longer depend on them.[1]

1

On 1 October 1882, Edward Henry Stanley, fifteenth Earl of Derby, took down his long foolscap Letts Office Diary, and began to record his puzzlement at the behaviour of one of his guests on the Sunday morning of a recent visit. 'Mr Arnold went with Lady D. to church', he wrote, 'which is a curious piece of conformity, his being an avowed agnostic.'[2] In trying to account for this perplexing behaviour, the peer concluded that it was perhaps the fact of his being 'a government official' that constrained him to such a display of public hypocrisy. The misapprehension of Lord Derby, a thoroughly orthodox peer, has been shared by many of Arnold's readers who, as has been argued above, have drawn too literal a conclusion from the 'melancholy, long withdrawing roar' of the Sea of Faith in *Dover Beach* and concluded that Arnold had rejected God.

Arnold's religious works of the 1870s – which perhaps hardly anyone now reads – could scarcely have been written by a man to whom Christianity meant nothing. Lord Derby's conservative instincts were right – Arnold was very far from being an orthodox Christian – but his attempt to reconcile Christianity with 'science' (by which he meant the application of reason rather than the scientific challenge from evolutionary theory) was fundamental even to his secular thinking. Like the twentieth-century Bishop of Durham, David Jenkins, Arnold tried to reformulate traditional Christian theology in terms that would convince a modern intelligence, and, also like David Jenkins, did so in language that was often both striking and highly controversial. Unorthodox, going too far for some, Arnold was certainly not 'an avowed agnostic', and remained a believer and a worshipper after his own fashion until – quite literally – the day he died.

The germ of *St Paul and Protestantism* (1870) was an article of the same name that appeared in two parts in the October and November 1869 issues of the *Cornhill* together with a further piece on *Puritanism and the Church of England* that appeared in the following February's issue of George Smith's organ, which normally declined articles on religious debate. In fact Arnold sought reassurance from Smith that it was not 'too grave a subject'[3] for the magazine. A couple of weeks later Arnold read an attack on his poems in the *Nonconformist* which accused them of 'immorality and irreligion'. He concluded: 'The Protestant Dissenters will more and more feel that it is war between us and that what I am doing strikes at the very root of their influence and power.'[4] When the first *Cornhill* piece appeared in October, Arnold thought he detected 'an extraordinary movement of unsettling'[5] in the Dissenting camp and clearly recognised his opportunity to drive home an argument. It seemed to him that there was 'a prevalent desire to get rid of much of the dogma which has covered itself with St Paul's authority' and that fact accounted for the 'extraordinary indulgence'[6] shown to the first article. 'It would have been no use publishing it if it were to have raised furious wrath: its chief merit is that it is opportune', he added.

While he was engaged on the next article in the series, Arnold heard of the death of Sainte-Beuve, whom he admired and had been strongly influenced by and had called 'the most delicate of living critics'.[7] Sainte-Beuve in turn described him as '*un étranger qui nous connait mieux que personne.*'[8] 'I have learnt a great deal from him, and the news of his death struck me as if it had been that of someone very near to me',[9] he told his mother. The end of the year was approaching and with it the ritual computation of the passing years. Arnold was keeping himself fit on his daily walks with Rover and by playing racquets. After an enthusiastic game with the son of Wyndham Slade he reported to his mother, with his hand still shaking, 'at Rugby I was very fond of the game and am still good enough at it to beat most of those I play with; and the exercise is splendid.'[10] Prone as he was to endless colds and bouts of flu, Arnold always loved being out of doors, walking and climbing and fishing and playing games. Yet he could describe at this time his old friend Walrond, who was a possible candidate for the new Rugby headmaster, as 'too old and *set*. He and I are the age Papa was when he ceased his working – we are too apt to forget this.'[11]

If Arnold's public profile as a writer remained high, his professional career remained becalmed, never quite reaching, in the years ahead, what his friends regarded as its proper destination. At a dinner party in November 1869, at the home of Baron Lionel de Rothschild at Gunnersbury, his superior at the Education Office, Lowe, had come over to speak to him after dinner, being civil yet 'expressing himself shocked to see me still an inspector'.[12] Arnold applied for a vacancy as Secretary in the Education Department but failed to get it, with, as usual, very mixed feelings. He saw certain things that needed to be done: 'But there would have been much which I should have felt oppressive and depressive in the situation – and if it had not been for Fanny Lucy, who has a true woman's notions about *getting-on*, and who was very anxious for this promotion I should have been decidedly averse to it. I more and more wish to turn my thoughts from all notions of advancement in official and public life and to go on quietly . . .'[13] But such protestations of turning his back on the world were contradicted by the reality that he was frequently to be found at the dining tables of the rich and the influential. Only days before the above declaration, he was at Latimer surrounded by the usual throng of Barbarians, including Disraeli 'in high force'.[14] Dizzy swung round to Arnold at one point in the conversation to say of some remark that had just been made: 'Sweetness and light I call that, Mr Arnold, eh?'

Far from feeling life 'oppressive and depressive', in fact, Arnold was in good humour, marked by his playful facetiousness with kindred spirits like Lady de Rothschild and Thomas Huxley. To the former on April Fool's Day he joked that Macmillan 'chooses this very suitable day to give a dinner to all his authors'[15] and from the latter came a brief note: 'My Dear Arnold – Look at Bishop Wilson on the sin of covetousness and then inspect your umbrella stand.'[16] His spirits were also lifted in the New Year by a letter read out by Flu at breakfast announcing that they had been left a £2,000 legacy by a distant cousin who was a brewer. 'The best thing money can give one is *freedom*',[17] he told his mother. The legacy would enable him to pay off all the family debts. 'Few people can have met with more kindness in money matters, or more escaped being ever actually driven to the wall, than I have', he went on, 'still the relief of clearing myself of all loans and obligations will be immense.' The legacy didn't quite compensate Flu for her husband's failure to get the Secretaryship, 'but it is a gleam of good fortune which gives her great pleasure, and since she married me she has had few of them . . . to Fanny Lucy it seems as if everyone who had done what I have was promoted, and I alone passed over. There is no good in letting one's mind run on these things, and I had rather she neither dwelt on them nor suggested them to me.'

Arnold's marriage to Flu seems to have been almost unreasonably happy but if there was any trace of tension in their relationship it would be found here, in Arnold's failure to rise more quickly and achieve a more secure income than the hand-to-mouth earnings of a Grub Street 'unpopular author' (Arnold never matched, with his income from writing, his official salary).. Flu had been brought up in very comfortable circumstances in Belgravia and was not used to having to struggle to make ends meet. She supported her husband as a writer, however, even if she did not always care for his subjects (accompanying him on his lecture tour of America, but, like her daughter, never having read Emerson on whom Arnold lectured many times), or feel happy with his alarming propensity to court controversy.

2

St Paul and Protestantism was published in book form in May. 'I hope it is starting pretty well; the Dissenters are pricked at heart and that is very good both for them and us',[18] he wrote to George Smith who was publishing it. The book can be seen in some sense as a continuation of Arnold's war against the Philistine by other means. It follows naturally on from *Culture and Anarchy* by striking at the heart of what Arnold saw as the Philistines' impoverished culture – their religion. 'The feeling of the harm their isolation from the main current of thought and culture does in the nation, a feeling that has been developed in me by going about among them for years, is the source of all I have written on religious political and social subjects',[19] he told his mother. In this aim he was very much his father's son, echoing the passionate conviction of the merits of a national church Establishment contained in Thomas Arnold's pamphlet, *Principles of Church Reform* (1833).

The book's main aim was to claw back what Arnold saw as the true nature of St Paul's fundamental ideas from 'the elaborate misconceptions with which Protestantism has overlaid them'.[20] In particular, he challenged the way in which the Puritans had taken their key terms *election* and *justification* from St Paul, giving them a meaning that Paul never intended them to bear and thus 'sophisticating simple religion of the heart into complicated theories of the brain'. To do this, he tried to apply what he called a 'scientific' or rational approach to the facts, to ask 'what is really Paul's account of God's proceedings with man, and whether this tallies with the Puritan account and confirms it'. His conclusion was that it did not and that Protestantism 'with its three notable tenets of predestination, original sin, and justification . . . has been pounding away for three centuries at St Paul's wrong words, and missing his essential doctrine'. In addition, Arnold was beginning to formulate his critique of 'the materialism of popular religion', its reliance on the notion of a personal God, and on miracles. He launches here, for the first time, the definition of God that would be elaborated more fully – and notoriously – in *Literature and Dogma* (1873): 'that stream of tendency by which all things seek to fulfil the law of their being'.

Arnold also wanted to challenge the fundamental premise of Dissent, that it must exist outside the national Church of England Establishment, an historical separation that Arnold regretted. In the second part of the book, 'Puritanism and the Church of England', he argues that the historical failure to keep the Puritans within the Establishment fold was a 'waste of power'. The Church of England, he believed, was right to resist the 'narrowness and tyrannousness' of the Puritan demands in the 1660s and far from their clash being the product of 'the lust of haughty ecclesiastics for dominion', it was a bid to keep the Church from narrowing its scope. And so it had proved, Arnold believed, with the Church of England now more amenable to 'a progressive development of Christianity' than the Nonconformists. Arnold had adopted the idea of 'development', or *Bildung*, from the German biblical critics who had been so influential on nineteenth-century religious thinking.[21] It fitted with the essentially progressive tendency of his thought, the idea that we are always moving forward to a better understanding of religion or thought or to a better ordering of society. The Church of England enjoyed its advantage because 'sects of men are apt to be shut up in sectarian ideas of their own, and to be less open to new general ideas than the main body of men'. In essence Arnold wanted to see, for the sake of 'the power of joint life', a union of all Protestants (and indeed an ecumenical Christendom that would incorporate the Catholics too – 'but this will not be in our day').

The final section of the book as it appears in the popular edition (though it formed the Preface to the original edition), 'Modern Dissent', argues that the spirit of the time, the *Zeit-Geist*, is moving against the Dissenters and that their return to the Establishment fold would be good for them and good for the Establishment whose danger is that it tends to become 'an appendage to the upper-class Barbarians'. Coming back to his distinction between Hebraism and Hellenism, Arnold produces a new sub-distinction, between 'Mialism' and 'Millism'. Edward Miall was a politician and Congregational minister who was the first editor of the *Nonconformist* and the founder in 1844 of the British Anti-State Church Association which regarded the Establishment as 'essentially vicious'.[22] John Stuart Mill, on the other hand, represented the excess of Hellenism as Miall represented the excess of Hebraism, both 'playing into one another's hands'. Since 'our only real perfection is our totality' no progress could be made until these partial mental states were replaced by a harmonious whole.

Arnold ends the book, which had largely eschewed, because of the solemn nature of its subject, his usual vivacity, with a brief flicker of fun as he represents the Nonconformists, smugly celebrating the confounding of science by exhibiting their enemy 'Professor Huxley in a white sheet, brought up at the Surrey Tabernacle between two deacons . . . and penitently confessing that *Science contradicts herself.*' Huxley immediately wrote to Arnold (though unfortunately we have no record of his reaction to this particular ghostly apparition) praising his argument about science gradually conquering the materialism of popular religion: 'It will startle the Puritans . . . These people are for the most part mere idolaters with a Bible-fetish, who urgently stand in need of conversion by Extra-Christian missionaries.'[23] He deplored their 'horribly absurd dogmas'.

3

In June 1870, Lord Salisbury, the new Chancellor of Oxford University, wrote to Arnold to say that he wanted to mark his installation by conferring on Arnold an honorary doctorate of Civil Law. 'Nothing could more gratify me, I think, in the way of an honour, than this recognition by my own University, of which I am so fond, and where, according to their own established standard of distinctions, I did so little',[24] he wrote to his mother. He also enclosed for her a letter from Richard Church, later Dean of St Paul's and historian of the Oxford Movement who, as a high churchman and 'more of a dogmatist than you are',[25] none the less liked *St Paul and Protestantism* which was selling well, exhausting its first printing in four months.

The Oxford ceremony, on a hot June day, was 'very jolly', Arnold reported to George Smith, 'though the grass was burnt up, and even the rivers of cup that were passing about could not freshen it'.[26] Arnold appreciated the warmth of the University towards him even if, in some sense, he expected it 'because there is so much of an Oxford character about what I have written'.[27] Salisbury told Arnold afterwards, with an allusion to 'sweetness and light', that he ought to have addressed him as *vir dulcissime et lucidissime*. Such courtesy, however, did not prevent Arnold from thinking him 'a dangerous man . . . chiefly from his want of any true sense and experience of literature and its beneficent function'. An awareness that men like Salisbury existed in such positions worried Arnold and made him hope that he might be able to act as 'a healing and reconciling influence' in what he saw as the troubled times ahead, 'and it is this which makes me glad to find – what I find more and more – that I *have* influence'.

In addition to his concern about the state of the nation's intellectual health, Arnold had more pressing domestic worries. The legacy was not enough to remove all financial anxiety. He told his mother during the summer that his total income from all sources was unlikely to exceed £1,200 a year and that any hopes of promotion in the educational sphere were now futile. 'I more and more accustom myself to feel that literature is what I have a turn for, and that one's happiness consists in doing what one has a turn for',[28] he concluded philosophically. Domestic economies were hard on Flu, for only the previous night he had observed: 'Flu in her new dress looked charming and is so good a hostess it is really a pity she has not more of such work to do.' Inspecting was also a distraction and he told his mother that what he needed to do was to focus his energies much more firmly, even if 'the power of self-management and turning one's circumstances to the best account is the hardest power in the world to acquire'.[29] He was now prepared to admit that it was 'absurd . . . that all the best of my days should be taken up with matters which thousands of other people could do just as well as I, and that what I have a special turn for doing I should have no time for'.[30] But the fact that he was bursting with ideas kept his mind active 'and prevents routine from jading me'.[31]

And life had its amusements. At the beginning of December, he went to see the Income Tax Commissioners at Edgware. Seeing his name bandied about in the newspapers they had assumed he was a high-earning author and assessed his profits at £1,000 a year. He went to put them right, declaring in his most Arnoldian manner: 'You see before you gentlemen what you have often heard of, *an unpopular author*.'[32] The taxmen accepted his plea and cut the assessment down to £200 but Arnold complained that even this would mean his having to write very many more articles to survive. No doubt catching the infection of irony in the air, the Chairman leaned across politely and declared: 'Then the public will have reason to be much obliged to us.'

4

On 29 November 1870 Arnold contributed the last of his satirical Arminius letters to the *Pall Mall Gazette* and then began to discuss with George Smith the possibility of bringing out as a book 'the literary remains of poor dear Arminius'.[33] They were to be grouped together with a mock editorial commentary by Arnold in his own name. 'It is rather fun making the notes',[34] he admitted to Smith. The collection, which was published as *Friendship's Garland* on 24 February 1870, is considerably more 'fun', we might feel, than the religious works that appeared before and after it. Although what one severe Marxist critic called Arnold's 'witty and malicious observation better suited to minor fiction',[35] may not have been to every taste (and Arnold himself worried that the letters may have been too 'chaffy'[36] for the seriousness of the times), the book has a lively and animated flavour that make it a welcome sorbet in the grave theological banquet of his writing of the 1870s.

It is framed with a dedicatory letter from Grub Street on Candlemas Day 1871 to 'Adolescens Leo Esq' – the young lion of the *Daily Telegraph* – recalling the now deceased Arminius von Thunder-ten-

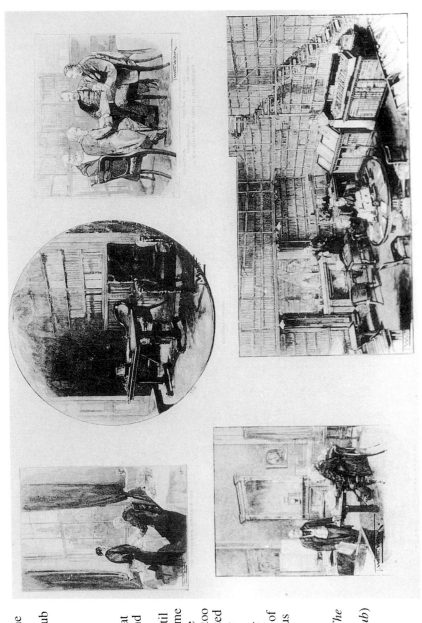

Scenes from the interior of the Athenaeum Club in Pall Mall which Arnold joined in 1856 and which became a treasured retreat from family and inspecting distractions until his growing fame made it a place where he was too easily recognised and courted by the leading intellectuals of the day. Many of his most famous essays were written in the library of the Athenaeum. (*The Trustees of the Athenaeum Club*)

Two caricatures of the famous man of letters. Spy's cartoon in *Vanity Fair* of 11 November 1871 where the caption accompanying the picture of the languid critic is from *Culture and Anarchy*: 'I say, the critic must keep out of the region of immediate practice.' (*Wordsworth Trust*)

And Max Beerbohm who has the small and priggish Mary Augusta Ward (the novelist Mrs Humphry Ward) asking her famous uncle: 'Why, Uncle Matthew, oh why, will not you be always wholly serious?' (*Wordsworth Trust*)

The photograph taken by the Victorian Oxford photographer Henry Taunt (1842–1922) of 'the stripling Thames at Bab-lock-hithe' (the old chain ferry looking west) one of the most evocative locations mentioned in *The Scholar-Gipsy*. (*Oxfordshire Photographic Archive, Oxfordshire County Council*)

And of another imaginary occupant of the scholar-gipsy country: 'Go, for they call you, Shepherd, from the hill.' Taunt's Berkshire shepherd (*Oxfordshire Photographic Archive, Oxfordshire County Council*)

Arnold with the
unmistakeable central parting
and bushy sidewhiskers
which were seized upon with
such glee by the caricaturists
at the time he was beginning
to be established as a leading
figure on the stage of public
controversy. (*Wordsworth
Trust*)

Lady Louisa de Rothschild
with her lapdog Elfie. Arnold
valued her liveliness and
intellectual companionship
throughout his life: 'I think
of you always in what I
write.'

Arnold's two daughters, Lucy and
Eleanor. The former married a
New York lawyer, Frederick
Whitridge, and the latter became
the Viscountess Sandhurst.
(*Moorman Collection*)

Arnold the middle-aged, and
slightly plumper, family man with
his daughter Eleanor and his two
dogs, Kaiser and Geist, whose
deaths would be recorded in
verse. A photograph which
reveals the strains imposed by the
conditions of Victorian studio
portraiture. (*Master and Fellows
of Balliol College*)

Arnold managing a rare smile for the camera. (*Trustees of the National Portrait Gallery*)

Arnold represented by the weekly magazine *Once a Week* in October 1872 as a trapeze artist skilfully leaping between the bars of poetry, philosophy and criticism. (*The British Library*)

Photographs of Bablock-hythe today.

Photographs of the churchyard at Laleham where Arnold and his wife are buried and close-ups of the family grave.

Tronckh, allegedly a descendant of Voltaire's Dr Pangloss. In the dedicatory letter, Arnold offers a mock-lament over the cost of his 'long warfare with the Philistines'[37] and sums up the acerbic message of Arminius to the British people: 'Your nation is sound enough, if only it can be taught that being able to do what one likes, and say what one likes, is not sufficient for salvation. Its dangers are from a surfeit of clap-trap, due to the false notion that liberty and publicity are not only valuable for the use to be made of them, but are goods in themselves, nay, are the *summum bonum!*'

The letters, in one sense, are a palatable way of acquiring some of those leading Arnoldian ideas expounded in works like *Culture and Anarchy*. One such is the notion of '*Geist*' or intelligence as the one thing needful for the English. 'The same idea is at the bottom of democracy; the victory of reason and intelligence over blind custom and prejudice,' Arminius notes. The satirical format enables Arnold to distance himself from some of his familiar criticisms by allowing himself to criticise, and to be criticised by, Arminius, and to put into the latter's mouth indictments of whose provenance his readers would be in no doubt. The public schools, for example, which Arnold was increasingly disillusioned with, telling his mother that 'Rugby is in an unhappy state: people will learn at last that it is an inferiority, not a superiority, to have your masters named by a set of private gentlemen instead of by a public Minister',[38] were described by Arminius as 'precious institutions . . . where . . . for 250*l.* sterling a year your boys learn gentlemanly deportment and cricket'.

Arnold also created some representative characters such as Mr Bottles, the Philistine bottle-manufacturer on the Reigate train, a radical of the Manchester school, a Liberal and a Dissenter brought up at the Lycurgus House Academy, Peckham under the earnest tutorship of its Principal, Archimedes Silverpump Ph.D. but now living at Laburnum House, Reigate. Bottles is a great believer in science and such technological marvels as the new Atlantic telegraph which Arminius dismisses as 'that great rope, with a Philistine at each end of it talking inutilities!' There is also the Reverend Hittall, a sporting parson, who, 'in the performance of his sacred duties never warms up except when he lights on some passage about hunting or fowling'. The chief object of the satire is the English infatuation with 'clap-trap' and the newspapers – particularly *The Times* and the *Daily Telegraph* – which feed that commodity to such as Mr Bottles in very large doses. Another, inanimate, character in this farce is Coles's Truss Manufactory, a building of superlative ugliness whose admirers boasted that it occupied 'the finest site in Europe' in Trafalgar Square. But for Arnold this was less a celebration at the heart of the Imperial capital of the thrusting spirit of Victorian commerce, than a monstrous architectural carbuncle.

Later editions of *Friendship's Garland* included the essay *My Country-men* which had first been published in the *Cornhill* in February 1866 and which had dealt with many of the same issues as the Arminius letters but with a little less levity. It develops the argument a little further by arguing that the lack of intelligence or 'Geist' in the English hampers their attempts to perform on the international stage and makes their foreign policy excursions frequently inept. And he contrasts the English middle class – 'drugged with business . . . its sense blunted for any stimulus besides except religion' – with the more civilised *bourgeoisie* of Europe.

My Countrymen is famous for including a passage of exasperated invective where Arnold lashes out at the Victorian self-satisfaction with a material progress that was unaccompanied by any intellectual cultivation: 'Your middle class man thinks it the highest pitch of development and civilisation when his letters are carried twelve times a day from Islington to Camberwell, and from Camberwell to Islington, and if railway trains run to and fro between them every quarter an hour. He thinks it nothing that the trains only carry him from an illiberal, dismal life at Islington to an illiberal, dismal life at Camberwell; and that the letters only tell him that such is the life there.'

Although Arnold's fears of legal proceedings from George Sala and the *Daily Telegraph* proved unfounded, he braced himself for criticism – not surprisingly in view of what he had been handing out. After reading Leslie Stephen's attack in the *Saturday Review* he wrote to George Smith: 'You see the *Saturday* does not find Arminius amusing, and it will be sad indeed if they persuade the public, as is too likely, to share their opinion.'[39] *Blackwood's Magazine* also doubted Arnold's humour and whether it would actually reach its target. The reviewer, the novelist Margaret Oliphant, wrote: 'Our satirist stands and mocks at the pit in a highly-refined small voice which never reaches beyond the orchestra stalls.'[40]

After spending the New Year at Folkestone Arnold returned to work to find that: 'They are proposing for me a *perfect* district: *Westminster*, and a small rural district round Harrow. And I have made no application, said not a single word!'[41] In 1871 he also became responsible for the first time for schools of all denominations in his district, following the passage of William Forster's Education Act of 1870. The inclusion of Catholic schools was an eye-opener. 'In the

Roman Catholic schools', he wrote in his annual report, 'the children do much more decidedly belong to the poor, and very many of them to the Irish poor, who are a class by themselves.'[42] The week before *Friendship's Garland* was published, the 'highly-refined' satirist was spending a week inspecting in the heart of Spitalfields during a severe outbreak of smallpox. He had the whole household vaccinated except the Welsh cook, Margaret Rees who refused because she was 'like all the Welsh, obstinate'.[43]

Meanwhile the political situation left Arnold rather disillusioned. He felt that Parliament had 'opened stupidly' with Disraeli's 'heavy pompous pounding' of the Prime Minister, Gladstone, who in turn responded with little more than 'emotional verbiage'.[44] A professed Liberal with a lifelong distaste for the Tories, Arnold had none the less little enthusiasm for many of the measures of the Liberals in the 1860s and 1870s and he felt that they were the prisoners of their most important constituency – the middle-class Dissenters. 'The old actors are worn out', he told his mother, 'and the public begins to tire of them; but the new actors do not yet appear.' A month later he greeted the days of the Paris Commune, not with the excitement with which he had observed the street protests of 1848 but with the mature disillusionment of a man approaching fifty: 'there is no way by which France can make the rest of Europe so alarmed and uneasy as by a socialistic and red republic,' he declared. 'It is a perpetual flag to the proletarian class everywhere – the class which makes all governments uneasy.'[45] He had little sympathy, however, for the aristocratic class, and a few weeks later reflected that, 'The Paris convulsion is an explosion of that fixed resolve of the working class to count for something and *live*, which is destined to make itself felt in the coming time . . .'[46]

One aspect of the new season, however, that never failed to excite him was the appearance of wild flowers – a subject about which he was passionate. Shortly after delivering himself of these bitter reflections on the political scene he set off down a turf lane on the south side of Harrow Hill to see if the violets were beginning to come out, and a week later noted with pleasure the imminence of many cowslips. He was also turning over in his mind yet another job offer. Froude had offered him the editorship of *Fraser's*, which he was giving up. The salary would be £400 a year and could be combined with the inspectorship. The drawback, however, was that it would take up Arnold's precious spare time with 'work for which I have a great distaste' and he had scruples lest 'my taking it would look greedy and as if I should not refuse £400 a year, in whatever shape it came'.[47] He decided against it, because having time to write meant more to him and because he was just about to reap the benefit of his perfect new inspectoral district: 'Westminster and the three Middlesex country parishes of Hendon, Barnet and Edmonton. This is as good as it can possibly be: for my London district the Athenaeum is the centre and for my country district this house', he wrote to his mother from Harrow.

When visiting London Arnold frequently borrowed a flat owned by George Smith at his firm's premises at 15 Waterloo Place, a stone's throw from the Athenaeum. This was far more convenient than K's house in Eccleston Square. His London life was thus made easier – even if he was to express genuine regret at losing the human contacts he had made in his trips around the country as an inspector. After lunch with some Hackney school managers in April 1871 he reflected that 'the place and the people were such as I should not have seen and known if I had not been an inspector . . . such as it is very good for one to have seen and known.' They in their turn expressed regret at losing a fair-minded and sympathetic inspector with a reputation for kindness and concern for individual teachers and pupils. 'My success has been due entirely to a naturally, I hope, humane manner, and then to the sense of my entire fairness',[48] he thought.

Although the death of Flu's mother, Lady Wightman, on 10 April was a blow, the Arnold's happy domestic life at Byron House continued. In addition to the cow and the sheep which he allowed a farmer to graze on part of his land, he kept a pig. One morning in June there was 'an alarm of pigs in the garden' as the piglets escaped through gaps in the fence from the field into the garden and the whole family 'with much laughter'[49] rounded them up. The previous day Arnold and Flu had celebrated their twentieth wedding anniversary and he wrote to his mother: 'It seems only a year or two ago we were married. It has been a great happiness ever since my marriage that you all took so to Fanny Lucy, and she to you.'[50] They spent the summer in the Alps ('The air is like champagne'[51]) where Arnold revisited Thun and then Paris. Afterwards, the family went on to Fox How. They were all 'very low'[52] at having to return to Harrow, however attractive the house was.

One day in the autumn, Arnold walked back across the fields after inspecting at Finchley:

> the walk was six miles and all over grass fields, up and down, with fine trees in all the hedges, and Harrow Hill and the sunset in front of me all the way: this is the sort of thing that keeps me going. The garden is a great pleasure to me, and

the cow; whenever I go into the garden she advances to the rail and expects me to give her an apple, a pear or a bunch of grapes, which she eats out of my hand.[53]

Arnold loved animals and possessed two cats, Blacky and Atossa, or Toss. The former shared a stall with the cow but the latter preferred to jump up on to the warm seat by the fire vacated by Flu when she went to bed. Arnold became disturbed when Blacky developed a limp and he decided to summon Thomas Huxley to his aid. After supper the great Victorian scientist, 'Darwin's bulldog', gravely shook out his table-napkin and gathered up the cat in its folds to examine its joints one by one, declaring eventually that a hip-joint was broken but that it would mend naturally.[54]

More serious matters also detained Arnold. He was now at work on a lecture to be delivered at the Masonic Hall Birmingham to the Birmingham and Midland Institute and which was to be published in later editions of *Essays in Criticism* (First Series). The essay, published in December in the *Cornhill*, compared an old Persian drama with the then very popular Oberammergau Passion Play, and was prompted by his reading of Gobineau's *Religion and Philosophy of Central Asia* (1865). It is interesting chiefly for its demonstration of Arnold's view – somewhat disparaging – of Islam in general and the Koran in particular. At Birmingham – where he had a good audience of 900, with 200 being turned away – Arnold met the novelist J. H. Short-house who urged him to write the great book which was worthy of him. Arnold replied with facetious bravado that ephemeral literature was so much easier and paid so much better[55] – he was paid £30 for the article by George Smith. He also found the audience, unlike an Oxford one, 'very animating' and was interested by the Birmingham people's passion for 'agitation' on the question of secular education: 'But things in England being what they are, I am glad to work indirectly by literature rather than directly by politics.'[56] This detachment was mocked by *Vanity Fair* which ran a cartoon by Spy the next month – during which Arnold delivered the same lecture to another audience at Leamington – showing a languid, monocled Arnold repeating his famous declaration that the critic must 'remain outside the area of immediate practice'. Arnold told his mother that the cartoon was 'so unlike; something of resemblance people find in the figure and attitude, but no-one, I think, finds any in the face'.[57]

Shortly after this burst of lecturing, Arnold wrote to Cardinal Newman who was then living at the Oratory in Birmingham, and whom he had just missed on his visit to the city, expressing his debt to

Newman, claiming that: 'In all the conflicts I have with Modern Liberalism and Dissent, and with their pretensions and shortcomings, I recognise your work; and I can truly say that no praise gives me such pleasure as to be told (which sometimes happens) that a thing I have said reminds people, either in manner or matter, of you.'[58] He also referred to the 'Tory, anti-democratic, and even squirearchical character' of the Church of England. Newman wrote back, courteous as ever, to imply that, much as Arnold's writing interested him, he did not quite see the nature of the debt, and was in fact 'sensitively alive to the great differences of opinion which separate us. I wish with all my heart I could make them less; but there they are, and I can only resign myself to them, as best I may'.

The liberal theology of Arnold was wholly at odds with the thinking of Newman and it is odd that Arnold does not seem to have seen how great the gulf was. His preoccupation with style – where there was a real debt – may have been getting the upper hand. Style was the subject of a letter he wrote to Tom at this time, prompted by Tom's precocious daughter Mary (the future novelist Mrs Humphry Ward). 'Tell her from me', Arnold wrote, 'an old and jaded man of letters, that her style showed too much of a determination *de se faire vif*: one should never *try* to be vif, but leave it to the subject to animate the style in the proper places.'[59]

5

Arnold's growing fame meant that caricatures like that in *Vanity Fair* (about whose 'badness and crudity' Browning had been 'open-mouthed'[60]) and parodies of his work abounded. But by far the shrewdest and most wicked satirist of Arnold was W. H. Mallock whose *The New Republic* (1877) targeted Arnold and many of his contemporaries. This work was preceded, however, by a much less well-known book, *Every Man His Own Poet: Or the Inspired Singer's Recipe Book*. Published in 1872 under the pseudonym of 'A Newdigate Prizeman' it was a witty send-up of various contemporary poets and how they went about composition. The entry: HOW TO WRITE A POEM LIKE MR MATTHEW ARNOLD reads:

Take one soulfull of involuntary unbelief, which has been previously well flavoured with self-satisfied despair. Add to this one beautiful text of Scripture. Mix these well together; and as soon as ebullition commences grate in finely a few regretful allusions to the New Testament and the Lake of Tiberius, one constellation of stars, half-a-dozen allusions to the nineteenth century, one to Goethe, one to Mont Blanc, or the Lake of Geneva; and one also, if possible, to some personal bereavement. Flavour the whole with a mouthful of 'Passions', 'finites' and 'yearnings'. This class of poem is concluded usually with some question, about which we have to observe only that it shall be impossible to answer.[61]

Arnold had indeed suffered a 'personal bereavement' at the start of 1872. Shortly after beginning his annual round of inspections (in the course of which he visited the de Rothschilds and met Disraeli who was 'very amiable' towards him and 'expressed great pleasure at meeting me'[62]), Budge, the fat, ungainly sixteen-year-old, was taken ill at school and put to bed with what seemed a bad cold. Unaccountably his condition worsened and he became light-headed, then sank into a kind of torpor, and died at five in the afternoon of 16 February, the third son of the Arnolds to die in childhood.

Arnold wrote to Tom in a state of dizzy unbelief at this latest tragedy: 'Blank astonishment at his being gone fills me and I could sit staring for hours if I had not work that must be done.'[63] Huxley wrote, from Thebes in Egypt, where he was staying for his health, a fine and sensitive letter of condolence. 'If such trouble befell me there are very few people in the world from whom I could bear even sympathy but you would be one of them',[64] he told Arnold – who had himself, a few weeks before the loss of Budge, written to Huxley's wife of her husband that 'there are few indeed among those with whom I have become acquainted in the later and colder years of life for whom I feel, and have felt from almost the first meeting with him, such affectionate liking and regard'.[65] Harriet Martineau also wrote to Fan at Fox How to say how the news grieved her 'unspeakably'.[66] The day before the funeral at Laleham, Arnold wrote to Browning: 'These poor children whom we call only children after the flesh – how much nearer and dearer they are to us than any others.'[67]

Both Arnold and Flu were deeply affected by the death of Budge and it may have been instrumental in their decision, taken after a summer holiday in Switzerland in August, to give up the lease on Byron House and move to Surrey in the early part of 1873. Arnold also decided to give up his planned book on Greek poetry and returned the advance of £150 to Macmillan, saying that he would put it off until his old age. Just before this all happened, Arnold had been tidying up the administration of his inspection district and reconciling himself to the fact that there was to be no promotion: 'I have now no desire for any change in the way of official preferment', he concluded, 'but am content to go on in this work which I know, and to be free, beyond it, for other work which I know also – instead of now changing my habits and my line of work altogether.'[68]

On the wider intellectual stage, however, he welcomed change and found 'the unsettled mind of the country' offered opportunities for it and was 'what makes the present time so interesting'. But he was worried that the Liberal secularists in Parliament were going too far in adopting a limiting Benthamite view of the business of the State with religion: 'the view is a shallow and unsound one, because it tends to look upon religion as powerful through men's delusions or ignorance, and not knowing the reality there is in it, does not know its real power'. Arnold was to make a similar point in *God and the Bible* and was anxious, as a critic of religious 'delusions' himself, not to be seen to be sharing the secularists' dismissal of religion. In fact he produced this year a book called *A Bible-Reading for Schools*, testimony to his powerful belief in the utility of the Bible.

As the year ended, a couple of days before his fiftieth birthday, Arnold met Henry Coleridge, whom he had not seen for years. Coleridge held on tightly to Arnold's hand as if he would never let it go, then at last declared: 'Matt!! – I expected to see a white-headed old man.'[69] Arnold replied gently that his white hairs were all internal. Arnold's fine head of black hair – which contributed to the impression even in his sixties that he was younger than his years – was often remarked upon. One day, his niece's husband, Thomas Humphry Ward, was walking down Bond Street when he was surprised to encounter Arnold standing in the street outside a hairdresser's shop. He asked Arnold what he was doing and the latter replied that he was waiting to see the hairdresser who looked after what he called, running his hand across his hair, 'this perpetual miracle'.[70]

6

At the beginning of February 1873 Arnold's most controversial book, *Literature and Dogma*, appeared. For his contemporaries, religious works were the most popular form of book, with a collection of sermons easily outselling fiction or any other kind of purely literary work. A work from a writer with a high reputation who was also the son of Dr Arnold, and no stranger to religious controversy, was assured of good sales. These eventually reached over 100,000, making it the best-selling work of this 'unpopular author'. The first two chapters had already appeared in the *Cornhill* in July and October 1871 but, after Arnold's critic Leslie Stephen took over as editor from George Smith in March 1871 with a marked distaste for such subjects, no further instalments appeared. Although Smith was eventually to publish the book, he had lost one of his most distinguished contributors. In future Arnold would publish his articles (the preliminary building blocks of all his books) for the *Contemporary Review* edited by James Knowles or, after March 1877, *The Nineteenth Century*, Knowles's new venture.

One of *Literature and Dogma*'s first readers was Alexander Macmillan who told Arnold that he had read every word with 'delight', adding: 'Of course it will make a row, but I think it will do good.'[71] Arnold wrote back that the book was 'sure to be much attacked and blamed'[72] – a fairly obvious prediction – and that 'the so-called orthodox position cannot, I think, ever again be precisely the same in England after the publication of this book'.

The argument of *Literature and Dogma* in essence was that Christianity could only survive if it jettisoned certain false dogmas – hostages to fortune that, if they were not got rid of would start to furnish people with excuses for abandoning Christianity altogether. Arnold knew that the middle classes were still punching their Bibles but the class beneath them, the increasingly confident attenders of the Working Men's Colleges that were springing up, was unlikely to remain satisfied with what Arnold referred to as 'the so-called orthodox theology'. Gazing into the future, as always, Arnold saw what was coming and sought to head it off, not by digging in, but by acknowledging what he called the *Zeit-Geist* – an irresistible force that it never seems to have occurred to him to think of resisting.

'Many of the most successful, energetic, and ingenious of the artisan class, who are steady and rise, are now found either of themselves rejecting the Bible altogether, or following teachers who tell them that the Bible is an exploded superstition',[73] he wrote in the Preface. He certainly did not believe that the Bible was 'an exploded superstition' and he wanted to save it, though conservative critics, then and now, have doubted Arnold's intentions. They were not convinced by such bold declarations as: 'For us, religion is the solidest of realities, and

Christianity the greatest and happiest stroke ever yet made for human perfection', preferring to concentrate on his dissent from theological orthodoxy.

Arnold made his position clearer still in *God and the Bible*, a review of objections to *Literature and Dogma* which was published over a year later: 'At the present moment two things about the Christian religion must surely be clear to anybody with eyes in his head. One is, that men cannot do without it; the other, that they cannot do with it as it is.'[74] One of the principal means he proposed was to get rid of Christianity's reliance on miracles and to base religion on a more intellectually secure foundation. 'For whatever is to stand must rest upon something which is verifiable, not unverifiable.' He wanted to 'give to the Bible a real experimental basis' and cut out both miracles and the notion of a personal God, described 'as if he were a man in the next street' or 'a magnified and non-natural man'.

Arnold had already, in *St Paul and Protestantism*, attempted a definition of God as 'that stream of tendency by which all things seek to fulfil the law of their being' and in the new book this was simplified to 'the Eternal, not ourselves, that makes for righteousness'. What these definitions have in common is a rejection of the notion of a personal God – the bearded patriarch – and an emphasis instead on 'righteousness'. His critics would argue that without a personal God the simple ordinary believer would be lost, unable to relate instead to an abstraction. For Arnold, religion was all about morality, it was 'morality touched by emotion', and as he famously asserted: 'conduct is three-fourths of life' (a figure subject to inflation for it was later to become four-fifths of life). By rejecting miracles – which he did not hesitate to describe, with scant regard for the susceptibilities of his audience, as 'fairy tales' – and similar supernatural delusions (he chose to use the German word *Aberglaube*) religion could concentrate on its real business of imparting 'the secret and the method of Jesus' which was about how to live, how to follow Christ, and how to love his temper, or *epieikeia*, his 'sweet reasonableness'. The 'secret' was defined as: 'He that will save his life shall lose it, he that will lose his life shall save it.'

In order to reach this point, however, what Arnold called in *God and the Bible* 'the dismal science' of theology, or 'that grotesque mixture . . . of learned pseudo science with popular legend', had to be confronted. Rejecting metaphysics, and boasting of his incapacity for abstract thought, Arnold claimed that the simple, self-evident truth that happiness flowed from right conduct was all we needed to know. Theology had interpreted the Bible too literally, forgetting that its language was poetic not scientific, that it had been 'thrown out' in an attempt to fix the mystery of God and could not be treated as a set of rigid axioms. The literary critic, he now argued, was the right person to attend to this tentative process of interpretation, because of his training in reading between the lines and listening out for nuance:

> This literary criticism, however, *is* extremely difficult. It calls into play the highest requisites for the study of letters; great and wide acquaintance with the history of the human mind, knowledge of the manner in which men have thought, of their way of using words and of what they mean by them, delicacy of perception and quick tact, and besides all these, a favourable moment and the 'Zeit-Geist'.

Leaving the particular argument aside, for a moment, we can note what a fine definition this is of what literary criticism, in the right hands, can be.

The final – and most difficult to focus – element of Arnold's argument in both these books is the contention that traditional Bible interpeters (and this is what made him ready to challenge the Bible canon itself) with their stolid literalism and respect for the scientific accuracy of the gospel reports of Jesus, were missing something. Being 'immured in the ideas of their time' and obsessed with accumulating evidence of miracles, the gospel writers missed the point – 'so immeasurably was Jesus above them'. Jesus was, as Arnold put it, 'above the heads of his reporters' and anyone who wanted to know him today therefore needed to jettison 'The misapprehending and materialising of his religion, the long and turbid stage of popular Christianity', in order to focus on the real message of Christianity: *he that will save his life shall lose it, he that will lose his life shall save it.*

Arnold was out of the country when the book was published. 'Huxley says I am going abroad to fly from the evil report of it',[75] he had joked to George Smith before setting off for France and Italy with Flu and the children. The immediate reaction was against Arnold's occasional flippancy (although by the standards of his non-religious works this was scarce) towards such eminences as the Bishops of Gloucester and Winchester and to his analogy – quickly dropped from all subsequent editions – of the Trinity as three versions of Lord Shaftesbury with, for example, God the Father as 'a sort of infinitely magnified and improved Lord Shaftesbury, with a race of vile offenders to deal with . . .' The most common reaction – typified by the leading Scottish theologian John Tulloch writing in *Blackwood's* – was that Arnold was an 'amateur'[76] theologian who had strayed off limits. That may be a fair judgement of Arnold's theology but more attention needs to be paid to his biblical scholarship. His familiarity with the Bible, and in its original texts (many of the quotations he uses are his own translations), is prodigious. His diaries throughout this period are so saturated with biblical texts, often in the original New Testament Greek, and with excerpts from works like the *De Imitatione Christi*, that some have seen the published *Notebooks* as nothing less than a devotional work.[77]

Arnold wrote to George Smith from Cannes to ask that any important letters be forwarded to him and suggesting that a note be put in the *Pall Mall Gazette* explaining that the author of *Literature and Dogma* was abroad – 'it might save a number of letters intended for my conversion being sent to me at Harrow'.[78] Arnold was enjoying himself at Mentone – 'a perfect Paradise' and told Smith: 'I am delighted to escape the first rush of lamentation and expostulation.'[79] Arnold was unimpressed by the reviews, observing: 'The English notices have for the most part been wholly unprofitable, concerning themselves with the mere fringes and externals of the book only.'[80] In spite of the critics, a month after publication the book was already in its third printing. At the end of March, the Arnolds had reached Rome where they were glimpsed lunching at a café by Henry James, who adulated Arnold as a critic, but who could not pluck up the courage to go up to him, waiting another five years for their first formal meeting in London. In Rome Arnold admired the Raphael frescoes in the Farnese Palace and at the Vatican museum chose to view the sculptures rather than the paintings.

He met an American sculptor called William Wetmore Story and his family in Rome which prompted that rarity now, a poem by Arnold which was published in the *Cornhill* in June and titled *New Rome, Lines Written for Miss Story's Album*. It is a harmless piece of light verse sparked off by an article in *The Times* criticising the dirt and inconvenience of Rome. Arnold wrote to his brother Walter admitting that 'verses I do not often bestow on the public now'.[81] The trip, which had proved expensive, but which was perhaps something the Arnolds felt they needed to treat themselves with after their recent unhappiness, ended in May. Arnold wrote to Tom on arrival at Dover on 19 May to say how much he had enjoyed Florence, a city which he conceded was even more beautiful than Oxford. His interest in visual art had also started to develop on this trip: 'never have I been so struck with the unapproached richness of Florence as regards pictures.' He was also struck by the extent to which Roman Catholicism in Italy 'is the church of the people' and 'a great power . . . but a blind one and a power that thickens the confusion of modern times instead of dispelling it'.[82] To George Smith, Arnold wrote: 'We have had a pleasant and long to be remembered tour' but it was probably the last, for: 'The Continent has become too expensive for little people.'[83]

7

In June 1873, on their return from the Continent, the Arnolds moved to Pains Hill Cottage, Cobham in Surrey which they rented from a Mr Leaf, who lived in a more spacious property with grounds next door, for £30 a quarter. Arnold was to live here for the rest of his life. 'Nowhere was Arnold so delighted and delightful as in his Surrey cottage, joyous in the play of warm home affection; in watching the cedars, flowers, blossoms, lawns of his skilfully tended garden; in the faithful salutation of favourite bird or dog . . .'[84] recalled John Morley rather cloyingly. The truth, however, was that in the first years at Cobham Arnold was as hard pressed as ever with work. Writing to Charles Appleton, editor of *The Academy*, a few months after moving in, he explained his refusal to contribute a piece to the magazine by saying: 'I am an *inspector of schools*, and a very slow worker into the bargain . . . Much I would willingly do I cannot even attempt and am obliged to husband my time and forces for the few things which are, or seem, the most necessary . . . I have to start every morning at 8 by omnibus to visit a school and do not get home till 7 at night. A little time for reading I may pick up on the way, but where am I to get the collectedness necessary for writing?'[85]

But even if Pains Hill Cottage was tiny compared with Byron House the move had been necessary. 'We had so much trouble and sorrow at Harrow that I was glad to leave it',[86] he told Lady de Rothschild. The cottage was 'charming' and when George Smith had to cancel lunch there at the last minute Arnold said his publisher had missed the sight of 'your literary friend in the character of the jolly farmer, going about amongst his hay'.[87] And he had his dogs, Kaiser, or Max in later years, to whom, as Mrs Humphry Ward conceded, he was 'too fondly devoted'[88] and whose attentions often distracted him from his guests.

The cottage had the benefit of mature trees and was definitely not 'the raw new sort of villa one has generally to take if one wants a small house near London'.[89] The 'great rambling village' itself, Arnold soon noted, had, in spite of the profusion of rich people in the neighbourhood, no working man's club or institute with the result that 'the public houses swarm'[90] but he was too busy to set about the improvement of the morals of the farm labourers.

Arnold's capacity for joy was never crushed by the relentless pressure of work and one lovely November morning, in the year he moved to Pains Hill Cottage, he described to Tom the sun rising opposite his window, filling the scene with light, and through the trees appearing the blue line of the Surrey hills: 'How beautiful things are and in spite of clouds within and without, may we go on feeling this to the end and die when we can no longer feel it!'[91] he exclaimed. He went on: 'It is my habit to walk to Weybridge station of a morning, three miles across St George's Hill; I assure you it is a kind of intoxication of delight, such fern such pines, such colours, such smells; and there is not a soul to be seen, except a woodcutter perhaps, and the squirrels and I have it all to ourselves.'

Arnold's pastoral rhapsody, however, was punctuated by the thought that he had to make a speech to the inaugural meeting of the Association of Public Elementary Teachers in Westminster at the weekend – 'the terrible "saying a few words" is inevitable'. He chose the occasion to hit back at a recent series of articles by his friend John Morley, editor of the *Fortnightly*, which had argued for the removal of religious instruction from State schools. After vigorously defending elementary schools against recent media sniping, and paying generous tribute to the teachers, Arnold argued that 'the facts and history of religion'[92] should be taught by teachers and that ministers should keep out of the schools and confine themselves to preaching. He also took a swipe at the system of payment by results, arguing that teachers should be allowed to get on and teach without being hampered by 'educational clap-trap, or political clap-trap, or politico-religious claptrap, the worst of all'. He told the teachers that 'a child's mind is a soil with its own powers . . . into which we have to put the right thing'.

On 30 September 1873, Arnold's mother died at Fox How, aged eighty-two. 'She had a clearness and fairness of mind, an interest in things, and a power of appreciating what might not be in her own line, which were very remarkable and which remained with her to the very end of her life',[93] he wrote to Lady de Rothschild. 'To many who knew my father her death will be the end of a period', he added. To

Fan, he promised: 'I shall try and keep up with you, too, my old habit of a weekly letter to her.'[94] He advised Fan to seek some consolation for her grief by reading regularly at some point in the day, a 'secret' that far too few people realised: 'Desultory reading is a mere anodyne; regular reading, well-chosen, is restoring and edifying.'[95] Emotionally articulate as the Arnolds could frequently be, death seems to have made them stoical and reserved. Arnold did not really reveal what he truly felt about his mother's death. He hinted at their disagreements (which were real, for Mrs Arnold could not understand her son's playful spirit in writing and skirmishing with his enemies) by praising her capacity to come to terms with ideas that she did not herself share. He also hinted that her respect for her husband's name was not merely dutiful and that she had a mind of her own when he quoted to Fan a letter from Stanley which said that Mrs Arnold 'retained the life-long reverence for your father's greatness, without a blind attempt to rest in the form and letter of his words'.[96]

8

The final collapse of Gladstone's Liberal administration after the general election of February 1874 – when Mr Bottles and his commuting friends in the Home Counties appeared to desert the Liberal Party in favour of the Conservatives[97] – did not seem to discountenance the 'Liberal tempered by experience, reflection and renouncement'. Arnold told K: 'I do not affect to be sorry at the change; the Liberal Party had no body of just, clear well ordered thought upon politics . . . now they will have to examine their minds and find what they really want and mean to try for.'[98] He elaborated to Lady de Rothschild on the departure of Gladstone and the arrival of her frequent dinner-party guest Disraeli as Prime Minister: 'You know that Liberalism did not seem to me quite the beautiful and admirable thing it does to the Liberal Party in general, and I am not sorry that a new stage in its growth should commence and that the party should be driven to examine itself, and see how much real stuff it has in its mind and how much claptrap.'[99] Arnold was clearly hoping that the Party modernisers would start to try to distance themselves from the influence of the Dissenters.

In March Arnold brought out a new book which consisted of the reprinted German chapters of his 1868 *Schools and Universities on the Continent*. He wanted to try and influence the debate that was currently taking place about Irish university education – in Prussia the government had already endowed Catholic universities within the State system – and the new book, *Higher Schools and Universities in Germany*, came with a freshly written Preface setting out his views about the proper relationship between Church and State. It also marked the beginning of Arnold's direct engagement with the Irish Question and showed him of the belief that 'Ireland has a right to a Catholic university, and that it is really expedient she should have one'.[100] Unfortunately the book did not sell well and seems to have had a very limited impact but Arnold was almost too busy to notice. 'My work just now is incessant',[101] he complained to Lady de Rothschild, and to the editor of the *Contemporary Review*, James Knowles, he voiced a similar lament: 'My schools keep me so busy day after day that I cannot get the collectedness necessary for giving literary form to what I have to say; all I can do is to keep on reading and thinking about my subject and, I hope, ripening myself to treat it easily and satisfactorily when I do treat it . . . Pity a poor jaded official instead of blaming him.'[102]

He was trying to supply Knowles with a new Preface to the latest reprint of *Literature and Dogma*. Further articles, that would eventually form *God and the Bible*, were promised later. 'I am beginning to think of retiring, even on such a beggar's allowance as is our retiring pension', he told Tom. 'But I shall probably be obliged to go on till I drop.'[103] Another possibility was to accept a rumoured Oxford Professorship of English Literature – 'But to say the truth I do not want a Professorship, or any lecturing and class work; I have had enough of them.' Arnold wanted only to write.

His pure dedication to writing, however, did not mean he was unaware of the practical effect he was having. 'But no-one knows better than I do how little of a popular author I am', he told Fan. 'But the thing is, I gradually produce a real effect, and the public acquires a kind of obscure interest in me as this gets to be perceived.'[104] When the first part of his review of the objections to *Literature and Dogma* appeared in the *Contemporary*, there was strong reaction, but Arnold protested to the editor that in truth: 'I really *hate* polemics.'[105] Leslie Stephen, now coming around to an appreciation of Arnold wrote to Charles Eliot Norton about the piece: 'It is Mat in excelsis – the very cheekiest production I have yet seen of his. Really I am fond of him. I fear he does not return the compliment.'[106] Arnold was aware of the risk he was taking by opposing miracles and comparing them to a belief in 'witches and hobgoblins'[107] but he told all his correspondents at this time that he was doing so with the sole aim of strengthening Christianity by putting it on a more verifiable basis: 'but I *must* try to do what I can to prevent a catastrophe which seems to me imminent,' he told Tom, adding, however, that: 'I would far sooner that the question should not have ripened in our time.' He added that the latest piece in the *Contemporary* 'ends the negative part of my work'.[108]

Arnold was cheered in the autumn by Dick's entry into Balliol. He had no high expectations of intellectual performance from any of his children and observed wryly to Lady de Rothschild: 'we hear a great deal about football, the river, and breakfast parties, and hardly a word about reading'.[109] He seems to have forgotten his own exploits with the Harriers at Oxford in the 1840s. His old friend Benjamin Jowett, the Master of Balliol, had welcomed Dick for his father's sake, and had taken the opportunity to say that many people at Oxford felt that *Literature and Dogma* should not have 'mixed up the ludicrous & the personal with the serious . . . but also I feel that no-one can prescribe for another how he ought to write, & I was very much amused at the ludicrous passages!'[110] Fan was clearly more offended by his tone. Arnold was obliged to write pointing out that: 'I write in the manner which is natural to me . . . But ponderous works produce no effect; the religious world which complains of me would not read me if I treated my subject as they say it ought to be treated'.[111]

With George Smith there were no constraints. When Arnold stayed up in London with him at 'No. 15' Waterloo Place they dined and played billiards together and swapped facetious jokes. Hearing that Smith was going to Liverpool with his daughter, Arnold wrote: 'Is Dolly going to be married to the mayor of that seaport? the only Mayor of Liverpool I ever knew was short and fat and not at all suitable.'[112] From Liverpool, too, came a letter from his brother-in-law and informal investment adviser, John Cropper, who lived with his sister Susy in a large house on the banks of the Mersey at the Dingle, to say that his father had died. Arnold's letter of condolence is oddly prophetic, even down to the city with which it is associated: 'to depart without a long and distressing failure of strength, spirits and faculties, is really the best one can wish for any man, and I am sure I should wish it for myself and for all whom I love'.[113]

9

'I think people get bored by one man and one subject going on too long',[114] Arnold had written at the end of 1874, after the appearance of the last part of what would be *God and the Bible*, published in March 1875 (although he felt the book contained 'some of the best prose I have written'). In fact he had one more religious book to come: *Last Essays on Church and Religion* (1877), gathering up his essays and addresses of 1876. The year began, however, with its usual prosaic load of grammar papers for marking. There was also news of the death of Charles Kingsley whom Arnold admired as a man, perhaps more than as a writer, telling his daughter that Kingsley was 'the most generous man I have ever known'.[115] As with Clough, however, Arnold never let his critical faculty be displaced by the demands of obsequy. In a franker letter to Max-Müller he said that Kingsley's poetry and prose both 'want something – want a *cachet* . . . without which no work done in letters seems to me quite serious'.[116]

The Arnolds decided to give themselves a break from Cobham in the winter and rented a tiny house at 3 Eccleston Square for the first three months of 1875. From there Arnold wrote to Alexander Macmillan – a far more thoughtful and appreciative reader of his work than the businessman George Smith – on the subject of money, always a delicate matter between author and publisher. Arnold was always conscious of financial constraints. He had children to educate and hefty annual life insurance premiums to pay and had begun to seek to tidy up his financial affairs. His relations with his publishers were confusing, for sometimes he published at what he called 'my own expense', taking royalties but also the risk of losing on an edition. At other times he sold an edition outright for cash, dispensing with royalties. In March 1875 he wrote to Macmillan querying his accounts and revealing that some of his literary friends, who knew Macmillan but whom he did not identify (Browning or Huxley might have been amongst their number) had told him over dinner that they thought he ought to be 'extremely dissatisfied'[117] with what he had received from Macmillan for his essays. Professing not to have taken much interest hitherto in the profit from his works, Arnold now told Macmillan: 'I am growing old and must attend a little more to my literary profits than I have hitherto done'. He thus proposed bundling his essays and 'belles lettres' together and taking them off to Smith & Elder. 'I do this without the least feeling of unfriendliness to you, or any complaint, but as the best way of changing a bad and careless system which I have too long followed.'

Macmillan replied three days later accepting that the accounts were a little awry but offering a little hard business wisdom about the poor profit from *Essays in Criticism*. 'But at the time they were published, my dear Arnold, your reputation was not so high as it has become since – or at least not so wide.'[118] He further pointed out that one of the reasons he had made more profit with Smith & Elder on *Culture and Anarchy* and *Literature and Dogma* was that George Smith had put a higher price on the books. As an inducement to keep his more purely literary works with Macmillan, the latter offered to publish a new edition of *Essays in Criticism* at a higher price (with another essay, *A Persian Passion Play*, bulking out the volume) and to pay Arnold £130 on publication. For this and various other projects Arnold found that £260 in total had been paid into his bank, Twining's in the Strand, at the end of the year. But no sooner had he settled with Macmillan than he was in dispute with George Smith to whom he had proposed scrapping royalties in favour of Smith buying the new editions outright and paying off his estimated profit share or royalty for the outstanding editions.

Arnold made the odious comparison with Macmillan who had now paid him £175 for 2,000 copies of *Essays in Criticism* which was £5 more than Smith was pretending to be the estimated profit (for himself and Arnold) for *God and the Bible* which, as a religious book, would sell far more copies. Conceding that Macmillan was probably making 'an unusually liberal offer'[119] to keep Arnold sweet, the hard-nosed critic let off a little more steam and then said he would accept an offer of £250 from Smith. He explained that what he wanted was to be able to estimate with 'some element of *certainty*' the future income from his books. 'This, I say, would be a comfort to my old age, and I do hope somehow and some day to arrive at it.' A few days later the two met and seemed to have smoothed things over. But in reality Smith was still sore about Arnold's aggressive letter and, after a further meeting in January 1876, at which Smith revealed that his first instinct had been to send Arnold packing, the latter wrote a very long, careful and patient letter explaining himself. 'I hated writing that letter to you',[120] Arnold confessed, apologising for comparing Smith unfavourably to Macmillan. 'Of course it makes a difference to me, particularly as I get older and feel the grind of school-inspecting more oppressive, what my books bring me,' he wrote, adding a wish that the 'sincere friendship I have for you' was not imperilled. 'My one desire is that my intercourse with you should continue to be just what it has always hitherto been – perfectly easy, cordial, and pleasant.'

But Arnold still intended to transfer his books to another publisher. Smith, realising that Arnold was both a good friend at the billiard table and a literary asset too valuable to let go to a rival, wrote back to make peace. The two men resolved, in Arnold's words, 'to hold a feast of Concord at our joint expense at the new place in Soho' and he promised not to return to the topic for ten years 'if the faulty valve of my heart continues to open and shut then' – the only recorded reference to his heart problem we have.

In May 1875 Arnold was invited to attend the inauguration of the first Chair of Celtic Studies at Edinburgh University – his responsibility for encouraging the academic study of Celtic literature and, more widely, his role as a begetter of the Celtic Revival, were increasingly acknowledged. Characteristically, he wrote back to Professor Stuart Blackie to say that he was too much of a dilettante to be an adornment to the occasion but asked: 'Have you a soul above guineas, or will you accept the guinea of a poor struggling English literary hack towards your new foundation?'[121]

Meanwhile, Dick was giving his father more anxiety. Reports from Oxford were not good and there was some doubt as to whether he would pass his Moderations. He seems to have inherited his father's undergraduate laziness without any of his latent intellectual gifts. A tutor at St Leonard's was prescribed for the summer, for Arnold knew from experience that a reading party 'would have many perils of idleness for him'.[122]

At about this time, Arnold discovered a talented working-class poet, living in Deptford, called Charles P. O'Conor, and wrote an unsigned review of his *Songs of a Life* in the *Pall Mall Gazette* for 25 June. O'Conor was Arnold's Leonard Bast – the talented young man from the working classes whom it was the duty of a progressive man to advance. His poetry reminded him of Burns and Arnold believed he had 'a real dash of genius'.[123] He tried to get him a job as a school board visitor and asked his friends to subscribe to the volume of poems O'Conor had published at his own expense. The review is a little condescending ('Mr O'Conor's poetry has many deficiencies'[124]) and draws attention to his poor grammar and spelling but concludes that the poems have 'gaiety, tune, pathos'. The review was an opportunity for Arnold to assert that: 'The right function of poetry is to animate, to console, to rejoice – in one word, to *strengthen*.' It is also the occasion for a paean to the Irish (leaving aside their nationalist 'Hibernian animosities'): 'What treasures of passion and tenderness are in this people; what natural music, what lyrical force, what gaiety!' Several years later, Arnold was to try to get a pension for the poet when he fell on bad times.

Advancing his own work, Arnold was revising both his essays and *Culture and Anarchy* for new editions and, as he did so, striking out some of the more personal attacks in them – 'as I draw near to my bitter end, the desire increases in me to die at peace with all men',[125] he told Alexander Macmillan. He was also pleased to receive a letter from Huxley acknowledging his point in the recently published *God and the Bible* about the 'charm and salutariness' of Jesus Christ (he told Fan that Huxley's apparent 'adhesion'[126] to religion was 'remarkable'). 'They are unquestionable, and it is kicking against the pricks to deny them . . . It is like denying that Lincoln Minster is grand, or wanting to pull it down, because the Bishop of Lincoln is an aggravating old woman.'[127] Arnold was also pleased that Huxley had detected the influence of Spinoza in the book: 'To him I owe more than I can say.'

10

'My life is very hellish (Goethe) as I have two lectures on Butler to give at Edinburgh in January and no leisure to get them ready',[128] Arnold had told Huxley at the end of 1875. The lectures were delivered, however, at the Edinburgh Philosophical Institution on 4 and 7 January 1876 and together formed the first essay in *Last Essays on Church and Religion* (1877) which was to be his farewell to explicitly religious writing. The day before the first lecture was delivered, Newman wrote from the Oratory at Birmingham thanking Arnold for sending him *Higher Schools and Universities in Germany* and his edition of Isaiah for schools. Newman was pleased with Arnold's advocacy of State support for a Catholic University in Ireland, although he took issue with much of the detail of Arnold's proposals, and ended a little mischievously: 'It is one of my prayers that you & your brother may become good Catholics.'[129]

The Edinburgh lectures went off well. 'The Scotch made an

admirable audience',[130] he told Mark Pattison, 'though the Free Church organ says that "a thrill of awe" ran through the assembly when I said, in the second lecture, that the Bible contained "plenty of truth and plenty of legend".' Arnold took a rather qualified view of his subject, the eighteenth-century theologian Bishop Joseph Butler, detecting about him a whiff of 'the somewhat arid air of the eighteenth century',[131] an epoch with which Arnold was notoriously out of sympathy. Butler's most famous theological work, the *Analogy of Religion* (1736) Arnold found 'a failure' because his reasoning was defective in Arnold's view as 'natural history', that is to say, it didn't fit with the facts of human nature, which he always believed was the basic test of convincing religious argument. 'It seemed once to have a spell and a power; but the *Zeit-Geist* breathes upon it, and we rub our eyes, and it has the spell and power no longer', he wrote. When the first part of *Bishop Butler and the Zeit-Geist* appeared in the *Contemporary*, Gladstone was so pleased with it he invited Arnold to have breakfast with him – an appointment the busy school inspector couldn't make. Carlyle also liked it, as did George Eliot, whose view that 'of all modern poetry mine is that which keeps constantly growing upon her',[132] Arnold reported to Fan when it was passed on to him. He added that it was 'a great and solid satisfaction, at fifty, to find one's work, the fruit of so many years of isolated reflection and labour, getting recognition amongst those whose judgement passes for the most valuable'.

On 22 February Arnold had to deliver another lecture, to the London clergy at Sion College, whose President, Henry Milman, had been trying to get Arnold to come and speak for some time. His address, which appeared in *Last Essays* as *The Church of England*, dealt boldly and without evasion, as usual, with the paradox that many of the clergy felt: how could a man like Arnold with such a cavalier approach to orthodox theology be such a passionate defender of the Established Church? 'Professed ardent enemies of the Church have assured me that I am really, in their opinion, one of the worst enemies that the Church has, – a much worse enemy than themselves',[133] he told his audience. Arnold was keen to dissociate himself firmly from the agnostic or anticlerical camp and branded the view of those false friends as 'totally erroneous' and based on 'an entire misconception' of what he had written.

He then offered his famous definition of the Church of England: 'I regard the Church of England as, in fact, a great national society for the promotion of what is commonly called *goodness*, and for promoting it through the most effectual means possible, the only means which are really and truly effectual for the object: through the means of the Christian religion and of the Bible.' But with his customary sweet indifference to the likely sensibilities of his listeners, Arnold went on to attack the class-based nature of the Church of England with the blunt assertion: 'the superstitious worship of existing social facts, a devoted obsequiousness to the landed and propertied and satisfied classes, does not inhere in the Christian religion'. He urged the clergy to make themselves more attractive to popular and progressive radicalism – if for no other reason than to hang on to their working-class congregations. In this way the rift with the Dissenters also might be closed.

Arnold said that he defended an Established Church because the Church of England was 'a *reasonable* Establishment' which went with the grain of the English people. The lecture contains some praise of the innate 'decency and integrity' of the English that suggests, not for the first time, a faint affinity between Arnold and George Orwell. He believed that 'the essence of religion is grace and peace' and that a new generation of Dissenters, growing up without 'the spirit of scruple, objection-taking and division' might come to rest under its shade, provided they were made welcome by the Establishment. 'And I, for my part, now leave this question', Arnold concluded, 'I hope for ever. I became engaged in it against my will, from being led by particular circumstances to remark the deteriorating effect of the temper and strifes of Dissent upon good men . . . However, as one grows old, one feels that it is not one's business to go on for ever expostulating with other people on their waste of life but to make progress in grace and peace oneself.'

In fact Arnold had one last outing for his battered standard, in July's *Macmillan's Magazine* when he took up the apparently arcane topic of the Denbighshire MP George Osborne Morgan's Burials Bill. This was intended to give certain rights to Dissenters over the way their burial services in parish churchyards were conducted that would avoid their being thrown to the mercies (sometimes exercised capriciously) of the Establishment clergy. Gladstone stopped Arnold in the street after it was published to congratulate him and try, once again unsuccessfully, for a meeting. 'You are the most inaccessible man I know',[134] exclaimed the former Prime Minister exasperatedly.

Arnold's argument, in the essay, was the rather condescending one that the traditional Anglican burial service was a thing of beauty that it was good for the Dissenters to be forced to submit to – particularly in view of the tendency of the Englishman to fall 'with great ease into vulgarity'. Those who always detected a streak of snobbery in Arnold's attack on Nonconformist culture felt to some degree vindicated by this stance (although he readily conceded that the clergy had been 'arbitrary, insolent, and vexatious' in this matter). It was Arnold's last blast against Dissent – of which he alleged there were now 138 varieties, naming some of them: 'Ranters, Recreative Religionists and Peculiar People'. Arnold's abandonment of his battle with the Peculiar People had come not a moment too soon. It was in danger of becoming at best a form of oppressive condescension, at worst petty. He perhaps never gave enough consideration to the reasons why the Nonconformists might have felt provoked or marginalised and his apparently reasonable advocacy of open, tolerant, civilised national cultural and religious institutions, glided over the means – that could be authoritarian or coercive – by which a national culture is maintained. Yet at the same time, by insisting on the fact that asserting one's difference is not the end of any matter, he can still give food for thought to today's debates about cultural separatism and the politics of personal autonomy.

The death of Arnold's youthful hero, George Sand, on 8 June, was deeply affecting as well as being a reminder of his own mortality. 'Her death has been much in my mind',[135] he told Fan, 'she was the greatest spirit in our European world from the time that Goethe departed. With all her faults and Frenchism, she was this.' But Arnold had more immediate worries. He had just written to Alexander Macmillan to see if £500 could be raised 'for a special purpose' on the strength of the future editions of his poems, given that the sales of his books were 'likely to increase rather than to diminish'.[136] Macmillan talked it over with his financial administrator George Lillie Craik and wrote back to say that £250 on the poems was all he could offer. Arnold accepted this, hinting darkly that he would explain when he saw him what he wanted it for. Arnold's embarrassment was due to the fact that Dick, in addition to being a poor scholar at Oxford, had gambled and run up some large debts. Always hopelessly indulgent towards his children, Arnold had little choice but to try and raise the money somehow by his own efforts. To make matters worse, Dick had a fall and had to be nursed at home during the summer (although Arnold managed to get away for some fishing at Chenies and in the Lakes later in the summer where he was delighted to find his *bête noire* Ruskin was on holiday and being referred to by the locals as Hoskins!).

The Arnolds left Cobham in the early part of 1877, as they often did, to rent a house (once again at 3 Eccleston Square) for the colder winter months until Easter. It was there that a letter was forwarded from Cobham, from Henry Nettleship, later Professor of Latin at Oxford, sounding him out about standing again as Oxford Professor of Poetry. Arnold declined to put himself forward, partly to give a chance to new faces but partly because of his instinct about how the Oxford establishment might these days regard him: 'I feel certain that if I stood, the religious question would be raised, and to have this question raised in an election to a Chair of Poetry would be, in my opinion, a bad thing for the University; to me myself it would be intolerable.'[137] Arnold could easily have pleaded his usual excuse of being too busy. He was preoccupied with the Preface to *Last Essays* which would be published in March, he had his inspector's general report for 1876 to finish, an article for the *Contemporary*, and a mass of correspondence.

In addition, he was discussing with Macmillan a selection of Wordsworth's poems. 'I suppose you would want a notion of Wordsworth to begin the volume',[138] he remarked casually of what was to turn out to be one of his finest critical essays on a single author. Macmillan suggested wittily that the target audience of the edition could be thought of as '*Bottles touched with emotion*'[139] – an allusion to the representative commuting Philistine of *Friendship's Garland* which his rival George Smith had published. Arnold added to Macmillan that he was pleased with the new order of his own poems in the latest edition: 'They seem much more *natural* and not so mournful.'[140]

The Preface to *Last Essays on Church and Religion* when the book appeared in March, was partly apologetic for the 'offence'[141] his writings may have caused, and partly valedictory. Arnold promised to return now to more purely literary writing, arguing none the less that 'the transformation of religion, which is essential for its perpetuance, can be accomplished only by carrying the qualities of flexibility, perceptiveness and judgement, which are the best fruits of letters, to whole classes of the community which now know next to nothing of them'. He argued that unless 'the obsolete religion of tradition' was superseded, Christianity would be eroded by the sort of liberal agnosticism which was leading progressive minds on the Continent to reject the Bible. It was more than ever vital to insist therefore on 'what I call the *natural truth*' of Christianity. Arnold bade farewell to his career as a religious controversialist with an assertion that ought to have been clear enough to convince even Lord Derby: 'Jesus Christ and his precepts are found to hit the moral experience of mankind, to hit it in the critical points, to hit it lastingly . . . I believe that Christianity will survive because of its natural truth.'

CHAPTER NINE:
APPROACHING AMERICA
[1877–1884]

On Friday I lecture at Salem, famous for its witches.[1]

1

In March 1877 Arnold went to Oxford to cast his vote for his old friend James Campbell Shairp as Professor of Poetry. Once again he had to dismiss allegations that it had been his original intention to stand but that he had pulled out simply to avoid the humiliation of defeat. He was happy to leave such honours to others – as he was to leave Browning to the Rectorship of St Andrew's later in the year. He had his hands full with commissions to write for the periodicals, including the new *Nineteenth Century*. The essays of this and the following year were collected as *Mixed Essays* in 1879, a volume which marked Arnold's return – welcome some might think – from religious to literary and cultural topics. He looked on the political world with his usual mixture of intense interest and deep disillusionment. The Liberal Party was in a state of confusion but this did not stop him being 'sincerely sorry that a charlatan like Dizzy should be Premier just now'.[2] Everyone was very agitated about 'the Eastern Question' – which amounted to how to respond to the Russo-Turkish War. Arnold had just taken his daughter, Nelly, to meet Carlyle who was 'very easy to get on with and very kind to Nelly' but he judged Carlyle's letter to *The Times* on the Eastern Question to be quite 'mad'.[3]

London literary circles were just now buzzing with a very sharp new satire called *The New Republic*, written by William Hurrell Mallock, the son of a Devonshire vicar, and a high Tory and high churchman. The book – one of the more lively and sparkling minor works of the Victorian period, which remains, like Arnold's *Friendship's Garland*, unaccountably out of print – was published anonymously and Arnold, who always loved being made fun of, eagerly recommended it to his family and friends. 'It seems generally thought that my verses are well parodied',[4] he told Flu, 'but I myself and my conversation are not well hit off. But then the writer did not know me personally, even by sight: and Ruskin, Jowett, Pater etc., he knew.' Subtitled *Culture, Faith and Philosophy in an English Country House*, the book (which it must be said is infinitely more subtle and skilled as satire than *Friendship's Garland*) consists of a series of lightly philosophical conversations in a country house between prominent (though pseudonymous) contemporary intellectuals such as Jowett, Huxley, Ruskin and Arnold – the latter disguised as 'Mr Luke'.

It is interesting in that it reveals in what light unsympathetic critics and the general public saw Arnold. He is represented as fastidious and foppish, with a pompous and rather extravagant air, and with a certain *hauteur* in his dismissals and sweeping judgements. His observations on culture slot neatly into the prepared stereotype: 'We the cultured – we indeed see. But the world at large does not',[5] minces Mr Luke. Mallock – who was clearly very familiar with Arnold's work – has some lethal touches, as when Mr Luke gives vent to some outrageous opinion 'in a voice whose tone seemed to beseech everyone to be sensible'. Mr Storks (Huxley) says that in any age other than the enlightened present he should languish. ' "I languish in this," said Mr Luke, looking up to the ceiling.' In general, it is precisely the fact that Mallock did not know Arnold in the way that he knew many of his other victims that makes his portrait so valuable. It is a rare insight into how Arnold was generally seen, a fixing of his public 'image' in the 1870s.

In October, Arnold wrote to a friend and wealthy Fox How neighbour, Victor Marshall, about the reviews of his new collected poems which were generally favourable: 'but why could they not come earlier, when I was young and full of life to enjoy them'.[6] To his niece's husband, Thomas Humphry Ward, he made the surprising admission, when discussing Ward's son's emigration: 'I should myself have preferred to try my hand even as a farm worker in Canada or New Zealand.'[7] Not long after he married, Arnold had talked with Flu about going to live in Italy, and now wistfully recalled another dream of escape. But in reality he was trapped. 'Alas', he lamented to Browning, 'day by day I inspect my school and depart to the train, only just getting twilight enough to drive home from the station without breaking my neck.'[8] Dick, at any rate, was planning to go to Australia – having done so miserably at Oxford to date that the Council Office would not be likely to take him in spite of his father's name. 'All the great men of business that I know say that he is doing the right thing in going',[9] Arnold told Tom.

Dick's father, meanwhile, was reconciled to his inspections and his intervals of rustic seclusion at Pains Hill Cottage where he was currently preparing another article for the *Quarterly Review* on Goethe. 'I always think of you when I am writing on an interesting subject, and wonder whether you will like what I say',[10] he told Lady de Rothschild. To Fan, he observed truthfully: 'Considering how much I have read of Goethe, I have said in my life very little about him.'[11] Reading what Carlyle had written on Goethe, Arnold reflected on how little of what Carlyle had said would stand. 'That is the thing – to write what will *stand*.'[12]

2

Arnold's *A French Critic on Goethe* duly appeared in the *Quarterly* in January and he was paid £31 10s. for it – his fees varying between £25 and £40 for an article at this time. The French critic in question was Edmund Scherer and the piece was a sequel to Arnold's article a year earlier on the same critic's view of Milton. Scherer was pleased with the article and wrote to Arnold from Versailles to say so – the two men had met, probably through the agency of Sainte-Beuve, during one of Arnold's educational missions in April 1859. Scherer revealed that he had been reading the new edition of Arnold's poems with 'intense and manifold interest' and that they led him back to his essays. 'I have more than once tried to get at the secret unity of your life as a theologian, a critic, and a poet',[13] he said, describing an all too rare ambition among those who have applied themselves to Arnold.

Arnold was now back in Eccleston Square until Easter, as usual, and from there he wrote to Lady de Rothschild: 'I thought of you when I gave my lecture on Equality at the Royal Institution, as I always look forward with pleasure and interest to being read by you.'[14] He added that he was 'astonished at the fervour with which this lecture has been received, even by those who might have considered themselves or their interests attacked by it; but the world is going very liberal'. The lecture was delivered at the Royal Institution in Albemarle Street at nine in the evening on 8 February and published the following month in the *Fortnightly*. Together with *Democracy*, it opened *Mixed Essays*, and marked Arnold's return to the concerns of *Culture and Anarchy*. Even more than the latter, it demonstrates the difference between Matthew Arnold and 'Mr Luke'. It shows how deeply committed Arnold was to the idea that 'No individual life can be truly prosperous, passed, as Obermann says, in the midst of men who suffer.'[15]

Once again he emphasised that culture confined to a narrowly circumscribed élite was worthless. It needed to be diffused throughout the *whole* of society and the 'wall of partition' dividing the classes in English society needed to be torn down. His proposals for creating equality are partly practical (he thought the law of entail needed to be changed to stop the concentration of land ownership and property in too few hands) and partly cultural. The present divisions of English society, he felt, were detrimental to all the classes. For inequality – which politicians like Gladstone actually recommended as a virtue – had 'the natural and necessary effect, under present circumstances, of materialising our upper class, vulgarising our middle class, and brutalising our lower class. And this is to fail in civilisation.'

Civilisation, he argued, was about 'the humanisation of man in society' and class divisions got in the way. Not that he believed in natural rights or in what he called 'socialistic and communistic schemes' because of the latter's 'fatal defect; they are content with too low and material a standard of well-being'. He looked to the more egalitarian and less class-obsessed society of France and turned for intellectual inspiration, not for the first time, to the writings of Burke, who argued that civil society – rather than the immature 'doing as you please' of Victorian laissez-faire – was necessary for progress in civilisation. Arnold ended the lecture, however, with a sanguine admission that the notion of social equality was still too far in advance of public opinion and 'the matter is at present one for the thoughts of those who think' – a clever way of ingratiating himself with his Royal Institution audience.

Arnold was also considering more ordinary methods of advancing the cause of civilisation. He was discussing with Alexander Macmillan a popular edition 'to hit the needs of the young student of English literature'[16] of Johnson's *Lives of the Poets*. It would also have the advantage of enabling him to pay off his £100 debt to Macmillan. This was the first of a number of projects aimed at putting out popular, well-edited selections of recent English literary texts such as Byron and Wordsworth or Burke's writings on Ireland. Arnold never had any doubts about the efficacy of literature and its moral worth. But even if, as an inspector of schools, he advocated in his annual reports the learning of poems by heart, he did so in a way that stressed the freedom of the imagination that reading poetry gave, rather than any severe disciplinary dividend. As he put it in his annual report for 1878: 'Good poetry is formative; it has, too, the precious power of acting by itself and in a way managed by nature, not through the instrumentality of that somewhat terrible character, the scientific educator.'[17]

The London winter ended sadly with the death of Arnold's brother, Edward. Like Willy, who had died in 1859, Edward was free from the weak heart that ought to have given both younger brothers greater longevity than their eldest. 'These losses arc blows which beat us down and age us', Arnold wrote gloomily to Lady de Rothschild, 'however good, in general, our health and spirits may be. I have now lost two brothers . . . both of them naturally called, as it seemed, to enjoy it longer than I should. I have come back [to Cobham] low and depressed.'[18] He hoped that Pains Hill Cottage and the spring flowers would somehow 'bring me round again'. And, of course, there was always fishing. At the beginning of May he got away and wrote to the romantic novelist Rhoda Broughton (whom he had met in London through Fanny du Quaire, sister of his old friend John Blackett MP): 'I have been away in Hampshire, indulging in one of the brutal pastimes of the people I call "Barbarians" – that is to say fishing.'[19] Later he wrote asking her for a copy of her novel *Goodbye Sweetheart* and gave her in return his poems and the selection of Johnson's *Lives*. Rhoda Broughton, who had just moved to Oxford, later became romantically entangled with Mark Pattison, the scholar who is thought to have furnished the model for Edward Casaubon in George Eliot's *Middlemarch*.

In the early summer of 1878 Arnold published a little selection of his poems in Macmillan's 'Golden Treasury' series, a serviceable little volume which was still in print in the 1930s (although it omitted some important poems like *Empedocles*). By the end of the year Macmillan was writing: 'Your little book has been doing wonderfully well of late & we are now in our third thousand, a fact that is edifying and encouraging'.[20]

Another essay appeared in the *Fortnightly* on *Irish Catholicism and British Liberalism* which showed Arnold's deep sympathy with the Irish. In a comment that would still serve today he observed: 'But even to the most self-satisfied Englishman, Ireland must be an occasion, one would think, from time to time of mortifying thoughts.'[21] The essay was sparked off by the refusal of the Government to support the endowment of a Catholic University in Ireland on the grounds that it could not risk upsetting public opinion. The Liberal opposition would not support it either, Arnold argued, because they were in hock to the Nonconformists whose hatred of Catholicism was overweening. Describing himself slyly as 'a humble follower of the true Liberal ideal' Arnold argued that if Liberalism could throw off the shackles of Nonconformist prejudice and return to its proper ideals it would see the transparent justice of the Irish case. Partly, no doubt as a stick to beat the Dissenters with, but partly because he believed it, Arnold praised Catholicism – in the way that he normally praised people and things, with plenty of stings in the tail – as a church 'with a great future before it', in spite of the 'mischiefs' that he was compelled to notice in its current practice. 'The Puritan churches have no beauty', he declared, comparing them unfavourably both to Catholicism and the Church of England Establishment in that respect.

He ended the essay with a bold – and somewhat disingenuous – assertion that, after all, he wished merely to transform the Puritan middle class which was 'with all its faults . . . still the best stuff in this nation'. More frank was his admission to Lord Houghton (Richard Monckton Milnes, the writer and politician) whom he had praised, in passing, for backing the Irish demand: 'That terrible middle class! But I begin to see the writing on the wall for them.'[22]

Arnold was preparing to collect all these essays when he received at the end of August a letter from George Smith disclosing the poor sales of his *Last Essays on Church and Religion*. 'It is a melancholy history you send me; I shall have to turn to ballad-singing and to leave the base mechanical art of prose',[23] he joked. But there may have been a more serious point here. Arnold's poems – in the recent collected edition and the new Golden Treasury *Selected* – were now attracting real interest and selling well. 'It is curious how the public is beginning to take them to its bosom after long years of comparative neglect',[24] he noted to his sister Susy Cropper. But he added wisely that: 'The writers of poetry have been better friends to me always than the mass of readers of poetry.' As to new work, he had still to struggle to find time to write and turned down a commission from Thomas Humphry Ward, as he had turned down a commission from John Morley to do Shakespeare for his 'English Men of Letters' series (which would have been a fascinating book to have had, given Arnold's sometimes controversial views on the Bard). 'Plans in which I could join if I were a man of letters purely and simply', he explained to Ward, 'I cannot join in now that I am a school inspector with a very limited time at my disposal for letters. I am obliged to keep, for work which has suggested itself to my own mind, the little time which I have free.'[25]

Arnold did, however, agree to a proposal from 'a strange American, Dr Wallace' to write a two-page introduction to the section on poets of a book of photographs of the hundred most remarkable men who had ever lived. At £50 a page it was an offer he could not refuse. Another offer came from Dick, who was just about to leave for Australia, and was promising gaily to pay back what he owed him and enable his (highly sceptical) father to retire. Retirement was seriously in Arnold's mind for he wrote to Huxley asking for advice 'to a poor, shiftless man of letters',[26] about the terms Macmillan were currently offering him. 'I hate fighting', he insisted to Huxley, 'and I have long acquiesced in being a little read author . . . But my things are selling much better now, and the comfort of my old age and my being able to retire on my pension at 60 [Arnold was nearly 56] greatly depends upon my getting a fair price for my publications.'

In spite, however, of the pressures on him, Arnold still felt compelled to carry on his fight for a proper educational system. In October the *Fortnightly* carried his *Porro Unum Est Necessarium*, a plea for the establishment of 'public schools for the middle classes' or a universal system of State-supported secondary education like the French. Arnold was always unashamed in his advocacy of the role of the State – as unfashionable in his day as it has become now – and he insisted that a civilised society should make the State 'the organ of its best self and highest reason of the community . . . an opinion not commonly held, I admit, in England.' Arnold had just refreshed his knowledge of French practice by a rather reluctant trip to Paris where Lucy demanded to be taken to see the Universal Exhibition. He was annoyed that the Liberals had no mention of the issue in their manifesto. He believed that 'perhaps our chief and gravest want in this country at present, our *unum necessarium*, is a middle class homogeneous, intelligent, civilised, brought up in good public schools and on the first plane'.[27]

Fighting off another commission from T. H. Ward, Arnold explained that 'one main reason why I am so little available for letters is that these educational questions have laid their hold upon me – in great measure from accident, in the first instance – and I cannot shake it off nor perhaps ought I to wish to'. This is the frankest description we have by Arnold of the clash between his literary career and his role as an advocate of educational reform. But it was to become franker still with the startling statement: 'What is a poem or essay more or less compared with the civilisation of the English middle class?'[28]

3

At the beginning of 1879 Arnold agreed with Macmillan to do a Golden Treasury selection of Wordsworth for £100 with a royalty of 9d a copy after the first 3,500 had been sold. 'I have always wished to arrange these poems in some natural and logical order, and I could hardly have believed how much their impressiveness and greatness would be brought out by their being so arranged',[29] he told Macmillan. He added that it would be 'a lovely book' and that 'it will help Wordsworth's fame'. Macmillan agreed that the book was looking 'attractive and bright'. Arnold told K that Wordsworth 'can show a body of work superior to what any other English poet, except Shakespeare and Milton can show'.[30] The Preface when it was written (after pleas for an extension of time 'as I am inspecting hither and thither over the face of the Earth and Saturdays and Sundays are the only days I can count on'[31]) was printed as an article in *Macmillan's*. The selection itself appeared in August – after many letters between publisher and author, the latter taking an interest in every minute detail of the process. Editing the selection seemed to have rejuvenated Arnold after his political polemics and he wrote eagerly to Macmillan: 'I have many hopes and plans.'[32]

That rare event now, a poem, came from his pen and was published in January's *Nineteenth Century*. The sonnet was inspired by Dick's successful voyage to Melbourne on the SS *Lusitania* and refers to a passage from Dante's *Inferno* whose tenor gave Arnold some anxiety until he received a card from Dick announcing his arrival at the Cape Verde islands. 'If ever anything makes me produce a new volume of poems it will be the inspiration of books of travel in countries which interest me',[33] Arnold told Macmillan after reading a new book from his list on the Atlas Mountains. But in truth his poetic inspiration was now all but dried up. Only *Westminster Abbey* and a few elegies for his pets were left to come.

In January *Mixed Essays* was published with a brief Preface which clearly signalled Arnold's having left explicitly religious subjects behind him. He said that this collection of essays – which contains writing as good as anything in the better-known critical works – had 'a unity of tendency'[34] which was to confirm that literature did not exist in isolation but had a social role. This was to contribute to civilisation, which in turn was defined as nothing less than 'the humanisation of man in society'. He recalled his concept of 'expansion' – the need of human beings to be free to grow and develop, a need which was thwarted by inequality and which therefore forced him as an essayist to dwell with frequent insistence on the manifold 'defects in the present actual life of our nation'. Most of the essays in the collection have already been discussed but it is perhaps worth while to single out one in particular, *Falkland*, an essay on the hero (for some) of the English Civil War, Lucius Cary, Viscount Falkland.

The essay was prompted by plans to build a monument to Falkland at Newbury where he had fallen in battle. But Arnold's reading at the time for a projected but never accomplished book on the Broad Church in the seventeenth century, also made the subject attractive. In the essay he quotes liberally from Clarendon's *History of the Rebellion* (1702–4) which represents Falkland as an ideal embodiment of sweetness and light – an interpretation that suited Arnold for here was another stick to beat the Nonconformists with. The latter had never forgiven Falkland for changing sides in the war of Cavalier versus Roundhead. Falkland, in Arnold's account, is, unlike the Puritans, 'amiable' and 'the sweetest mannered of men'. He was also a tragic figure of great gifts who died early at the age of thirty-four and seemed 'a man in the grasp of fatality' and 'surely and visibly touched by the finger of doom' – as we know Arnold, without voiced complaint, often felt himself to be. Arnold's attacks on English Puritanism were usually on its contemporary manifestations. Here he attacked it historically, finding the same character in the seventeenth-century Puritans 'which makes one shiver: its hideousness, its immense ennui'. Falkland, by contrast, admitted the complexity of things, doubted the value of what he called 'great mutations' and was always for 'compromise and adjustment'. What made him, in Arnold's eyes, 'truly tragic' was his recognition that whichever party he backed he could not be sure that it would prove to have either the truth or the future on its side. This struggle to contest wrong-headed ideas in his time, and his 'lucidity of mind' are 'what make him ours; what link him with the nineteenth century'.

The characterisation of Falkland has led many to see in it a partial self-portrait, with Arnold casting himself as one of those 'gifted outsiders' who lead important movements of thought. He writes of Falkland: 'He was the martyr of lucidity of mind and largeness of temper, in a strife of imperfect intelligences and tempers illiberal.' But Arnold was perhaps more wilful and determined, more confident in his public engagements, than this complex, thwarted figure whose demeanour is more obviously tragic than the demeanour presented by the scourge of Mr Bottles.

Just before *Mixed Essays* appeared, Arnold was invited to address the Ipswich Working Men's College, the largest of its kind in England where he delivered his address, *Ecce, Convertimur Ad Gentes* ('Lo, we turn to the Gentiles', St Paul's words in *Acts* to the Jews who would not listen to the Word of God), on 8 January. His subject was the establishment of 'public schools for the middle classes' with the working men standing in for the Gentiles who would listen to a message the middle classes themselves were not disposed to listen to. He explained to Fan, who liked the address, that he had deliberately refrained from his customary 'irony and playfulness' because these were generally misunderstood 'by people who have not had a literary training'.[35] Six hundred people filled the hall and though there were some subdued 'signs of irritation',[36] probably from the middle-class section of the audience, it was a success. Arnold had to fight off local newspapermen who wanted a copy of the speech because he had promised it exclusively to John Morley for the *Fortnightly*.

Arnold was trying to interest the working class in the notion of establishing a system of public education for the middle classes using the argument that 'the working class suffered most by not having a more civilised middle class to rise into'. He told Susy that 'the working men, the hands in the great factories for agricultural implements' in Ipswich were 'said to be an intelligent sort, and I do not despair of making them follow me'.[37] Arnold believed he was pressing for a great democratic reform but protested to K: 'And they call me a bad Liberal, or no Liberal at all!'[38]

Liberalism, however, did not mean a rejection of imperialism. Arnold welcomed the news from Africa, where British troops had just been repulsed at Isandlana, on the grounds that it would lead to 'a more thorough subjugation of the Zulus, and to a more speedy extension of the Englishry . . . its spread is the spread of future civilisation.'[39] There were good reports from another part of the Empire, too, with news that Dick was doing well in Australia, but his long-suffering father was sanguine: 'It is early days to be throwing up one's hat and huzzahing.'[40]

On 5 April, Arnold went to address an 'agreeable' audience at Eton (the President of the Literary Society having twisted the arm of a pupil, Francis Sorell Arnold, Tom's eighth child, to procure his uncle to speak). 'The Eton boys received me beautifully', he told George Smith, 'and the compliment to the Eton bathing brought down the house'.[41] One wonders, however, how attentive the boys were to a long disquisition on the Greek word *eutrapalia* (flexibility), however dear to the heart of their lecturer the concept was. It was a welcome break for Arnold whose official work was piling up again, as he explained in a letter to his French correspondent M. Fontanès. Arnold valued his French readers, he said, because English writing, owing to England's 'insularity and eccentricity', rarely crossed the Channel: 'In general, we English write for the English-speaking public, and expect no other; this public is now a very large one, and an author may well be satisfied with it; still, the civilised European nations ought to understand one another and to share one another's thoughts . . .'[42]

By now Arnold had succumbed to the pressures of Thomas Humphry Ward and agreed to write an introduction to Ward's proposed anthology of *The English Poets*. This was to become one of Arnold's most famous essays, *The Study of Poetry*. It opened the 1888 collection of *Essays in Criticism* and it constitutes a kind of *summa* of Arnold's beliefs on the nature and purpose of poetry. 'More and more mankind will discover that we have to turn to poetry to interpret life for us, to console us, to sustain us',[43] he wrote. 'Without poetry our science will appear incomplete; and most of what now passes with us for religion and philosophy will be replaced by poetry.' This famous declaration has tended to be received inhospitably by critics but if we take 'poetry' in the large sense that Arnold always implicitly assigned to it – embracing literature and art in general – there is a sense in which it is not bad prophecy. At the end of the twentieth century, it is in the contemplation of art and literature rather than in religion, that the most serious imaginative and intellectual experiences of the secular *literati* occur. Critics who have not, like Eliot (who deplored Arnold's prophecy), explicitly embraced Christian orthodoxy, have tended in this century to approach literature with the earnest intensity once reserved for religion.

Arnold also argued in this essay that 'we must also set our standard for poetry high' for 'the best poetry is what we want'. Poetry was both 'salutary' and 'formative', an influence for good. In trying to find the best we should avoid personal or historical estimates and concentrate solely on intrinsic poetic merit. Arnold's test of poetic value, the use of 'touchstones', has attracted as much adverse comment as the suggestion that poetry will replace religion. Once again, close attention to what he actually says may help to indicate that he was not suggesting that touchstones be applied as if they were some sort of greenhouse thermometer that simply had to be hung up on a nail and its reading noted down. He said that the touchstones – lines of indisputably great poetry – would work '*if we have tact and can use them*' [my italics]. In other words, if the wider contexts from which those moments of intense poetic expression were wrenched were always borne in mind, then the touchstone might yield dividends, bringing the reader into living contact with the imaginative pitch of the original work of which the quoted line was merely a summary or reminder. For a man like Arnold, widely read in the poetry of half a dozen languages, the notion of the touchstone made sense. For a schoolboy or schoolgirl of necessarily limited reading it might well have less force and educationists, perhaps understandably, have rarely shown much enthusiasm for Arnold's idea.

The third controversial contention of this essay is Arnold's assertion that Dryden and Pope were mere 'masters of the art of versification' and not poets. 'Dryden and Pope are not classics of our poetry, they are classics of our prose', he wrote. The judgement, which few would endorse wholly today (although there is a grain of truth in it) shows that Arnold, for all his classicism, was a Romantic at heart, who placed a poetry of feeling above a poetry of decorum.

Dismissing the prevalent argument that an era of mass culture was approaching with its 'multitudes of a common sort of readers, and masses of a common sort of literature' churned out as 'a vast and profitable industry', Arnold believed that serious literature would never lose its supremacy even if it was backed into a corner by the mass media. His cultural optimism was rooted in one thing – reiterated so many times in so many contexts that we could call it his basic philosophy of life – and that was that moral virtue and the desire for the best in art alike derived their motivating power from 'the instinct of self-preservation in humanity'.

The essay would appear as an introduction to Ward's book in May the following year but for now, he told him in September, after returning from a holiday in the Gower peninsula ('so new and remote') where he stayed at Fairy Hill, Swansea, home of Flu's relatives, the Bensons,[44] 'I have no notion of what I shall say, but Providence will, I hope, make my way plain before my face.'[45] Meanwhile, the Wordsworth selection was selling well – over 2,000 copies in little over a month – but compared with the marketing potential of theology it was insignificant. Arnold wrote to Dean Farrar to marvel at the latter's latest work on St Paul (which *The Times* wanted Arnold to write about but over which he was unwilling to break his resolution to abjure theological subjects). 'I cannot help envying you your sale – you have sold *10,000* copies, and that large book! We think ourselves lucky to have got rid of 2,000 of our poor little undersized one.'[46]

4

Early in 1880 Arnold wrote to his friend M. Fontanès about Burke, towards whom Arnold was characteristically ambivalent, and about whom John Morley had just written a book in the English Men of Letters series which Arnold commended. The Liberal in Arnold, the advocate of freedom or 'expansion' (but who received coolly the general election victory of 1880 which returned Gladstone as Prime Minister), disliked Burke's conservatism: 'The old order of things had not the virtue which Burke supposed',[47] he told Fontanès. Arnold felt that he was too much an advocate of authority or 'concentration' and was too harsh on the French Revolution which Arnold, while alive to its negative aspects, believed to have been necessary. As Arnold's interest in Ireland grew, however, during the 1870s and 1880s he was drawn more and more to Burke's writings on that subject and eventually edited a selection of them for Macmillan in 1881. In a letter early in 1880 to Tom, who was planning to edit Burke himself, he called him 'an English classic of the very first order, and editing him would be a delightful and edifying task. If I were not so over-driven I would attempt it myself.'[48]

Over-driven as he was, Arnold was pressing ahead with his Introduction to the *English Poets*, joking to Ward that whatever its quality 'as the Americans observe "there is a set of critics in England who seem to be perpetually hostile to Mr Arnold" '.[49] He had also agreed to write introductions to the selections on Gray and Keats. Preparing the Gray had involved a great deal of reading in the eighteenth century which had been Purgatory for Arnold. Not merely was this epoch impossibly dreary to Arnold, Gray himself was 'a very depressing' man. 'It will be weeks before I recover from him,'[50] he wailed. And Tennyson was still producing affronts to Arnold's critical sensibility: 'Tennyson ought to be placed in confinement to prevent any more such exhibitions as his poem in this last XIX Century', he told Ward (presumably referring to *De Profundis*[51]). But for now: 'I have certain things I want to do this year', he told Ward, 'and I am getting fearfully old and the time is short.'

He was preparing for Smith & Elder a selection of his prose writings and asked Ward if he could remember where it was he had said that poetic expression was superior to other forms of expression (for the record, it was in his essay on Heinrich Heine). 'That is the worst of having written so much!' he lamented at this faulty recall. More significantly, he hoped that the prose selection would bring in some money 'to help me pay Dick's debts'. This is the only explicit reference we have to Arnold's real reason for embarking on his trip to America in 1883–84: to clear his son's gambling debts incurred at Oxford.

In the spring of 1880 Arnold had written to Tom (who had first become a Catholic in 1856, then lapsed, and was now in the fold again and subjected to his older brother's teasing on the matter) that everything he said about the Catholics was said 'most sincerely, though I know that if they had power again they would burn me'.[52] Shortly afterwards, Arnold had his first meeting with the most famous Catholic in England, Cardinal Newman. Arnold was of course himself a celebrity. He was just about to sit for the portrait painter G. F. Watts and was so much in demand that his diary records 22 social engagements between 12 February and 27 March 1880. But his admiration for the now ancient and venerable Cardinal, aged nearly eighty, was of long standing. A picture of Newman hung in Pains Hill Cottage next to Emerson.

Arnold had received a card from the Duke of Norfolk, summoning him, at Newman's own prompting, to the Duke's house in St James's Square. 'I went, because I wanted to have spoken once in my life to Newman, and because I wanted to see the house',[53] Arnold later told Fan. Newman was not in his full Cardinal's rig but 'a sort of vest with gold about it and a red cap' and he was placed in state at the far end of the room between the Duke and a chaplain. People, mostly women, filed before him 'as before the Queen', dropping down on their knees and kissing his hand. No son of Dr Arnold was going to get down on his knees before a Catholic cardinal but Arnold managed what he called 'a deferential bow'. The ageing Cardinal took one of Arnold's hands briefly in his own and said: 'I ventured to tell the Duchess I should like to see you.' Newman said nothing of import except to ask briefly how Tom was getting on and then Arnold was swept on by the crowd of devotees; 'but I am glad to have spoken to him and shaken hands with him', he told Arthur Stanley, 'The sentiment of him, of his sermons, of his position in the church and in English religion, filled Oxford when I was there; it suited the place, and I am glad, and always shall be glad, to have been there at that moment, and grateful to Newman for the atmosphere of feeling he then created for me.'[54]

By now Arnold was beginning to put aside his initial reluctance to participate in Ward's *English Poets* and was becoming quite absorbed in the project. 'Lord Houghton tells me he hasn't done a word of his Landor yet',[55] he gossiped to Ward in May on his return from a fishing-trip to Chenies, and Swinburne's introduction to Collins was an 'outrage'. Arnold felt he should have been given Byron to do, and, besides, Collins was not much of a poet: 'The *Ode to Evening* leads nowhere . . .' He was to receive £50 from Ward for the introductions to Gray and Keats and his selection from Byron for Macmillan was soon to appear, following close on the heels of the Wordsworth selection. Accordingly, he asked Macmillan to pay £100 into his Twining's account on the 29th May to cover his annual life insurance premium.

Arnold took a welcome holiday on his own in Northern Italy and Switzerland in September, where he none the less seems to have run into various politicians and officials on holiday such as Sir Francis Sandford, Secretary to the Education Department and Anthony Mundella, newly appointed Vice-President of the Committee of Council on Education. He was obliged to lobby the latter on various educational matters and told Sandford that 'nowhere else in Europe is there to be found a Minister exhorting his subordinate official to write more poetry'.[56] Describing his tour to Fan, Arnold wrote: 'I never write a journal, but I tell my story in letters, which is the better and pleasanter way.'[57] For Arnold's copious letters – scattered and un-collected as they are – posterity must be properly grateful for they are the only personal writings we have, his diaries consisting merely of reading-lists, uplifting quotations, and the occasional note of an engagement. He also wrote to Flu to tell her how much he had enjoyed the Morteratsch Glacier: 'I have seldom enjoyed anything more, and I did a good deal of botanising . . . I did not see a soul.'[58]

One trivial incident on this trip showed how Arnold, as well as loving the Alpine scenery, also loved animals to a fault. He reported back to Flu for the benefit of the girls how he had witnessed a beautiful Swiss cat with a bell around its neck being run over and killed by a four-horse carriage: 'the sudden end of the poor little cat quite afflicted me',[59] he wrote sadly. And shortly after his return a rare brief note in his pocket diary records on 31 October: 'Dear little Geist [Dick's dachshund] died.' This resulted in a poem, *Geist's Grave*, which was written shortly afterwards and published in the *Fortnightly* in January 1881, as well as being privately printed in a very limited edition, bound in lavender paper wrappers, for friends. Arnold, it seems, was making the most of a rare visit by the Muse ('And so there rise these lines of verse / On lips that rarely form them now'). This charmingly innocuous verse which sees in the family pet's 'liquid, melancholy eye' a suggestion of Virgil's *lacrimae rerum*, has more than a hint of the prosaic Augustan manner that Arnold was so quick to disparage in Gray's contemporaries. It was a far cry from the experimental verve of *Empedocles*.

For the first time, in the autumn of 1880, Arnold read *David Copperfield*, published thirty years previously, and loved it so much that he drew heavily on it for his argument in *The Incompatibles*, the first essay in *Irish Essays* (1882). He also read passages of it to Nelly in the evenings. He was an enthusiastic reader of novels but rarely wrote about fiction – a late essay like that on Tolstoy being a rare exception. He was also reading a lot of Chaucer and Burns as part of the preparation for *The Study of Poetry*, and ended, he told Fan, with *King Lear*, 'before I finally write my Introduction in order to have a proper taste in my mind while I am at work'.[60] When the essay on Gray appeared, Flu said she liked it, and her husband wrote to her in Ireland, where she was visiting K and William, now the Chief Secretary for Ireland in the Gladstone Government, admitting that the eighteenth century was 'very interesting, though I should not like to have lived in it'.[61]

In October, Huxley had given an address (the text of which he sent Arnold) on 'Science and Culture' at Birmingham at the opening of Sir Josiah Mason's new Science College which made an explicit reference to his friend as 'our chief apostle of culture'.[62] In a forerunner of a more famous twentieth-century debate on 'the two cultures', Huxley criticised Arnold for assuming that a liberal education founded on the classics was adequate and that a scientific education was somehow insufficient.

Arnold would eventually confront the topic in his 1882 Rede Lecture at Cambridge on *Literature and Science* but for now he wrote privately to Huxley strongly underlining his belief that science was very much part of his definition of culture: 'the dictum about knowing "the best that has been known and said in the world" was meant to include knowing what has been done in science and art as well as letters', he explained. 'I remember changing the word *said* to the word *uttered*, because I was dissatisfied with the formula for seeming not to include art, and a picture or statue may be called an *utterance* though it cannot be called a *saying*: however, I went back to *said* for the base reason that the formula runs so much easier off the tongue with the shorter word. But I never doubted that the formula included science.'[63] Arnold valued his friendship with Huxley too highly to risk any real breach between them and wrote: 'I have plenty to make me melancholy – public affairs, the approach of old age, the general cussedness of mankind – but your goodwill and sympathy act always as a cordial.'

In November Arnold was once again approached to stand as Oxford Professor of Poetry. 'I see the *World* this week says that the only contemporary poetry that will be read a century hence is Tennyson's earlier work and my poetry generally',[64] he was to write to Macmillan a few weeks later but for now he was adamant and refused for a second time to stand, telling the author and politician James Bryce who had offered to propose him that despite 'a great memorial from the undergraduates'[65] he regarded himself as under a pledge not to stand – though Palgrave had indicated that he would release him from the pledge and stand aside himself.

5

Arnold was now fifty-eight and beginning to feel his age. On 2 January 1881 he wrote to Lady de Rothschild, thanking her for her annual Christmas gift of pheasants from the Aston Clinton estate: 'What a number of years it is since you first gave me pheasants and how far too seldom in the rapid course of all these years have I seen you.'[66] The following day he wrote to Tom: 'We are growing so old that we ought to make it a rule to meet every six months, at least.'[67] Tom was once again trying to get a post, this time as an examiner for the Catholic University in Ireland. 'The stupid management of the Irish by the English is more provoking to me than the faults of the Irish themselves', Arnold wrote, adding that he was not impressed so far by William Forster's performance as Chief Secretary for Ireland: 'Poor William Forster has not made a success of his proconsulate.' In the first half of 1881 Arnold was to write several of the essays on Ireland that would eventually be published the following year as *Irish Essays*. He was also at work on his selection of Byron, writing the Introduction in the cold early months of the year: 'Amidst snow and ice, I have done that volcano Byron',[68] he wrote to Macmillan's literary adviser (and later author of the *Dictionary of Music and Musicians*) George Grove. The book was published in June.

In February, Arnold met Disraeli again at Lady Airlie's house in London. Disraeli took Arnold to the end of the drawing room and indicated a settee, declaring: 'The poet's sofa!'[69] They sat down for 'a long talk' which Arnold reported to Fan: 'He went on to say that he read me with delight, that I was doing very great good, and ended by declaring that I was the only living Englishman who had become a classic in his own lifetime.' Arnold, however, was shrewd enough to see through this flattery and to grasp that what impressed Disraeli was Arnold's gift for coining phrases – such as sweetness and light or Philistines and Barbarians – that quickly gained currency. As a clever politician Disraeli appreciated Arnold's mastery of the telling and memorable phrase which quickly establishes itself as a term of public debate. He brushed aside his hostess's reservations about such a gift (which were that people merely picked up the catchphrases and then thought they knew all about Arnold's work). 'Never mind', exclaimed Disraeli, 'it's a great achievement!'

As well as politicians, Arnold was being pursued by portrait painters. George Frederick Watts, the famous painter of eminent Victorians (his cadaverous painting of Cardinal Manning was to be painted the following year), was anxious to meet the deadline of the first week of April for the annual Royal Academy Exhibition and wrote to Arnold requesting 'some immediate sittings'.[70] Watts submitted five portraits, Arnold's and Frederic Leighton's being singled out for particular praise. The *Annual Register* noted: 'That of Mr Arnold, somewhat coarse and markedly Semitic in aspect, was nevertheless a striking likeness.'[71] The success of the portrait meant another unwelcome speaking engagement for Arnold who always professed to dislike having to 'say a few words'.

He was invited by Leighton, President of the Royal Academy, to propose part of the toast at the Royal Academy Banquet to 'Science and Literature'. Sir William Grove took responsibility for Science and Arnold spoke for Literature. Leighton introduced him as 'a writer in whom a keen and Attic spirit finds utterance in speech more than usually chastened, bright and supple'.[72] There were cheers when he called Arnold to speak with the words: 'a seeker after light, the foe of all Philistines – Matthew Arnold!' Adopting the mock-rueful tone of the writer in an age that regarded literature as 'less interesting and ornamental' when compared with science, Arnold looked round at 'this brilliant company of Princes, Ministers of State, noble and wealthy patrons of art' and wondered to the President 'what can have induced you to import among them such an inutility as a poor man of letters'. Never one to flatter an audience when he could sweetly disconcert it, Arnold suggested that what constituted the common bond between Literature and Art was the need to struggle against the odds to achieve anything in either field, a struggle unknown to these 'wealthy patrons' and arts nabobs: 'What do they know of it, these favourites of fortune, for whom existence, at any rate, has been always secure and easy . . .?'

With his controversial religious writings behind him, Arnold was now trying to acquire a calmer perspective on such matters and wrote to Fontanès describing what he saw as a 'revolution' taking place in England in the late 1880s which was replacing the 'too large and absorbing a place in human life' occupied by religious ideas and discussions, with a new feeling that man is 'a more various and richly endowed animal than the old religious theory of human life allowed'.[73] This loosening up of people's minds, their greater disposition to go out and enjoy themselves, the 'awakening demand for beauty, a demand so little made in this country for the last century' was creating a new climate and was 'like all inevitable revolutions, a salutary one'. The result was that 'the great centre-current of our time is a *lay* one'. Arnold was positioning himself yet again alongside the *Zeit-Geist*. He also revealed to Fontanès his thoughts about Carlyle who had just died: 'I never much liked Carlyle. He seemed to me to be "carrying coals to Newcastle," as our proverb says; preaching earnestness to a nation which had plenty of it by nature, but was less abundantly supplied with several other useful things.'

Arnold was now reading ever more widely in Burke, whose conservatism did not appeal to him, but whose insight into the problems of Ireland very much did. He produced for Macmillan in June a selection of Burke's writings – which he sent to the politician

John Bright. The latter replied that it was strange that a man who 'could see so clearly in the case of Ireland should run so blind & mad in the case of France'.[74] Arnold drew on his writing heavily for a two-part essay in the April and June numbers of the *Nineteenth Century*. The essay, *The Incompatibles*, was prompted by Gladstone's forthcoming Irish Land Bill which aimed – very inadequately in Arnold's view – to redress some of the injustices of the absentee landlords. Arnold's view of the Irish Question was, in essence, not that the Irish should be given their freedom but that the English should be nicer to them. 'We find ourselves the object of a glowing, fierce, unexplained hatred on the part of the Irish people',[75] he wrote, but the terrible injustices done to the Irish did not warrant 'a separation which will bring confusion and misery to Ireland, danger to us'.

For Arnold the idea of Ireland separating itself from England was as absurd as the Scots, Welsh or Cornish – who were 'really blended in national feeling with us' – seeking to do so. After all, he went on, 'the English conquest of Ireland took place a little more than a century after the Norman conquest of England' and 'almost all countries have undergone conquest and confiscation' and have managed to put it behind them. Yet at the same time he was fully alive to the history and present prospect of 'Irish misery' and, in lavishly praising Burke as one who 'traces the reason of things in politics', Arnold agreed with his verdict that 'Irish misery and discontent have been due more to English misgovernment and injustice than to Irish faults'. But the obstacle to removing that misery turns out to be 'our terrible friend the British Philistine'. The refusal of the Philistines behind the Liberal Party to countenance the real reforms needed to deal with bad landlords, their religious prejudice against the beliefs of the Irish, and their 'pedantic' obsession with unhelpful nostrums rather than trying to see the situation as it really was, all contributed to the present impasse and the view that the English and the Irish were 'incompatible'.

For Arnold: 'The thing is to bring Ireland to acquiesce cordially in the English connection. This can be brought about only by doing perfect justice to Ireland.' Arnold credited the Irish with having more attractive manners than the English and enjoined his fellow-country-men once again to do something about improving their own.

In his reading of *David Copperfield* he saw in the portrait of Salem House school and Mr Creakle the incarnation of the middle-class Philistine who blocked the way to light in Ireland. Claiming that the middle class was 'improvable' Arnold argued that at the present time: 'All its members seem of one type of civilisation to an Irish eye, and that type a repulsive one. They are all tarred with one brush, and that brush is Creakle's.' Cromwell, too, 'whom we earnest English Liberals reverentially name "the great Puritan leader" ' stood before the Irish imagination as 'a glorified Murdstone' – although Arnold himself was clear, as always, that Government should act swiftly and decisively to repress disorder in Ireland with a Cromwellian implacability. In short: 'The Irish quick-wittedness, sentiment, keen feeling for social life and manners, demand something which this hard and imperfect civilisation cannot give them.' Aware perhaps that his audience might be feeling that it had heard all this before, when he offered 'public schools for the middle classes' as his remedy for this unlovely civilisation, Arnold conceded that his hearers would say: '*There! he has got on his old hobby again!*' Astride this mount, he offered a change of attitude on the part of the English, brought about by their improving their mental culture and their social demeanour so as to think again and with more under-standing and sensitivity about 'the down-trodden, hated, despised Irish', as the means that the Irish might come to love them and see the folly of separation as a solution to their undeniable problems.

A more immediate and practical Irish Question was the fate of the poet O'Conor. Arnold wrote to Gladstone, forbearing to send his Burke ('of Irish matters you have only too much'[76]) but enclosing his new Byron selection and asking for consideration to be given to a pension for O'Conor whose 'small vein, but a genuine one' continued to impress Arnold. He stressed the fact that O'Conor had lived by his hands and educated himself. Gladstone's secretary wrote back to say that the case was already listed and in September O'Conor was granted a civil list pension of £50. In thanking Gladstone, Arnold said it would relieve O'Conor of his 'great present danger, which is that he is tempted to work this vein much too fast and too hard in order to get a living by contributing verses to the newspapers'.[77] The comment reveals Arnold's personal insight into the struggles and compromises of the life of a Grub Street writer.

While he was busying himself with the fate of this struggling poet another young poet wrote to him enclosing his first volume of poems and testifying to 'the constant source of joy and wonder that your beautiful work was to all of us at Oxford' and referring to 'this great art in which you are a master illustrious and supreme'.[78] The author of these extravagant compliments was the 26-year-old Oscar Wilde (who was later to have one of his characters in *The Critic as Artist* (1890) mock one of Arnold's cardinal critical precepts by asserting, 'The primary aim of the critic is to see the object as it really is not.'). Arnold replied gracefully that: 'Your volume and note were put in my hands as I was leaving the Athenaeum last night.'[79] He had not had time to look at the poems properly but saw in them already 'the true feeling for rhythm, which is at the bottom of all success in poetry'. Arnold always appreciated the praise and respect of fellow-writers as the consolation of the 'unpopular' author. 'I have not much to thank the *public* for', he told Wilde, 'but from my fellow-workers, both in poetry and prose, I have met with kindness and recognition such as might satisfy any man.'

In September Arnold went to stay with K and William at the latter's official residence in Phoenix Park, Dublin – his first visit to Ireland in spite of the flow of essays on Irish subjects that had come from his pen recently. When he got back he received a letter from Cardinal Manning, Archbishop of Westminster, thanking him for sending him the Burke selections. 'The state of mind of my English, & even Catholic friends towards Ireland is a pain & a perplexity to me', he wrote. 'It is a people which has been pollarded and stunted by England. We have never civilised it, and we have refused to let it civilise itself.'[80] Another recipient of the book, Lord Derby, wrote to Arnold that Burke 'seems to me to excel all writers in the art of giving lasting interest to temporary controversies'.[81]

Although Arnold was preoccupied in gathering up the essays that would be published early the following year as *Irish Essays*, he was also worrying about Dick. 'He was idle at Oxford', he told the Australian man of letters, Robert Dudley Adams, bluntly, 'and I sent him to Melbourne that he might learn what regular work was.'[82] Although good reports were filtering back from the Union Bank at Melbourne where Dick worked, his son felt that a bank clerk's post had no future and he wanted to come home. Arnold decided to do what did not come easily to him, use his influence to get Dick a job. He wrote to the Home Secretary, Sir William Harcourt, first in February, joking that if nothing could be done for Dick 'I shall have to make him a printer's devil',[83] and later in October, with a little more awkwardness: 'I never before asked for anything. Either for myself or one of my belongings . . . I write with an overwhelming sense of the disappointments and rebuffs to which the makers of such applications are by common report said to be liable . . .'[84] He was after a factory inspectorship for Dick which he eventually got, although it is not clear whether it was through Harcourt's efforts.

Just before Christmas Swinburne sent Arnold his new tragedy *Mary Stuart* which Arnold promised to read during the holiday after his 'drudgery' of inspecting and training school examinations was over. 'I congratulate you', he told Swinburne, 'I who have never been able to do even the one poor play from Roman History which I schemed more than thirty years ago'[85] – a reference to the never-completed tragedy on Lucretius.

6

In January 1882 a fresh poem from Arnold's pen appeared in the *Nineteenth Century*. It was written to commemorate the death of Arthur Stanley on 25 July 1881 and had been written in the first weeks of November of that year. *Westminster Abbey*, which can only be described in Hopkins's sense as a Parnassian exercise, celebrates Stanley as a Broad Churchman, reflecting Arnold's view, expressed to Fontanès after Stanley's death, that 'What is clear is that the Broad Church *among the clergy* may be almost said to have perished with Stanley'.[86] The poem draws on a legend that in the early seventh century St Peter miraculously appeared at the consecration of Westminster Abbey, asking to be rowed across the Thames by a fisherman, accompanied by a heavenly choir of angels. St Peter secretly consecrated the church, with the result that Mellitus, Bishop of London, informed by the fisherman of what had happened, and finding the signs of consecration in the church, abandoned his own plans to perform the ceremony and merely celebrated Mass. Stanley is seen as 'a child of light' at a time when the Broad Church tendencies were under strain from a Church 'grown strait in soul' with 'folly revived' and 'refurbished sophistries'. Like most of Arnold's attempts at panegyric the heavy sense of a duty to be performed seems to crush any spontaneous poetic life.

In Arnold's last decade the entries in his pocket diaries show that his reading was as extensive and thoughtful as ever. He was still reading the Bible and the *Imitation of Christ*, and Goethe, as well as the classics and more modern thinkers such as George Sand and Vauvenargues whose *Réflexions et Maximes* furnish many quotations. Alongside the biblical saws and high-toned maxims he noted, under the heading *Our Ancestor*, a passage from Darwin's *The Descent of Man* (1871): 'A hairy quadruped furnished with a tail and pointed ears, probably arboreal in its habits.'[87]

This beast was soon to make a brief apperance in the lecture *Literature and Science*. Arnold had told Fan at the beginning of the year: 'If I live to be eighty I shall probably be the only person left in England who reads anything but newspapers and scientific publications.'[88] He told her that during 1881 he had been more successful than usual in meeting at least some of the target of books listed for reading in his diaries. 'The importance of reading, not slight stuff to get through the time, but the best that has been written, forces itself upon me more and more every year I live; it is living in good company, the best company, and people are generally quite keen enough, or too keen, about doing that, yet they will not do it in the simplest and most innocent manner by reading.'

As far as the public's disposition to read his own work went, Arnold could not be certain. 'I always feel that the public is not disposed to take me cordially; it receives my things, as Gray says it received all his except the *Elegy*, with more astonishment than pleasure at first, and does not quite make out what I would be at',[89] he confessed to Fan. He worried, in particular, about *Westminster Abbey*, and whether, like *Thyrsis*, people would complain of a lack of 'direct personal effusion as to the departed and as to my feelings towards him'. Edmund Gosse, the writer and critic who would the following year give Arnold's name as a reference when applying to give the Clark Lectures at Cambridge, liked the poem, but Arnold told him that 'it is one which poets will like rather than the great public, which indeed never did like me much and never will'.[90] The public just now, he complained, was 'in a realistic mood and relishes poems about the suicide of agnostic operatives, or perhaps the Wimbledon poisoning case'.

However unkind the public might be – and Arnold was wrong about posterity's interest in his poems for popular selections of his verse continue to the present day to pour from the presses while only one complete prose work is in print – his domestic life at Pains Hill Cottage was happy. 'I do very much enjoy the life at home', he wrote to Fan, 'with half an hour in the garden every morning, and two hours in the lanes every afternoon'.[91] To Fontanès, he described himself and his wife and daughters as 'the hermit and the hermitesses of the Mole'.[92]

In March *Irish Essays* appeared with a Preface suggesting that the three essays on Ireland with which the collection starts had not been well received: 'Practical politicians and men of the world are apt rather to resent the incursion of a man of letters into the field of politics; he is, in truth, not on his own ground there, and he is in peculiar danger of talking at random.'[93] He said that almost all the essays – even those not explicitly dealing with Ireland – were about 'the need of a changed and more attractive power in English civilisation' as a means of healing the breach with Ireland. His diagnoses and cures were scarcely unfamiliar. Arnold has a rare entry in his diary recording some direct criticism of his own work, a review in *The Century Magazine* by Andrew Lang in April of *Irish Essays* which says that: '*Sohrab and Rustum* or *The Sick King in Bokhara*, does more for culture than a world of essays and reviews, and disquisitions on the hideous middle class.'[94] Arnold has headed the extract, 'Prose and Poetry' and its appearance in this place suggests that it was a criticism he intended to take to heart and reflect on.

A little later in the year he would write to Swinburne, who had sent him his latest volume, recalling once more his aborted poetic drama on Lucretius and declaring that if his 'daily grind at school inspecting ever ceases' he would return to it: 'But I daresay I shall die in harness, and do no more poetry.'[95] Arnold, however, continued to push the new volume, sending a copy to Gladstone drawing attention to the essay on *Copyright*, arguing that copyright really ought to extend longer after the author's death than it did. George Smith had also decided to reprint *Culture and Anarchy* which Arnold admitted was 'rather a favourite child of mine'.[96] Smith was also going to act as a referee for Dick, who, having charged his father's account for the ticket home, was back from Australia and sitting the Civil Service examinations 'and in an awful stew'.[97] In the end he was successful and was located as a factory inspector in Manchester. The appointment, his father wrote to Tom, was 'in all the newspapers, as if he had been made ambassador at Constantinople'[98] but the salary was still not enough to marry on.

Arnold, meanwhile, continued his prose skirmishes with the Philistine, and delivered to a crowded audience in the Senate House at Cambridge on 14 June, the Rede Lecture on *Literature and Science*. This was later adapted for delivery (29 times!) on his American lecture tour the following year. 'I do think my works are at last taking hold, or have even taken hold of this precious public of ours', he told Macmillan. 'I was greatly pleased at a third edition of *Culture and Anarchy* being wanted.'[99] James Russell Lowell, the United States Minister to England, was in the Cambridge audience and liked the address. Arnold wrote to him saying that a lecture tour of America would be 'a horrid way of seeing the country' but that if he was to have any hope of retiring comfortably, he would first have to pay off 'a largish sum of money I borrowed to pay [Dick's] Oxford debts and to send him out to Australia'.[100] A lecture tour was therefore looking very likely even if he had been advised that the financial return would not be great. He made the same point to Charles Eliot Norton, saying that his plans to tour America had been put on ice and they would anyway be 'an odious business, and tolerable to me only in view of making a certain sum of money to enable me to take my small pension and retire'.[101]

Just before departure to Fox How for the summer, Arnold wrote to Gosse about his essay on Gray, conceding that Gray was 'one of the most interesting figures in our literary history' and observing: 'His scantiness of production was a misery to him, but has it hurt his fame?'[102] It is impossible to avoid silently asking the same question about Arnold himself. He believed that Tennyson over-produced and that if he had not written so much on Arthurian themes it might have been better for his reputation. Arnold wrote to Gosse again when he had arrived at Fox How to say that once he had met all his current periodical commissions: 'I contemplate leaving off writing for periodicals altogether before the public are quite sick of me.'[103]

Arnold's first task after the holiday was to deliver an address at the opening of the new term of the Liverpool University College, whose President was Lord Derby with whom he stayed at Knowsley Hall. The trip had enabled Arnold to visit Dick in Manchester, although he was distinctly off-form – a fact seized upon by the local press. 'I was much bothered by my discourse, and very bilious',[104] he reported to Flu from Knowsley on the Sunday morning after the speech. He had sat up until 5 a.m. working on the text and then slept for a few hours before being taken to the train by Dick. On arrival at Liverpool he was whisked off to a champagne reception for doctors at Rodney Street and thence to the St George's Hall where Lord Derby and a crowd of 1,200 was waiting patiently.

Arnold had, only a few months previously, published a collection of essays which included *The Future of Liberalism* which contained some rather satirical remarks about the former Tory MP who had switched to the Liberals in 1880. The essay cited Lord Derby as one of those Liberals who talked endlessly of personal liberty and free trade yet 'at his own gate' in the industrial grime and misery of St Helens – not to mention Bolton and Wigan – there was, in spite of these ebullient celebrations of material success 'little satisfaction to [man's] instinct for beauty, and to his instinct for a fit and pleasing form of social life and manners'. St Helens, in short, was 'eminently what Cobbett meant by a *Hell-hole*'.[105] Arnold also managed to suggest that the Liberal rhetoric about being free from the stifling aristocratic embrace might have been received a little ironically by any inhabitant of industrial south-west

Lancashire who chose to cast an eye on Knowsley Hall. Lord Derby, however, seemed to have taken no offence and introduced his guest handsomely.

When Arnold rose to his feet, not in the best of health and having had little sleep, he apologised for not being the 'eminent man of science' they had been promised and launched into an unsettlingly downbeat account of himself which must have given the cue to the hostile reporters present:

> You have . . . many people would tell you, a nearly worn-out man of letters, with one nostrum for practical application, his nostrum of public schools for the middle classes; and with a frippery of phrases about sweetness and light, seeing things as they really are, knowing the best that has been thought and said in the world, which never had very much solid meaning, and have now quite lost the gloss and charm of novelty.[106]

He said he wished he could change his phrases but: 'What has been the burden of my song hitherto, will probably have, so far as I can at present see, to be the burden of it till the end.' He did, however, pay generous tribute to Liverpool's educational achievements – 'a gratifying, an animating history' – and hoped that 'the spirit of lucidity' would be the end product of all this educational activity.

Although Arnold told Flu that he thought he had been well received and that the speech 'gave satisfaction'[107] (a view confirmed by Lord Derby in spite of his accurate judgement that it was 'not very new') the *Liverpool Daily Post* was unimpressed. The paper described him as 'a gentleman of quiet and not very distinguishable appearance, who reads monotonously from a paper and never attempts an oratorical effect either by voice or action'. He had 'the elocution of a worn and weary curate – a mechanical clerical delivery . . . His manner shows extreme lassitude, and when in his languid way he vindicates some of his old utterances, you wonder how he could ever have had the courage to utter them.'[108] That this was not wholly unjust is confirmed by the reports that were soon to be made of his first attempts at lecturing American audiences.

The stay at Knowsley was, however, a consolation. The house, he told Flu, was 'full of interesting things and the perfection of comfort'. He particularly liked Lady Derby who was 'very nice, though shy at first'. He was shown the pictures and the library and walked around the park. 'He has a fair share of literary vanity, repeats with pleasure compliments paid to himself & inviting them: but the desire of praise this shows is simple, natural & does not offend',[109] Lord Derby wrote in his diary. Still thinking about him two days later, he wrote: 'He made a good impression on the whole party, talking much, but pleasantly & unaffectedly.'

In the latter part of October Arnold wrote his penultimate poem, *Poor Matthias*, published in December's *Macmillan's Magazine*. The poor deceased canary, Matthias, bought in Hastings eight years previously, is celebrated in rhyming tetrameter couplets whose lightness removes the risk of bathos that might have come had a grander manner been attempted (the poem was successfully parodied in *Punch*, to Arnold's amusement – he suspected the author to be 'that demon Traill'[110]). It also mentions the lost dog Rover, the cat Atossa and the dachshund Geist. Looking at his two current dogs, Max and Kaiser, playing on the lawn, Arnold reflects that they could now outlive him: 'But, as age comes on, I know, / Poet's fire gets faint and low.' He remarks on the fact that birds are a species much harder for man to know than cats and dogs and that in the same way human suffering might not properly be appreciated by us even if it exists in our vicinity. The poem's deceptive slightness is augmented by a genuine sense of sadness on the part of Arnold who is clearly possessed by an intuition that his end cannot be far away. Shortly after it was finished he wrote to John Morley that he intended to retire in Easter 1883: 'Gladstone will never promote the author of *Literature and Dogma* if he can help it, and meanwhile my life is drawing to an end, and I have no wish to execute the Dance of Death in an elementary school.'[111]

7

As it turned out, Arnold had over three years to go before retirement and there was no let-up in his duties and professional engagements. He always spent the first few weeks of January dealing with training-school examination papers and in his 1883 diary for January he set himself a target which included 'five papers before breakfast' and '5 papers before bed'.[112] Another end-of-year ritual was the arrival of the Aston Clinton pheasants. Lady de Rothschild provided Arnold with a lifelong friendship and their intellectual sympathy as much as anything else was what made them so fond of each other. Writing to thank her, both for the game and her kind words about *Poor Matthias*, Arnold confessed: 'there is no one whose liking for what I write gives me more pleasure than yours does – hardly anyone whose liking for it gives me so much'.[113] It is clear that, deep as was his love for Flu, and close as their companionship was, she was not his intellectual equal (although she generally read his work, once forcing George Smith to forward another copy of the *Pall Mall Gazette* containing a piece which she was anxious to see) in quite the same sense that Lady de Rothschild continued to be. A couple of months later, when the latter's brother Nathaniel died, Arnold wrote a letter of condolence that shows how important she was to him: 'My heart turns to you very often, and, above all, it turns to you when suffering or sorrow befall you.'[114]

In the early spring of 1883 Arnold was faced with an unpleasant duty: delivering a lecture to the Wordsworth Society, in response to the solicitations of its President, Professor William Knight of the University of St Andrews, who also wanted Arnold to stand for the Rectorship of Edinburgh University – an offer which Arnold declined with alacrity. The lecture itself was launched into a sea of other papers, all 'awfully boring' as he reported to Flu, who was visiting a sick relative at Bournemouth. 'The grave would have been cheerful compared to the view presented by the Westminster Chamber and the assembled Wordsworth Society when I came upon the platform',[115] he added. He took consolation from the fact that 'now I have no more speechifying in prospect'.

Arnold's public profile continued to grow and he was increasingly having to deal with invitations to lecture, to 'say a few words' at literary occasions, and reply to correspondence, often unsolicited, from a variety of correspondents. Sometimes this persuaded him into interesting off-the-cuff revelations as when a certain Alfred Arthur Reade wrote apparently asking advice from the man who said 'conduct is three-fourths of life' about how to handle wine consumption. 'As a general rule', wrote Arnold easily, 'I drink water in the middle of the day; and a glass or two of sherry and some light claret mixed with water at a late dinner; and this seems to suit me very well. I have given up beer in the middle of the day, not because I experienced that it did not suit me, but because the doctor assured me it was bad for rheumatism, from which I sometimes suffer . . . But in general, wine used in moderation seems to add to the *agreeableness* of life, for adults at any rate; and whatever adds to the agreeableness of life adds to its resources and power.'[116] Small wonder that Arnold abhorred the Puritans' tea-meetings.

To another correspondent he stressed the importance of 'the training to think and feel' which came from the study of poetry (a point he had made in his address on *Literature and Science*) and described it as 'perhaps the best reward one gets from making it, at least I am sure that in my own case I have found it to be so'.[117] As well as enjoying literature and good wine, Arnold – in spite of his strictures on the poor quality of the contemporary English theatre contained in the essay, *The French Play in London* – enjoyed the theatre quite as much as he enjoyed novels (and not always highbrow ones). He had just started to contribute to the *Pall Mall Gazette* a series of anonymous theatre reviews or 'letters' which were collected long after his death in a book as *Letters of an Old Play-goer* (1919). In a letter to the magazine's editor, John Morley, at the end of May enclosing his latest review, he announced: 'I must now prepare for the invasion of America.'[118]

At last his mind was made up. This most reluctant lecturer was about to embark on a gruelling six-month tour. He quipped to Morley: 'If I make my lowly grave by the banks of the Connecticut River, you will sometimes remember me?' There were, however, some hurdles to be got over. The Education Office made some difficulties about granting leave and Sandford was unwilling to carry on paying his salary while he was in the States and grant 'privileged leave'. At one point this made Arnold consider deferring the whole trip until he could retire properly. In the meantime Andrew Carnegie, the great industrialist and philanthropist who did so much to make the eventual trip a success, hosted a dinner at the Grand Hotel in London to enable Arnold to meet some influential Americans. During the summer the obstacles were finally resolved and Arnold wrote with prophetic insight to James Lowell: 'I am very dubious about much success as a speaker and lecturer, but at all events I shall see and learn something.'[119] Arnold's preliminary view of the Americans seems to have been that they were not unlike the coarse, self-satisfied, materialistic English middle-class Philistines, and thus in need of liberal quantities of sweetness and light.

In August, Arnold was surprised to be offered, out of the blue, a civil list pension of £250, by Gladstone 'as a public recognition of service to the poetry and literature of England'.[120] Arnold hesitated to accept and took advice from friends on what to do. He was worried that a man already drawing a salary of nearly £1,000 a year as a public servant would attract disapproval for claiming an extra £250 from the public purse. He seems to have been unusually sensitive throughout his public career to such accusations. He had a very keen sense of the disposition of the newspapers towards him. In the event, his friends were unanimous that he accept and, apart from some predictable press mutterings, the public did not seem outraged. The extra money would clearly enable him now to retire as planned. Arnold offered Lady de Rothschild a slightly different explanation of Gladstone's generosity: it was his way of saying that 'he does not intend to promote me in the public service'.[121] Once the new Code devised by Anthony Mundella, Vice-President of the Committee of Council on Education, had been safely launched, Arnold would be glad to go 'and have a few years, if so it may be, for my own pursuits'.

Just before Arnold was due to leave he wrote to K saying bluntly: 'I hate going to America.'[122] He told her: 'I have nearly broken my heart over my first discourse [*Numbers*]', the second would be the recast Rede Lecture on *Literature and Science*, and of the third, on *Emerson*, he had 'not written a line'. He was too distracted in his last week to do anything more than read and reread Emerson. 'I have always found him of more use than Carlyle, and I now think so more than ever', he told K. Arnold was beginning to hear 'all sorts of promising reports about America'. A recent visitor had a report from a railway contractor there 'that all the railway porters and guards have read my books!'[123] This last letter from England, to Fan, expressed the anxiety that: 'I feel as if, after once starting from here, I should never be alone again till my return (if I live to return) in the spring.'

8

Arnold left, with a very excited Flu and Lucy, for America on 13 October 1883. They sailed from Liverpool on the Cunard boat SS *Servia* and set foot on American soil after a rough crossing and a brief quarantine delay at Staten Island, on 22 October. 'How delightful it will be to find oneself entering the mouth of the Mersey on our return',[124] wrote the reluctant lecturer after a day at sea, having earlier told his Education Department colleague Joshua Fitch: 'I don't like going, I don't like lecturing, I don't like living in public – and I wish it was all well over.'[125] Arnold had made use of the voyage to continue his attempt to advance his reading of Emerson – the *Essays* and the correspondence with Carlyle – with the result, as he wrote to Fan, that:

'My lecture on Emerson is pretty well formed in my head, and the passages marked which I mean to use for it – but oh, my dear Fan, how and when am I to write it? The blaring publicity of this place is beyond all that I had any idea of.'[126]

A little fatigued by the voyage, the Arnolds were swept off by Andrew Carnegie and deposited in a suite at the Windsor Hotel in New York where in the evening they attended a reception of three hundred people at the hotel. The rooms were decorated with plants and flowers and picked out in brightly coloured blossoms were the names of Arnold's best-known works. In the first days Arnold gave many interviews to the American newspapers and was quoted variously as saying: 'I hope I shall like America, but after all I think there is no place to live in like dear smoky old London' and 'I expect fair criticism, and care not how much I get'.[127] An injudicious piece of vivacity about Staten Island – 'Just like Richmond and not a single Mohican running about!'[128] – was overheard by a reporter and widely broadcast. Arnold was simply not prepared for the public exposure and complained to Fan that he was 'hardly able to do more than the writing of my name, the demand for my autograph being incessant'.[129]

The publicity, however, had begun even before Arnold left, with a flattering piece in the newspaper the author had treated with such disrespect in the past, *The Times*: 'In sending our foremost critic to America we are sending one who is no stranger to the American public, for there are few Englishmen who are more read in the United States or about whose personality more curiosity is felt.'[130] The paper predicted that Arnold would conduct himself with 'the happy mixture of audacity and urbanity, to which he has long accustomed us'. It added that there was much more appetite in the United States for the literary man and much more eagerness to turn out and listen to him than would be the case in England. Arnold's tour promoter – Richard D'Oyly Carte of the Savoy Theatre – must have hoped that this prediction would prove correct.

Even more enterprising was the *Pall Mall Gazette* whose reporter had the bright idea of interviewing Arnold at St Pancras with one foot on the Liverpool train. Arnold, said the reporter, was easy to spot: 'He is very like his photographs – tall with a large nose and mouth, brown mutton chop whiskers and hair almost jet black, carefully-trimmed and parted in the middle, and brushed smoothly over his broad, but not particularly lofty forehead. The habit of poring over books had made him slightly bent, but he seems a great deal younger than his real age, and is evidently in his intellectual prime.'[131] The reporter then persuaded Arnold to step off the train and adjourn to a waiting room where he declared: 'I am a poor man, only a poor schoolmaster [*sic*], with a small Government appointment, and could never have afforded to undertake the journey in the ordinary way, so I am preparing a few lectures which I hope will be successful and give me the means of retiring, for I should like to write one or two more books.' Remarks like these may well have persuaded the US public, who had just been treated to accounts of his civil list pension, that Arnold was coming over purely to make money out of them (the *Chicago Tribune* accused him of lecturing for 'filthy lucre'[132]) and could have explained the occasionally qualified reception of a speaker who, in what he said, was not willing to bend over backwards to flatter his listeners.

Arnold's first public engagement was by all accounts a disaster. It took place on the evening of 30 October at the Chickering Hall in New York City. His comment later to Fan that: 'The lecture itself is all right, but I am not sure about my delivery of it',[133] was a masterly understatement. Arnold was used to lecturing in small rooms and he seems to have been unable to appreciate the demands of a large hall. When he began to speak he was inaudible beyond the first four rows and the chairman, Wayne MacVeagh, scribbled on the back of a visiting card the word: LOUDER and passed it to Arnold. The fact that he read rather than spoke his lecture, and swallowed the end of his sentences, was reported mercilessly by the local media. 'Mr Arnold's style is academical', said the *New York Daily Tribune*, 'and though his enunciation is clear, he has the common defect of the English clergy among whom he was educated – the habit of dropping his voice at the end of a sentence, which renders it inaudible'.[134] The *New York Herald* was more specific: 'He held his manuscript in his left hand, nearly level with his face, and glancing at it to catch a sentence or two lowered it and glanced over the audience as he spoke the words deliberately and with a not very marked British inflection. In this way he delivered the whole lecture except that two or three times he appeared to speak for a minute extemporaneously.' The *Herald* concluded: 'He says he will do better next time.'

These reports filtered back to London where *The Times* reported: 'Mr Arnold's imperfect delivery was a great disappointment.' *Punch*, which had marked Arnold's visit with a piece of merry doggerel parodying the argument of *Numbers*: 'Nothing so good as a merry minority, / Very few people are sure to be right / Down with the power of the tyrant majority / Wanting in sweetness and lacking in light',[135] asked: 'He began by lecturing on "Numbers", but if he goes on like this, will he end up by lecturing to Numbers?' Several newspapers remarked on the contrast between Arnold's relaxed and charming personal manner – 'simple, cordial and unaffected'[136] the *Christian Union* of New York put it – and his lacklustre performance as a public orator. There was a marked contrast with Dickens who had taken America by storm with his powerful and dramatic (and immensely lucrative) readings, fifteen years earlier, as part of the explosion in the 1860s of British lecture-tours, supported by specialist agencies. This could not have been more marked.[137] The *Daily News* in London observed that Arnold's visit was more likely to excite interest in the United States than a reciprocal one: 'Lectures are to America what the opera is to Italy, and the theatre to France – the great popular intellectual enjoyment and relaxation.'[138] Although there was some evidence that the tour was stimulating Arnold's sales, he was clearly not going to make his fortune.

The subject Arnold chose for his first address – *Numbers; or, the Majority and the Remnant* (later published in *Discourses in America* [1885]) – was a characteristically bold choice (as was his later, and highly critical lecture on Emerson which he prudently declined to deliver in the latter's home town). He had evidently decided to 'do some good' to the American public by drawing attention to the deficiencies of the mass democracy their society celebrated. At least one member of the audience, however, was reported to have been expecting a lecture on the Book of Numbers. Arnold, as has been noted above, was a dyed-in-the-wool democrat and a believer in equality. But here he entered dangerous waters by suggesting that the majority was not always right. There was no question of his endorsing the wrong sort of politics and he took care to make himself very plain:

> It may be better, it is better, that the body of the people, with all its faults, should act for itself, and control its own affairs, than that it should be set aside as ignorant and incapable, and have its affairs managed for it by a so-called superior class, possessing property and intelligence.[139]

But although Arnold realised that there was no better political system than democracy to live under, he was not prepared to accept that everything the majority thought or did was beyond reproach. Quoting both Plato, who talked of the 'very small remnant' of the truly wise, and the Hebrew prophets who also believed in a remnant, or a group of enlightened individuals who perceived what was wrong with their society, Arnold argued that: 'States are saved by their righteous remnant.' That remnant, however, needed to be very large to be effective, and, in the United States, it certainly was large enough: 'what a remnant, I say, – what an incomparable, all-transforming remnant, – you may fairly hope with your numbers, if things go happily, to have!' Perhaps conscious of the risk of being too critical of his hosts, Arnold's chief illustration of his thesis was drawn from France, where he alleged that the popular literature of that numerous democracy was falling into the worship of the Goddess Aselgeia, or Lubricity. For those who managed to hear him, it was a challenging lecture that was founded, not in any incipient desire to launch a cultural *putsch*, but in a profound belief – testifying to the underlying religious strain which unified his thinking – in 'this great law that moral causes govern the standing and the falling of men and nations' and that the moral should speak out.

When Arnold gave his next lecture a week later on 7 November at Boston there had been a change. Arnold had submitted to the discipline of a professor of elocution at the Andover Theological Seminary, the Reverend John Wesley Churchill, who came over to Boston and took Arnold to an empty hall for two sessions to put him through his paces. Churchill believed his pupil, who had none of the natural instincts of a public speaker, and was perhaps too old to be reformable (although he appeared 'the youngest looking man of sixty I ever saw'[140]) was none the less much improved as a result of his efforts. Arnold began to relax and delivered some of the lectures from memory, although his jerky swivelling back to the lectern periodically to check his notes was not very smoothly accomplished. The New York promoters took care to advertise his next lecture there with the following: 'Special notice. – The Management beg to assure the public that Mr Arnold will be distinctly heard in all parts of the hall.'[141] It was Churchill who made the unsubstantiated claim that Arnold had made $10,000 out of the trip. Arnold himself speculated half-way through the trip that £1,000 might be nearer the mark but there is no record of what he did actually make.

Arnold sent regular bulletins to Fan throughout the trip, and was clearly irritated by the over-emphasis in the British media on his deficiencies as a speaker. In a letter to George Washburn Smalley, the London correspondent of the *New York Tribune* who had helped him plan the trip he tried to make light of it by saying: 'I get on much better now, but am a little bored by my own eloquence.'[142] Given the number of times that each lecture was delivered, his boredom can easily be understood. A hostile comment in the *New York Tribune* gives some idea of how his unsympathetic US critics saw him: 'He is a poet whose fine qualities have never appealed very strongly to the popular sense, and a critic who has addressed himself almost ostentatiously to the refined and cultivated few . . . he has taken a daring delight in shocking popular prejudices, jeering at popular idols, and showing contempt for the popular intellect.'[143] To another newspaper which asked whether he had no religious belief Arnold replied that his position was clear in his books. 'I will say, however, that no-one who has read my *Literature and Dogma* . . . can call me a Unitarian or an atheist.'[144] Always a connoisseur of sermons Arnold went to hear the preacher Ward Beecher, whom he had once called 'a heated barbarian'. To his embarrassment the preacher insisted afterwards on being introduced to Arnold who immediately began to apologise. 'No, no,' cut in Beecher, 'not at all. I deserved it all, and it did me good.'[145]

Arnold's busy schedule soon meant that he could not meet some of those people he had been anxious to see. He wrote to the novelist William Dean Howells that they would have to defer a meeting until he was in London when he could come and see him at Cobham 'at a small hovel I have in Surrey where I have never yet succeeded in decoying Henry James'.[146] To George Smith he complained of the newspapers and their invented quotes. 'I am surprised people come to hear me, for my three lectures are all of a grave sort – one of them decidedly dull, I think – at least it bores me very much to give it.'[147] If Arnold was bored, however, Lucy was having the time of her life. 'Lucy is a great success here, owing very much to that *ball-dress*', he told Smith. As well as the three discourses, Arnold gave occasional poetry readings which seem to have been a little more successful. The *Pall Mall Gazette* reported at the end of the year at Boston a successful reading: 'And, finally, when the audience still asked for more, Mr Arnold read his recently published verses on his dog "Geist" '.[148]

Women flocked in some numbers to his lectures and a report in *The Literary World* of Boston of a lecture to the Aesthetic Society of Jersey City was headed: HE DELIVERS HIS LECTURE SURROUNDED BY BEAUTIFUL LADIES.[149] Arnold, who seldom failed to take note of attractive women, told the *Detroit Times*: 'Your women are gayer, dress better, and on the whole are more attractive than English-women.'[150] As he toured the States, his monocle was remarked upon disparagingly in Cleveland and the thrumming of a piano from a nearby dancing class affected the proceedings at Detroit. The *Ottawa Citizen* decided that: 'Mr Arnold . . . looks anything but a typical poet or philosopher as he faces his audience.'[151] He told Tom: 'They make a fuss with me here which in the old world is reserved for princes and politicians.'[152]

In the course of his trip, Arnold admired the way that the ordinary people seemed happier and to have more of a share of the good things of life than their English counterparts and the middle classes, too, 'have, compared with our middle class at home . . . buoyancy, enjoyment, and freedom from constraint', all of which proved his point about how 'the aristocratic class acts as an *incubus* upon our middle class at home'.[153] He found everyone very kind, loved the abundance of fresh fruit and ice (although he balked at 'an immense beefsteak'[154] given to him for breakfast by the President of Amherst College) but disliked the feverish activity and 'publicity' and longed for some peace and tranquillity.

He passed as far south as Richmond, Virginia, where he was very struck by the black servants and where he went to see 'the schools of coloured children – dem little things'.[155] He found the black children 'neater and better dressed than the Irish scholars in Boston' and found 'astonishing . . . the line of demarcation between the white and the negro in the South still'.[156] He was fascinated by the schools and told K: 'I could have passed hours there.' He loved Virginia and left resolving to see more of the South, as well as California, if he ever returned to the United States. On Christmas Day he went to meet the President at the White House and found him 'a good-looking man with pleasant, easy manners'.[157]

By the start of 1884, Arnold was beginning to show signs of impatience with the effectiveness of D'Oyly Carte as a promoter. He wrote home to Macmillan complaining of his neglect: 'The consequence is, my visit *cannot* produce the returns in money which it might have produced and I do not know whether to laugh or cry when I hear the rumours from England as to what I am making.'[158] At the end of January Arnold and Flu pressed on to Canada but Lucy returned to 'the gaieties of New York'.[159] On the way he lectured at Illinois where the enterprising local promoter advertised him as 'the only living compeer of Dickens and Thackeray', both of whom had made successful tours of the United States. From Chicago, he wrote to Nelly to say that the lecture tickets had *Matthew Arnold troupe* printed on them. He was beginning to feel like a travelling player or showman. He told her that a Detroit newspaper 'compared me, as I stood now and then to look at my manuscript on a music stool, to "an elderly bird picking at grapes on a trellis".'[160] After Chicago, which was 'a great uninteresting place',[161] with less than a month to go, Arnold wrote to Fan: 'When I think of England, the desire to be back rises sometimes into a passion.'[162]

In Ottawa he was given a reception at Government House and loved the snow-furred sledge that took him there. Everyone was skating and tobogganing and he wrote to Fan: 'Tobogganing is going down an ice-slide on a thing like a shutter . . .'[163] In a letter to Yates Thompson, owner of the *Pall Mall Gazette*, Arnold quoted a newspaper account which managed to confuse him with Edwin Arnold (no relation) who wrote *The Light of Asia* and which described him as 'son of Tom Brown of Rugby'. And another, under the heading: E HAVE SEEN HIM ARRIVE! offered this cameo of Arnold: 'He has harsh features, supercilious manner, parts his hair down the middle, wears a single eyeglass and ill-fitting clothes.'[164] Arnold went on: 'Sometimes, in the dead unhappy night, I pour a little whisky which yet remains to me into a glass of milk which I have carried to my room, and things wear a milder aspect. But the life is diabolic.' Arnold was growing tired. More used than Flu and Lucy to this peripatetic existence, from his years as an inspector, he was none the less beginning to weary of the tour. Eventually, on 5 March the Arnolds set sail for England on the SS *Servia* once more. Arnold summed up the expedition neatly to George Smalley: 'I paid off the debt I wanted to discharge, and I saw and learned a great deal.'[165] It was not, however, to be his last experience of stepping westward.

CHAPTER TEN:
LAST WORDS
[1884–1888]

What a long way back it is to the School Field at this
season, and the withered elm leaves, and the footballs
kicking about, and the November dimness over
everything.[1]

1

Arnold returned from the United States to Pains Hill Cottage,
Cobham, to resume what he hoped would be his life of rural
seclusion. In fact, the demands for public appearances, dinners,
speeches, and articles do not seem to have lessened and he was
constantly on the train to London. It was this phase of his life that
his niece, Mrs Humphry Ward, recalled when she wrote of his 'pretty
cottage beside the Mole'[2] where she and her husband came out from
London to talk to 'Uncle Matt' – when they could secure his attention
from the dogs and cats who took precedence over any human visitors
(towards whom they were often hostile). 'Nobody who knew the
modest Cobham cottage while its master lived will ever forget it',
wrote Mrs Humphry Ward. 'The garden beside the Mole, where every
bush and flower-bed had its history; and that little study-dressing room
where some of the best work in nineteenth century letters was done.
Not a great multitude of books, but all cherished, all read, each one the
friend of its owner. No untidiness anywhere; the ordinary litter of an
author's room was quite absent.'
Arnold told his French friend M. Fontanès on his return that: 'I saw

and learnt a great deal, but I am not going to write a book'.[3] He did, however, publish the three lectures he had given so many times in the United States as a book, *Discourses in America*, the following year. Lucy had enjoyed America so much that she had found a husband there, Frederick Whitridge, a New York lawyer. Lucy and Fred were married on 9 December. And on 17 April 1884 Dick married Ella Ford, the girl with whom he had fallen in love in Australia. Her new father-in-law described her to Sir Charles Dilke, whom he was lobbying for a better job for Dick, as 'an exceedingly nice person who will not, however, make him any richer'.[4] Arnold hoped that Dilke, who was in the Cabinet as President of the Local Government Board, would be able to get Dick a place as a Poor Law Inspector. 'He was idle at Oxford', his father admitted, 'but learnt to work in Australia, gets on very well with people and is a good man of business.' Even in such an important formal letter as this, however, Arnold could not forbear to be facetious, telling Dilke that Dick 'has no turn for letters, but perhaps he consoles himself by thinking that such a turn has not made his father prosperous'.

Arnold's niece, who was married to Thomas Humphry Ward, the editor who had elicited from him *The Study of Poetry*, was also coming to his notice as a writer. One of the last books he read was her best-selling novel *Robert Elsmere* in 1888. Arnold was always a strict critic of Mary and when he read an essay she had written on Keats he suggested that she might have done well to 'swallow down an article of this kind'[5] and hold her fire a little longer. In a wise reflection on literary continence he advised her husband that: 'One should swallow down scores of possible articles; out of the compost thus gradually made, a far better article in time will grow – and health is preserved.' In the world of literary hack-work a writer of conscience must always feel from time to time that he or she has written too much. Arnold's slow habits of working and the press of other duties, however, spared him this particular fate.

Arnold's continuing interest in the theatre brought him into contact with Henry Arthur Jones, a late-Victorian playwright, whose *Chatterton* he had just seen. Although he conceded there was 'good writing' in it, Arnold disliked the theme of passive suffering and told Jones: 'I feel so strongly the defects of a situation where "everything is to be endured, nothing to be done," that I suppressed a dramatic sketch [*Empedocles on Etna*] of my own on that account; and though I afterwards restored it at Mr Browning's request, I restored it for reading only – I would never have restored it for representation.'[6]

During the summer the Arnolds visited Fox How, Scotland and Swansea where they stayed with Flu's relatives, the Bensons at Fairy Hill. This enabled him to visit Brecon where Constance de Rothschild – Lady Battersea, wife of the MP for Brecon and daughter of Lady de Rothschild – was staying. In Constances's journal 24 September was described as: 'A red letter day for it brought us dear Mr Arnold. What a delight!'[7] By the time Arnold returned to London in October he had started to think of another trip to America. It had been suggested that, with a more dedicated and less costly agent than Richard D'Oyly Carte, he might make a little more out of the tour, and, much as he loathed lecturing, he had clearly not discharged all his debts. It is also true that he had been intrigued by America – though he claimed that Quebec was the most interesting part of the 1883 trip – and wanted to see more of the country. But the most obvious reason was the desire to see Lucy in New York.

'I shall probably return to America this year',[8] he told Percy Bunting, editor of the *Contemporary Review*. In the event he did not go until May 1886. Arnold was aware that his religious books were better received in the United States where the audience for them was less likely to be outraged by their progressive content. Writing to Charles Eliot Norton about his 1883 selection from Isaiah (a reading for schools which presented the chapters not used in his 1872 Isaiah edition), Arnold said that it was hard to make an impression in England with such a book for 'the old world profoundly distrusts the dealings with it of an innovator such as I am, wants no change in its ideas on the subject, and draws its bedclothes over its ears'.[9] His religious books, however, were still selling well, and on reviewing *God and the Bible* for a new edition Arnold told Norton that 'I seem to find some chapters in it to be the best prose I have ever succeeded in writing'. He agreed with Norton that 'the influence of poetry and literature appears at this moment diminishing rather than increasing' and blamed the newspapers for monopolising the attention of the potential reading public (ironically, because their quality had improved) – 'yet reading a book – a good book – is a discipline such as no reading of even good newspapers can give.'

At the end of October, Arnold went to the Kinnaird Hall at Dundee to give *Literature and Science* yet again to an audience of over 2,000 (stopping off on the way to see Dick and Ella at Manchester which necessitated a 'windy and dismal'[10] wait on the railway platform at Wigan). He thought this the dullest of the American discourses yet it usefully sets out his view that science – while vitally important and requiring the attention of the literary scholar – could not in the end usurp literature as a central humanistic discipline. He took up the challenge of his friend Huxley – 'the very prince of debaters'[11] – by saying that such polemical opponents of literary studies generally took them to be mere *belles lettres* whereas his idea of literature was 'something more than a superficial humanism, mainly decorative', it was altogether more rigorous and disciplined – 'a genuine humanism is scientific'. He made clear, what he had already made clear to Huxley in private correspondence, that his 'best that has been thought and said in the world' formula very definitely included 'what has been done by such men as Copernicus, Galileo, Newton, Darwin'. But he drew the line at science replacing the humanities as the central part of the educational curriculum.

The natural human tendency to seek an organic unity in knowledge – 'the need of relating what we have learnt and known to the sense which we have in us for conduct, to the sense which we have in us for beauty' – to couple knowledge to the moral and aesthetic sense, would always defeat the monopoly of science, Arnold believed. 'Such is human nature', he declared, summoning up once again his old argument about 'the instinct for self-preservation in humanity'. The importance of 'humane letters', moreover, grew as the scientific spirit grew and as old superstitions died, making the need for a new framework of belief more urgent. 'The majority of men will always require humane letters', he argued. 'The appeal is to experience.'

The lecture demonstrates at once the strength and the weakness of Arnold's thought. His argument is lucid, attractive and persuasive – and enviably optimistic – but its philosophical foundations are fairly tenuous. A simple appeal to experience, to 'the instinct of self-preservation in humanity', to a gut feeling that right was on the side of liberal humanism, we might feel now, in the more embattled intellectual climate of the late-twentieth century, is simply not sophisticated enough. But at the time he wrote, as the letter to Charles Eliot Norton shows, Arnold was confident that 'humane letters' were not seriously under attack. He could not have foreseen the intellectual uproar of the academy a century later as literary theory – rather than the natural sciences which, no doubt owing to Huxley's good influence, he always respected – began to attack the notion of humane letters, and even the person of Matthew Arnold himself as their representative figure, from within.[12]

Just before giving the Dundee lecture, Arnold wrote to K to say that Huxley was not well: 'I have a real affection for him though we seldom meet; it brought the tears into my eyes to see him.'[13] Huxley had told Arnold that he had consciously given thought to the art of public speaking and worked on it in a way that seems not to have occurred to Arnold who told K: 'How very right you were about what you called my too "solemn" and poor Mr Carnegie my "ministerial" manner in speaking. Since I have spoken so much, I have perceived that it is my great defect, inasmuch as it strikes everyone.' He quoted the opinion of *Harper's Magazine* that in fact he should consider giving up public speaking altogether because of his deficiencies.

Lucy's wedding made a happy end to the year – although it played havoc with his deadlines – and, as he reported to Tom 'it is the first time "a Lady" as the people say has been married in Cobham for 20 years, and the excitement and the triumphal arching are great'.[14] Lucy and Nelly had more or less grown up in Cobham where they had lived for eleven years now and the local people, rich and poor, came forward with presents. The tradespeople made Lucy an address in which they said how proud they were to have 'a man of her father's literary reputation and character (mark *character*, my boy) an inhabitant of their village'. Arnold drew the conclusion that such an event showed how far popular education had come – 'would this have been possible from village tradespeople to a man of letters in Pope's time or Johnson's?'

2

From the depths of his end-of-year examination marking, Arnold broke off each day to scan *The Times* for news of Lucy's safe arrival at New York. He wrote to say that he would send her a letter to 12 West Tenth Street every Monday for 'you are so far off, and so dear to my heart'.[15] He offers her a picture of his daily routine – working until lunch (on *A Word More About America* for the *Nineteenth Century* now that the examination papers were finished), pottering in the shrubberies, paying local calls, working again, and then finishing the day with a new novel, *Mansfield Park*. He was anxious that his piece on America did not cause problems for Lucy in New York if it turned out to be too critical – 'Mamma, however, is in a thousand agonies, I need not say', for she knew full well where her husband's vivacity sometimes took him. He told Lucy how he had just then looked up from his writing to see her pony, Lola, walking past the window 'with the sun shining on her back'. His next letter described the pony rolling on her back in the paddock and kicking her heels and the snowdrops and primroses appearing in the garden. Arnold's care to paint a picture of life at Cobham shows how much he missed Lucy's presence in the scene.

To another correspondent he described his attempts to grow, not merely the wild daffodil from Fox How, but 'the *cypressus semperviva* which is such a feature of the Italian landscape' and to nurture in Surrey this symbol of Abroad 'amid the crash of States'.[16] He went on: 'To pass from this poetry of nature to my own poor productions: you will be glad to hear that my poems sell better than ever, though they have now been in the world some thirty years.' Macmillan was just about to bring out a three-volume library edition of the poems, which were indeed selling well in their existing editions, helped perhaps by the consolidation of Arnold's reputation now on both sides of the Atlantic as a senior man of letters. Macmillan offered him £500 for the three volumes, of which he printed 2,000, priced at 7/6 per volume. 'Your offer for the Poems was above what I expected – an unusual avowal, I suppose, for an author to have to make to a publisher',[17] Arnold wrote to Craik, Macmillan's assistant. The *Discourses in America*, also to be published during the summer, had a smaller print run of 1,250 and Arnold was paid £75 for the English and American editions. This shows that in spite of the high public profile of Arnold the prose controversialist, it was his poems that enjoyed more commercial success.

Eighteen months later Macmillan was writing to say that sales of the three-volume edition (he had also reprinted the popular one-volume selection made by Arnold in 1878 which was reissued more or less annually) had been 'very good. It is the most permanent & important of all the books.'[18]

Meanwhile the letters to Lucy continued to flow. He urged her not to lose the habit of reading: 'Keep always something going besides the novel of the hour . . . you will find the resource more and more precious.'[19] He told her that Knowles of the *Nineteenth Century* wanted him to sit for the portrait painter Weigall for his collection of star contributors: 'there will at last be as many portraits of me as of Ruben's wife'. Arnold loved his daughter but was also sentimental with her in these letters. 'Your letters are delightful, my child', he wrote. 'I always cry when they are read to me; but it is a happy cry.' In his next letter he revealed how pressed he was by a deadline for the *Contemporary* – 'you know how these things worry me and upset me and I am more pressed than usual'.[20] At the same time invitations to dine were raining down on Pains Hill Cottage – four arriving in the space of one day.

Arnold was so busy that even reports that a new opera called *The Mikado* at the Savoy Theatre was '*simply irresistible*'[21] could not tempt him, even though Richard D'Oyly Carte was offering him a box whenever he wanted one. He was going through *Merope* for the new edition of the poems and showed a touching loyalty to it and a conviction that it could be staged. Everyone told him it couldn't be: 'But it will be put on the stage some day by a royal or wealthy amateur, after I am dead.' He told Lucy that at a grand dinner party the previous evening he had been observing Flu 'and was particularly struck by her resources of conversation'. We learn more than usual of the detail of Arnold's social engagements at this time – the dinners with Henry James, Edward Burne-Jones, and various titled Barbarians – because he knew that Lucy loved such things and wanted to hear about them.

At Easter, Arnold appears to have been approached yet again about standing as an Oxford Professor. 'No, nothing would induce me to become a professor now . . . The métier of a school inspector is not one to rejoice the heart perhaps, but I prefer it to that of a professor',[22] he wrote to Tom. He proposed Tom as an alternative (but was told by Jowett that this would be 'impossible'). The fact that it was a post other than Poetry Professor (over which approaches would be made to him in the autumn) is confirmed by a passage in the memoirs of George Charles Brodrick, Warden of Merton College, Oxford, who recalled that when the Merton English Professorship was founded that year, he was deputed to make some private approaches to Arnold to sound him out about taking on the job. 'He at once decided against it, telling me that he regarded himself as a more or less ornamental lecturer, who might deliver a few well-finished discourses in each year, but who could not undertake the weekly drudgery of teaching.'[23]

Not that his inspecting was anything other than drudgery – he barely found time to attend the wedding of Tom's daughter Julia to Huxley's son, Leonard, at Oxford this month – and a letter to Yates Thompson indicates that the old routine was still pushing hard at the 62-year-old: 'I write this at 7am; a school in Pimlico all the morning, a luncheon in Holland Park at 1.30, a sitting to Weigall at 3; down here [Cobham] again to reports and letters at 5.20. Add to this a pain across my chest when I walk, which is probably the beginning of the end.'[24] Arnold's doctor, Sir Andrew Clark, decided it was not the heart but indigestion (perhaps all that dining out was taking its toll). He put Arnold on a strict diet of soup, sweet things and fruit, 'and, worst of all, all green vegetables entirely forbidden, and my liquors confined to one small half-glass of brandy with cold water, at dinner'.[25] To a fit and active man like Arnold, who was just about to set off for some fishing on Lord Tavistock's estate at Chenies with Dick, who shared his father's passion for angling, this was irksome. 'At present I feel very unlike lawn tennis, as going fast or going up hill gives me the sense of having a mountain on my chest; luckily, in fishing, one goes slow and stands still a great deal', he reported to Dick. In spite of the diet, however, he managed a dinner with the Archbishop of Canterbury on 3 June ('which I always think a gratifying marvel, considering what things I have published'[26]).

Arnold was relieved to learn that Lucy was coming to Europe this summer which spared him the necessity of crossing the Atlantic: 'I am very well pleased that it is settled so because I am rather tired by my final year of school inspection, and do not wish to have the American fatigue to face again so soon. I think, too, it will be better to let another year elapse before I again try the patience of American audiences.'[27] He told Carnegie that 'as my family is full of heart complaints, my father and grandfather having both died of it long before reaching my age, the doctors insist on my taking care of myself'.[28] During the long summer drought of 1885, Arnold patiently went out into his garden each day to water his Italian cypress and dreamed of one more trip to Italy. He told Grant Duff that after America 'if the Blind Fury permits me, I will see Italy again and get done one or two long projected things in verse'.[29] Before this, however, the Education Department had found one last task for him to perform before retiring on Lady Day 1886, 'that I might go round the Training Schools and report on the literary instruction in them'.[30] This would take him to Germany, France, and Switzerland across the winter of 1885–6.

After a summer break during which he stayed at Mountain Ash in South Wales with Lord Aberdare in order to attend the annual Eisteddfod and make a short speech (he found the audience to be 'a wonderful sight'[31]) and was later the guest of Lord Rosebery at Mentmore, Arnold visited the President of Corpus at Oxford prior to resuming his inspecting in the vicinity. He learnt that plans were afoot to ask him to stand yet again as Oxford Professor of Poetry, following the death of Shairp, with signatures being gathered, but he had no wish to accept and get in the way of Palgrave who wanted to stand. 'On Friday', he told Fan, 'I got out to Hinksey and up to the hill to within sight of the Cumner firs. I cannot describe the effect which this landscape always has upon me – the hillside with its valleys, and Oxford in the great Thames valley below.'[32] Ten days earlier he had told her: 'I think Oxford is still, on the whole, the place in the world to which I am most attached.'[33] But not enough to be a professor there again.

Arnold was moved by the gestures of support but once again, although he seems to have come close to considering it, he feared that the contest would stir up a hornet's nest of very Oxfordian contention. He told Thomas Humphry Ward: 'I do not feel quite secure, if I do stand, against a whipping up of the clergy and a blowing of trumpets in *The Guardian*, against the author of *Literature and Dogma* – a thing which would be very unpleasant to me.'[34] Palgrave, clearly thinking that Arnold was going to stand against him, sent his alleged rival a long 137-word telegram 'which will severely curtail his profits from the first year's income of the Chair'.[35] Arnold decided enough was enough and that any contest would now be 'detestable'. He told Ward that he was 'deeply gratified because I am so fond of Oxford, and because I know, too, how apt the dear place is to be sniffy'.[36] He wrote to Lucy saying that 400 undergraduates had sent a memorial recommending him, in addition to that sent by the heads of colleges and tutors. 'Everyone is kind as one grows old, but I want my Lucy.'[37] In his next letter to her he revealed that his Jane Austen fit was still upon him: 'We all agree that Mr Woodhouse in *Emma* is rather like *me*; in particular so far as his sayings to and of his daughters are concerned.'[38]

3

At the beginning of November, Arnold set off on his third and last foreign schools mission before retiring for good. It was a splendid way to go, for he loved travelling on the Continent and the subject was one he cared about. It was twenty years since he had undertaken a similar mission. He had told Mundella, his superior, that he wanted to ascertain what the literary instruction in teacher-training schools amounted to; whether aid to higher and secondary institutions had increased similarly to that to primary institutions, and how the new free primary schools were working. 'It is just the sort of mission that interests me, one is enabled to see so many persons and things in the most thorough manner',[39] he told Lucy. All his expenses were paid, his salary would continue to be drawn, and there would be £50 for the eventual report. Originally it seemed that it would be a quick six-week mission reporting by Christmas, but he went back for more information in the early part of 1886. One immediate casualty was the article on Sainte-Beuve for the *Encyclopaedia Britannica* which had to be postponed, though it was to be finished later.

Arnold described his journey from Calais to Berlin for the benefit of Flu – in the course of which he realised when talking to some wealthy German businessmen on a train who insisted on filling the carriage with cigarette smoke, that his German was 'shocking'.[40] He also found Alphonse Daudet's *Sapho* 'shocking' (presumably for its 'lubricity') and had to read the *Odyssey* the following day 'to take the taste out of my mouth'. In Berlin, Arnold had the chance to go and see Bismarck speaking in the Reichstag and observed: 'Bismarck has all the faults of a bad, untrained speaker; holds himself ill, keeps his head down, does not speak out, makes awkward little pokes with his hands; but the authority of the man and the weight with which he speaks, make up for everything.'[41] When he came home at Christmas to find Gladstone 'proposing to give the Irish a Parliament' the contrast in the weight of the two politicians struck him forcibly. While still in Germany he wrote back to Flu – always a keen student of the political scene – about the British elections, the first after the extension of the suffrage to the agricultural labourers, which were just about to replace Gladstone with Lord Salisbury. 'How I wish we could talk about them together',[42] he wrote from Berlin. Arnold's disillusionment with the Liberals was growing, even if: 'I have . . . no confidence at all in the Tories.'[43] He actually preferred the Tory candidate in Westmorland 'though I should never myself vote for a Tory'.[44]

In Berlin, Arnold met the Crown Prince and Princess of Prussia, having been summoned by an anonymous courtier, 'a tall personage in black'.[45] He talked to them about the elections. They were the privileged possessors of a telephone which was connected to the Opera. 'The Prince showed me how to put it to my ears, and I heard every word of the recitative, which was then going on distinctly, and presently the music also.' There was a great deal of theatre-going and dressing for dinner with important personages during this first phase of Arnold's mission and relatively slow progress in educational inquiry. He wore a decoration with his evening dress one night, almost certainly the order bestowed on him by the King of Italy in recognition of his kindness to the Prince of Savoy in the days at Harrow, and went to see the King himself. He had to call on the services of a chambermaid to tie the order behind him 'which she accomplished with much tittering, and with a lively interest in my making myself *hübsch* [beautiful], because I was going to speak with *der König*, and to speak with him *allein*, too!'[46] He and the King spoke, stiffly and rather briefly, in stilted French.

Arnold returned home for Christmas to Cobham where he wrote to Lucy that he would be coming to see the United States again in the summer of 1886 and that this time he would perhaps give just a few lectures 'which would pay our expenses without my having the fatigue of a campaign . . . Then I should return home to be free from my inspectorship and to try and get one or two literary schemes accomplished – much more to my taste than lecturing.'[47]

Arnold left for Paris and the second half of his educational mission on 21 January 1886. He had enjoyed the break and the skating on Pains Hill Lake which, as he explained to Fan 'did not bring on the chest pain'.[48] It was walking up a hill or struggling through snow that brought it on. Every day he had read five pages of the *Greek Anthology* 'looking out all the words I do not know; this is what I shall always understand by *education*, and it does me good, and gives me great pleasure'.[49] Those were characteristic words and could stand as Arnold's motto for the purpose of art: *it does me good, and gives me great pleasure.* He could not conceive of a separation between the aesthetic and the moral, between profit and delight, and was thus in a direct line running back to Sir Philip Sidney's *An Apologie for Poetrie* (1595) who himself drew his defence of the imagination from classical sources such as the privileging by Aristotle of *praxis* over *gnosis*. Such an explicit moral approach to the aesthetic tends to find less favour in the present day – which is why Arnold's criticism and his judgements on individual poets are sometimes held at arm's length by modern critics. Yet the political readings which have often replaced it can seem just as insistent or dogmatic. Art for art's sake is just as far off as it was in Arnold's day now that texts are subjected to the harsh rigour of political interrogation. Arnold himself has been caught up in what Edward Said calls, in another context, this 'rhetoric of blame',[50] a retrospective censure of writers from the past who transgress against late-twentieth-century nostrums.

Just before he left again for Germany, Arnold wrote to the historian Goldwin Smith in Toronto to explain his intention to retire in May when he became entitled to his pension: 'I have had five and thirty years of inspecting, and I should like to retire from it before I drop. One or two things in verse which all my life I have wished to do I am now probably too old to do well.'[51] One of those 'things' was 'a Roman play with Clodius, Milo, Lucretius, Cicero, Caesar in it'. Arnold also shared with Goldwin Smith his dismay at Gladstone's Home Rule Bill for Ireland and was planning an article on *The Nadir of Liberalism*. Arnold, keenly sensible as he was of the wrongs done to Ireland, still hated the idea of separation from England. In particular, he was concerned that Gladstone's plans 'merge Ulster in Celtic Ireland when, in any plan for local government, it should be kept distinct as a centre of natural Englishism and loyalty'. To Thomas Humphry Ward he also talked about his retirement and the regaining of liberty at last – 'but how late in life, alas, how far, far, too late!'[52]

Arnold spent three weeks in Switzerland and Germany where he heard from Flu the news of the death of the pony, Lola. 'I could indeed say, "Let my last end be like hers!" for her death must have been easy . . . The tears come into my eyes as I write.'[53] He wrote to Flu again from Munich where he had seen Wagner's opera *Tristan and Isolde*. Unable to appreciate the music, Arnold wrote: 'I may say that I have managed the story better than Wagner. The second act is interminable and without any action.'[54] He loved Nuremberg, where he saw the house of Dürer, and noted with relief, as he walked the streets, the absence of his pain. Closing a letter to Fan from Paris at the end of this trip he asked simply: 'I wonder if I shall ever get anything more done in poetry?'[55] The answer was that he had only one more poem to write – yet another elegy for the death of one of his pets whom he always addressed in anthropomorphic terms when alive and treated with the affection that he would treat a family member. Arnold seems to have resigned himself to the final extinction of his gift, which for a poet must always be the most precious one, whatever literary distinction is achieved in other fields. The myth that Arnold in his last years grew more and more melancholy has absolutely no foundation. There was no slackening of his animation and joy in living. His passionate enthusiasm, even for an official educational mission at the very end of his life, is entirely characteristic of a man who, it is true, complained of the pressures on him, but who never let them depress his spirits and who found life constantly interesting and full of promise. And no sooner had he returned from the Continent and penned his report than he was off again on his second trip to America.

4

In a letter to William Gordon McCabe, founder of McCabe's University School in Petersburg, Virginia, Arnold promised to confine himself to lecturing in 'three or four of the great cities'.[56] He had no wish to repeat the gruelling demands of his first trip in 1883. He added: 'It will go hard with me if I do not manage to set eyes on Virginia somehow – the most attractive of all the States.' That generosity was reciprocated in the twentieth century when the University of Virginia became one of the most important centres of Arnold scholarship. Arnold told Carnegie that he would offer an address called ' "A last word about America", or something of that kind.'[57] He was sending Flu and Nelly on ahead of him, for the real reason for his trip was to be present during the birth of Lucy's child and Lucy was not well, sending 'piteous appeals'[58] to her mother. They set off for Liverpool on 2 April. He himself was coming on later, from Southampton, when he had finished his report. He was due to retire officially on 19 April.

Although Arnold did not relish the long sea voyage he admitted to Carnegie that he was 'glad at the thought of seeing America and my friends there once more; it will be the last time! The effort and the interruption of work and habits are too great.' In the end Arnold had to delay his departure because, in addition to the report and an article for the *Nineteenth Century* on *The Nadir of Liberalism*, he was required to answer questions at a session of the Royal Commission on the workings of primary schools since the 1870 Education Act. The architect of the Act, K's husband William Forster, had just died on 5 April. Arnold told Charles Eliot Norton that, tragic as the loss of William was: 'Whether he who is gone or any of those who remain had or have the power to extricate us from our present difficulties and dangers is another question.'[59]

In the middle of dinner on Saturday 17 April came a telegram announcing the birth of Lucy's first child, a girl whom Flu christened 'the little midget'.[60] This made Arnold more than ever determined to get away. 'I shall strain every nerve to get out by her [the SS *Servia*], for, as you say, "we are too old for these separations", and I cannot bear them',[61] he wrote to Flu.

In the event he set off on the Cunard Royal Mail Steamship *Umbria* from Liverpool on 22 May, seen off by Dick, and frustrated by the fact that he would be at sea during the critical passage of Gladstone's Home Rule Bill 'but probably I shall be too sick to care'.[62] By the copious use of lemons and soda water he defeated his sea-sickness, and struggled to write letters as the screw of the *Umbria* shook the vessel. The ship's captain insisted on his famous passenger taking the chair at a concert one night in aid of the Liverpool Sailors' Orphanage and, though the concert was 'terrible',[63] and most of the performers sea-sick, the collection was good. Arnold stoically performed his duty until the concert was over and he could go up on deck and get a good breath of fresh air, steadying himself by grabbing a rope. 'On board ship I quite lose the taste for wine', he reported to Fan, 'even for claret, and like nothing so much as iced soda water or iced lemonade without sugar.' At New York Arnold was met by Lucy and Fred and the little midget. 'My Lucy's baby is a real pleasure to me and I nurse it a great deal',[64] the doting grandfather reported to Fan soon afterwards.

Arnold received news in New York of the collapse of the Home Rule Bill. 'A load is taken off my spirit', he told Fan. In a letter to K, however, he showed the complexity of his actual position. He was not in fact against 'Home Rule' on principle, as William had been. He was opposed to Gladstone's idea of a separate national parliament for Ireland but he was very much in favour of 'giving real powers of local government' to the Irish. He was thus a devolutionist but not a separatist. The Americans, however, he felt, could not grasp the distinction because 'they are not closely informed on Irish matters'.[65]

Arnold deliberately gave himself a light schedule and turned most of the trip into a family visit. Fred's father drove Arnold around Massachusetts during which trip he noted that the Americans talked a great deal of the beauty of the State and its buildings 'because it is their own place where wealth and luxury are in full possession, and where the scumbling, ugly, half-finished side of American life is not visible'.[66] He then got the Chicago express train to Buffalo, hugely impressed by having covered 440 miles in less than eleven hours. The address he gave was a low-key one on 'some points in foreign education'[67] as he described it to Carnegie. He also spoke in Philadelphia but from the end of June he gave no more lectures. The *Pall Mall Gazette* reported a letter read out to a meeting in New York of the Irish Loyal and Patriotic Union which Arnold couldn't attend. His letter uses the analogy of what would happen if the Southern States decided that the only way to get 'effective government by Southerners' was to establish a Southern Congress at Richmond which would then eclipse the Washington Congress given the Southern talent for politics and oratory. Exactly the same would happen in Ireland with their Parliament challenging the Imperial Parliament. 'Let, however, "the principle of giving Ireland an effective Government by Irishmen" be your principle as firmly as it is Mr Gladstone's',[68] he concluded. The collapse of the Liberals did not make Arnold an enthusiast for the new Tory Government under Lord Salisbury but he predicted that: 'we have some really interesting and fruitful political work before us – the establishment of a thorough system of local government.'[69]

Once the speeches were over Arnold concentrated on exploring the country. He and Flu went to the Niagara Falls where they boarded a steamer, the *Maid of the Mist*, and, dressed in sailor's waterproofs, sailed close through the spray to see 'the pale green sheets of water, the depth of a great ship, they say, pouring over the semi-circular rock for ever'.[70] His heart had started to give him trouble again, partly as a result of the summer heat, so he looked forward to returning to England at the end of August. He had a bad scare while bathing, just before he left, and it took him a week to get over the attack and to get back to that walking which meant so much to him. His general judgement of the United States after his second visit was that its 'capital defect' was that 'compared with life in England it is so uninteresting, so without savour and without depth'.[71] He also disliked the 'badness and ignobleness' of the newspapers: 'They are the worst feature in the life in the United States, and make me feel kindly even to the *Pall Mall Gazette*'.[72] And he told Charles Eliot Norton that he was 'more than doubtful about your pullulating colleges and universities'.[73] One can see here the foundations being laid for much subsequent English criticism of American culture.

On 4 September the Arnolds set sail from New York on the *Aurania*. A letter from Lucy had followed them on board and they wept over it. 'These pangs of longing pass off, but the intense love and fondness do not relax for a moment,'[74] he wrote to her from sea. The Arnolds were a very close and happy family and such separations were not easy for them. The voyage home, however, was a little better than the voyage out. Flu spent all day on deck and Arnold sat out there in the moonlight until 10 p.m. Flu busied herself administering grapes and pears to 'the suffering steerage passengers'[75] and soon they arrived at Liverpool on 13 September to be greeted by Dick and Ella, or 'the Dicks' as Arnold called them. They went straight to Manchester with Dick and Ella and then to Fox How where the Westmorland air seemed to perk Arnold up. Flu and Nelly were very anxious about his pains, and tried to 'keep me in leading strings', but one morning he managed to give them the slip – one of the servants called him 'Mr Fox' – and got out on the fells. He took the ascent slowly and, as he reported to Lucy: 'I had not a minute of pain all the way.'[76] He even managed some fishing at Rydal Head and in the Wharfe and then returned at last to Cobham at the beginning of October where it was still warm enough to take a rocking chair out on to the lawn and sit there with Kaiser at his side, in the gentle autumn sunshine.

Although Arnold has often seemed to be one of the presiding spirits in the academic study of English Literature, he responded to the enthusiasm of John Churton Collins, an early propagandist for the foundation of the academic discipline of 'Eng. Lit.', with some caution. He told Collins that: 'I have no difficulty in saying that I should be glad to see at the Universities not a new school established for Modern Literature or Modern Languages, but the great works of English Literature taken in conjunction with those of Greek and Latin Literature in the final Examination for honours in *Literae Human-iores*.'[77] Arnold believed too strongly in the value of Greek to be able to agree to a school of pure English Literature. His prescription for the direction of literary studies might have turned out to be an interesting one, and to have given the discipline greater breadth.

At the end of October, Arnold wrote to K about the political situation in a way which revealed his disillusionment at the 'drift' that seemed to be taking place. He said he wanted to write another political piece for Knowles 'simply to try to be of use by keeping people's eyes fixed on main issues'[78] and indeed: 'I should like to write one political article a year – only one – and an article of this nature.' He also revealed that although his leisure in retirement was now 'delightful' he could as yet 'hardly turn round, I have so many letters to answer and promises to fulfil'. And because they had been abroad for four months everyone wanted to invite them to dinner. 'The dining will abate presently,'[79] he wrote, hopefully, to Fan at the end of October. To Lucy in New York, he wrote: 'I am delighted with my new existence and when I have done making my adieux to my schools I shall go up [to London] but once a week.'[80] While he finished off various small writing tasks – such as an introduction to the stories of Mary Claude which he had promised her brother he would do – Flu was 'pottering about' the village selling copies of the parish magazine. He told Lucy that the following week 'my teachers give me something or other in silver and I should have to make a speech, alas!'

The speech was Arnold's farewell to a lifetime of school inspecting, the career that he had pursued with diligence for thirty-five years, and which had turned him, in addition to all his other public roles, into a leading advocate of universal State-aided education, an advocacy that today would make him seem too progressive by far, with even socialist parties in Britain eagerly embracing the private and partial solutions he regarded as the source of the problem that State education was to solve. That advocacy – during the debate about 'payment by results' – could easily have cost him his job for speaking out against his political masters, and in the long term may have explained his failure to win advancement. He was held in great affection by the teachers and students who had dealings with him and his annual reports – published in 1899 with an introduction by Lord Sandford and more fully as *Reports on Elementary Schools* in 1908 – were models of a clear and forceful prose rare in official documents.

On the evening of 12 November a group of friends and colleagues from Arnold's Westminster district gathered in St Peter's School, Lower Belgrave Street, under the chairmanship of E. T. Morgan, Headmaster of St James's School Westminster, to pay tribute to Arnold and to present him with a silver claret jug and salver. Knowing that he was among friends, Arnold was frank. Reviewing his obligations he began where they were least. 'To Government I owe nothing',[81] he declared to cheers and laughter, adding that although his work might have been more highly valued had he been an educationist abroad he might not have survived so long because of his outspokenness: 'Our Government here in England takes a large and liberal view of what it considers a man's private affairs, and so I have been enabled to survive as an inspector for 35 years.' He paid generous tribute to individual officials who were also personal friends, and to his assistants: 'And the teachers!'

In trying to account for the affection and goodwill of the teachers towards him he said that 'one cause of it was certainly that I was my father's son' and another was the deference paid to him as one 'more or less known to the public as an author'. But there were two much more important factors: as a believer in the true critical spirit, 'I from the first sought to see the schools as they really were', and secondly 'I got the habit, very early in my time, of trying to put myself in the place of the teachers whom I was inspecting'. That humane empathy was clearly his secret with the teachers. His remarks about the early inspecting days have already been noted but he concluded with a warm endorsement of the teachers' trade union, the National Union of Elementary Teachers – 'Some people would say it was too strong. I do not think so' and said it should use its strength to campaign for a Minister of

Education. He ended by describing the teachers as possessing an influence 'for good; it helps morality and virtue'.

Reporting the 'touching' evening to Lucy he wrote: 'I was afraid of a tea service . . . I could get through life with a wooden spoon and platter, but the jug and salver they have given me will look well on the sideboard.'[82] He also wrote to Tom: 'You must come and drink out of the teachers' claret jug.'[83] Arnold's remarks were reported in *The Times* and prompted a letter from Mundella at the Education Department protesting at some of his strictures about the behaviour of the Government towards him. Arnold wrote a placatory letter back, paying tribute to Mundella himself but insisting that the pension from Gladstone was not for his official work but for his literary achievements and that he was right in saying what he did. But he was prepared to let the matter go: 'Literature is henceforth my business, if at sixty-three it is not presumptuous to speak of having still a business.'[84]

With retirement now officially established, Arnold was looking forward to getting free of various obligations to editors – including his nephew Ted Arnold at *Murray's Magazine* – but expected this would not happen much before Easter 1887. 'I call it being free when one writes only what one is self-moved to write, not plagued into writing', he explained to Tom. In spite of the workload – which included a piece for Ted on the life of General Grant, a Preface for the popular edition of *St Paul and Protestantism*, and an entry on Sainte-Beuve for the *Encyclopaedia Britannica* – Arnold was able to tell Lucy as the year drew to a close: 'I am quite my old self again – walked about London all yesterday in the fog without choke or pain.'[85] But he did complain to Fan that the November fog under Box Hill at Dorking on a walk caused him some breathing difficulties. And on Christmas Day he skated on Pains Hill Lake to celebrate his having reached the age of 64. Thanking George Smith for a present (presumably something for the dinner or drinks table) he wrote that the gift would enable him 'when I have young people to dinner, even now in my extreme old age, to assume the airs of the rake and the man of pleasure'.[86]

5

Retirement to his cottage garden and the care of his fruit trees had not signalled the end of Arnold the controversialist and the January 1887 issue of the *Nineteenth Century* appeared with a critical article which in its title alluded to his onslaught on Liberalism the previous year. *The Zenith of Conservatism* (which was to be followed by two more articles on Lord Salisbury's Government later in the year) was a review of the current political situation which began with a skilful presentation of the author as 'an aged outsider'[87] who merely wished to be 'doing some little good by saying what many quiet people are thinking and wishing outside of the strife, phrases, and routine of professional politics'. In fact it was another excuse for Arnold to ride his hobby-horses rather than being a representative expression of the views of 'the plain people outside of the rivalry of parties'. It repeated his views on Ireland (local government but no separate Parliament, immediate suppression of the *United Irishman* as 'an incitement to crime and outrage') and a new topic he was just beginning to broach, Church Disestablishment in Wales. Arnold continued to tread the fine line between rejecting utterly the current mode of rule in Ireland – and the Protestant ascendancy, which he regarded as 'doomed'[88] – and advocating a system of local government which allowed for the continued connection with England. In America this position had even caused one newspaper to declare: MR ARNOLD SUPPORTS HOME RULE. He told Lord Suffolk that: 'Neither party will like what I have said in the *Nineteenth Century*',[89] but insisted that they needed to take account of the plain people if they wished to survive.

Arnold's own survival was increasingly exercising him. He was still skating 'though with a good deal of reluctance to try figures or skating backwards'[90] and in a letter of condolence to the American poet Mrs Florence Earle Coates on the death of her grandmother he observed: 'One should try to bring oneself to regard death as a quite natural event . . . For my part, since I was sixty I have regarded each year, as it ended, as something to the good beyond what I could naturally have expected.'[91] He revealed that he had thought 'my time was really coming to an end' during the summer in America but that, back in England, the pain brought on by the heat had diminished 'and now, in the friendly air of this dear, stupid old country, it has almost entirely disappeared'. Throughout these last years Arnold had regularly declined approaches from various literary societies to join or preside over their proceedings. Now that he was retired from official duties he felt entitled to regain some control over his life rather than for its shape to be determined by public demands. 'I am refusing every invitation to lecture and to make addresses this year, or I shall never establish my freedom',[92] he told Sydney Buxton MP.

To another correspondent he revived the fantasy of his youth of going to live in Italy: 'I have sometimes talked of ending my days in Florence, but somehow when it comes to uprooting myself from my cottage and garden here, I cannot do it.'[93] Not that this meant rustic seclusion. 'We dine out every night but one',[94] he reported to Lucy in the middle of March from London where the Arnolds had, as usual been spending the two worst winter months. Lucy, in turn, reported on the 'six little teeth in the mouth of the midget'. One of those dinners was attended by Gladstone who 'talked a great deal, but looked white, worn and old, and his voice quite gone – husky and extinguished'.[95]

After a brief visit to Hastings in the hope of easing an attack of lumbago, Arnold was back at Cobham in May to receive Lucy and Fred who had come over on the *Umbria* and who stayed for the summer. In June he wrote a long letter to the scholar Sidney Colvin, who had just published his book on the poet in the English Men of Letters series. Arnold had already given his view of Keats in his introduction to Ward's *English Poets* in 1880 (later included in the second series of *Essays in Criticism* (1888)) where he praised Keats's strength of character and 'lucidity' and argued that in his 'natural magic' he could rank with Shakespeare but that he lacked Shakespeare's 'faculty of moral interpretation' and the crucial gift of 'architectonics', the grand structure which lifts poetry above mere local felicity of expression. Arnold told Colvin that his praise for *La Belle Dame Sans Merci* 'is simply annoying to me',[96] although he liked the book in general. He approved the remarks on Keats and Spenser and recalled, in an observation interesting in that Arnold generally said very little about the Latin poets: 'How true it is that one's first master, or the first work of him one apprehends, strikes the note for us; I feel this of the 4th Eclogue of Virgil, which I took into my system at 9 yrs old, having been flogged through the preceding Eclogues and learnt nothing from them.' Arnold admitted that he had scribbled next to Colvin's reference to Keats loading every rift with ore the word 'dangerous'. He was keeping faith with the argument of the 1853 Preface.

His own poetry, he knew, would never come again after the last poem was written in April on the death of Kaiser the mongrel dachshund who left now only Max as an ageing companion for his master. *Kaiser Dead*, Arnold's last poem, was published in the *Fortnightly* in July, and as a last poem probably deserves our indulgence in spite of its occasional banality ('Six years ago I brought him down / A baby dog, from London town'). The 'plain stave' contains, however, some amusing digs at Tennyson and Gladstone and shows how much animals meant to Arnold for their companionship: 'To us, declining tow'rds our end, / A mate how dear!' He wrote to Grant Duff that his friend's regard for his verse grew more precious 'as one begins to apprehend in every fresh thing one attempts, the flagging and failure of old age'.[97] 'I do not know whether I shall do any more poetry, but it is something to be of use in prose',[98] he wrote philosophically to Charles Eliot Norton. These remarks imply that Arnold may have been trying to write more poetry in his last years but he was clearly unsuccessful for we have nothing between *Poor Matthias* in 1882 and *Kaiser Dead* five years later.

Arnold was even less successful in his laments for human beings. He had to decline a request from the widow of Shairp for a contribution to a memoir because, as he explained to Professor William Knight, he had failed in a similar request concerning Theodore Walrond and 'it does not come naturally to me to speak of my dead friends in this fashion, and what one does not do naturally one never does well'.[99] This echoes his difficulties with Clough, and explains the only qualified successes of his elegies for his father and for Stanley. As far as memoirs of himself went, he had to write to Percy Bunting, editor of the *Contemporary*, to quash a rumour that he was writing an autobiography in the leisure of his retirement at Cobham.

Arnold spent the last summer holiday of his life at Fox How (after visiting K in Yorkshire), in Scotland and in South Wales. He was finding it difficult now to climb mountains but his passion for fishing was undiminished. George Venables, brother of Richard Venables, vicar of Clyro, in Radnorshire in Mid-Wales, who figures frequently in the pages of the diary of the Reverend Francis Kilvert, had a house at Llysdinam, in Powys (where Kilvert often stayed in the 1870s). 'On my way to pay a visit in Glamorganshire', he wrote to Venables, 'I want to turn aside and see something of the upper parts of South Wales which I have never visited. When I am in that land of rivers I shall want to fish.'[100] After a week with Lord Coleridge at Ottery St Mary in Devon the Arnolds were heading for the Bensons at the Gower but Arnold wanted to detach himself from the party and go off on his own to fish the upper Wye. 'I like fishing because I so much like rivers, or like rivers because I so much like fishing, but I rather think the former; hardly anything gives me so much pleasure as to see a new and beautiful river', [101] he wrote to Venables in accepting the offer of a few days' hospitality in October at Llysdinam on the Wye. Later that month, Arnold wrote to Tom from Fairy Hill, Swansea: 'I have at last done what I have for more than forty years wanted to do – have seen the Upper Wye. I have a passion for beautiful rivers in general, and for the Wye, that "wanderer of the woods" in particular . . . I am full of desires to take some house still further up next summer, and to explore the lateral valleys; the tourist is still almost unknown in these blessed regions.' [102] Arnold, however, would not see another summer.

Returning to Cobham he resumed work on an essay on Shelley, and in December an essay on *Count Leo Tolstoi* appeared in the *Fortnightly*. It was the only article, apart from that on George Sand, which Arnold devoted to a novelist, though he was a keen reader of novels. Tolstoy was now sixty and in his phase of religious simplicity. After a summary of *Anna Karenina*, Arnold discusses this aspect of the man who was a 'great soul and a great writer' and playfully suggests that, in an English village like Cobham, Tolstoy's ascetic injunction to 'the satisfied classes' to earn their bread by the work of their hands would cause 'dismay' to the local tradesmen who would say: 'pray stick to your articles, your poetry, and nonsense; in manual labour you will interfere with us, and be taking the bread out of our mouths'. [103] A similar robust scepticism from the lifelong admirer of Swift and Voltaire is present in his essay on *Amiel*.

At the end of November, Arnold wrote to Lady de Rothschild: 'after Christmas I mean to boycott my Editors', [104] an aspiration that was unlikely to be fulfilled.

6

At the beginning of January 1888, Arnold wrote to George Brodrick, the Warden of Merton College, Oxford to say: 'I am just off for the North to make a horrid discourse about America at Hull and at

Bradford; I have then to prepare a horrid discourse about Milton, and a horrid article on Welsh Disestablishment – all before the middle of February.'[105] Arnold was supposed to be in retirement, devoting himself to those literary projects which came naturally to him rather than at the importunate command of editors or public men. But he was not to be let off so lightly, and indeed might well have reflected that his best work in prose had come about precisely in response to those pressures. For a Grub Street writer (the designation which Arnold was so fond of using) freedom may not be merely illusory. It may actually be undesirable. He confided to Lady de Rothschild that the first of these 'horrid' performances was on 'a very ticklish subject'[106] – the quality of civilisation in America. Before this, however, she was reading his latest essay in the *Nineteenth Century*. 'You know how I like to think of your reading what I write', he told her.

The essay was prompted by Professor Edward Dowden's life of Shelley which Arnold deplored as the very worst kind of literary biography – overblown, over-written, speculative, prurient, and lacking in critical and moral judgement. Unfortunately, Arnold had little to say about Shelley's poetry that might expand on his famous throwaway remark at the end of his essay on *Byron*: 'Shelley, beautiful and ineffectual angel, beating in the void his luminous wings in vain.'[107] The essay shows the powerful influence of Sainte-Beuve – the modern critic Arnold admired above all others – in its mixture of relaxed summary, generous quotation, biographical emphasis and acute criticism. In particular, Arnold took issue, on moral grounds, with Dowden's biassed account of Shelley's affair with Mary and of his cruel treatment of Harriet Westbrook. 'After reading his book, one feels sickened for ever of the subject of irregular relations.' For all his considerable love of life and its pleasures and his marked distaste for the ascetic, Arnold had a very old-fashioned attitude to the presentation of anything other than strict morals in art and literature.

The first of the New Year's horrid discourses was delivered on 31 January at the Literary and Philosophical Society at Hull, at the Philosophical Society at Bradford three days later, and again at Bristol on 8 March. It was published as *Civilisation in the United States* in the April number of the *Nineteenth Century*. Following two earlier pieces (*A Word about America* and *A Word More about America*), the address returned to Arnold's theme of the shortcomings of American civilisation. In his opening remarks to the Hull audience he joked about being inclined to follow the example of the Greek moralist Theophrastus, 'who waited, before composing his famous *Characters*, until he was ninety-nine years old'.[108] His argument was that the United States had solved 'the political and social problem' but there was still work to do on 'the human problem' or as Plato put it: *how to live?* Arnold admired much in the USA, including its more democratic, less hidebound flavour and manners, the lack of English snobbery and stiffness – 'we on the contrary are so little homogeneous, we are living with a system of classes so intense, with institutions and society so little modern, so unnaturally complicated, that the whole actions of our minds is hampered and falsified by it; we are in consequence wanting in lucidity, we do not see clear or think straight, and the Americans have here much the advantage of us.'

But Arnold would not leave it there. He felt that in the area of spiritual perfection the Americans left something to be desired and were, like Mr Bottles, a little too good at congratulating themselves on how well they had done materially, forgetting the more important characters of civilisation. Arnold attacked the ugliness of the names of US towns and the nature of their newspapers. He was no doubt still smarting from the rough treatment they had handed out to him, including the famous Chicago hoax during his 1883 trip when a New York paper fabricated a criticism of Chicago purporting to have been written by Arnold, which was picked up and reported in the *Pall Mall Gazette*. Arnold argued that the cult of the average man in US democracy was the enemy of 'what is elevated and beautiful, of what is interesting' – in a reprise of the argument of *Numbers*.

He also warned that England would increasingly feel the influence of American civilisation such that the problem would become hers, too. 'As our country becomes more democratic', Arnold argued, the US malady would replace his now much-iterated English cultural malady of 'an upper-class materialised, a middle-class vulgarised, and a lower-class brutalised' with a new malady: 'the predominance of the common and ignoble, born of the predominance of the average man'. With his customary plain speaking Arnold had identified a problem that would only grow during the rest of his century and throughout the twentieth century, the conundrum that lies at the heart of democracy – how can a legitimate system of rule by the many rather than the few (and Arnold never doubted its legitimacy for an instant), nevertheless succeed in, as Arnold put it elsewhere, 'keeping high ideals'. A few weeks before he died, Arnold returned to this theme in an address on Milton who possessed, he believed, the rare excellence of a great style which he owed to 'that bent of nature for inequality which to the worshippers of the average man is so unacceptable'.[109]

To Alfred Austin, editor of the *National Review*, Arnold now promised a piece on *Disestablishment in Wales* which would appear in the March number and which offered a characteristic compromise. The undeniable injustice of an Anglican Establishment, with its property, tithes and privileges, in a country large parts of which worshipped in another Church, could be remedied, Arnold believed, not by disestablishment, but by making Welsh Presbyterianism the Established Church in those areas of Wales where it was the majority religion and leaving the others in the Anglican Establishment. After delivering this piece (for a Tory paper, expressing the hope that the Tories in their present incarnation were more open and reasonable than they had been for a long time) Arnold told Austin: 'then I turn to Lucifer'.[110]

He told Lucy that he was reading the later volumes of the correspondence of George Sand and would like to write an article on her old age. Instead, he was being harried for an address on Milton to be delivered at the installation of a memorial window at St Margaret's Church, Westminster. 'I hate delivering things,' he told Lucy, 'and I hate to have a subject found for me instead of occurring of itself to my mind.'[111] To the American poet Florence Coates, he disclosed another principle with him, not to write about 'the literary performances of living contemporaries or contemporaries only recently dead. Therefore I am not likely to write about Tourguenieff, though I admire him greatly'.[112] This was an unfortunate prohibition – for an essay on Tennyson, for example, would have been most valuable and might have explained the roots of Arnold's objection to him. It would have been equally interesting to have had his considered view on Swinburne, Browning and Clough as poets he knew and admired in varying degrees.

7

Towards the end of March, Arnold made his last visit to see Lady de Rothschild at Aston Clinton and then began to look forward eagerly to the arrival of Lucy and her child, Eleanor. 'I long to have the Midget here,' he wrote just before she and Fred left New York on the *Aurania*, hoping to arrive at Liverpool by Sunday 15 April. Arnold and Flu left Cobham on Saturday 14 April for Liverpool where they stayed with the Croppers at their large house at Dingle Bank next to the Mersey. The previous Thursday they had attended the funeral in Leicestershire of Mary's husband.

Arnold's younger sister, Susy, had married John Cropper, a Liverpool businessman, in 1858 and Cropper advised Arnold on financial investments from time to time.

The Croppers were an odd family, descending from James Cropper, the son of a yeoman farmer, who was born in the eighteenth century at Winstanley, near Ormskirk in the Lancashire hinterland of Liverpool. He bought the 30-acre site of Dingle Bank in 1823 and built the house at a time when he was growing fabulously wealthy as a ship-owner. His wealth, however, was accompanied by a strong Quaker philanthropic streak and he was prominent in the anti-slavery movement and other 'unconventional and sometimes weird philanthropic experiments'[113] as his biographer puts it. At Dingle Bank – described by Arthur Stanley after a visit as 'the Paradise of the North' – the Croppers in John's father's day were constantly reminded of the evils of slavery by a dinner-service on which the pleading faces of chained black slaves would look up, each holding up his hands to exclaim, variously: 'Am I not a man and a brother?' or 'Remember them that are in bonds.' A visitor to the house reported that it was 'impregnated with holiness'. By the time Arnold was a visitor the perfervid atmosphere had probably lifted and he was reported on this weekend to be lively and playful.

On the fine Saturday evening of 14 April he went for a walk with John Cropper and, after what the *Liverpool Courier* later called 'one ineffective attempt',[114] succeeded in leaping gaily over a low, three-foot iron railing near the house 'with the lightheartedness of a boy'. (This recalled a similar leap, back in the 1840s as a Balliol undergraduate, when he had jumped over the spiked railings at Wadham.) This exertion was, for a long time, taken as the occasion of Arnold's final seizure, but in fact he had nearly another twenty-four hours of eager anticipation at Lucy's imminent arrival and of dining and letter-writing ahead of him.

The next morning Arnold attended a service at a nearby Presbyterian Church, in Sefton Park, in accordance with his habit of always seeking out an interesting sermon from whatever pulpit – this time from the Reverend John Watson – and returned on foot to Dingle

Bank for what another local newspaper called 'a hearty dinner'[115] after which he scribbled a note and, hearing that the *Aurania* had docked, set off eagerly for the landing stage. The day before setting off for Liverpool, Arnold had been seen at the Athenaeum 'conversing with many friends . . . and showing no signs of failing health or of any lack of power' and all day Saturday had been 'as happy and bright as he always was when with his family'.[116] He set off with Flu, walking briskly along Dingle Lane to catch a tram to the docks, probably over-excited at the prospect of seeing Lucy and the Midget, when he suddenly fell forward and collapsed, just opposite the old Toxteth Chapel. Although he had dropped outside the house of Dr William Little (the latter aroused by a 'violent ringing at his front door bell') there was little the doctor could do. A crowd had gathered in the street as Arnold was carried into Dr Little's study and laid on his couch. He was still alive, though unconscious, but, in spite of having spirits poured down his throat, after a few minutes Little pronounced him dead at 2.45 p.m. The doctor's view was that the state of excitement Arnold was in, rather than his physical exertion the previous night, was the immediate cause of the heart attack. The doctor told the press that Arnold was 'a fine-looking man of probably about seventeen stone weight, with refined features'.

The body was taken back to Dingle Bank where the distraught family retreated – even from the Lord Bishop of Liverpool, Dr Ryle, who left his calling card. They were joined by Dick who had just been getting out of his cab 'when my uncle met us with the sad and dreadful news'.[117] Dick was bereft at the loss of his indulgent father who had so often bailed him out of his financial difficulties: 'My dear father', he wrote several days later to Professor William Knight, 'I can scarcely yet realize what I have lost and that I shall never hear his voice or have his advice and help again: to his children he was not only the kindest, most indulgent of fathers, but the dearest most intimate of friends as well.' Flu, with the kind of quiet clarity and dignity her husband would have admired, wrote simply to Browning: 'He was all in all to me and to his children, and the world seems indeed empty. I can only thank God I was with him when the end came, and that he passed away as he had wished – in a moment!'[118]

At 9.45 a.m. on Tuesday 17 April the coffin was placed in a closed hearse and driven to Lime Street Station where fate had one last trick to play on the man who, a quarter of a century earlier had criticised both the ugliness of English names and the brutality of a brief newspaper report of a young inmate of a workhouse who had just killed her baby by quoting the words: 'Wragg is in custody.'[119] The clergyman standing on the steps of the railway station at 10.20 a.m. to receive the coffin was the Reverend J. T. Slugg. Four railway porters carried the coffin to the brake van at the back of the saloon attached to the 11.05 London train and, after stopping briefly a few minutes later at Edge Hill station to collect Flu and the rest of the family, the remains of Arnold set off on the journey back to Cobham.

On the morning of Wednesday 18 April – a lovely spring day alternating bright sun and showers – a special train left London's Waterloo Station at 10.45 a.m. for Staines carrying the mourners who drove the final stage from Staines to Laleham. Those who had glanced over breakfast at *The Times* – a newspaper which in its cruder days in the 1860s Arnold had so frequently attacked – would have read a generous tribute in that morning's edition which concluded: 'The whole educated intelligence of England will stand in spirit among the mourners today by the open grave at Laleham.'[120] As the hearse made its way by road from Staines to Laleham some old villagers who had known Arnold in his youth came out to pay their respects to Dr Arnold's son. The service itself was bleak and unadorned. No hymns were sung; no music was played. The signs of grief among the congregation were noted by the newspapers and, as they moved outside, the renewed rainfall, combined with the cracked, emotional voice of Arnold's old friend, Archdeacon Farrar, who was conducting the service, intensified what the *Liverpool Echo* headlined the AFFECTING SCENE.

Young Stephen Coleridge, the son of another lifelong friend, Lord Coleridge, found himself standing at the graveside between the Master of Balliol, Jowett, and the historian, Lecky. 'Never before nor since has there been gathered together in that little church such a concourse of famous men as met there to pay the last tribute of honour and affection to this universally beloved man of genius',[121] he later wrote. Browning, too, was at the graveside, with George Smith, Mundella, Lord Sandford, Augustus Hare, Yates Thompson, the Arnold family, a friend from Liverpool, George Melly (great-uncle of the writer and jazz singer of the present day), and many others. The ex-President of the National Union of Elementary Teachers and representatives of the Westminster Teachers 'Association were also there. And the bulky form of Henry James threaded its way through the mourners. The oak coffin was covered in floral wreaths from Tennyson, Millais, Lady de Rothschild and many other famous men and women. But perhaps the most moving tribute of all read simply: 'from St Stephen's School,

Westminster, where Matthew Arnold's annual presence, genial, kindly, encouraging, discriminating in sympathy, was welcomed as sunshine in the monotony of school life'.[122]

8

In the weeks and months following Arnold's death the obituaries and assessments were copious and generous. A recurring theme was the sense that somehow Arnold had not received his just deserts, at least in terms of public recognition of his achievement. *The Times* put its finger on the issue: 'The best the State ever did for him was to set the poet, the thinker, the analyst of beauty, the subtle theorist, to the task of examining national schoolchildren in spelling, the rules of arithmetic, and plain sewing.'[123]

Flu lived on at Pains Hill Cottage, initially keeping her husband's room and its contents just as they had been when he was alive (the cottage was demolished in the late 1960s without anyone making much of a fuss). The year after her husband's death Nelly was married and Flu wrote to Browning on that occasion: 'You can, I am sure, imagine all it is to me to be without him, and all the conflict of feeling in my heart just now.'[124] Lucy's second child, a boy, was born two months after the funeral but died twenty-four hours later and was buried next to his grandfather in the grave at Laleham.

Shortly afterwards, Flu wrote: 'I have often thought that from the austere tone of some of his poems, those who did not know him, could never have imagined his really bright, genial, loveable nature and that he, indeed, was "consoled by spirits gloriously gay" and his knowledge of the uncertain state of his health never depressed him. I *cannot* write of what it is to be without him.'[125]

Dick and Ella later moved to Worcester, where, keen amateur musicians, they befriended a young unknown composer who was to reward Dick with immortality by making him the dedicatee, as 'RPA' (Richard Penrose Arnold) of one of his *Enigma Variations*. Tom married again after the death of his first wife, Julia, and lived until 1900. Fan, the lone survivor at Fox How, lived on until she was nearly ninety – dictating her last letters in the 1920s and signing them in a spidery hand.

She saw the Great War come and go, and with it some of the high-minded faith in the future that characterised Arnoldian liberalism. In the spring of 1915 she wrote: 'I try not to be cowardly and weak, but when you are nearly 82 it is very difficult to keep brave while the world you have known so long is lying in ruins around us. It is a great help to look up at the everlasting hills and to be reminded by them of the help and strength which "cometh from the Lord".'[126]

9

'I always think that, beautiful and graceful as his prose is, he will be best remembered by his poetry',[127] Flu wrote a few months after her husband's death. In the years after Arnold's death that prophecy more and more came to be fulfilled. He could certainly have wished to have written more poetry but what he did write will live as long as the language. The nature of his busy and varied life meant that he wrote less but also that he wrote less that was indifferent. Many more productive poets would trade a little of their bulk for a *Scholar-Gipsy*, a *Dover Beach*, a *Forsaken Merman*.

Arnold's life – lived as we now know under the permanent shadow of a hereditary heart disease that gave him little expectation that he would survive for as long as he did – has a satisfactory completeness. He died as he wished to die, in the full possession of his energies and his faculties, having completed a body of literary work – in poetry and in criticism – that has become more impressive with time and is perhaps only now beginning to emerge into full view from behind the shadow of partial neglect and partial or partisan misreading. Arnold himself – in spite of his airs and his *chutzpah* – grows likewise in stature as the life he led, a life dedicated in all its facets to writing and the life of the mind, comes to seem exemplary. Not content to achieve success in one field or to turn his back on the society in which he lived for the sake of mere personal ambition, Arnold brought to an age of transition, a modern age, trying to find its way through uncertainty and rapid change, a voice that it needed to hear, that could, in a characteristic term from the lexicon of Victorian high seriousness, 'help' it.

It was not the dreamy, romantic voice of Newman heard from an

Oxford pulpit in the 1840s which he had idealised. It was a recognisably modern voice – graceful, intelligent, thoughtful, deeply enmeshed in the messy, contingent detail of modern society, but defending its own right to speak freely, pertinently, and without being cowed by the conventional wisdom. No society is ever over-endowed with such voices. No society – whether it be that of the mid-Victorian period or our own – can afford not to listen to what such voices feel compelled to say.

NOTES

Abbreviations

Allott	*The Poems of Matthew Arnold* (1979), ed. Kenneth Allott, second edition, rev. by Miriam Allott.
Balliol MS	Manuscript letters at Balliol College, Oxford.
Bodleian MS	Manuscript letters in Bodleian Library, Oxford.
Bonnerot	*Matthew Arnold – Poète* (1947), Louis Bonnerot, Paris.
British Museum MS	Manuscript letters in the British Library.
Brotherton MS	Manuscript letters, diaries, Arnold family papers, Special Collection, Brotherton Library, University of Leeds.
Buckler	*Matthew Arnold's Books: Towards a Publishing Diary* (1958), W. E. Buckler, Geneva.
CL	*The Letters of Matthew Arnold to Arthur Hugh Clough* (1932), ed. H. F. Lowry.
Clough, Letters	*Correspondence of Arthur Hugh Clough* (1957), ed. F. L. Mulhauser.
CPW	*The Complete Prose Works of Matthew Arnold* (1960–77), ed. R. H. Super (11 vols), Ann Arbor, University of Michigan.
Davis	*Matthew Arnold's Letters: A Descriptive Checklist* (1968), Arthur Kyle Davis, Charlottesville, University of Virginia.
Guthrie	*Matthew Arnold's Diaries, The Unpublished Items: A Transcription and Commentary* (1957), unpublished thesis by William Bell Guthrie, University of Virginia.
Honan	*Matthew Arnold: A Life* (1981), Park Honan.
L	*Letters of Matthew Arnold, 1848–88* (1895), ed. G. W. E. Russell (2 vols).
Liverpool City Libraries MS	Manuscript diaries of Lord Derby.
Microfilm UVA	Copies of letters in the A. K. Davis Collection, Alderman Library, University of Virginia.
Notebooks	*The Notebooks of Matthew Arnold* (1952), ed. H. F. Lowry, K. Young, W. H. Dunn.
Tinker & Lowry	*The Poetry of Matthew Arnold: A Commentary*

	(1940), C. B. Tinker and H. E. Lowry.
Trilling	*Matthew Arnold* (second edition, 1949), Lionel Trilling, New York.
UL	*Unpublished Letters of Matthew Arnold* (1923), ed. Arnold Whitridge, New Haven, Yale.
Ullmann	*The Yale Manuscript* (1989), ed. S. O. A. Ullmann, Ann Arbor, University of Michigan.
University of Birmingham MS	Harriet Martineau papers in Special Collection.
Yale MS	Collection of MA's manuscript letters, notebooks, diaries, etc.

Preface

1. E. M. Forster, *Two Cheers for Democracy* (1951), p. 202.
2. Steiner's alleged indictment of Arnold for failing to anticipate the horrors of the twentieth century is reported in Stefan Collini, *Matthew Arnold: A Critical Portrait* (1994), p. 133. In a private communication to the present author, Professor Steiner says: 'I simply pointed out the differences between a "local" thought and sensibility of stature and that of a "world-rank" thought such as Nietzsche's or Marx's contemporary with it. Notably in reference to the nearing collapse of the "Hebraic–Hellenic" order of values.'

Chapter One

1. Balliol MS, 20 December 1864. Letter to Mrs Arnold.
2. Brotherton MS. Mrs Arnold's Diary.
3. See 'Introduction', Arnold Whitridge, *Doctor Arnold of Rugby* (1928), p. xviii.
4. *On the Study of Celtic Literature*, CPW.I.
5. See Brian Cheyette, *Constructions of 'The Jew' in English Literature and Society* (1994).
6. Lytton Strachey, *Eminent Victorians* (1918).
7. See Arthur Stanley, *Life and Correspondence of Thomas Arnold* DD (1884), Ch. IX, p. 340, where the doubts appear to be 'whether the Epistle to the Hebrews did not belong to a period subsequent to the Apostolical age' and 'the indiscriminate use of the Baptismal and Burial Services'.
8. Whitridge, *op. cit*. See also Stanley, *op. cit*.; N. Wymer, *Dr Arnold of Rugby* (1953); T. W. Bamford, *Thomas Arnold* (1960); M. McCrum, *Thomas Arnold* (1989) – a more acute analysis of the educationist.
9. Rev. T. Mozley, *Reminiscences: chiefly of Oriel College and the Oxford Movement* (1882), p. 52.
10. Edith Morley (ed.), *The Correspondence of Crabb Robinson With the Wordsworth Circle* (1927), p. 6.
11. J. Bertram (ed.), *New Zealand Letters of Thomas Arnold the Younger* (1966).

12. Goldwin Smith, *Reminiscences* (1910), pp. 70–71.
13. Whitridge, *op. cit.*, p. 204.
14. 'Maurice de Guérin' in *Essays in Criticism*, 1st series.
15. 'Joubert' in *Essays in Criticism*, 1st series.
16. 'Pagan and Mediaeval Religious Sentiment', *Essays in Criticism*, 1st series.
17. Brotherton MS. July 1836 addendum to *The History of Jane's Life*.
18. Wilfrid Ward, *Aubrey de Vere: A Memoir* (1904), p. 68.
19. Balliol MS. Letter to Tom, 24 February nd.
20. John Morley, *Recollections* (1917), p. 125.
21. See, for example, A. L. Rowse, *Matthew Arnold: Poet and Prophet* (1976), p. 12.
22. See, for example, Bonnerot, p. 39. For Bonnerot, Arnold was 'un poète dont l'intelligence prévaut souvent sur la sensibilité'.
23. Rev. A. B. Baldwin (ed.), *The Penroses of Fledborough Parsonage* (1933, Hull).
24. *Ibid*.
25. Philip Guedalla, *Mary Arnold* (1928).
26. Tom Arnold, *Passages in a Wandering Life* (1900), p. 2.
27. Clough, Letters, 30 July 1852, p. 319.
28. Balliol MS. Letter to Mrs Arnold, 9 November 1862.
29. Balliol MS. Letter to Mrs Arnold, 16 December 1868.
30. Balliol MS. Letter to Mrs Arnold, 1 August 1868.
31. *The Strayed Reveller*, ll. 180–83: 'They see the ferry / On the broad, clay-laden / Lone Chorasmian stream . . .'
32. See Laurie Magnus (ed.), *Poems of Matthew Arnold*, nd, Introduction, where a suggestive distinction between the 'thalassic' and the 'potamic' imagination is drawn.
33. Balliol MS. Letter to Tom Arnold, 19 October 1887.
34. Brotherton MS. Mrs Arnold's diary, 1828.
35. See Lionel Trilling, *Matthew Arnold* (1939) for the symbolic significance of the christening (p. 36), Keble and Dr Arnold representing the two worlds, one dead, one powerless to be born.
36. Brotherton MS. Mrs Arnold's diary, 1824.
37. Brotherton MS. Mrs Arnold's diary, 1825.
38. Brotherton MS. 1836.
39. Brotherton MS. Mrs Arnold's diary, 1824.
40. Brotherton MS. Mrs Arnold's diary, 1826.
41. Brotherton MS. Mrs Arnold's diary, 1826.
42. Brotherton MS. *History of Jane's Life*, 1836.
43. Trilling, *op. cit.*, p. 72 calls it 'the Rugby Iliad'.
44. Wymer, *op. cit.*, p. 8.
45. *Ibid.*, p. 85.
46. *Ibid.*, p. 90.
47. Brotherton MS. Mrs Arnold's diary, 1828.
48. Wymer, *op. cit.* p. 91.
49. *Ibid.*, p. 109.
50. Brotherton MS. Mrs Arnold's diary, February 1830.

51. Brotherton MS. Mrs Arnold's diary, 22 October 1829.
52. Brotherton MS.
53. Letter in 'An Arnold Family Album', *The Arnoldian*, 1989–90, Vol. XV, No. 3.
54. Brotherton MS, 18 October 1831.
55. Brotherton MS, 21 March 1832.
56. Brotherton MS, 28 July 1832.
57. Balliol MS., 23 September 1832. Letter from Tom Arnold.
58. Tom Arnold, *op.cit.*
59. Arnold Family Album, 19 September 1832, *loc.cit.*
60. Henry Crabb Robinson, *op.cit.*
61. Quoted by Stephen Gill in *William Wordsworth: A Life* (1989), p. 347.
62. *Letters of William Wordsworth*, ed. Alan Hill (1984), pp. 313–14.
63. Brotherton MS, Mrs Arnold's diary, February 1837.
64. Quoted in Mrs Humphry [Mary Augusta] Ward, *A Writer's Recollections* (1918), p. 77.
65. Brotherton MS, 21 March 1832.
66. Stanley, *op. cit.* Letter to Rev. John Tucker, p. 197, February 1833.
67. Tom Arnold, *op. cit.* p. 10.
68. Microfilm UVA, Letter to Trevenen Penrose, 15 December 1833.
69. For the texts of these early poems see Allott, p. 612 ff.
70. Yale MS. Letter to Martha Buckland, 14 May 1836. Also in Allott, pp. 617–18.
71. Brotherton MS. See also Allott, pp. 618–20.
72. Brotherton MS. Letter to Willy and Susy Arnold, 10 July 1836.
73. Brotherton MS. Mrs Arnold's letter, nd, but see also Allott, p. 621.
74. Balliol MS. Letter to Tom Arnold, 7 December [1884?].
75. Bamford, *op.cit.* p. 108, quoting letter of Thomas Arnold to Sir Thomas Pasley, 15 April 1835.
76. Brotherton MS. Mrs Arnold's 1836 diary. Full text in Allott, pp. 622–3.
77. Tom Arnold, *op. cit.*, p. 14.
78. Sir Llewellyn Woodward, *The Age of Reform* (1938, 2nd edn, 1962).
79. Balliol MS. 1837 Travel Journal of Matthew Arnold.
80. Clough, Letters, 26 August 1837, p. 63.
81. Balliol MS. 'Rugby School Fifth Form 1837' notebook. Text in Allott, pp. 714–16 with prose translation by Francis Cairns.
82. Brotherton MS. Dr Arnold's diary 1837.
83. Mrs Humphry Ward, *op. cit*, p. 23.
84. Yale MS. Letter from Fanny Lucy [Mrs] Arnold to Arthur Galton, 24 August 1894.
85. The Fox How poems are in Allott, p. 624ff.
86. Balliol MS. Typescript unsigned but attributed to Mrs Humphry Ward (Moorman collection).
87. Brotherton MS. Dr Arnold's diary, 1838.
88. Tom Arnold, *op. cit.* p. 38.

89. *Ibid.*, p. 45.
90. *Ibid.*, p. 47.
91. Brotherton MS, September 1839. Partial text in Wymer, *op. cit.* p. 151.
92. Dr Arnold quoted in Wymer, p. 186.
93. Edmund Gosse, *Athenaeum*, 28 April 1888, No. 3157, pp. 533–4.
94. E. H. Bradby, *Pall Mall Gazette*, 2 January 1892.
95. Brotherton MS. Letter of Mrs Arnold, 15 May 1840.
96. Brotherton MS, 30 August 1840. Letter to 'My Dear Aunts'.
97. K. Lake (ed.), *Memorials of William Charles Lake* (1901), p. 161, quoting letter from Dr Arnold to Lake, 17 August 1840.
98. Clough, Letters, 16 November 1840, p. 73.
99. Honan, p. 46, quoting *The Times*.
100. *Ibid.*, p. 186.
101. Allott, pp. 632–3.
102. Brotherton MS. Diary of Dr Arnold, 8 July 1841.

Chapter Two

1. *Thyrsis*, 11.141–2.
2. CPW. XI.382. 8 March 1888. 'Remarks at University College, Bristol'.
3. Clough, Letters, 10 November 1841, p. 84.
4. Quoted in E. K. Chambers, *Matthew Arnold: A Study* (1947), p. 6.
5. Mrs Humphry Ward, *A Writer's Recollections* (1918), p. 11.
6. UL.59. Letter from J. H. Newman to MA, 3 December 1871.
7. *Discourses in America*, 'Emerson', CPW. X.175.
8. E. G. Sandford (ed.), *Memoirs of Archbishop Temple by Seven Friends* (1906).
9. E. H. Coleridge (ed.), *Life and Correspondence of John Duke Lord Coleridge* (1904), p. 76.
10. *Ibid.*, p. 76.
11. Tom Arnold, *Passages in a Wandering Life* (1900), p. 59.
12. G.W.E. Russell, *Matthew Arnold* (1904), p. 204.
13. Friedrich Max-Müller, *My Autobiography: A Fragment* (1901), pp. 272–73.
14. Tom Arnold, *op. cit.*, p. 58.
15. George Sand, *Indiana* (trans. Sylvia Raphael, 1994), p. 191.
16. For a more extensive account of this widespread influence see Patricia Thomson, *George Sand and the Victorians (1977)*. Also Ruth apRobert, 'Matthew Arnold and George Sand', *Essays and Studies* (1988), pp. 96–107.
17. *Mixed Essays*, CPW.VII 'George Sand'.
18. *Ibid.*
19. Balliol MS. Letter to Mrs Arnold, 16 October 1869.
20. *Discourses in America* (1885), 'Emerson', CPW.X.165.
21. CL.111.
22. See James Simpson. 'Arnold and Goethe' in *Matthew Arnold*

(1975), ed. K. Allott, pp. 286–318.

23. UL, 65–66.

24. CPW.III.110.

25. Thomas Arnold, *Introductory Lectures on Modern History* (1842), p. 52.

26. Text in Allott, pp. 635–36.

27. Quoted by Tom Arnold, *op. cit.* p. 56.

28. Brotherton MS, Notes by A. P. Stanley, Rugby, 5 December 1841.

29. Brotherton MS, 2 February 1842.

30. Quoted by Alan Harris, 'Matthew Arnold: The Unknown Years', *The Nineteenth Century*, April 1933, p. 501.

31. Tom Arnold, now identified as the author of 'Matthew Arnold, by One Who Knew Him Well'. Obituary notice in the *Guardian*, 18 May 1888.

32. Friedrich Max-Müller, *Auld Lang Syne* (1898), p. 124.

33. Tom Arnold, *loc. cit.*

34. Microfilm UVA. Letter to Archibald Tait, 3 August 1842.

35. Max-Müller, *Auld Lang Syne* (1898), p. 111.

36. J.C. Shairp, *Glen Dessary and Other Poems* (1888), ed. F. Palgrave.

37. Warren Anderson, 'Arnold's Undergraduate Syllabus', *The Arnoldian* [now ceased publication], Winter 1979, pp. 2–6.

38. Coleridge, *op. cit.*, p. 126.

39. Wilfrid Ward, *William George Ward and the Oxford Movement* (1899), p. 432.

40. Tinker and H. F. Lowry, *The Poetry of Matthew Arnold: A Commentary* (1940), p. 325.

41. Coleridge, *op. cit.*, Letter to John Duke Coleridge, 2 March 1843, p. 124.

42. John Morley, *Nineteenth Century Essays* (1970), ed. Peter Stansky, p. 351.

43. Tom Arnold, *Guardian*, *loc. cit.*

44. *Culture and Anarchy*, Chapter 6, CPW.V.217.

45. Anthony Kenny (ed.), *The Oxford Diaries of Arthur Hugh Clough* (1990).

46. Coleridge, *op. cit.*

47. Tom Arnold. *Guardian, loc. cit.*

48. Coleridge, *op. cit.*, Letter to John Duke Coleridge, 28 July 1844, p. 145.

49. Max–Müller, *Auld Lang Syne*, pp. 111–12.

50. Max–Müller, *My Autobiography*, p. 272.

51. See for example George Watson, *The Literary Critics* (1962), p. 152 who deplores his 'high-bred disdain'.

52. Tom, Arnold, *Guardian, loc. cit.*

53. Goldie Levy, *Arthur Hugh Clough* (1938), p. 13. See also Katherine Chorley, *Arthur Hugh Clough: The Uncommitted Mind* (1962) and Robindra Kumar Biswas. *Arthur Hugh Clough: Towards A Reconsideration* (1972).

54. Levy, *op. cit.* p. 18.
55. *Ibid.*, p. 26.
56. *Ibid.*, p. 34.
57. *Ibid.*, p. 37.
58. F.L. Mulhauser, (ed.), *The Poems of Arthur Hugh Clough* (1974), pp. 292–94.
59. Balliol MS Letter to Mrs Arnold, June [1844] Sunday.
60. Balliol MS Letter to Mrs Arnold, Thursday [1844].
61. Clough, Letters. 21 July 1844, p. 97.
62. Clough, Letters. 31 July 1844, p. 98.
63. *Ibid.*
64. Mrs Humphry Ward, *op. cit.* p. 44, quoting letter by Mary Arnold of 1849. See also Allott, p. 31n.
65. Clough, Letters, 11 November 1844, p. 104.
66. Clough, Letters, 18 November 1844, p. 105.
67. Clough, Letters, 28 November 1844, p. 107.
68. K. Lake, (ed.), *Memorials of William Charles Lake* (1901), p. 72.
69. Yale MS. 1845 diary. Tinker 25.
70. Clough, Letters, 8 February 1845, p. 109.
71. T. S. Eliot, *The Use of Poetry and the Use of Criticism* (1933), 'Matthew Arnold', p. 105.
72. Kenneth Allott, 'Matthew Arnold's Reading-Lists in Three Early Diaries', *Victorian Studies*, March 1959.
73. Tom Arnold, *Guardian, loc. cit.*
74. A. G. Butler, *The Three Friends* (1900), p. 64.
75. Margaret Woods, 'Matthew Arnold', *Essays and Studies*, Vol. XV, 1929 pp. 7–19.
76. CL.55–57.
77. CL.58–59.
78. Clough, Letters, 2 April 1845, p. 111.
79. Balliol MS. Letter to Trevenen Penrose, 8 April 1845.
80. Tom Arnold, *Guardian, loc. cit.*
81. *Mixed Essays*, CPW.VII. 'George Sand'.
82. ii.131. To Fan, June 1876.
83. Mrs Humphry Ward, *op. cit.* p. 41.
84. C. W. E. Russell, *Portraits of the Seventies* (1916), p. 294.
85. *Irish Essays*, CPW. IX, 'The French Play in London'.
86. CL.81.
87. Clough, Letters, 14 February 1847, p. 178.
88. Clough, Letters, 22 February 1847, p. 178.
89. Clough, Letters, 7 March 1847, p. 144.
90. Microfilm UVA. Letter to Lord Shelburne, 2 February 1863.
91. Arnold Family Album, *The Arnoldian, loc. cit.* Letter to MA from Lord Lansdowne, 8 December 1854.
92. Balliol MS. Typescript by T. H. Ward (Moorman collection).
93. Charles Lacaita (ed.), *An Italian Englishman, Sir James Lacaita*, p. 93.
94. Balliol MS. Baron Bunsen letter to Mrs Arnold, 28 April 1847.
95. Clough, Letters. Tom Arnold to Clough, 16 April 1847.

96. Clough, Letters, 18 April 1847.
97. *Schools and Universities on the Continent* (1868) CPW.IV.318.
98. Thomas Hardy, *Jude the Obscure*, Part 2, Chapter 1, p. 99 (Wessex edition).

Chapter Three

1. *Absence*, Allott pp. 144–45.
2. Yale MS. The envelope survives but not its contents.
3. *Culture and Anarchy*, 'Introduction' (CPW.V.88), ed. J. Dover Wilson (1932), p. 41.
4. L.i.2.
5. Balliol MS. Letter to Tom Arnold, 28 February 1848.
6. L.i.4.
7. L.i.5.
8. CL.63.
9. *Ibid.*
10. CL.65.
11. CL.69.
12. CL.68.
13. CL.72.
14. Quoted in CL.73n.
15. CL.74.
16. L.i.5.
17. Balliol MS shows that L.i.5 has substituted 'feebleness' for 'purblindedness'.
18. L.i.4. and CL.75.
19. CL.74.
20. *Prose Remains of Arthur Hugh Clough*, i.119.
21. CL.66.
22. *North American Review*, CLX, July 1853, pp. 22–23.
23. Clough, Letters, p. 215.
24. L.i.7.
25. CL.78.
26. L.i.9.
27. L.i.10.
28. Clough, Letters, p. 196.
29. CL.76.
30. *Ibid.*
31. Balliol MS. Letter to K, 31 July [1848].
32. CL.84.
33. W.D. Arnold, *Oakfield; or, Fellowship in the East*, edited with an introduction by Kenneth Allott (Leicester, 1973).
34. CL.86.
35. CL.88–89.
36. CL.86.
37. Clough, Letters, p. 215.
38. CL.84.

39. Clough, Letters, p. 215.
40. See, for example, Isobel Macdonald, *The Buried Self* (1949).
41. I. Sells, *Matthew Arnold and France* (1935), p. 99.
42. CL.91.
43. CPW.III.3.
44. Balliol MS. Letter to K, 11 May [1850].
45. Park Honan in his *Matthew Arnold: A Life* (1981) takes a very different view of the identification of Marguerite. See also Honan's argument in *Victorian Poetry* (1985), pp. 144–59, a rejoinder to Miriam Allott, pp. 125–43.
46. Elsie Duncan-Jones thinks the kerchief a 'socially unambitious headgear'. Private communication with the author.
47. Bertram (ed.), *New Zealand Letters of Thomas Arnold the Younger* (1966), pp. 118–20.
48. Microfilm UVA. Letter to Lucy Arnold, 29 October 1886.
49. CL.91–93.
50. *Metamorphoses*, Book X.
51. Clough, Letters, p. 224.
52. Clough, Letters, p. 221.
53. CL.95.
54. CL.97.
55. Quoted in Mrs Humphry Ward, *A Writer's Recollections* (1918), *op. cit.*, p. 44.
56. Quoted *ibid.*, p. 45.
57. Quoted *ibid.*, p. 42.
58. Balliol MS. Letter to Mrs Arnold, 10 April 1849.
59. Balliol MS. Letter to Mrs Arnold, nd [1849].
60. Ullmann, p. 114. See also C.B. Tinker, 'Arnold's Poetic Plans', *Yale Review*, 22, 1933, pp. 782–93.
61. Balliol MS. Letter to K, 'Thursday'. Ullmann suggests 1849 on handwriting evidence.
62. UL.13.
63. *Ibid.*, pp. 14–17.
64. Brotherton MS. Letter to Tom Arnold, 11 April 1849.
65. Mrs Humphry Ward, *op. cit.*, p. 34.
66. CL.99.
67. CL.101.
68. CPW.III.30.
69. UL.18, wrongly dated 1853.
70. T. S. Eliot, *The Use of Poetry and the Use of Criticism* (1933), p. 119.
71. Clough, Letters, p. 251.
72. UL.14.
73. L.i.11.
74. Clough, Letters, p. 243.
75. Clough, Letters, p. 270.
76. Tinker and Lowry, *op. cit.*, *Commentary*, p. 49.
77. CL.109–11.
78. Clough, Letters, p. 274.

79. UL.13.
80. Balliol MS. Letter from K to Tom, 23 November 1849.
81. CPW.V. 295.

Chapter Four

1. CPW.XI.374. Arnold's retirement speech, 12 November 1886.
2. Clough, Letters, p. 286.
3. Clough, Letters, 425n.
4. Clough, Letters, p. 460.
5. G.W.E. Russell, 'Comments by the Way', *The Pilot*, 6 July 1901, pp. 13–14.
6. Clough, Letters, p. 290.
7. Mrs Humphry Ward, *A Writer's Recollections*, p. 52–53.
8. Russell, 'Comments by the Way'.
9. Edward Quillinan, Letter to Crabb Robinson, 16 January 1851. *Crabb Robinson's Correspondence with the Wordsworth Circle*, (1927) ii.769. Also quoted in Allott, p. 239.
10. William Rossetti, *The Germ*, No. 2, February 1850.
11. CL.115.
12. Tom Arnold, *The Guardian*, 18 May 1888.
13. Quoted in *Commentary*, p. 169.
14. Mrs Humphry Ward, *op. cit.* p. 52.
15. Balliol MS. Undated letter to K, Tuesday [1850?].
16. Balliol MS. Letter to K, 11 May [1850].
17. Quoted in Mrs Humphry Ward, *op. cit.* p. 46.
18. *Ibid.*, p. 65.
19. But Honan quoting from 'a typescript in possession of an Arnold descendant' transcribing a letter written by Mary Arnold has a description of the event which omits any reference to Arnold being present, as Mrs Humphry Ward (*op.cit.*) claimed he was.
20. CL.117. Translation by Lowry.
21. Alan Harris, citing 'Matthew Arnold: The Unknown Years', The Nineteenth Century, (1933) MA's 1851 diary.
22. L.i.13.
23. Charlotte Brontë, letter to James Taylor, 15 January 1851. Quoted in Winifred Gérin, *Charlotte Brontë* (1967), p. 461. See also Elizabeth Gaskell, *The Life of Charlotte Brontë* (1857), chapter xxiii, quoting an opinion of Harriet Martineau that 'Mr. A' was 'a combination of the antique Greek sage with the European modern man of science' encased in 'marble'.
24. L.i.14
25. L.i.15.
26. L.i.16.
27. Microfilm UVA. Letter to James Penchey, 10 March 1851.
28. MA diary of 1851. Quoted by Honan, p. 223.
29. Clough, Letters, p. 289.
30. MA diary of 1851. Quoted by Honan, p. 224.

31. Clough Letters, p. 290.
32. Balliol MS. Letter to K, 10 May 1851.
33. Clough Letters, p. 291.
34. F. Walcott, *Michigan Alumnus Quarterly Review* LX 243–8, 'Matthew Arnold: Her Majesty's Inspector of Schools'.
35. Balliol MS. Letter to Tom, 2 July 1851.
36. L.i.17.
37. L.i.17.
38. Sir Joshua Fitch, *Thomas and Matthew Arnold and Their Influence on English Education* (1897), p. 171.
39. Quoted by Fitch *ibid.*, p. 173.
40. CPW.XI.377. Speech, 12 November 1886, at Westminster.
41. Irvin Stock, *William Hale White* (1956), p. 3n.
42. L.i.18.
43. See CL.173 [Appendix].
44. CL.118.
45. J. Bertram (ed.), *Letters of Thomas Arnold the Younger*, 1850–1900 (1980), pp. 21–2.
46. Yale MS. 1852 diary.
47. See L.i.21.
48. Clough, Letters, pp. 310–11.
49. CL.119.
50. CL.122.
51. L.i.19.
52. CL.92.
53. L.i.20.
54. Clough, Letters, p.319.
55. L.i.20.
56. Balliol MS. Letter to Mrs Arnold, 19 August 1852. Russell prints only a partial text of this letter.
57. Edith Morley, (ed.), *Correspondence of Crabb Robinson with the Wordsworth Circle (1927)*, p. 789.
58. Bodleian MS. To Secretary of Committee. 29 September 1852.
59. *Reports on Elementary Schools* (1908), ed. F.S. Marvin, pp. 3–4.
60. L.i.22.
61. CL.124.
62. L.i.22.
63. Yale MS., quoted in Allott, p. 154.
64. Ullmann, p. 135.
65. Yale MS., quoted in Allott, p. 156.
66. For a very valuable discussion of this poem and Arnold's 'exasperating' rejection of it see Frank Kermode, *Romantic Image* (1957), pp. 12–20.
67. A. H. Clough, *North American Review*, No. CLX, July 1853.
68. CL.126.
69. Balliol MS. Letter to Mrs Arnold, 25 November 1852.
70. Balliol MS. Letter to Mrs Arnold, 25 November 1852. Russell partial text only.

71. L.i.23.
72. L.i.23.
73. CL.128 and CL.132.
74. L.i.26.
75. L.i.26.
76. L.i.26.
77. L.i.27.
78. L.i.27.
79. Clough, Letters, p. 128.
80. CL.131–33.
81. Clough, Letters, p. 401.
82. Clough, Letters, p. 437.
83. CL.135.
84. CL.135.
85. CL.142.
86. CL.144.

Chapter Five

1. CL.144.
2. L.i.29.
3. L.i.30.
4. *Ibid.*
5. CL.139.
6. Clough, Letters, p. 463.
7. E. H. Coleridge (ed.) *Life and Correspondence of John Duke Lord Coleridge* (1904), p. 210.
8. Clough, Letters, p. 463.
9. CL.145.
10. Clough, Letters, p. 470.
11. L.i.31.
12. Bonnerot, p. 518. Letter of 6 January 1854.
13. Clough, Letters, p. 467.
14. Letter quoted in Mrs Humphry Ward, *A Writer's Recollections* (1918), p. 54.
15. Clough, Letters, p. 467.
16. CL.146.
17. CL.144.
18. CPW.I.1.
19. UL 18–19.
20. UL 19–21.
21. UL 21–23.
22. Microfilm UVA [John Rylands MS], 18 November 1853.
23. Clough, Letters, p. 477.
24. *Reports on Elementary Schools*, p. 23.
25. *Ibid.*, p. 34.
26. L.i.34.
27. L.i.37.

28. UL 24–25.
29. L.i.38.
30. L.i.39.
31. Clough, Letters, p. 496.
32. CPW.I.16.
33. L.i.41.
34. L.i.47. Russell wrongly dates as 12 December 1855 not 1854.
35. Quoted in Mrs Humphry Ward, *op.cit*. p. 52.
36. Clough, Letters, p. 497.
37. Microfilm UVA. 17 January 1855.
38. L.i.43.
39. Balliol MS. Letter to Tom Arnold, 28 March 1855.
40. L.i.46.
41. Yale MS. Letter to J.W. Parker, 20 March 1855.
42. Yale MS. Letter to J.W. Parker, 11 April 1855.
43. L.i.44.
44. UL 26–29.
45. Arnold Family Album. Letter to MA from Mrs Gaskell, 25 May 1855.
46. Microfilm UVA [John Rylands MS].
47. L.i.44.
48. Balliol MS. Letter to Mrs Arnold, 3 June 1855.
49. L.i.46.
50. CL.147.
51. L.i.49.
52. L.i.51.
53. Microfilm UVA [Trinity College, Cambridge MS].
54. L.i.50.
55. UL 30.
56. L.i.54.
57. L.i.51.
58. For an analysis of the intellectual significance of the club see Stefan Collini, *Public Moralists: Political Thought and Intellectual Life in Britain 1850–1930* (1991).
59. UL 31.
60. Arnold Family Album, *loc. cit*. Letter to MA, 6 October 1859.
61. L.i.53.
62. Clough, Letters, p. 523.
63. Balliol MS. Letter to Mrs Arnold, 2 November 1856.
64. *Ibid*.
65. *Notebooks*, p. 4.
66. Balliol MS. Letter to Mrs Arnold, 16 January 1857.
67. L.i.55.
68. Herbert Paul, *Matthew Arnold*, (1902) p. 51.
69. Mrs Humphry Ward, *op.cit*., p. 55.
70. Sir John Coleridge. *A Memoir of the Reverend John Keble* (1874) p. 211.
71. Mrs Humphry Ward, *op.cit*., p. 54.

72. Balliol MS. Letter to Mrs Arnold, Sunday [May 1857].
73. *Ibid.*, but also quoted in part in Mrs Humphry Ward, *op.cit.*, p. 56.
74. Bodleian MS. Froude letter to MA, 1 June 1857.
75. Balliol MS. Letter to Mrs Arnold, Sunday [May 1857].
76. Yale MS. Unpublished 1857 diary.
77. L.i.57.
78. *Ibid.*
79. Clough, Letters, p. 534.
80. CPW.I.18.
81. E. Morley (ed.), *Correspondence of Crabb Robinson with the Wordsworth Circle* (1927), p. 826.
82. Kenneth Allott, *Matthew Arnold; Writers and Their Background* (1975), quoting his unpublished notes on *Merope*, p. 114.
83. Microfilm UVA [Herts County Record Office]. Letter to William Leake, 23 December 1857.
84. CPW.I.39.
85. L.i.58.
86. L.i.58.
87. UL 41–43.
88. Balliol MS. Letter to Tom Arnold, 11 February 1858.
89. L.i.59.
90. UL 34–40.
91. L.i.60.
92. Microfilm UVA [Fitzwilliam MS]. Letter to Herbert Hill. 7 January 1858.
93. Arnold Family Album. Letter to MA, 8 January 1858.
94. Clough, Letters, p. 546.
95. Clough, Letters, p. 540.
96. Clough, Letters, p. 544.
97. Arnold Family Album. Letter to MA, 10 January 1858.
98. Microfilm UVA. Letter to Alfred Arthur Reade, 4 November 1882.
99. Balliol MS. Letter to Mrs Arnold, 16 May 1858.
100. *Ibid.*
101. *The Times*, 17 June 1858, p. 12.
102. Balliol MS. Letter to Mrs Arnold, 30 May 1858.
103. L.i.62.
104. L.i.116–17.
105. L.i.75.
106. Balliol MS. Letter to Mrs Arnold, 23 October 1858.
107. L.i.76.
108. L.i.75.
109. Balliol MS. Letter to Mrs Arnold, 1 December 1858.
110. L.i.77.
111. L.i.77.
112. L.i.78.
113. Balliol MS. Letter to Mrs Arnold, 28 March 1859.
114. L.i.80.

115. L.i.86.
116. L.i.89.
117. Balliol MS. Letter to K, 22 May 1859.
118. L.i.90.
119. L.i.92.
120. L.i.96.
121. *The Function of Criticism at the Present Time*, CPW.III.275.
122. L.i.98.
123. Balliol MS. Letter to K, 22 May 1859.
124. Balliol MS. Letter to Mrs Arnold, 11 July 1859.
125. Balliol MS. Letter to Mrs Arnold, 19 August 1859.
126. L.i.102.
127. Clough, Letters, p. 570.
128. British Museum MS. Letter to Gladstone, 5 August 1859.
129. Balliol MS. Letter to Mrs Arnold, 4 August 1859.
130. L.i.106.
131. L.i.108.
132. L.i.108.
133. Clough, Letters, p. 573.
134. Balliol MS. Letter to Edward Walford, 4 December 1859.
135. L.i.110.
136. L.i.112.
137. L.i.113.

Chapter Six

1. University of Birmingham MS. Letter to Harriet Martineau, 24 July 1860.
2. *Notebooks*, pp. 10–11. Translation by present writer.
3. CPW.I.86.
4. L.i.114.
5. L.i.115.
6. Yale MS. Letter to J.W. Parker, 1 June 1860.
7. University of Birmingham MS. Letter to Harriet Martineau, 30 July 1860.
8. L.i.118.
9. L.i.122.
10. Balliol MS. Letter to Tom, 26 August 1995.
11. L.i.124.
12. L.i.126.
13. Balliol MS. Letter to Mrs Arnold, 19 November 1860.
14. L.i.127.
15. Robert Bernard Martin, *Tennyson: The Unquiet Heart* (1983), p. 535.
16. Ibid.
17. CL.154.
18. L.i.128.
19. CL.151.

20. CPW.I.97.
21. CL.153.
22. Balliol MS. Letter to Mrs Arnold, 16 January 1861.
23. Balliol MS. Letter to Mrs Arnold, 28 February 1861.
24. CL.154.
25. CL.152.
26. L.i.129.
27. Balliol MS. Letter to Mrs Arnold, 13 February 1861.
28. Balliol MS. Letter to Mrs Arnold, 28 March 1861.
29. Microfilm UVA [Wellesley College MS]. Letter to Herbert Hill, 18 February 1861.
30. Microfilm UVA [Trinity College MS]. Letter to Rev. W. Hewell, 6 March 1861.
31. L.i.132.
32. L.i.134.
33. L.i.136.
34. CPW.II.11.
35. T. S. Eliot, *The Sacred Wood* (1920), p. 1.
36. Balliol MS. Letter to Mrs Arnold, 29 May 1861.
37. Microfilm UVA. Letter to Lady de Rothschild, 27 June 1861.
38. CL.155.
39. Yale MS. MA's 1861 diary.
40. Balliol MS. Letter to Mrs Arnold, 20 July 1861.
41. L.i.138.
42. Fitzjames Stephen, *Saturday Review*, 27 July 1861, xii, 95–96.
43. L.i.139.
44. Balliol MS. Letter to Mrs Arnold, 30 October 1861.
45. L.i.140.
46. L.i.142.
47. Balliol MS. Letter to Fan, 9 October 1861.
48. L.i.152.
49. CL.159.
50. CPW.I.170.
51. *The Function of Criticism at the Present Time*, CPW.III.258–85.
52. L.i.154.
53. Balliol MS. Letter to Mrs Arnold, 11 December 1861.
54. L.i.156.
55. L.i.157.
56. Balliol MS. Letter to Mrs Arnold, 21 December 1861.
57. Microfilm UVA. Letter to Lady de Rothschild, 28 December 1861.
58. Balliol MS. Letter to Mrs Arnold, 1 January 1862.
59. L.i.158.
60. L.i.162.
61. CPW.II.216.
62. CPW.II.246.
63. L.i.167.
64. CPW.II.250.

65. CPW.II.260.
66. CPW.II.249.
67. L.i.157.
68. L.i.159.
69. *Notebooks*, 15.
70. *Ibid.*, 17.
71. Balliol MS. Letter to Mrs Arnold, February 1862.
72. L.i.166.
73. Balliol MS. Letter to Mrs Arnold, 26 March 1862.
74. L.i.168.
75. Balliol MS. Letter to Mrs Arnold, 26 March 1862.
76. L.i.169.
77. Balliol MS. Letter to Mrs Arnold, 18 April 1862.
78. Balliol MS. Letter to Mrs Arnold, 28 April 1862.
79. CL.160.
80. Balliol MS. Letter to Mrs Arnold, 28 April 1862.
81. Balliol MS. Letter to Mrs Arnold, 3 May 1862.
82. Balliol MS. Letter to Mrs Arnold, 14 June 1862.
83. L.i.172.
84. Balliol MS. Letter to Mrs Arnold, 13 October 1862.
85. Balliol MS. Letter to Mrs Arnold, 1 November 1862.
86. Balliol MS. Letter to Mrs Arnold, 9 November 1862.
87. Balliol MS. Letter to Mrs Arnold, 10 November 1862.
88. Balliol MS. Letter to Mrs Arnold, 27 November 1862.
89. L.i.175.
90. Balliol MS. Letter to Mrs Arnold, 10 November 1862.
91. Balliol MS. Letter to Mrs Arnold, 9 December 1862.
92. L.i.177.
93. Balliol MS. Letter to Mrs Arnold, 21 January 1863.
94. L.i.179.
95. Balliol MS. Letter to Mrs Arnold, 21 January 1863.
96. L.i.182.
97. L.i.193.
98. L.i.183.
99. L.i.191.
100. L.i.195.
101. Balliol MS. Letter to Mrs Arnold, 26 June 1863.
102. L.i.201.
103. Balliol MS. Letter to Mrs Arnold, 21 October 1863.
104. L.i.204.
105. L.i.207.
106. L.i.208.
107. Buckler, p. 167.
108. CPW.IX.66.
109. L.i.210.
110. *Lady de Rothschild*, ed. Constance Battersea, nd, p. 82.
111. Lucy Cohen, *Lady de Rothschild and Her Daughters* (1935), p. 194.
112. *Ibid.*, p. 41.

113. Algernon West, *Contemporary Portraits* (1920), pp. 57–64.
114. L.i.213.
115. Balliol MS. Letter to Tom, 1 December 1863.
116. CPW.II.316.
117. L.i.230.
118. Microfilm UVA. Letter to R. W. Emerson, 19 June 1864.
119. L.i.222.
120. Microfilm UVA. Letter to George Smith, 26 May 1864.
121. Balliol MS. Letter to Mrs Arnold, 10 June 1864.
122. Balliol MS. Letter to Mrs Arnold, 22 July 1864.
123. *Ibid.*
124. L.i.234.
125. L.i.239.
126. L.i.238.
127. L.i.239.
128. L.i.241.
129. L.i.243.
130. Microfilm UVA. Letter to George Smith, 7 December 1864.
131. Balliol MS. Letter to Mrs Arnold, 1 December 1864.

Chapter Seven

1. Balliol MS. Letter to Mrs Arnold, 5 December 1867.
2. Microfilm UVA. Letter to Alexander Macmillan, 28 July 1864.
3. Microfilm UVA. Letter to Alexander Macmillan, 2 August 1864.
4. Microfilm UVA. Letter to Lady de Rothschild, 24 October 1864.
5. Léon Edel, *Henry James, The Untried Years*, p. 182.
6. *North American Review*, July 1865, No. CI. pp. 206–13. Unsigned review (also in ed. Carl Dawson and John Pfordrisher *Matthew Arnold: the Critical Heritage*, p. 144).
7. L.i.248.
8. L.i.248.
9. L.i.246.
10. L.i.247.
11. L.i.246,
12. *North British Review*, No. XLII, pp. 158–82, March 1865.
13. L.i.249.
14. CPW.III.287.
15. T.S. Eliot, *The Sacred Wood* (1920), 'The Perfect Critic' p. 1. For a corrective view of Eliot's rendering of Arnold see F. R. Leavis, 'Arnold as Critic', *Scrutiny*, December 1938.
16. This second formulation first used in the Preface to *Culture and Anarchy* ed. J. Dover Wilson (1932), p. 6.
17. Microfilm UVA. Letter to Alexander Macmillan, 25 February 1865.
18. Balliol MS. Letter to Mrs Arnold, 1 April 1865.
19. L.i.251.
20. Balliol MS. Letter to Mrs Arnold March [1865].

21. L.i.253.
22. Balliol MS. Letter to Mrs Arnold, 1 April 1865.
23. L.i.254.
24. L.i.254.
25. L.i.256.
26. L.i.261.
27. L.i.271.
28. L.i.272.
29. L.i.280.
30. L.i.288.
31. L.i.293.
32. L.i.296.
33. Balliol MS. Letter to Mrs Arnold, 17 September 1865.
34. Microfilm. UVA. Letter to George Smith 30 July 1865.
35. Balliol MS. Letter to Mrs Arnold. 3 November 1865.
36. Balliol MS. Letter to Mrs Arnold. 25 November 1865.
37. Microfilm UVA. Letter to Lady de Rothschild, 28 November 1865.
38. Balliol MS. Letter to Mrs Arnold, 4 December 1865.
39. Balliol MS. Letter to Mrs Arnold, n.d.
40. Balliol MS. Letter to Mrs Arnold, 23 January 1866.
41. Balliol MS. Letter to Mrs Arnold, 6 January 1866.
42. Balliol MS. Letter to Tom Arnold, 16 January 1866.
43. Balliol MS. Letter to Mrs Arnold, 17 January 1866.
44. Balliol MS. Letter to Mrs Arnold, 10 February 1866.
45. Microfilm UVA. Letter to Alexander Macmillan, 30 March 1866.
46. Balliol MS. Letter to Mrs Arnold, 15 February 1866.
47. L.i.320.
48. L.i.323.
49. Balliol MS. Letter to Mrs Arnold, 31 March 1866.
50. L.i.327.
51. L.i.325.
52. L.i.327.
53. L.i.331.
54. Balliol MS. Letter to Tom Arnold, 10 June 1866.
55. Balliol MS. Letter to Mrs Arnold, 19 June 1866.
56. L.i.328.
57. Microfilm UVA. Letter to Herman Kindt, 2 June 1866.
58. Balliol MS. Letter to Mrs Arnold, 10 July 1866.
59. L.i.335.
60. *The Spectator*, 3 February 1866, p. 125.
61. Balliol MS. Letter to Mrs Arnold, 19 August 1866.
62. L.i.337.
63. Microfilm UVA. Letter to Lady de Rothschild, 24 September 1866.
64. Microfilm UVA. Letter to Alexander Macmillan, 30 September 1866.
65. Microfilm UVA. Letter to George Smith, 13 November 1866.

66. L.i.341.
67. Balliol MS. Letter to Mrs Arnold, 11 August 1866.
68. L.i.342.
69. Balliol MS. Letter to Mrs Arnold, 1 December 1866.
70. Balliol MS. Letter to Mrs Arnold, 8 December 1866.
71. Balliol MS. Letter to Mrs Arnold, 22 December 1866.
72. L.i.344.
73. Balliol MS. Letter to Mrs Arnold, 18 January 1867.
74. For a fuller account of Arnold's relationship with his publishers see William Buckler's invaluable *Matthew Arnold's Books: Towards a Publishing Diary* (1958) which prints many interesting letters between all the parties.
75. Balliol MS. Letter to Mrs Arnold, 2 February 1867.
76. Yale MS. Flu's diary, 1867. Honan transcribes this remark as: 'But pleasant'.
77. L.i.350.
78. Buckler, p. 19. Letter to George Smith, 1 March 1867.
79. British Library MS. Letter to Gladstone, 20 April 1867.
80. Arnold Family Album. Letter of Disraeli, 25 April 1867.
81. L.i.360.
82. L.i.359.
83. L.i.362.
84. Balliol MS. Letter to Mrs Arnold, 31 March 1867.
85. Buckler, p. 85. Letter to George Smith, 1 June 1867.
86. L.i.361.
87. James Macdonnell, *Daily Telegraph*, 8 September 1866. In Dawson and Pfordresher, *op. cit.*, pp. 163–66.
88. Buckler, *op. cit.*, p. 84. Letter to George Smith, 15 June 1867.
89. L.i.332.
90. Microfilm UVA. Letter to George Smith, 3 September 1866.
91. CPW.III.
92. W. Gareth Evans, 'The "Bilingual Difficulty": Her Majesty's Inspectorate and the Welsh Language in the Victorian Age', *The Welsh History Review*, December 1993, Vol. 16 No. 4, pp. 494–513. The article also demonstrates that some native Welsh speakers, such as the Reverend Shadrach Pryce HMI, shared Arnold's views. See also Rachel Bromwich, *Matthew Arnold and Celtic Literature* (Oxford, 1965) for a more sympathetic account of Arnold's contribution to Celtic studies.
93. Yale MS. Flu's diary, 6, 7 June, 1867.
94. Buckler, p. 85. Letter to George Smith, 1 June 1867.
95. Buckler, p. 85. Letter to George Smith, 9 June 1867.
96. Yale MS. Flu's 1867 diary.
97. L.i.364.
98. L.i.368.
99. Dawson and Pfordresher, *op. cit.*, pp. 209–24.
100. Buckler, p. 86. Letter from Alexander Macmillan, 25 July 1867.
101. L.i.361.

102. Buckler, p. 34. Letter of Alexander Macmillan, 25 July 1867.
103. Yale MS. Letter to Henry Dunn, 12 November 1867.
104. Review of *New Poems* in *Essays and Studies* (1876), pp. 123–83.
105. L.i.371.
106. Balliol MS. Letter to Mrs Arnold, 23 November 1867.
107. L.i.376.
108. Microfilm UVA [Harvard MS]. Letter to R. W. Emerson, 30 July 1867.
109. Balliol MS. Letter to Mrs Arnold, 31 October 1867.
110. L.i.372.
111. L.i.376.
112. Balliol MS. Letter to Mrs Arnold, 4 July 1867.
113. Balliol MS. Letter to Mrs Arnold, 'Thursday morning' [1867?].
114. Balliol MS. Letter to Mrs Arnold, 16 July 1867.
115. British Library MS. Letter to A.C. Swinburne, 10 October 1867.
116. L.i.372.
117. L.i.390.
118. L.i.387.
119. L.i.377.
120. L.i.379.
121. Balliol MS. Letter to Mrs Arnold, 23 November 1867.
122. Balliol MS. Letter to Mrs Arnold, 5 December 1867.
123. Balliol MS. Letter to Mrs Arnold, 19 December 1867.
124. Balliol MS. Letter to Mrs Arnold, 23 November 1867.
125. CPW.IV.290.
126. L.i.382.
127. Balliol MS. Letter to Mrs Arnold, 14 February 1868.
128. L.i.382.
129. L.i.385.
130. Balliol MS. Letter to Mrs Arnold, 14 February 1868.
131. L.i.394.
132. L.i.388.
133. L.i.387.
134. L.i.389.
135. Balliol MS. Letter to Mrs Arnold, 2 June 1868.
136. Birmingham MS. Letter to Harriet Martineau, 11 April 1868.
137. L.i.391.
138. Balliol MS. Letter to Mrs Arnold, 12 July 1868.
139. Balliol MS. Letter to Mrs Arnold, 25 July 1868.
140. Conclusion to *Culture and Anarchy*, ed. J. Dover Wilson. p. 203.
141. Balliol MS. Letter to Mrs Arnold, 25 July 1868.
142. L.i.400.
143. CL.162.
144. Balliol MS. Letter to Mrs Arnold, 24 September 1868.
145. Balliol MS. Letter to Mrs Arnold, 3 October 1868.
146. L.i.401.
147. Balliol MS. Letter to Mrs Arnold, 16 December 1868.

148. Examples are too numerous to cite, but see for example Robert Hughes, *Culture of Complaint* (1994), p. 92: 'Matthew Arnold . . . who believed universities should preserve the best that has been thought and said, but as an *antidote* to the spreading values of liberal democracy.' Bryan Appleyard (representative of newspaper cultural pundits) in the *Independent* (18 November 1993) accuses Arnold of 'an ever-more paranoid assertion of the need for an inner cultural priesthood that would protect the highest and the best from the lowest and the worst'. See also reply by present author, 19 November 1993.

149. CPW.V.86ff. But the edition preferred here for its greater accessibility is Dover Wilson (Cambridge, 1932).

150. *Independent*, 12 August 1995, p. 15.

151. See also an acute and almost-sympathetic account of Arnold by Raymond Williams in *Culture and Society* (1958), Chapter 6, which worries that 'Culture was a process but he could not find the material of that process . . .'

152. F.W. Maitland (ed.), *The Life and Letters of Leslie Stephen* (1906), p. 380.

153. Quoted in Dawson and Pfordresher, *op. cit.*, p. 242.

154. Buckler, p. 91. Letter from Alexander Macmillan, 3 February 1869.

155. Balliol MS. Letter to Mrs Arnold, 23 January 1869.

156. L.ii.1.

157. Balliol MS. Letter to Tom Arnold, 11 March 1869.

158. L.ii.6.

159. Balliol MS. Letter to Mrs Arnold, 13 February 1869.

160. L.ii.9.

Chapter Eight

1. Balliol MS. Letter to Mrs Arnold, 27 October 1874.

2. Liverpool City Library MS. Lord Derby's 1882 diary.

3. Buckler, p. 99. Letter to George Smith, 5 September 1869.

4. Balliol MS. Letter to Mrs Arnold, 25 September 1869.

5. Balliol MS. Letter to Mrs Arnold, 2 October 1869.

6. Balliol MS. Letter to Mrs Arnold, 16 October 1869.

7. CPW.I.102.

8. Balliol MS. Letter to Mrs Arnold, 25 January 1865.

9. Balliol MS. Letter to Mrs Arnold, 16 October 1869.

10. Balliol MS. Letter to Mrs Arnold, 25 September 1869.

11. Balliol MS. Letter to Mrs Arnold, 23 October 1869.

12. Balliol MS. Letter to Mrs Arnold, [November 1869].

13. Balliol MS. Letter to Mrs Arnold, 25 December 1869.

14. L.ii.23.

15. L.ii.29.

16. L. Huxley (ed.), *Life and Letters of Thomas Henry Huxley* (1900), p. 311. Letter to Arnold, 8 July 1869.

17. Balliol MS. Letter to Mrs Arnold, 16 January 1870.
18. Buckler, p. 102. Letter to George Smith, 23 May 1870.
19. Balliol MS. Letter to Mrs Arnold, 21 November 1869.
20. CPW.VI.1ff.
21. For a much more extensive consideration of Arnold's religious thought and the way in which it acted as an organising principle across the whole range of his intellectual concerns see the indispensable *Arnold and God* (1983) by Ruth apRoberts.
22. A. Miall (ed.), *Life of Edward Miall* (1884), p. 51.
23. Huxley, *op. cit.*, p. 329. Letter to MA, 10 May 1870.
24. L.ii.31.
25. Arnold Family Album. Letter from RW Church to MA, 6 June 1870.
26. Microfilm UVA. Letter to George Smith, 24 June 1870.
27. L.ii.35.
28. Balliol MS. Letter to Mrs Arnold, nd [July 1870?].
29. L.ii.39.
30. L.ii.43.
31. Balliol MS. Letter to Mrs Arnold, 30 November 1870.
32. L.ii.47.
33. Buckler, p. 94. Letter to George Smith, 6 January 1871.
34. Buckler, p. 94. Letter to George Smith, 1 February 1871,
35. Raymond Williams, *Culture and Society* (1958), p. 126.
36. Yale MS. Letter to Frederick Greenwood, 14 August 1870
37. CPW.V.1ff,
38. Balliol MS. Letter to Mrs Arnold, 25 December 1870.
39. Microfilm UVA. Letter to Dean Farrar, 13 March 1871.
40. *Blackwood's Magazine*, April 1871, CIX, pp. 440–64. In *Matthew Arnold: The Critical Heritage*, ed. Carl Dawson and John Pfordresher (1979), *op. cit.*, p. 252.
41. L.ii.48.
42. *Reports on Elementary Schools*, p. 151.
43. Balliol MS. Letter to Mrs Arnold, 11 February 1871.
44. L.ii.49.
45. L.ii.52.
46. L.ii.57.
47. Balliol MS. Letter to Mrs Arnold, 25 February 1871.
48. L.ii.53.
49. L.ii.58.
50. L.ii.59.
51. L.ii.63.
52. L.ii.64.
53. Balliol MS. Letter to Mrs Arnold, 8 October 1871.
54. Balliol MS. Letter to Mrs Arnold, 1 November 1871.
55. CPW.VI.449, quoting *Life and Letters of J.H. Shorthouse*, ed. Sarah Shorthouse (1905), p. 328.
56. L.ii.67.
57. Balliol MS. Letter to Mrs Arnold, n.d., Harrow, Sunday [1871].

58. UL.56
59. Balliol MS. Letter to Tom Arnold, 29 November 1871.
60. Balliol MS. Letter to Mrs Arnold, 4 December 1871.
61. W. H. Mallock, *Every Man His Own Poet* (1872), pp. 11–12.
62. L.ii.76.
63. Balliol MS. Letter to Tom Arnold, n.d., Sunday [1872].
64. Huxley *op. cit.*, Letter to MA, 10 March 1872.
65. Microfilm UVA. Letter to Mrs Huxley, 13 January 1872.
66. Arnold Family Album. Letter to Fan, 18 February 1872.
67. Brotherton MS. Letter to Robert Browning, 21 February 1872.
68. Balliol MS. Letter to Mrs Arnold, February [?] 1872.
69. L.ii.90.
70. Algernon West, *Contemporary Portraits* (1920), pp. 57–64.
71. Buckler, p. 95. Letter to MA. 15 February 1873.
72. Buckler, p. 96. Letter to Alexander Macmillan, 6 March 1873.
73. CPW.VI.140ff.
74. CPW.VII.140ff.
75. Microfilm UVA. Letter to George Smith, 12 January 1873.
76. J. Tulloch, *Blackwoods*, June 1873, CXIII, pp. 678–92, quoted in Dawson and Pfordresher, *op.cit.*, pp. 286ff.
77. The view of the editors of the *Notebooks* (p. xiii).
78. Microfilm UVA. Letter to George Smith, 24 February 1873.
79. Microfilm UVA. Letter to George Smith, 9 March 1873.
80. Yale MS. Letter to Charles Appleton, 12 September 1873.
81. L.ii.103.
82. Balliol MS. Letter to Tom Arnold, 19 May 1873.
83. Microfilm UVA. Letter to George Smith, 13 May 1873.
84. John Morley, *Recollections* (1917), p. 125.
85. Yale MS. Letter to Charles Appleton, 16 November 1873.
86. Microfilm UVA. Letter to Lady de Rothschild, 12 June 1873.
87. Microfilm UVA. Letter to George Smith, 16 November 1873.
88. Balliol MS. Unsigned typescript by [?] Mrs H. Ward.
89. L.ii.111.
90. Microfilm UVA. Letter to Sir Anthony de Rothschild, 22 December 1873.
91. Balliol MS. Letter to Tom Arnold, 30 November 1873.
92. CPW.VII.84.
93. L.ii.108.
94. Balliol MS. Letter to Fan [October 1873?].
95. L.ii.110.
96. L.ii.108.
97. See Richard Shannon, *The Crisis of Imperialism* (1974), p. 97: 'Significant shifts occurred all over the middle-class commuting constituencies of the Home Counties created by railway development . . . all of which had been overwhelmingly Liberal in the 1850s.'
98. L.ii.112.
99. L.ii.113.

100. CPW.VII.128.
101. Microfilm UVA. Letter to Lady de Rothschild, 10 May 1874.
102. Yale MS. Letter to James Knowles, 6 May 1874.
103. Balliol MS. Letter to Tom Arnold, 16 May 1874.
104. L.ii.117.
105. Yale MS. Letter to James Knowles, 26 October 1874.
106. F. W. Maitland (ed.), *The Life and Letters of Leslie Stephen* (1906), p. 245. Letter to Charles Eliot Norton, 12 October 1874.
107. Bodleian MS. Letter to Dean Farrar, 19 October 1874.
108. Balliol MS. Letter to Tom Arnold, 27 October 1874.
109. L.ii.118.
110. Arnold Family Album. Letter to MA, 20 June 1873.
111. L.ii.120.
112. Microfilm UVA. Letter to George Smith, 9 December 1874.
113. Microfilm UVA. Letter to John Cropper, 11 November 1874.
114. Yale MS. Letter to William Knowles, 16 December 1874.
115. L.ii.122.
116. Bodleian MS. Letter to Friedrich Max-Müller, n.d. [January 1875].
117. Buckler, p. 23. Letter to Alexander Macmillan, 12 March 1875.
118. Buckler, p. 24. Letter to MA, 15 March 1875.
119. Buckler, p. 27. Letter to George Smith, 12 December 1875.
120. Buckler, p. 30. Letter to George Smith, 27 January 1876.
121. Microfilm UVA. Letter to Stuart Blackie, 20 May 1875.
122. Microfilm UVA. Letter to T. H. Ward, 29 May 1875.
123. Microfilm UVA. To unidentified correspondent, 18 June 1875.
124. CPW.VII.1ff.
125. Microfilm UVA. Letter to Alexander Macmillan, 13 July 1875.
126. L.ii.123.
127. Microfilm UVA. Letter to Thomas Huxley, 8 December 1875.
128. *Ibid.*
129. Arnold Family Album. Letter to MA, 3 January 1876.
130. Bodleian MS. Letter to Mark Pattison, 20 January 1876.
131. CPW.VII.16ff.
132. L.ii.126.
133. CPW.VII.63ff.
134. L.ii.132.
135. L.ii.131.
136. Buckler, p. 21. Letter to Alexander Macmillan, 4 June 1876.
137. L.ii.135.
138. Buckler, p. 132. Letter to Alexander Macmillan, 22 January 1877.
139. Buckler, p. 133. Letter to MA, 22 January 1877.
140. Buckler, p. 42. Letter to Alexander Macmillan, 25 January 1877.
141. CPW.VII.148ff.

Chapter Nine

1. L.ii.232.
2. L.ii.137.

3. L.ii.139.
4. L.ii.140.
5. John Lucas (ed.), *The New Republic* (1877), by W. H. Mallock. Victorian Library edition (1975 Leicester), p. 27.
6. Microfilm UVA. Letter to Victor Marshall, 18 October 1877.
7. Microfilm UVA. Letter to T. H. Ward, 6 October 1877.
8. Brotherton MS. Letter to Robert Browning, 26 November 1877.
9. Balliol MS. Letter to Tom Arnold, December 1877.
10. Microfilm, UVA. Letter to Lady de Rothschild, 25 December 1877.
11. L.ii.143.
12. L.ii.144.
13. Arnold Family Album. Letter to MA, 2 February 1878.
14. Microfilm UVA. Letter to Lady de Rothschild, February 1878.
15. CPW.VII.277ff.
16. Buckler, p. 126. Letter to Alexander Macmillan, 18 March 1878.
17. *Reports on Elementary Schools*, p. 187.
18. L.ii.145.
19. Microfilm UVA. Letter to Rhoda Broughton, 12 May 1878.
20. Buckler, p. 51, Letter to MA, 24 December 1878.
21. CPW.VII.321ff.
22. Trinity College Cambridge MS. Letter to Lord Houghton, 15 July 1878.
23. Buckler, p. 159. Letter to George Smith, 25 August 1878.
24. L.ii.148.
25. Yale MS. Letter to T. H. Ward, 22 October 1878.
26. Microfilm. UVA. Letter to Thomas Huxley, 22 November 1878.
27. CPW.VII.368.
28. Microfilm UVA. Letter to T. H. Ward, 26 October 1878.
29. Buckler, p. 136. Letter to Alexander Macmillan, 16 April 1879.
30. L.ii.157.
31. Buckler, p. 139. Letter to George Grove, 10 May 1879.
32. Buckler, p. 140. Letter to Alexander Macmillan, 22 May 1879.
33. Microfilm UVA. Letter to Alexander Macmillan, 4 February 1879.
34. CPW.VII.370ff.
35. L.ii.153.
36. L.ii.152.
37. L.ii.151.
38. L.ii.153.
39. L.ii.154.
40. Microfilm UVA. Letter to George Smith, 12/19 April 1879.
41. *Ibid.*
42. L.ii.158.
43. CPW.IX.161ff.
44. See Joan Harding, *From Fox How to Fairy Hill* (1986 Cowbridge). A very useful study of the Benson family in relation to Arnold.
45. Yale MS. Letter to T. H. Ward, 11 September 1879.
46. Bodleian MS. Letter to Dean Farrar, 24 September 1879.

47. L.ii.165.
48. Balliol MS. Letter to Tom Arnold, Saturday [spring, 1880?].
49. Microfilm UVA. Letter to T. H. Ward, 8 February 1880.
50. Yale MS. Letter to T. H. Ward, 1 May 1880.
51. C. Ricks (ed.), *The Poems of Tennyson* (1969), p. 1281.
52. Balliol MS. Letter to Tom Arnold [spring 1880?].
53. L.ii.169.
54. Arnold Family Album. Letter to Arthur Stanley, 13 May 1880.
55. Microfilm UVA. Letter to T. H. Ward, 20 May 1880.
56. L.ii.176.
57. L.ii.174.
58. L.ii.175.
59. L.ii.178.
60. L.ii.185.
61. L.ii.187.
62. T. Huxley, *Science and Culture and Other Essays* (1881), p. 8.
63. Microfilm UVA. Letter to Thomas Huxley, 17 October 1880.
64. Microfilm UVA. Letter to Alexander Macmillan, 2 December 1880.
65. Bodleian MS. Letter to James Bryce, 5 November 1880.
66. Microfilm UVA. Letter to Lady de Rothschild, 2 January 1881.
67. Balliol MS. Letter to Tom Arnold, 3 January 1881.
68. Microfilm UVA. Letter to George Grove, 24 January 1881.
69. L.ii.188.
70. Arnold Family Album. Letter from G. F. Watts, 22 March 1881.
71. *Ibid*, p. 55n.
72. CPW.XI.370.
73. L.ii.190.
74. Arnold Family Album. Letter from John Bright, 18 June 1881.
75. CPW.IX.238ff.
76. British Museum MS. Letter to Gladstone, 6 July 1881.
77. British Museum MS. Letter to Gladstone, 26 September 1881.
78. Richard Ellmann, *Oscar Wilde* (1987), p. 143.
79. *Ibid*.
80. Arnold Family Album. Letter from Cardinal Manning, 19 October 1881.
81. Arnold Family Album. Letter from Lord Derby, 21 October 1881.
82. Microfilm UVA. Letter to Robert Dudley Adams, 7 July 1881.
83. Bodleian MS. Letter to Sir William Harcourt, 25 February 1881.
84. Bodleian MS. Letter to Sir William Harcourt, 25 October 1881.
85. British Museum MS. Letter to A.C. Swinburne, 7 December 1881.
86. L.ii.193.
87. *Notebooks*, p. 377.
88. L.ii.196.
89. L.ii.197.
90. British Museum MS. Letter to Edmund Gosse, 16 January 1882.
91. L.ii.198.

92. L.ii.199.
93. CPW, IX.312.
94. *Notebooks*, p. 385.
95. British Museum MS. Letter to A.C. Swinburne, 26 July 1882.
96. Microfilm UVA. Letter to George Smith, n.d., 1882.
97. Microfilm UVA. Letter to George Smith, 1 May 1882.
98. Balliol MS. Letter to Tom Arnold, 12 June 1882.
99. Microfilm UVA. Letter to Alexander Macmillan, 21 May 1882.
100. Microfilm UVA. Letter to James Russell Lowell, 11 August 1882.
101. Yale MS. Letter to Charles Eliot Norton, 31 August 1882.
102. British Museum MS. Letter to Edmund Gosse, 11 August 1882.
103. Brotherton MS. Letter to Edmund Gosse, 24 September 1882.
104. L.ii.205.
105. CPW.IX.136ff.
106. CPW.X.75ff.
107. L.ii.206.
108. CPW.X.473n, quoting *Liverpool Daily Post*, 4 October 1882.
109. Liverpool City Libraries MS. Lord Derby's 1882 Diary,
     30 September and 2 October.
110. L.ii.209.
111. L.ii.207.
112. Yale MS. Arnold's 1883 Diary. Guthrie transcription.
113. L.ii.210.
114. L.ii.210.
115. L.ii.211.
116. Microfilm UVA. Letter to Alfred Arthur Reade, 4 November
     1882.
117. Microfilm UVA. Letter to R. D. Adams, 5 June 1883.
118. L.ii.212.
119. Microfilm UVA. Letter to James Russell Lowell, 8 August 1883.
120. L.ii.215.
121. Microfilm UVA. Letter to Lady de Rothschild, 3 September 1883.
122. L.ii.217.
123. L.ii.220.
124. Balliol MS. Letter to Fan, 14 October 1883.
125. Microfilm UVA. Letter to Joshua Fitch, 9 October 1883.
126. L.ii.221.
127. *Daily News*, 23 October 1883. This and many other press quotes
     from Nelly's scrapbook of cuttings October 1883 – February 1884
     [Microfilm UVA].
128. L.ii.221.
129. L.ii.221.
130. *The Times*, 11 October 1883.
131. *Pall Mall Gazette*, October 1883.
132. L.ii.225.
133. L.ii.222.
134. See Harriet Holman, 'Matthew Arnold's Elocution Lessons', *New
     England Quarterly*, Vol. XVIII, No. 4, December 1945.

135. *Punch*, 10 November 1883.
136. Quoted in *Pall Mall Gazette*, 22 November 1883.
137. See Malcolm Bradbury, *Dangerous Pilgrimages* (1995), pp. 114–15.
138. *Daily News*, 22 October 1883.
139. CPW.X.143ff.
140. Holman, *loc.cit.*, p. 483.
141. *Ibid.*, p. 486.
142. Microfilm UVA. Letter to George Smalley. 27 November 1883.
143. *New York Tribune*, 22 October 1883.
144. *The World* (New York), 23 October 1883.
145. Nelly's scrapbook.
146. Microfilm UVA. Letter to W. D. Howells, 3 December 1883.
147. Microfilm UVA. Letter to George Smith, 16 December 1883.
148. *Pall Mall Gazette*, 13 December 1883.
149. *Literary World*, 3 November 1883.
150. *Detroit Times*, 18 January 1884.
151. *Ottawa Citizen*, 18 February 1884.
152. Balliol MS. Letter to Tom Arnold, 30 November 1883.
153. L.ii.229.
154. L.ii.239.
155. L.ii.245.
156. L.ii.246.
157. L.ii.249.
158. Microfilm UVA. Letter to Alexander Macmillan, 1 January 1884.
159. Microfilm UVA. Letter to Goldwin Smith, 30 January 1884.
160. L.ii.254.
161. L.ii.254.
162. L.ii.257.
163. Balliol MS. Yates Letter to Fan, 24 February 1884.
164. Yale MS. Letter to Yates Thompson, 31 January 1884.
165. Microfilm UVA. Letter to George Smalley, 2 April 1884.

Chapter Ten

1. Balliol MS. Letter to Tom Arnold, 30 November 1886.
2. Mrs Humphrey Ward, A *Writer's Recollections* (1918), pp. 241ff.
3. L.ii.266.
4. British Museum MS. Letter to Dilke, 18 May 1884.
5. Microfilm UVA. Letter to T. H. Ward, 11 April 1884.
6. L.ii.267.
7. Lucy Cohen, *Lady de Rothschild and her Daughters* (1935), p. 203.
8. Microfilm UVA. Letter to Percy Bunting, 9 October 1884.
9. L.ii.268.
10. L.ii.270.
11. CPW.X.53ff.
12. See for example Chris Baldick, *The Social Mission of English Criticism 1848–1932* (1983), who, exactly a hundred years after Arnold's lecture writes on 'Arnold's Innocent Language', pp. 18–57.

13. UL.54.
14. Balliol MS. Letter to Tom, 7 December 1884.
15. Microfilm UVA. Letter to Lucy, 12 January 1885.
16. Microfilm UVA. Letter to Grant-Duff, 4 March 1885.
17. Buckler, p. 58. Letter to G. C. Craik. 12 April 1885.
18. Buckler, *op.cit.*, p. 59. Letter to MA, 7 October 1886.
19. L.ii.273.
20. Microfilm UVA. Letter to Lucy, 17 March 1885. This passage not in L.ii.275.
21. Microfilm UVA. Letter to Lucy, 24 March 1885.
22. Balliol MS. Letter to Tom, Easter Sunday 1885.
23. George Brodrick, *Memories and Impressions* (1900) pp. 262–63.
24. Yale MS. Letter to Yates Thompson, 15 May 1885.
25. L.ii.278.
26. L.ii.280.
27. Microfilm UVA. Letter to Goldwin Smith, 19 June 1885.
28. Microfilm UVA. Letter to Andrew Carnegie, 21 June 1885.
29. Microfilm. UVA. Letter to Grant-Duff, 7 August 1885.
30. Microfilm UVA. Letter to Andrew Carnegie, 21 June 1885.
31. L.ii.284.
32. L.ii.286.
33. L.ii.285.
34. Microfilm UVA. Letter to T. H. Ward, 24 October 1885.
35. Microfilm UVA. Letter to T. H. Ward, 31 October 1885.
36. Microfilm UVA. Letter to T. H. Ward, 24 October 1885.
37. L.ii.290.
38. L.ii.288.
39. Microfilm UVA. Letter to Lucy, 20 October 1885.
40. L.ii.291.
41. Microfilm UVA. Letter to Grant-Duff, 24 December 1885.
42. L.ii.299.
43. Microfilm UVA. Letter to Goldwin Smith, 19 June 1885.
44. L.ii.304.
45. L.ii.298.
46. L.ii.306.
47. Microfilm UVA. Letter to Lucy, 28 December 1885.
48. L.ii.315.
49. L.ii.316.
50. Edward Said, *Culture and Imperialism* (1993), p. 19. Said is using the term in a specific application to the relationship between post-colonial cultures and their former colonisers, but it is a phrase that seems to admit of wider application, in its call for something more generous – a more objective critical spirit – to replace the rhetoric.
51. Microfilm UVA. Letter to Goldwin Smith, 13 January 1886.
52. Microfilm UVA. Letter to T. H. Ward, 19 January 1886.
53. L.ii.319.
54. L.ii.321.
55. L.ii.325.

56. Microfilm UVA. Letter to Gordon McCabe, 27 March 1886.
57. Microfilm UVA, 29 March 1886.
58. Microfilm UVA. Letter to Lady de Rothschild, 12 April 1886.
59. L.ii.327.
60. Yale MS. Letter to Mrs George Smith, 4 May 1886.
61. L.ii.329.
62. Yale MS. Letter to Yates Thompson, 17 May 1886.
63. Balliol MS. Letter to Fan, 28 May 1886.
64. L.ii.332.
65. L.ii.333.
66. Balliol MS. Letter to Fan, 26 June 1886.
67. Microfilm UVA. Letter to Andrew Carnegie, 4 June 1886.
68. CPW.XI.374.
69. L.ii.340.
70. Balliol MS. Letter to Fan, 4 July 1886.
71. L.ii.340.
72. L.ii.347.
73. L.ii.346.
74. Microfilm UVA. Letter to Lucy, 5 September 1886.
75. Microfilm UVA. Letter to Lucy, 7 September 1886.
76. Microfilm UVA. Letter to Lucy, 24 September 1886.
77. Microfilm UVA. Letter to John Churton Collins, 24 October 1886.
78. L.ii.349.
79. L.ii.351.
80. Microfilm UVA. Letter to Lucy, 29 October 1886.
81. CPW.XI.374–9.
82. L.ii.351.
83. Balliol MS. Letter to Tom, 30 November 1886.
84. Microfilm UVA. Letter to Anthony Mundella, 26 November 1886.
85. L.ii.354.
86. Microfilm UVA. Letter to George Smith, 30 December 1886.
87. CPW.XI.122ff.
88. L.ii.367.
89. Balliol MS. Letter to Lord Suffolk, 4 January 1887.
90. L.ii.361.
91. L.ii.363.
92. L.ii.364.
93. L.ii.364.
94. Microfilm UVA. Letter to Lucy, 14 March 1887.
95. Microfilm UVA. Letter to Lucy, 2 April 1887.
96. Fitzwilliam MS. Letter to Sidney Colvin, 26 June 1887.
97. Microfilm UVA. Letter to Grant Duff, 7 July 1887.
98. L.ii.368.
99. Microfilm UVA. Letter to William Knight, 2 July 1887.
100. National Library of Wales MS. Letter to George Venables, 22 September 1887.

101. National Library of Wales MS. Letter to George Venables, 30 September 1887.
102. Balliol MS. Letter to Tom, 19 October 1887.
103. CPW.XI.282ff.
104. Microfilm UVA. Letter to Lady de Rothschild, 25 November 1887.
105. Brodrick, *op.cit.* Letter to MA, dated 26 January 1888.
106. L.ii.371.
107. CPW.IX.217ff.
108. CPW.XI.350ff.
109. CPW.IX.328ff.
110. Microfilm UVA. Letter to Alfred Austin, 22 January 1888.
111. L.ii.375.
112. L.ii.376.
113. See Frances Conybeare, *Dingle Bank; the Home of the Croppers: A Recollection* (1925), Cambridge.
114. *Liverpool Courier*, 17 April 1888.
115. *Liverpool Daily Post*, 17 April 1888.
116. *The Times*, 17 April 1888.
117. Microfilm UVA. Letter to William Knight, 21 April 1888.
118. Brotherton MS. Letter to Robert Browning, 21 April 1888.
119. *The Function of Criticism at the Present Time* (1864).
120. *The Times*, 19 April 1888.
121. Stephen Coleridge, *Memories* (1913), p. 51.
122. *Liverpool Echo*, 20 April 1888.
123. *The Times*, 19 April 1888.
124. Microfilm UVA. Letter to Robert Browning, 21 May 1889.
125. Microfilm UVA. Letter to Arthur Galton, 15 August 1888.
126. Microfilm UVA. Letter to Arthur Galton, 15 May 1913.
127. Microfilm UVA. Letter to Arthur Galton, 15 August 1888.

ACKNOWLEDGEMENTS

In writing this book I have drawn extensively on unpublished manuscript material, some of it available to a biographer for the first time. I have therefore incurred incalculable debts to the following libraries and special collections where I have been made welcome and given every assistance and to whom I would like to express gratitude for permission to quote from unpublished material: to the Master and Fellows of Balliol College, Oxford and Frederick Whitridge; the Special Collections at the Brotherton Library, University of Leeds and at the University of Birmingham; the Bodleian Library, Oxford; Liverpool City Libraries; the British Library; the National Library of Wales. I would also like to thank the Wordsworth Trust at Grasmere, both for allowing me to see its collection of Arnold family papers and for assistance with illustrations. I am also indebted to the resources and unfailing helpfulness of the staff of the London Library.

In the United States I am grateful to the Alderman Library at the University of Virginia for giving me generous access to the outstanding Arthur Kyle Davis collection of Arnold letters on microfilm (the reservoir from which a projected multi-volume collection of Arnold's letters edited by Cecil Y. Lang will soon be drawn) and for giving me the opportunity to spend several weeks in the delightful spring sunshine of Charlottesville. I am also grateful to the Beinecke Rare Book and Manuscript Library at Yale University for granting access to its collection of Arnold papers.

I would also like to thank all those who have assisted me so generously and so enthusiastically with advice, suggestions for further research, and encouragement. I am particularly grateful for the kindness and encouragement of Arnold's pioneering modern biographer, Park Honan. The Reverend Doreen Harrison kindly allowed me to visit Fox How, a private residence not open to the public. And finally, I would like to acknowledge my debt to the great Arnold scholar, Kenneth Allott, who first introduced me to the study of Matthew Arnold when I was an undergraduate at Liverpool University in the early 1970s and who himself embodied something of the lively intellectual energy and fairness of mind of the writer whose qualities he communicated with such verve to his students.

INDEX